Between Sarmatia and

The Life and Works of
Johannes Bobrowski

AMSTERDAMER PUBLIKATIONEN ZUR SPRACHE UND LITERATUR

in Verbindung mit

PETER BOERNER, BLOOMINGTON; HUGO DYSERINCK, AACHEN; FERDINAND VAN INGEN, AMSTERDAM; FRIEDRICH MAURER†, FREIBURG; OSKAR REICHMANN, HEIDELBERG

herausgegeben von

COLA MINIS†
und
AREND QUAK

139

AMSTERDAM - ATLANTA, GA 1999

Between Sarmatia and Socialism

The Life and Works of
Johannes Bobrowski

by

John P. Wieczorek

⊚ The paper on which this book is printed meets the requirements of "ISO 9706:1994, Information and documentation - Paper for documents - Requirements for permanence".

ISBN: 90-420-0756-7
©Editions Rodopi B.V., Amsterdam - Atlanta, GA 1999
Printed in The Netherlands

CONTENTS

PREFACE

This study is an attempt to continue and deepen interest in the English-speaking world for an author whose works can be all too easily overlooked in the cultural development of the new and united German Federal Republic. Johannes Bobrowski (1917-1965) was an author from the German Democratic Republic, the 'wrong' part of Germany. He wrote poetry and prose of considerable complexity, and he devoted much of his productive life to writing about areas even further to the East – the great open and flat landscape he called, using the classical name given to Eastern Europe, 'Sarmatien'. As an 'Ossi' and an esoteric he is already doubly damned. He lacks even the saving grace of having been a distinguished dissident or of having suffered significantly at the hands of the East German authorities: his works were published uncensored.[1]

Equally unpromising was the attitude Bobrowski displayed to the areas about which he wrote, his highly critical view of the role played by his fellow-Germans and his public acceptance of the post-1945 German boundaries in the East. He refers to a 'lange Geschichte aus Unglück und Verschuldung'[2] and maintains that the 'German East' (i.e. East and West Prussia) is 'mit allem Recht verloren'.[3] To write of such areas *at all* at this period was to break the taboo of silence in East Germany; to write of them *thus* was to offend the many in the West, refugees, 'Heimatvertriebene', 'Umsiedler', who rejected these borders and called vociferously for a return to the borders of 1937. Their political voice, we must remember, was much more powerful in the 1950s and early 1960s than it is now.

---

[1] There is one ironic exception: the early poem 'Pruzzische Elegie' was initially refused publication by Bobrowski's *West* German publishers because of his all too free use of the word 'Volk'.

[2] See the note for Hans Bender's anthology *Widerspiel – deutsche Lyrik seit 1945*, reprinted in Johannes Bobrowski, *Gesammelte Werke in sechs Bänden*, ed. Eberhard Haufe and (vol. 6) Holger Gehle, Berlin/Stuttgart 1987ff., 4:335. Further references to these collected works, including the *Erläuterungen* (vols. 5 and 6) will appear in the text.

[3] See the letter to Karl Schwedhelm of April 30 1959, quoted in *Johannes Bobrowski: Selbstzeugnisse und neue Beiträge über sein Werk*, ed. Gerhard Rostin, Berlin 1975, p.134. Further references to this volume will appear in the text under *SZNB*.

Out of these many negatives there arises paradoxically an impression of something unusual and positive: a difficult East German writer whose first volume of poetry was thematically suspect in the East and politically highly incorrect in the West, and yet was published almost simultaneously in East and West in 1961, the very year in which the Berlin Wall was built. Such works, one might well conclude, must surely have some qualities, literary or otherwise, that merit continued attention. For readers in the British Isles on the rim of Europe, let alone still further west in America, the issues involved may appear historically, geographically and linguistically remote. Perspectival foreshortening turns the rich complexity of Lithuanian, Latvian, Estonian, Polish and Russian history and culture that Bobrowski wrote of into an undifferentiated 'Eastern European' mass. The genuine ambivalence of German relations with the East is all too easily reduced to the expansionist catchword of a Teutonic 'Drang nach Osten'. The history and geography of Bobrowski's few square kilometres of spiritual homeland, the so-called 'Memelland', are now rarely accorded more than an academic footnote.[4] Bobrowski's language itself, difficult enough for many Germans, may appear impenetrable to unaccustomed Anglo-Saxon ears.

Despite such real and apparent remoteness, British and American writers have responded with a number of monographs and academic articles, from the early and seminal *Johannes Bobrowski* by Brian Keith-Smith (1970) to the recent summarising and popularising *Understanding Johannes Bobrowski* (1995) by David Scrase. Bobrowski's poetry has also been translated by poets and translators as distinguished and varied as Michael Hamburger and Ruth and Matthew Mead and Christopher Middleton. The reasons for this are far from parochial. Bobrowski may have written poems on Thomas Chatterton, Dylan Thomas and the Anglicised Pole Joseph Conrad, as well as translating T.S.Eliot. Much more important is, however, the evident aesthetic quality of his works, a sense of intensity of expression giving meaning

---

[4] The Memelland was a narrow strip of land across the River Memel/Niemen at the extreme Eastern border of East Prussia. Although settled by Germans for several centuries, it was placed under international control by the Versailles Treaty but later annexed by Lithuania. Hitler restored it to German rule in March 1939 shortly after his entry into Prague. The word Memel occurs in fact in the first stanza of the German national anthem ('Von der Maas bis an die Memel'), but this is a curious historical remnant, and this stanza is never officially sung.

to the saw that 'dichten' = 'dicht machen'. This poetic quality has ensured that praise for Bobrowski's works from whatever source cannot be dismissed as praise of 'Gesinnungsästhetik', and an appreciation of their value has, if anything, increased since the literary blood-letting of the post-unification 'Literaturstreit' surrounding such East German luminaries as Christa Wolf, Stephan Hermlin and Monika Maron. Anglo-Saxon distance has made it easier to avoid the more violent swings of opinion concerning the value of GDR literature, and the occasionally strident implication of the victory of West German culture over the derided East carries less conviction outside Germany itself.

At the centre of Bobrowski's works, both temporally and in terms of significance, stand the two volumes of poetry *Sarmatische Zeit* (1961) and *Schattenland Ströme* (1962). Together these constitute the 'Sarmatian' cycle on which his fame has rested. His work in general, both poetry and prose, has been seen in terms of this core. Pre-Sarmatian and post-Sarmatian works are frequently ignored or viewed as a considerably weaker body of work than the main cycles, and the novels in particular have been much criticised.[5] Such concentration on the one 'Sarmatian' aspect runs alongside a further frequently unstated assumption of a lack of poetic development. This is supported in general by Bobrowski's own reluctance to discuss his development, and by the relatively short period of his major publications from 1961 to 1965.

The current study is emphatically chronological, both in its approach and in its arrangement. After a biographical survey it examines Bobrowski's pre-Sarmatian works, the existence of large sections of which he denied. It analyses the well-researched odes to Lake Ilmen and Novgorod but also draws attention to a small number of other poems in which a second theme may be seen developing, that of a neo-Romantic longing for a view of reality less subordinate to any divisive dualism. Although submerged under the Sarmatian task, this will play a new role in the late poems. The two Sarmatian volumes are then examined as a continuous whole, but within them the study examines the development concealed behind the cyclical arrangement.

---

[5] See especially Hans Christian Kosler, *Kritisches Lexikon zur deutschsprachigen Gegenwartsliteratur*, Munich 1978ff.: 'Der lange Atem des Epikers war ihm fremd'.

In its analysis of a number of poems reflecting different aspects of Sarmatia, it emphasises the movement from personal lament at the loss of a homeland to an acceptance of the passage of time and a determination to build positively on this. With particular reference to a poem to Mickiewicz it emphasises the role of love and resignation.

Bobrowski's Sarmatian world included a number of poems to or about artists and fellow-writers whom he 'kidnapped'. As well as the British authors mentioned above these included St. John Perse, Alexis Kivi, Hans Henny Jahnn and many others. These Bobrowski used in a process of self-orientation. In a separate chapter the study looks at three of the most important names for Bobrowski's poetic development, Hamann, Klopstock and Celan.

In Bobrowski's last and only post-Sarmatian volume of poetry, *Wetterzeichen*, the study sees a contradictory development. On the one hand stand a number of poems which hold fast fleeting moments of epiphanic experience; on the other stand a number of poems concerned with Bobrowski's own position in the GDR. The specifically historical dimension of Sarmatia falls away and Bobrowski appears to return to pre-Sarmatian themes, in particular an emphasis on the language of nature as an expression of the unity of existence. Such an emphasis contains an implied criticism of the dogmatic Marxism Bobrowski encountered in his daily life. He offers instead a richness and diversity of existence encompassing the rational and the irrational.

The study devotes chapters to Bobrowski's short stories and to his two novels. In the short stories it sees the development of an ever clearer tactical dimension, as Bobrowski attempted a dialogue with the GDR. Earlier Sarmatian frames of reference are abandoned. In separate chapters on the two novels *Levins Mühle* and *Litauische Claviere* I analyse the extent to which, behind the apparent continuation of interest in the theme of the Germans and their Eastern neighbours, these works constitute attempts to raise very specific aesthetic issues with the GDR authorities. They contain implicit defences of his own pluralistic beliefs and suggest correctives to the dogmatism that surrounded him.

With this combination of the temporal and the spiritual, the metaphysical and the openly tactical a picture of Bobrowski emerges that shows him as a much more complex figure than the remote and ahistorical 'poet of Sarmatia'. I have made use where relevant or illuminating of all material available, unpublished works, letters, early drafts of poems, published and unpublished. I have attempted to shed light on a number of individual poems of varying complexity, which I have also reviewed for their significance within the key volumes. No amount of background material or detailed textual analysis will turn Bobrowski into an 'easy' writer: judicious contextualisation and cross-referencing between earlier and later works, earlier and final versions, may, however, open fresh channels of understanding.

The transfer of much of Bobrowski's 'Nachlaß' from his home in Ahornallee, Berlin, to the Deutsches Literaturarchiv in Marbach promises a new freedom for scholarly research, while the publication of the volume *Landschaft mit Leuten* (1993)[6] and, more recently, two volumes of 'Erläuterungen' as volumes 5 and 6 of the *Gesammelte Werke* has given an indication of the wealth of material available. This study makes considerable use of this 'Nachlaß', to which I had access during visits to Ahornallee in the early 1970s, and I remain grateful to Bobrowski's widow, Frau Johanna Bobrowski, for allowing me the freedom to use what I chose. Much new material has also been rediscovered and is present in the archives at Marbach, and I am grateful also to Brian Keith-Smith for allowing me to see copies of important parts of Bobrowski's correspondence.

Finally I am grateful to my family and to all those friends and colleagues, past and present, who have had patience and have given me time and space to complete this work.

The University of Reading   John Wieczorek
July 1999

[6] *Johannes Bobrowski oder Landschaft mit Leuten*, ed. Reinhard Tgahrt, Marbach am Neckar 1993. Further references will be made in the text under *Marbach*.

1

BIOGRAPHY

Johannes Bobrowski (full name Johannes Konrad Bernhard Bobrowski) was born on April 9 1917 in Tilsit (now Russian Sovetsk), on the River Memel (Niemen/Nemona) on the extreme eastern border of the then East Prussia.[1] His father Gustav Bobrowski was an official with the German railways. In spring 1919 the family moved from Tilsit to Graudenz (now Polish Grudziądz) in the then West Prussia, but within a year experienced the geographical and national instability of the area, as the Treaty of Versailles transferred Graudenz to Polish sovereignty. The family moved back to Tilsit for a while, before Bobrowski's father was transferred in 1925 to Rastenburg (now Polish Ketrzyn) and then in 1928 to nearby Königsberg (now Russian Kaliningrad). Here they stayed, until his parents moved to Friedrichshagen in the relatively leafy suburbs of south-eastern Berlin in 1937 and 1938. The family then stayed in Berlin until their deaths.

Bobrowski's childhood and youth were marked by these moves – from Tilsit to Graudenz, to Rastenburg, to Tilsit, and then to Königsberg. There he experienced a large cosmopolitan city with a significant philosophical and cultural history. It had been the home of the Enlightenment philosopher Immanuel Kant (1724-1804) and the 'Magus im Norden' Johann Georg Hamann (1730-1788), and before that of the Baroque 'Königsberger Dichterkreis', and it was the experience of Königsberg that most deeply affected Bobrowski's intellectual development, even though he saw Tilsit as his 'Vaterstadt', the title of a poem from November 1946 (2:81-3).

From October 1928 Bobrowski attended the Stadtgymnasium Alt-stadt-Kneiphof ('Kant-Gymnasium' or 'Dom-Schule'), a school with a long humanist tradition courageously maintained for much of the early National Socialist period. While a pupil there he started to read precociously. He read Kant and Hamann, and also Johann Gottfried Herder (1740-1803), Friedrich Gottlieb Klopstock (1724-1803) and Friedrich Hölderlin (1770-1843). Here too he made the acquaintance of Alfred

---

[1] Biographical details are taken from Eberhard Haufe's *Bobrowski-Chronik: Daten zu Leben und Werk,* Würzburg 1994, references to which will occur in the text under *Chronik.*

Brust (1891-1934), an Expressionist writer and apologist for Old Prussian culture, especially in his novel *Die verlorene Erde* (1926). It was a personal contact that was instrumental in helping Bobrowski develop his individual interpretation of Prussian history and his iconoclastic attitudes towards the 'Ordensstaat' of the Teutonic Knights and its glorification both by historians such as Treitschke and in National Socialist propaganda.

Of particular significance for Bobrowski's later poetic world was his maternal grandmother, Agnes Lydia Bertha Witzke (1876-1954). After separating from her first husband, Bobrowski's grandfather Ludwig Albert Witzke, in 1920 she had married an estate owner Max Fröhlich in the small village of Willkischken, on the Jura, just over the border on the Memelland side of the River Memel. Later they moved to the nearby hamlet of Motzischken, and the estate proper was taken over by Agathe Fröhlich, Bobrowski's aunt. From 1929 to 1937 Bobrowski regularly spent time in his school holidays in this Memelgebiet. His visits there and to relatives and acquaintances on his own side of the Memel provided him with vivid childhood memories and supplied material for many of his works. The area also showed him an ideal of harmonious life to which he later occasionally referred:

> Aufgewachsen auf beiden Seiten der Memel, zeitweise auf dem Kleinbauernhof der Großeltern im damaligen Memelgebiet (Litauen), in einem Landstrich, wo Deutsche in engster Nachbarschaft mit Litauern, Polen, Russen lebten, in dem der jüdische Bevölkerungsteil sehr hoch war. (*SZNB* 14)

Although his grandparents on both sides had come from West Prussia, Bobrowski's more distant ancestry was much more varied, and in a letter of October 9 1956 he explained his poetic intentions with, among other things, a reference to the complexity of this history:

> Ich komme [...] aus einer Familie, in der Polnisches und Deutsches wunderlich gemischt ist. Ich wuchs auf in ständigem Umgang mit Litauern, Juden – einfachen Menschen und allerlei Landadel usw. Nachzutragen: daß ich den Weg meiner Sippe durch ein gutes Jahrtausend verfolgen kann. Ich kann also – ohne zu konstruieren – in meiner eigenen Existenz die Ostvölker [...] mit den Deutschen konfrontieren. (*SZNB* 132)[2]

---

[2] The claim involves less poetic licence than it seems. Just over a year before, in August 1955, Bobrowski had written a summary history of his family (4:318-26). The Bobrowskis (the Slavonic name appears to refer to badger-hunting and possibly arose in the 6th to 8th century) formed part of the Jastrząb, later Jastrzębiec, tribe. In the late C10

It was indeed a mixed ancestry, and Bobrowski could relate his own family to the conflicts of the last thousand years, where 'Bobrowskis' had been Poles, Lithuanians and Prussians (even English, if we stretch a point with Joseph Conrad), Catholics and Protestants, oppressors and oppressed.

In addition to his voracious reading, his holiday experiences in the Memelland and this sense of the complexity of his family history, Bobrowski was deeply affected by his Protestant family background and upbringing.[3] In Königsberg he experienced at first hand the attempts of the National Socialist 'Deutsche Christen' to take over the German Protestant community. In opposition to this he remained as a pupil an active member of the 'Bund Deutscher Bibelkreise' (the Federation of German Bible Circles) until it disbanded itself in February 1934 in order to escape compulsory integration into the Hitler Youth Movement.[4] He

---

they had distinguished themselves in fighting as Christians the heathen Pruzzi and Polani tribes, and they remained active in subsequent campaigns. Others from the family were involved in 1080 in the murder of Stanislaw, Bishop of Cracow. Of particular importance was a Burg Bobrofh, also Bobrau, Bobrowo, Boberow and Boberowe, mentioned in deeds of 1222 as being transferred by a Masovian Duke Konrad to the Teutonic Knights as reward for their assistance against the Pruzzi. It was situated in the Strasburg district of West Prussia, later used as the setting for *Levins Mühle*. The inhabitants of the village Bobrofh, the Bobrowskis, had evidently earlier been forced out by pressure from the heathen Pruzzi.

In the Thirteen Year War (1453 to 1466) members of the wider family supported the Teutonic Knights against the eventually victorious Polish King. The Masovian Bobrowskis later largely converted to Protestantism, as did much of Poland, and in 1606 took part in the *Rokosz* against the counter-reformation of Zygmunt III Wasa. With the defeat of that uprising, this section of the family lost its significance. In his summary, Bobrowski quotes with evident relish a nineteenth-century text which refers to the Bobrowskis as 'altpolnisch' (4:324).

There were, however, further references to *Catholic* Bobrowskis in Masovia, and other Bobrowskis occurred in the Catholic Galician areas and in Lithuania, while a Count Bobrowski was active in 1846 as leader of insurgents in West Galicia. Joseph Conrad (whose mother was born a Bobrowski) came from this branch of the family.

[3] His paternal grandmother, Olga Charlotte Bobrowski née Laudien, (1864-1902) was descended from a Huguenot family; his paternal grandfather Carl Johann Bobrowski (1861-1927) was a Baptist. His immediate family was also largely church-going.

[4] The 'Bund' was formed in the 1880s as an organisation devoted to Bible study but also to group and social activities. By the 1920s it had developed a programme that included folksong evenings, hikes and displays of local patriotism. As an organisation with missionary intentions it was involved both with charitable aspects of the church and also

then joined the 'Bekennende Kirche' (the Confessing Church), a group within Protestantism set up specifically in opposition to the encroaching dogma of the 'Deutsche Christen' with their extreme nationalism and segregationalism, their 'leadership principle' and their rejection of the Old Testament and 'Jewish', 'degenerate' elements of the New Testament.[5] In opposition to this the 'Bekennende Kirche' emphasised a conscious return to the whole Bible and to the Creeds of the Reformation.

In April 1937 Bobrowski was called up for six months compulsory 'Reichsarbeitsdienst', after which he volunteered immediately for military service in order to complete his two years as soon as possible. Inevitably, this service was prolonged by the invasion of Poland in September 1939 and the outbreak of the Second World War. He served first as a private in the communications regiment 501 of the Third Army and travelled with this regiment through Krasne (4:256f.), Rozan (see 'Der Tänzer Malige' and *Levins Mühle*), Ostrow, Siedlce, Przemysl, Brzozow and Mielce (see 'Else Lasker-Schüler'). Later he visited Czestochowa and saw the famous Black Madonna. After the conclusion of the Polish campaign he was transferred to Bad Bertrich on the Mosel as part of the new 16th Army in preparation for the invasion of France. In the course of this campaign he visited Cap Gris-Nez and Guînes near Calais, (see 'Ich will fortgehn', 'Dunkel und wenig Licht', 'Französisches Dorf', 'Guines Sept. 1940'). In April 1941 he was transferred back to the East in preparation for the attack on the Soviet Union on June 22 1941.

The following years spent in the Soviet Union brutally confirmed Bobrowski's critical view of his fellow Germans. On June 28 1941 he witnessed the infamous massacre of 3,800 Jews in Kaunas (see 'Kaunas 1941'), a city he knew from earlier visits to an uncle who worked there. The event, in the course of which many hundreds of Jews were bludgeoned to death by prisoners who had been released and armed with iron bars, scarred him emotionally for life (see *Marbach* 467). By August 1941 he was stationed at Korosztyn on Lake Ilmen, near the beautiful and ancient Russian city of Novgorod, and by early September he had visited it and witnessed its devastation. This visit, like visits to other

---

with discussions with atheists. Bobrowski's later prose piece 'Fortgeführte Überlegungen' (4:158-60) refers to this time.

[5] See Arthur C. Cochrane, *The Church's Confession under Hitler*, Pittsburgh 1976, esp. pp.222f.

devastated Russian towns and villages behind the front, was reflected directly in poems written at the time.

On a semester's study leave from December 1941 he studied art history in Berlin with the intention of enrolling on a full course at a later date. He returned to the Russian front near Lake Ilmen in April 1942 and apart from occasional home leave was stationed here until December 1943, when he was moved to Karsava, on the eastern borders of Latvia. In 1943 he also married Johanna Budrus, daughter of the neighbours of his step-grandfather Max Fröhlich. In spring and summer 1944 he was stationed on the River Dvina (Düna) near Riga, until Soviet advances forced his regiment westwards in October. He was then cut off with the rest of the troops near Kandava until the German capitulation, when he was taken into captivity on May 8 1945.

Initially he worked in labour camps at Novoshakhtinsk in the Rostov area. Here he was active in the 'Kulturbrigade Lager 4' (informally the 'Bunte Palette'), contributing songs, short theatrical sketches and his own versions, reconstructed from memory, of various plays. In summer 1947 and in 1949 he attended courses of anti-fascist education, which took him to Rostov itself and to Gorky (now Nizhniy Novgorod), before he was finally released from captivity in December 1949. He returned to his family in East Berlin in the newly founded Deutsche Demokratische Republik. It was a decision prompted obviously by convenience, but also by conviction, and early letters from Berlin indicate a period of sympathy for communism deeply shocking to the rest of his family.

After working for a short period at the Berliner Volksbühne, he was appointed (February 22 1950) reader for the Altberliner Verlag Lucie Groszer, a private publishing house specialising in children's literature. Here he remained until September 1959, when he took up a post as 'Lektor für Belletristik' at the Union Verlag, the publishing house of the East German Christlich-Demokratische Union. He held this post with changing conditions of service until his death six years later. His position there involved considerable personal advancement, but it was also one of great irony: Bobrowski had been born and spent much of his youth on the easternmost border of East Prussia and had frequently crossed the virtually open border of the River Memel into the mixed community of the Memelland. With the Union Verlag, however, his office was in a building commanding a view across – after August 13 1961 – one of the most dangerous borders in the world, that between East and West Berlin. This border itself was a symbol of communal dis-

harmony and a freezing of relations which contradicted virtually everything for which he wrote. The difference to the border he had known as
a child could not have been greater.

Bobrowski had written poetry from an early age, and his claim
(4:335) that he only started to write 'am Ilmensee' was untrue. He had
even sought publication before the war, sending poems in March 1936
to Heinrich Ellermann for *Das Gedicht: Blätter für die Dichtung*. They
were rejected. In March 1944, however, he did achieve his first
significant publication, of poems reflecting his Russian experience, in
the journal *Das Innere Reich* (1943/44, vol. 4). A further publication in
Das Innere Reich was planned, but the standing type was destroyed in a
bombing raid on Munich in December 1944. After the war ended, and
again completely contrary to his claims, Bobrowski continued to write
poetry, both as a prisoner and after his release, but he made no attempt
to publish until April 1954, when he unsuccessfully offered eight poems
to *Akzente* in Munich.

In the following year five poems were finally published in Peter
Huchel's prestigious *Sinn und Form* (1955, vol. 4). The response was
disappointing, however, perhaps because their subject matter was
unusual and their intentions misunderstood. In a letter of October 27
1955 to Huchel Bobrowski complained: '[es] herrscht auf den zahl-
reichen Sitzungen, Besprechungen usw, die ich im Namen der Jugendli-
teratur zu überstehen hab, ein – wie mir scheint – ziemlich eisiges
Schweigen'.[6] In the GDR in the mid-1950s it is easy to imagine reasons
for this. Bobrowski's subject-matter was the East, viewed from the
perspective of someone brought up there. As such it ran the risk of
keeping alive memories the East German authorities considered taboo.
In another letter to Huchel of June 1 1956 Bobrowski, echoing Goethe,
coined the phrase he was to use to describe the poetic project that
occupied him in various forms for the next five years. He was writing,
he wrote, 'eine Art Sarmatischer Divan' (p.12).

Publication of works from this project followed regularly but, from
Bobrowski's point of view, excruciatingly slowly. He secured just one
publication of a small selection in each of the years 1956,[7] 1957[8] and

---

[6] *Johannes Bobrowski: Peter Huchel: Briefwechsel*, ed. Eberhard Haufe, Marbach am
Neckar 1993, p.11. Further references will be to *Bobrowski/Huchel Briefwechsel*.

[7] In *Das Gedicht: Jahrbuch zeitgenössischer Lyrik*, ed. Rudolf Ibel, Hamburg 1956/57.

1958,[9] and letters in the period from 1955 to late 1959 indicate his frustration at the failure to achieve the sort of publishing breakthrough that would clarify his poetic intentions. In December 1957 he wrote to a new acquaintance Peter Jokostra, thanking him for his praise and encouragement:

> Leute, die hierorts etwas sind – Huchel, Arendt, Hermlin, vielleicht noch Eva Strittmatter, [...] Heiner Müller – sagen einem, wenn man sie alle Jahre einmal trifft, etwas Freundliches. [...] Aber damit hat sich's, meine alten Freunde halten mich für einen guten Kerl, der an seiner Poeterei wie an einer verschleppten Knabensünde leidet. Genug davon, ich werd es zu keinem Gedichtband bringen. (*Marbach* 28)

Attempts to avoid misunderstandings by having his 'Divan' published as a whole met with repeated rejection: in June 1958 by the East Berlin publisher Rütten & Loening, by S. Fischer Verlag in late spring 1959, and by the Hanser-Verlag in late 1959, while in December 1959 a project with V.O.Stomps' Eremiten-Presse also came to nothing. In December 1959 he set himself an ultimatum of December 31 1960:

> Sind bis dahin die nötigsten Dinge nicht gedruckt, so schließe ich die ganze Poeterei unwiderruflich ab. Als einen Irrtum des Publikums oder meinerseits. Und ohne Tragik. (*Marbach* 58)

In 1959/1960 finally came the breakthrough, with a significant number of publications in journals and newspapers[10] and, more importantly, with a contract for the volume *Sarmatische Zeit*, which

---

The section 'Junge Lyrik aus der DDR' contained five poems by Bobrowski, also selected by Huchel.

[8] In *Sinn und Form* vol. 4, three poems.

[9] In *Sinn und Form* vol. 3, two poems.

[10] 1959: eight poems broadcast by Süddeutscher Rundfunk; eight poems in *Eckart*, together with the essay 'Deutsche Lyrik auf der anderen Seite' by Ad den Besten (which marked the first critical review of Bobrowski's works in a journal); November 8 1959, *Neue Zeit*, one poem ('Die Droste'); December 1959 *Alternative: Blätter für Lyrik und Prosa*, two poems; February 1960, *Neue Zeit*, one poem ('Auf den jüdischen Händler A.S.'); July 1960, *Merkur*, two poems; August 1960, *Neue Zeit*, one poem ('Gedächtnis für einen Flußfischer'); September 1960, *Jahresring 60/61*, seven poems; October 1960, *Merkur*, six poems; autumn 1960, *Alphabet*, three poems; November 1960, in Ad den Besten's anthology *Deutsche Lyrik auf der anderen Seite*, thirteen poems. Not that the echo after these poems was particularly loud. The first reference to Bobrowski as a lyric poet in East Germany appeared in *Neue Zeit* in June 1959.

appeared in February 1961 in the West German Deutsche Verlags-
anstalt, and in the Union Verlag towards the end of the same year.[11]
Within a very short time he had completed his second volume of poetry
Schattenland Ströme, before, pressed from many sides, he concentrated
so intensely on prose-writing that his third volume of poetry, *Wetterzeichen*, was only published posthumously. By the time of his death he
had completed the two novels *Levins Mühle* (first published 1964) and
Litauische Claviere (published posthumously in 1966) as well as over
30 short stories. He had also completed a number of satirical quatrains,
including some for the Stockholm Catalogue of the Gruppe 47. His
significant publishing projects for the Union Verlag in these last years
included the volume *Entkleidung und Verklärung*, an anthology of the
works of Hamann edited by Martin Seils (1963), and an edition of Jean
Paul's *Leben Fibels* (1963), while for the East Berlin Eulenspiegel-
Verlag he edited his own personal anthology of mildly erotic verse *Wer
mich und Ilse sieht im Grase* (1964). He received literary awards in all
four German-speaking countries: the Alma-Johanna-Koenig-Preis,
presented in July 1962 in Austria; the prize of the Gruppe 47 in October
1962; the East German Heinrich-Mann-Preis in March 1965, and the
Swiss Charles-Veillon-Preis in May 1965.

With the September 1959 move to the Union Verlag, Bobrowski was
caught up in ever more frequent political and cultural activities, and it
was inevitable that he should eventually (May 1960) join the East
German CDU, one of the block parties that constituted the National
Front in co-operation with the Communist SED. This move, like the
post with the Union Verlag, had its more and less appealing sides:
instead of being the outsider working for a small private publisher, he
was exposed much more to demands for party discipline, and especially
after being awarded the prize of the Gruppe 47 he was expected to use
his prestige in the West to support East German protests against
assumed or real West German wrong-doings. Together with the
increasing frequency of his publications the move led to a steady growth
in public commitments, both on behalf of his employers and for himself
as a writer, and in the 1960s he increasingly appeared almost over-

---

[11] This achievement – to publish the same work at more or less the same time in East
and West – was not simply a personal breakthrough. Such parallel publication in both
countries was previously almost unheard of, though with time it became more common.

whelmed by competing responsibilities. There were private commitments too, especially his duty towards his growing family, with children born 1951, 1952, 1957 and 1964.

The tensions inherent in his situation are exemplified in his dealings with two very different organisations: the Gruppe 47 and the Berlin 'Evangelische Akademie' (see *Marbach* 105-76). In November 1960 he attended a meeting of Hans Werner Richter's Gruppe 47 in Aschaffenburg, the first East German writer to do so since Peter Huchel in 1954. Despite considerable success at this meeting, with his poems praised by Walter Jens, Walter Höllerer and Günter Grass, he was not invited in October 1961, the year of the building of the Berlin Wall. After his next reading in October 1962 at Wannsee he was awarded the group's prize. This confirmed his position as a leading poet, but also – in the shadow of the Cuba crisis and virtually in the middle of the 'Spiegel-Affäre' – put him in an exposed position, open to criticism from East and West if he failed to respond to issues he would almost certainly rather have ducked.[12] He was invited to the 1963 meeting held in Saulgau on October 25-27, but events of the past twelve months led the East German authorities to grant him a travel visa so late that he could not arrive on time, while in September 1964 he was prevented from attending the Stockholm meeting altogether, although he was allowed to attend the subsequent 'Stockholmer Woche der Gruppe 47'. He died before the next annual meeting of the group in October 1965.

A series of 'Schriftstellertagungen der Evangelischen Akademie Berlin-Brandenburg', which he attended regularly from June 1959 till February 1965 led to even greater tensions. At the conference held in December 1962, after being awarded the Gruppe 47 prize, Bobrowski delivered a topical and controversial speech on 'Benannte Schuld – gebannte Schuld?' (4:443-8), in which, as he later commented to Christoph Meckel, he discussed 'die Machtlosigkeit der Literatur' (*Marbach* 113). The next of these meetings, held January 25-27 1963, provided the spark for Bobrowski's most serious disagreement with the East German authorities and the dogmatic need for party discipline. The

---

[12] Particularly embarrassing was a letter to members of the Gruppe 47 he signed in November 1962 protesting at the treatment of Bruno Apitz in West Germany (see *Chronik* pp.157f.). In a letter to Peter Huchel of February 1963 he distanced himself from it as based on 'eine unredliche Unterrichtung' (*Bobrowski/Huchel Briefwechsel*, p.26).

conference had as its theme 'Sprache im technischen Zeitalter', and a number of West German and West Berlin writers and critics attended, including Klaus Wagenbach, who talked on Günter Grass's *Die Blechtrommel*. Hans Mayer gave a paper on 'Brecht und Dürrenmatt'. Bobrowski himself contributed nothing, but the meeting coincided unfortunately with a hardening of ideological attitudes in the East after the VI 'Parteitag' of the SED of January 15-21 1963. The authorities took disciplinary measures against a number of leading cultural figures. At the end of 1962, after almost a decade of skirmishing, Peter Huchel had been forced to resign as editor of *Sinn und Form*. Bobrowski showed his solidarity with him by refusing to allow his own works to be published in *Sinn und Form*, but his subsequent reticence led to a cooling in their relations.[13] Stephan Hermlin was another victim of this hardening of the party line: after a spectacularly controversial poetry evening of December 11 1962, which Bobrowski attended and later praised in *Neue Zeit* (4:462), he was forced out of his post as secretary of the poetry section at the Academy of Arts. In the bitter ideological climate of the time, all these evidences of independent cultural policy were criticised: Huchel's editorial policy for *Sinn und Form*, Hermlin's forum for controversial poets (including Wolf Biermann), and the freedom of discussion between writers of East and West evident at the Evangelische Akademie. All were condemned as symptoms of 'ideologische Koexistenz', inadequate investment in the ideological warfare that was to accompany peaceful coexistence between the two opposing political blocks.

Bobrowski's Berlin-Brandenburg meeting was then criticised at the 'Beratung des Politbüros der ZK der SED mit den Kulturschaffenden' on March 25/26 1963 (*Marbach* 116/247), was the issue at a CDU meeting of March 29 1963 and was thrashed out on April 18 at a meeting of the 'Arbeitsgemeinschaft Kulturpolitik des Hauptvorstandes der CDU'. Here Bobrowski was savaged by the CDU leadership 'im Ungeist stalinistischer Kulturpolitik' (*Marbach* 248). This series of measures was finally concluded in Weimar at the 'Tagung des Präsidiums des Hauptvorstandes der CDU mit christlichen Kulturschaffenden' on June 16/17 1963 where Bobrowski was expected to contribute a paper. Avoiding the officially dictated theme ('Wie unterstützen wir die oppositionellen und humanistischen Schriftsteller Westdeutschlands in ihrem Kampf gegen die reaktionäre Kunst- und Kultur-

---

[13] See *Bobrowski/Huchel Briefwechsel*, esp. pp.26-29.

politik der Bonner Ultras?') he delivered the speech later presented in a more politically correct form as 'Die Koexistenz und das Gespräch' (4:449-55). It is no surprise that he was under police surveillance on suspicion of 'Betreiben von staatsgefährdender Propaganda und Hetze', 'illegale Gruppenbildung' and 'verdächtige Verbindungen, besonders nach Westdeutschland'.[14]

Alongside such politically sensitive meetings, Bobrowski read from his works on numerous occasions in East and West: in the 'Zinke' in West Berlin (from October 1959), in the 'Komma-Klub' in Munich (December 1962, together with Günter Kunert) and in the Baltic resort of Ahrenshoop, where he often spent his summer holidays. He spoke in Klaus Völker's 'Keller' in West Berlin (January 26 1961) and addressed the Jena Studentengemeinde and students of theology in Naumburg (May 24/25 1965); he visited the 'Studentensiedlung Eichkamp' in West Berlin (December 11 1963) and the West Berlin student village 'Sigmundshof' (November 13 1964 and February 5 1965). Other visits involved the East Berlin 'Klub der Kulturschaffenden Johannes R. Becher'[15] (February 20 1962, April 11 1963, May 13 1965), the 'Institut für Literatur Johannes R. Becher' in Leipzig (June 1962), and a meeting at the 'Kammer für evangelisches Schrifttum' in Hirschluch (April 26 1960). Other readings were organised by Eberhard Haufe (December 12 1962, September 19 1963), by the 'Weimarer Akademie' (June 1962, September 1963 and November 1964), and the conference of Christian 'Kulturschaffende' at the University of Greifswald (July 1965). Some of these readings were organised by the CDU, others by the Union Verlag, while in other cases Bobrowski appears to have been responding to personal invitations, often in Christian contexts. It was a full programme punctuated by illness and stress and there was little escape outside the Germanies. Indeed, apart from the delayed 1964 visit to Stockholm and

---

[14] Joachim Walther, *Sicherungsbereich Literatur: Schriftsteller und Staatssicherheit in der Deutschen Demokratischen Republik*, Berlin 1996, pp.448f. The 'illegale Gruppenbildung' referred to Bobrowski's 'Friedrichshagener Dichterkreis', which served as a totally unserious frame for convivial social activities. Elsewhere Bobrowski was suspected of supporting the 'ideologische Konzeption' of the Gruppe 47 (p.449). The full list of crimes Bobrowski was suspected of (p.448) is even more ominous.

[15] Despite the association in the name with Johannes R. Becher, whom Bobrowski described in an epigram (1:236) as 'der größte tote Dichter bei Lebzeiten', the club was run by the more acceptable 'Deutscher Kulturbund', the successor to the 'Kulturbund zur demokratischen Erneuerung Deutschlands'.

the short and much delayed visit to Vienna in 1962 to collect his Alma-Johanna-Koenig Prize, Bobrowski's only significant foreign visit took place in June 1964, to an International Writers' Seminar in Lahti, Finland (*Marbach* 235). One last conference at least he appears to have enjoyed: that held in May 1965 to commemorate the 20th anniversary of the end of the Second World War and the 30th anniversary of the First International Writers' Conference for the Defence of Culture of June 1935.

As his health deteriorated – almost inevitable consequence of his experiences as a prisoner of war and of the pressures and tensions to which he was subjected during these years – he was able to renegotiate his contract and needed to attend the publishing house for only three days in the week. His ill health continued, however, and on July 30 1965 he was admitted to hospital in Berlin-Köpenick with a ruptured appendix. Characteristically he had mistaken early signs of this for cirrhosis of the liver and, in fear of this diagnosis and its effect on his life-style, had refused to go to a doctor. He died September 2 1965 of a stroke. His funeral was attended by the Cultural Minister of the GDR Hans Bentzien, and by writers as politically and artistically disparate as Erich Arendt and Ingeborg Bachmann, Uwe Johnson and Hubert Fichte, Wolf Biermann and Hermann Kant.

2

THE PATH TO SARMATIA

In his speech at Bobrowski's funeral, Stephan Hermlin claimed that Bobrowski 'begann sofort, und zwar nicht mehr so jung, als ein großer Dichter'.[1] For some time this remained a commonly accepted view, though even Bobrowski, while still concealing significant parts of his poetic apprenticeship, admitted that it had been considerably longer. In an autobiographical note for an anthology he claimed: 'Zu schreiben habe ich begonnen am Ilmensee 1941' (4:335), and in an interview with Irma Reblitz in March 1965 he went into details:

> Ich wollte, und das ist der Anfang meiner Schreiberei, damals – das ist 1943/44 gewesen, im Kriege – die russische Landschaft festlegen. Es gibt da Schilderungen nicht nur bei Paustowski, sondern schon bei Tolstoi, diese Winterschilderungen, wo versucht wird, diese Landschaft wirklich in den Griff zu bekommen, außerhalb der einfachen Beschreibung. [...] Ich habe es mit Zeichnen und dann mit Prosa probiert. Schließlich fand ich ein Hilfsmittel: die griechische Ode in der von Klopstock bis Hölderlin versuchten Eindeutschung. In dieser Form also, in der alkäischen, sapphischen Strophe entstanden meine ersten Versuche.
> Dann habe ich das Schreiben wieder bleibenlassen eine ganze Zeit. Erst nach der Gefangenschaft, also erst 1952 [...] habe ich es noch einmal aufgenommen. (4:480)

It is a politically very correct scheme, emphasising the war-time odes written under the influence of the Russian landscape, and then switching to Sarmatian works written after 1952. In reality, however, the period up to 1952 was much more complex, with four distinct phases: a phase of true juvenilia until 1941; the period of experimentation with the German forms of the Greek ode from 1941 to 1945; a period of 'Heimatlieder' which he wrote as a prisoner of war between 1945 and 1948, using generally rhyming forms to preserve memories of his distant 'Heimat' and of the European culture that accompanied it; and, from 1950 to 1952, a period of artistic and existential self-questioning in his new socialist Germany. In 1952, with the writing of 'Pruzzische Elegie' (1:33-5) and 'Städte sah ich' (2:221), the first version of 'Unter dem Nachtrand' (1:124), Bobrowski discovered almost by chance the style

---

[1] Quoted in *Johannes Bobrowski: Selbstzeugnisse und Beiträge über sein Werk*, Berlin 1967, p.202.

and subject-matter to which he dedicated himself until he completed his 'Sarmatischer Divan'.

Bobrowski started to write as a teenager in the mid-1930s and first offered poems for publication as early as 1936.[2] Some poems from this earliest period have survived, and a few have been published in the *Gesammelte Werke*.[3] Almost without exception they are short, two or three stanzas long, with (often impure) rhyming quatrains, expressing conventional sentiments on love, death and transience. There is little to indicate his later themes or poetic intention. Some occasional verses reflect his holidays with his father, in particular a trip to Würzburg and Heidelberg. Evening tones prevail:

> Ein Turm. Ein goldnes Dach.
> O Bild ohn' Maßen!
> Du willst es halten ach –
> und mußt es lassen.
>
> Bald ist dir alles fern
> wie niegesehn.
>   'Flußfahrt' (2:9f.)
>
> Leise kam der Stundenschlag,
> und der Tag ist hingeschwommen.
>   'Würzburg/abends' (2:10)
>
> Seltsam scheint der Wein erhellt –
> Morgen bist du fortgezogen.
>   'Heidelberg/abends' (2:11)
>
> O große Schwermut dieser Sommertage.
>   'Sommerabend' (2:12)

In 'Kaspar Hauser' (2:13) he criticises conventionally the heartlessness and the 'feigen kleinen / Selbstherrlichkeiten' of his contemporaries. There is a distant anticipation of future themes in the poem 'Euch, von

---

[2] In *Das Gedicht: Blätter für die Dichtung*. The poems were rejected as lacking 'das einmalige unverwechselbare – Schicksal' (*Marbach* 285). They were considered pleasant but derivative.

[3] A significant number of these very early poems have not been published. Apart from individual poems on loose leaves, they are to be found in two hand-written collections: an early but undated 'Hauspostille', and a '1943 Ausgabe letzter Hand', containing works written between the 1930s and, despite the title, 1944.

denen ich ...' (2:13), in which he sees the continuing presence of those who have gone before both in natural things ('in der Spieg'lung eines Sees, [...] im Erglühn der Früchte') and also in works of art and shared human experiences ('im Klang / alter Lieder, [...] im Verblühn der Hoffnungen'). Surviving poems hardly ever treat specifically East Prussian material, and where this is used, as in 'Parwe' (2:12) (the title refers to a short East Prussian river), the vocabulary of the East, especially the key word 'Kalmus', is quite lost in otherwise conventional images of a summer scene.

Stylistically, the poems of this period show little originality. They are rhyming, the lines usually end-stopped, avoiding enjambement, and they contain occasional echoes of Trakl in their calculated use of unconventional word order[4] to place the verb at the end of the line:

> Die Spinne Trauer dich einspinnt. (2:10)

> [...] Frohen Gruß
> Wanderer mit Wandrern tauscht. (2:11)

> Sonne den Mittag beginnt. (2:12)

> Lustig Winde sich drehn. (2:12)

Reflecting his classical education, a significant number of poems use classical mythology or references: the unpublished poems 'Aphrodite', 'Apoll', 'Herostrat' (who set fire to the temple of Artemis in Ephesos in 356 B.C. in order to give his name a sad immortality), 'Alkibiades' and 'Die Horen', as well as the published 'Der Gott der Tore' (i.e. Janus), (2:21), 'Orpheus' (2:21), 'Amors Wege' (2:27) and 'Thanatos/ Aphrodite' (2:29). Surviving poems contain no reference to the officially fostered Nordic mythology of the time, and the rhyming poems in general contain no intimation of the change to odic forms in 1941.

Apart from the poem 'Die Küssenden (Steinbild an einem Haus in Saint Antonin)' (2:15), poems from the first two years of the war (i.e. from the invasions of Poland and France) are almost unrepresented in the published works, and the unpublished 'Nachlaß' is not much more forthcoming, although it does include a poem 'Kobylka', about a small

---

[4] See, for example, 'Winterdämmerung' in Georg Trakl, *Das dichterische Werk*, Munich 1972, p.14.

town near Warsaw,[5] and a semi-philosophical essay and poem on the French town Guînes.[6] These references are quite different in character. 'Kobylka' is a remarkably clear-sighted short poem, dealing directly (and literally) with a moment of self-reflection:

> Ließ der stille See
> mich ein Bild erblicken:
> wie der Tod ich geh,
> auf dem müden Rücken
> trage ich die Sense.
>
> Aller Traum verloht,
> seit ich mich gesehn
> wie der Tod, der Tod
> durch die Felder gehn.

It is a slight but highly revealing work. Through the cliché of death as the reaper, Bobrowski's expression of self-reproach at his involvement attains a directness not achieved again for many years. He is more circumspect in writing of Guînes. In the essay he describes the town as

> der Rahmen und der Zeuge einer Schicksalsgemeinschaft der Menschen, die sie ja schufen, die Vielseitigkeit menschlicher Verhältnisse tief offenbarend. Und da wir es so sahen, ergriff uns das brüderliche Los der Menschen, darüber die Geißel des Kriegs nun ging.

The hackneyed images of 'brüderliches Los' and the 'Geißel des Kriegs' gloss over the historical fact of German aggression and Bobrowski's (admittedly involuntary) part in it.

The move from France to the Russian front through Lithuania and the events of Kaunas marked a new phase in the war for Bobrowski, and this move is clearly visible in the form and subject-matter of poems written from now on. In a later letter to Ina Seidel (February 20 1944) Bobrowski referred to a 'gewisse Inflation des Menschlichen' (1:xxix), that he had experienced in France. In Russia he had no such problems. His poems turn instead to the immediate experience of this new landscape, of which for him the two most significant elements were Lake Ilmen, on which he was stationed, and Novgorod, which he visited

---

[5] The town is mentioned in passing in *Levins Mühle* (3:64).

[6] 'Über die Abhängigkeit der Beurteilung von der Dauer der Erfahrungen mit dem Gegenstande des Urteils (am Beispiel einer nordfranzösischen Stadt)'.

shortly after it fell. Bobrowski's poetic development in these Russian years can be followed through the cycles of poems that he devoted to each of these two subjects. A letter home from the time links them:

> Einige Zeit liegen wir nun schon fast hier am hohen Ufer des Ilmensees. Über den weiten See, ein Binnenmeer erscheint er fast, sieht man fern die Reste Nowgorods ragen, das einmal eine bedeutende Stadt war. Der lärmende Tag, den wir dort verbrachten, belehrte uns darüber. Der See ist schon die Hauptsache hier, und wir stehen oft am Ufer, wenn auch der Wind schneidend daherfährt.[7]

In this new environment Bobrowski turned almost immediately to odes, generally three stanzas long, occasionally linked to form a short cycle. In view of the overwhelming size and formlessness of the Russian landscape[8] such a move to tight formal structures is not surprising. A number of respectable though now largely unread German poets had reverted to classical metres in the 1920s and 1930s in reaction both against the conventional formlessness of Expressionist poetry from the 1910s and the poetically understated forms of 'Neue Sachlichkeit' from the 1920s. In particular Rudolf Alexander Schröder (1878-1962), Josef Weinheber (1892-1945), Friedrich Georg Jünger (1898-1977) and the Nazi bard Erwin Kolbenheyer (1878-1962) had rediscovered the discipline of the classical poets and their German imitators.[9] These poets looked back to the achievements of Klopstock and also Hölderlin, whose elevation to the status of national poet of the Germans was com-

---

[7] Quoted in Eberhard Haufe, 'Zur Entwicklung der sarmatischen Lyrik Bobrowskis 1941-1961', *Wissenschaftliche Zeitschrift der Martin-Luther-Universität Halle-Wittenberg* 24 (1975), no. 1, 53-74 (p.55).

[8] In another letter to Seidel (March 30 1943) he commented:

> Das Erste, was wir hier lernten, ist das Sehen. Die Landschaft, immer wieder abgesucht, kam uns mit nichts entgegen. Die Endlosigkeit der Ebene, die auch ein Fluß und der (zudem meist niedrige) Wald nicht unterbrechen konnten, wollte uns immer mit einem Gefühl von Verlorenheit betrügen, und so befand sich der Blick immer wieder bei der Fahrt der Wolken, den Farben des Abends und bei den Sternen. Aber da hielten die Worte nicht mit. (*Marbach* 271)

[9] Karl Krolow commented on this phenomenon: 'Form wird Zuflucht, Rettung vor der Überwältigung durch Trostlosigkeit oder Überschwang', in *Das innere Reich* 44 (1934), p.431. Quoted by Roland Rittig in 'Zur Bedeutung der klassischen Odentradition für Johannes Bobrowski', in *Erworbene Tradition: Studien zu Werken der sozialistischen deutschen Literatur*, eds. Günter Hartung, Thomas Höhle and Hans-Georg Werner, Berlin and Weimar 1977, 148-193 (p.153).

pleted under National Socialism.[10]

Bobrowski had read Klopstock and Hölderlin at school and was well aware of poetic developments between 1920 and 1939. That he should turn to these metres in an exercise of poetic self-restraint is not therefore surprising. Nor is his reference in the interview with Reblitz quoted above to using the alcaic and sapphic forms. More mystifying from a later viewpoint is his clear reverence for Klopstock, whom he described to Hans Bender as his 'Zuchtmeister' (4:335). There is simply much more Hölderlin in his works than Klopstock. A possible reason for this comment may, however, be found in 'Der Ilmensee' (2:16f.), the first cycle of poems about Lake Ilmen and arguably the starting point for all these poems in classical metres. The metre for this poem, with the admittedly important exception of the first line, follows very closely that created by Klopstock in another poem about a lake, namely 'Der Zürchersee', and it is possible to see the young and inexperienced Bobrowski imitating Klopstock here in order to write about 'his' lake too.[11] Certainly, seeing 'Der Zürchersee' as providing the pattern for the first Ilmensee ode would in part explain the later insistence on Klopstock as a 'Zuchtmeister'. He would indeed have provided the direct pattern for an important component of this poem.

This earliest Ilmensee poem owes, however, little else to 'Der Zürchersee'. It is a conventional landscape poem, presenting the lake chronologically through scenes of a typical day, and the subject is treated without historical or social dimension or any reference to the destruction already experienced. The invasion of the Soviet Union and Bobrowski's contribution as a soldier are reduced to 'der / strenger fordernde Tag, Rufen [...] und Geklirr,' for which 'der Spindel heimliches Wunder' (a snail-shell) provides some compensating happiness. The poem echoes classical motifs in its description of the sun's movement ('und aufleuchtet die Hore / grell'), while the Russian landscape at night is finally reduced, in images reminiscent of Rilke and Stefan George, to 'die marmornen Gärten der Nacht', full of the 'Lied' of the

---

[10] 'Wir ehren und verehren in Hölderlin den größten Sprachgenius unseres Volkes,' Josef Weinheber, 'Anmerkung zur Erscheinung Friedrich Hölderlins', (written 1940) in *Sämtliche Werke*, Salzburg 1955, vol.4, p.56.

[11] Bobrowski's 'Ilmensee' has a distych in the first two lines; Klopstock's 'Zürchersee' has two pentameters. Lines 3 and 4 are virtually identical in both poems, though Bobrowski shows more freedom in the interchange of dactyls and trochees.

shores and 'der Sterne klare Strophen'. In the stanzas in which he presents the evening scene at the lake, he implies a possible disquiet ('ein Grüßen,– / doch aus unendlichen Fernen von Eis'), but even here the mood is more that of conventional evening melancholy than of an immediate threat or danger.

Many other poems from the period 1941-1943 have survived in the ring-folder '1943 Ausgabe letzter Hand', and some have been published in the *Gesammelte Werke*. In a few cases different versions indicate Bobrowski's poetic development during this period, especially the cycles 'Östliche Landschaft 1941' (2:18-21), which was reworked from an earlier 'Erde und Wind (Östliche Landschaft, Juli 1941)' (*Marbach* 271f.), and the two Novgorod cycles, 'Nowgorod 1941' and 'Nowgorod 1943'. The two different versions of the 'Östliche Landschaft' cycle show an increasing determination to follow metrical structures more accurately and introduce more movement into his poetry, and although such changes are almost certainly the result of natural poetic development and improvement they too demonstrate the possible influence of Klopstock, who insisted in his essay 'Von der Darstellung' on the need for movement within poetry.

More significant were the two Novgorod cycles, the first written under the impact of his arrival and the second representing a later reworking. The differences between these two cycles demonstrate the development from the initial confrontation with these events to their final summary. In its layout the cycle 'Nowgorod 1941' (2:49-51) is almost exactly imitated by 'Nowgorod 1943'[12] (1:222f.; 2:53). 'Nowgorod 1941' has five sections with the titles 'Ikone', 'Anruf', 'Klosterkirche', 'Kreml' and 'Abend', while the 1943 cycle replaces 'Ikone' with 'Steinkreuz'. The most significant differences lie in the increased use of more dramatic visual imagery to express the destruction seen, and in the correspondingly reduced profile of the poetic persona. In the 1941 'Anruf' (2:49) the description of the destruction is weakened by consciously clever word-play:

> Doch wie die Nähe, da nun der Tag anstieg,
> sich nähertat mit vieler Verweigerung [...]

while the poetic persona (as an 'ich' or 'du') reflects distinctly and derivatively on his problems.

---

[12] Largely published in *Das innere Reich* (1943/44, vol. 4).

The 1941 'Abend' (2:51) in this cycle had started reflectively and with an imitation of Jünger's 'Der Taurus':

> Euch such ich heut, Alkäen, daß ihr ins Maß
> das Herz mir leitet wieder und meinem Mund
> die Worte alle nehmt.[13]

Bobrowski's urgent questions in this poem ('Wo ist [...] Wo ist [...] und wo [...] irgendwo...') are also derivative – from the repeated 'Wo?' of Jünger's 'Die Trennung',[14] and indeed the first words of the second stanza 'Doch wie!' are also derivative, as Fritz Minde has pointed out, echoing the first words of the second stanza of Hölderlin's 'Mnemosyne': 'Wie aber liebes?'[15] In the 1943 'Abend' (1:223) the destruction is expressed more directly:

> Zerstörten Treppen gleichend das Ufer geht,
> ein Trümmerfeld von Häusern, aufleuchtend weiß
> und rötlich, stumm hinab. Ein Turm. Dort
> grünlich ein Stück noch von Kirchendächern.

The 1943 'Klosterkirche' (1:222f.) shares the concern with the telling concrete image, replacing the too obviously Christian 'fiel ein rettendes Licht' of 1941 with the more tactile 'es wäscht der / Regen zerbrochnes Gerät des Frommseins'. The 1943 'Kreml' (2:53), arguably the weakest of this cycle and not included in the poems published in *Das innere Reich*, almost reverses the direction of the 1941 'Kreml' (2:50). The earlier version had highlighted the mountain, which was 'unzerstörbar'. In 1943 the emphasis lay on the destruction:

---

[13]   Alcäen ihr, gerüstet wie Krieger, euch
       Erkor ich zu dem kühneren Fluge mir.
       Friedrich Georg Jünger, *Sämtliche Gedichte*, Frankfurt/M.1974, p.52.

Later Bobrowski re-cycled the image in 'Der Strom' (2:67f.), with the lines:

       So nehmt doch zorngerüstet, Alkäen, ihr
       mein Herz in eure leuchtenden Schwünge ein.

Rittig (p.152) calls these cycles in general 'ein Gewebe von Echos'.

[14] *Sämtliche Gedichte*, p.61.

[15] Fritz Minde, *Johannes Bobrowskis Lyrik und die Tradition*, Frankfurt/M. 1981. In the same context Minde points to the coincidence of the line from the 1943 'Anruf' (1:222) 'Noch sinne ich das wohl' with Hölderlin's 'Noch denket mir das wohl'. (p.725, FN 764).

> Kein Weg des Todes, den du geschritten nicht,
> Vernichtung keine, die dir vorüberging
> [...]
> Der Dächer und der Kreuze beraubt [...]

Behind both cycles lies Bobrowski's response to what he saw in and around Novgorod. In the earlier, however, the emotional response and his accompanying thoughts are made explicit, while in the later, as a significant reduction in the number of references to an 'ich' or ich-substitute indicates, he concentrates on the visible and presents his response *through* his description, rather than as comments separate from it. It is a characteristic that will become ever more pronounced in the Sarmatian poems.

These Novgorod cycles anticipate the thematic material of the destruction of Russian church architecture that constitutes an important part of the later cycles. Other poems published in *Das innere Reich* express Bobrowski's sense of the threat to his own existence, using the very appropriate topos of the end of autumn. This sense of transience is ultimately outweighed by elements of a Christian faith, as in the Novgorod cycles, but also in, for example, 'Welebitzy' (1:220) and 'Der Friedhof' (1:221). 'Welebitzy' in particular ends with an almost passionate affirmation of religious exaltation:

> Dann aber reißt der Himmel den Blick empor.
> Da lodern Feuer auf und da steigt ein Wald
> so mächtig, daß die Erde drunten
> trüb nur mehr scheint und ein blinder Spiegel.[16]

The most common form for the 1941-1944 poems had been the short ode. Whilst stationed in Latvia in the final year of the war Bobrowski wrote a number of poems which anticipate later developments, including 'Die Memel' (2:62f.) and the longer 'Kandauer Herbstgedicht' (2:71f.), as well as 'Wiederkehr (Lettland 1944)' (5:259-61). With some of these poems he also set himself a new aim, which he expressed in a letter of September 16 1944 to Ina Seidel:

> [Ich gehe an ein] die bisher angenommenen Grenzen weit übersteigendes Vorhaben: Aus den vielen und vielfältigen Einzelbildern das eine Bild, gleichsam

---

[16] Minde comments on the image of the mirror: 'Die irdische Wirklichkeit erscheint ihm als uneigentliches Abbild einer transzendenten', in *Johannes Bobrowskis Lyrik und die Tradition,* p.419.

das Prinzip etwa des Stroms, der Ebene usw. zu fügen. (*SZNB* 120)

The products of this attempt include the weak odes 'Der Strom' (2:67f.) and 'Die Ebene' (2:69f.). 'Der Strom' was clearly influenced by Jünger and Weinheber and reads as a pale imitation of Hölderlin's river-poems. It starts:

> Ihr hundert Ströme! einmal erfuhr das Herz
> in euern Bildern allen den einen Strom

echoing Weinheber's ode 'Beschreibung eines Himmels', which itself starts

> Viele Himmel sah ich. Aber immer
> seh ich nur den einen

and which ends:

> Daß er mir im Herzen nie verglute!
> Hundert Himmel war er, immer neu. [17]

'Die Ebene' fails to rise above the description of a walk in the country until it attains a dubious climax in a rhetorical assertion of the individual's sense of security in a 'motherly' earth:

> wie diese unbegreiflich weite
> Erde uns mütterlich sein muß, endlos. [18]

The 'Kandauer Herbstgedicht' deals at length with an autumn day in Kandava. As in the 'Russian' odes, the poem reflects the transience of autumn, but where autumn in the earlier poems had been presented as the harbinger of winter and death, 'Kandauer Herbstgedicht' presents a picture of autumn's 'mellow fruitfulness', which ends in the comforting act of holding out a hand to another, though whether to friend or deity is

---

[17] *Sämtliche Werke*, vol. 2, p.382. The next but one poem in this collection is, coincidentally, entitled 'Der Strom'. In his freer use of enjambement, both in his odes and in his (few) elegiac couplets, Bobrowski is considerably closer to Weinheber than to Jünger, who avoided enjambement from pentameter to hexameter. For Bobrowski this is routine.

[18] See also 'Sommerabend' (2:65):

> Oh Erde, Erde, nicht zu enge,
> viel, viel zu reich, viel zu gütig bist du!

unclear.[19]

Bobrowski's intention to present 'das Prinzip' ran counter to his development and was unproductive for the future, despite the later 'Stromgedicht' (1:54f.) and 'Die Sarmatische Ebene' (1:30f.). Of much greater immediate significance for his future work was the Sapphic ode 'Die Memel' (2:62f.), in which, distant from home, he is moved by the 'stumm-gewalt'gen Bildes Erinnerung' to think of his home river and to long for a rejuvenating union with it: 'Da die Fluten teilen und untertauchen / ganz in deine Heiterkeit'. The poem is the first surviving ode from this period to take up the theme of childhood experiences and tackle subject matter other than that of transience in general or of the 'Russian' experience.

'Wiederkehr (Lettland 1944)' is another longer work, anticipating the weary march home of the 'Heere der Söhne' as they think of their homeland and increasingly recognise similarities between this and the route of their retreat:

> Wie aber wird es sein? Freund, befragst du dich
> nicht oft in Nächten, wenn dir das Übermaß
> der Sterne scheint versöhnlicher und
> näher, weil Dörfer und Gärten, Straßen
>
> und jene unvergeßliche hohe Reih'
> von Bäumen ruhn darunter, fast heimatlich?[20]

Their thoughts are already with their homes, and the poem ends as the joy of such thoughts brings forth a 'lösende Träne'.

Throughout most of this 'classical' phase Bobrowski also occasionally wrote rhyming verses continuing the style of his pre-war works. After capitulation and his own capture this strand became predominant in a large number of the poems collected or reconstructed from memory in 1950 in a hand-written anthology 'Heimatlieder'. The reference to 'Lieder' in the title underlines the turn from the strict metrical conventions of the ode, which Bobrowski now used almost exclusively

---

[19] This poem, together with a number of other works from this short period, later contributed imagery to the poem 'Der lettische Herbst' (1:156) which Bobrowski wrote shortly after the building of the Berlin Wall in 1961.

[20] The 'Kandauer Herbstgedicht' had praised the flesh of an apple in similar terms as 'den kräftigen [...] den *heimatlichen*' (my italics).

for social or occasional works – 'Ode an eine Hutnadel' (2:84f.), 'Klassizistische Ode' (2:116-8) or in the deliberate bathos of 'Die Kälber von Nowo-Shachtinsk' (2:78).[21] Instead these poems present a range of forms, including in particular a number of longer, conventional, normally rhyming cycles, with strong echoes especially of works by Weinheber. Although 'Blumen und Kräuter' (2:87-101), 'Geliebtes Jahr' (2:119-28) and 'Konzert für Klavier und Orchester' (2:140-4) present poetically skilful but uninspiring versions of conventional topoi, the long 'Backsteingotik' (2:106-13) is more personal, illustrating a continued interest in East and West Prussian architectural themes, and 'Der Maler Keßler' (2:133-7) is devoted to a minor eighteenth-century painter from Bobrowski's 'Vaterstadt' Tilsit.

These poems were written under the harsh conditions of life as a prisoner of war, and their value is arguably therapeutic rather than aesthetic.[22] They appear frequently to be attempts at cultural stock-taking, preserving memories of the 'Heimat', the other element of the title 'Heimatlieder', and the length of many is the result not of lyrical development but of simple accumulation of remembered facts. 'Blumen und Kräuter' lists and describes thirty-five different plants in a 'leichtes Angebinde / von Blumen, Laub und Gras'; the cycle 'Geliebtes Jahr' is addressed conventionally to a fictional Elise and summarises, unsurprisingly, the monthly joys of 'ein volles rundes Jahr / aus Streit und Küssen'.[23]

The less obviously conventional but incomplete 'Backsteingotik' cycle details architectural elements from castles, cathedrals, the church

---

[21] An exception is the love-poem 'Sommernacht' (2:130).

[22] Rittig interprets this development as an attempt on Bobrowski's part to close the gap between himself and his audience: 'er [überwand] [...] die abgrenzende und gesell-schaftsferne Haltung der frühen Oden [...] und begann, mit klangvollen volksliedhaften Formen positive Beziehungen zu sozialer und natürlicher Umwelt herzustellen' (p.154).

[23] The re-publication of some of these poems in a recent book on the Memelland indicates both their quality and their potential to be misunderstood. Ulla Lachauer, *Land der vielen Himmel: Memelländischer Bilderbogen*, Berlin 1992 includes a selection from the 'Blumen und Kräuter' with a necessary explanatory note:

> Niemand anders hat in den ersten Jahren der Entwurzelung seinem Heimweh so zarten Ausdruck gegeben: so innig noch einmal festgehalten, was er liebte, und es so unmißverständlich klar losgelassen, weil er die deutsche Schuld am Verlust anerkannte und auf sich nahm. (p.104)

The individual poems from this period make *nothing* 'unmißverständlich klar'.

of St. Georg in Rastenburg, and the Hoher Chor of Königsberg Cathedral,[24] while other works of art are fixed in the long poem 'Keiner verdunkelte euch' (2:102-5), which could also easily have been presented as a cycle and in which works by artists as disparate as Baldung, Velazquez and Gauguin are presented as visiting the poet in his dreams. While such memories increase the suffering of the writer, Bobrowski still insists on the validity of such praise of beautiful objects: they are not 'verdunkelt'.

Individual poems of considerable length also fix happy memories of 'Heimat'. In the introductory work 'Heimatlied' (2:74-6) it is memories of, above all, his childhood spent beside the 'Fluß', almost certainly the Jura, which in this poem is clearly distinguished from the 'Strom', i.e. the Memel, into which it flows.[25] In 'Die Vaterstadt' (1:81-3) it is memories of Tilsit, and Bobrowski here makes his listing intentions clear, but also his continued indebtedness to Rilke and George:

> Unendlichs Glück, die letzte deiner Straßen
> im Traum zu wandern.
> [...] Ohne Maßen
> geliebte Stadt, so alt und schön geworden,
>
> rühm ich dich auch, ich rühm dich nie genug.
> Wie soll ich alles nennen: die Alleen,
> den herbstlich-alten Park.

Other poems from the time, in particular 'Die Kurische Nehrung' (2:77f.), at least present more austere aspects of East Prussia:

> Die harten Halme klirren, wenn der Wind
> sich fröstelnd, wie in Wellen, niederschlägt.
> Aufstiebend Sand. [...]
> schmucklos und roh und kalt.

Bobrowski later drew on material from many of these works, and the poem 'Die Kurische Nehrung' appears to anticipate 'Pruzzische Elegie', with one line in particular demonstrating the starting point for the development of the historical and moral dimension later to be so

---

[24] It also provides an unusually early critical appraisal of the Teutonic Knights, whose 'Burg' was of stone and thus 'getreuer / und heimatlicher ihren Herzen'.

[25] In a later letter of January 22 1963 to Alfred Kelletat Bobrowski makes this distinction explicit: 'Also Wiederkehr, das ist an der Jura, welche ein Fluß, nicht an der Memel, die heißt immer Strom' (*Marbach* 470).

characteristic. In 'Die Kurische Nehrung' one finds the lines: 'wenn sich die Wasser ebnen, flüsternd schleichen, / bleibt lang der Ton noch im Geäst der Kiefern'. This refers to the sound of the waves breaking. In 'Pruzzische Elegie' he has the line, referring to an old linden-tree, 'Wie hing Gerücht im Geäst ihr'. This, however, involves not the physical sound of the waves but the historical knowledge of the Old Prussians still echoing through the East Prussian landscape. The shift of emphasis marks the move into the moral world of the 'Sarmatischer Divan'.

Bobrowski's own evaluation of his 'Heimatlieder' at the time showed considerable lack of judgement. In a postcard of July 30 1948 from captivity to his wife Johanna he expressed his relief at the survival of a list of titles she had sent him from the '1943 Ausgabe letzter Hand': 'Die mitgeteilten Titel nehmen mir ein paar Sorgen ab, wenn sie auch gegenüber dem hier Entstandenen wie Vorarbeiten höchstens anmuten werden' (*Marbach* 273). Later he recognised the extent to which these poems were, as he put it, 'konventionell', and drew 'ihren ganzen Wert von ihrem unerschöpflichen Thema' (4:315).

Few of the poems from the 'Heimatlieder' deserve particular mention, except the untypical 1948 poem 'Kentauren' (2:132f.), which, anticipating a later issue, baldly interprets the mythical Centaurs in terms of the inadequacy of attempts to create artificial divisions within a united totality. Centaurs are 'Menschengeist und Kreatur', an embodiment, for the poet, of the fact

> daß mir Hand, Gehör, Gesicht,
>
> Seel, Geist – alles gleichermaßen
> teilhaft ist und zugetan,
> daß ich mit der Seele fassen,
> mit den Händen fühlen kann.

In emphasising the indivisibility of spirituality and physicality, of 'Geistiges' and 'Sinnliches', to the extent that the vocabulary of body and soul can be interchanged, Bobrowski rejects the divisiveness of an age dedicated to 'Verstand' ('Der Verstand bekämpft die Mythen'), in which the 'truth' of 'Sagen', 'Lieder', 'Märchen' and 'Steine' is denied:

> ihr lebt!
>
> Lebt für den, der unverlierbar
> in der Phänomene Flucht
> Marmorbilder, unbeirrbar

> Sagen weiß und Lieder sucht,
>
> der in Märchen und in Steinen
> sein Geschick entdecken kann.

The verses, dedicated to those who are 'ins Kontroverse / unsres Daseins eingeengt', insist on an alternative vision to the strict dualism to which Bobrowski, as a prisoner of war in the process of anti-fascist re-education, was exposed.[26] Later this list of elements containing their own form of 'truth' is resurrected in the 'Pruzzische Elegie', but here is located in concrete historical reality:

> Namen reden von dir,
> zertretenes Volk, Berghänge,
> Flüsse, glanzlos noch oft,
> *Steine* und Wege –
> *Lieder* abends und *Sagen.*

Almost the same list recurs later in the definitive statement of Bobrowski's Sarmatian intentions in his letter to Hans Ricke of October 9 1956: 'Dazu muß alles herhalten: Landschaft, Lebensart, Vorstellungsweise, *Lieder, Märchen, Sagen,* Mythologisches, Geschichte' (*Marbach* 320). The 'truth' of these 1948 Centaurs casts an unexpectedly long shadow.

On December 24 1949 Bobrowski returned from captivity to his family in East Berlin. This late return meant that he saw little of the relative freedom in cultural matters of the years 1945-1949, when cultural policy in the Soviet Zone of Occupation were largely determined by the non-dogmatic 'Kulturbund zur demokratischen Erneuerung Deutschlands'. Instead he was confronted with East Germany's Stalinist campaign against 'formalism', and his own talks on 'Das Kinder- und Jugendbuch' (1951) and 'Über Illustration in Kinder- und Jugendbuch' (1952) (4:406-22) themselves employ the rhetoric of the Cold War. Despite this, his poetic works of the time contributed nothing to this rhetoric, tending instead towards sensitive poetic appreciations of artists or various works of art.

---

[26] See Franz Fühmann's *Der Sturz des Engels*, Munich 1985, with its reference to his own period spent as a prisoner of war: there was no problem that could not be encompassed 'in ein duales Koordinatensystem. [...] Die Welt zerfiel in Weiß und Schwarz' (p.57). It was a 'völlig duales Weltbild' (p.58).

It was a period involving a number of experiments and false starts before in March 1952 he finally praised 'Städte sah ich' (2:221) as 'mein bestes Gedicht' (*Marbach* 317) and as representing the 'Anfang eines "Landschaften-Projekts"' (*Marbach* 319). By December of the same year, he could express his pride at a short cycle of poems on North German composers and musicians 'Der Regenbogen: Improvisationen über alte Musik' (2:206-11):

> Es ist vielleicht etwas schwierig, aber ich hoffe sehr, die Beschäftigung damit möchte sich lohnen; vielleicht enthält's meine künstlerischen und sonstigen Möglichkeiten und Einstellungen sozusagen in nuce und vereinigt. (*SZNB* 403)

The two works anticipate two of the most significant strands of his later poetry: his 'Sarmatian' landscape works and the works to or about fellow artists. Before this became clear to him, however, Bobrowski still had a long way to go.

As with the poems written in war and captivity, earlier works of this period betray a number of influences. Delicate and sensitive interpretations of works of art such as 'Zu einer Bildniszeichnung Julius Schnorrs von Carolsfeld' (2:169f.) and 'Friedrich Overbeck, Jünglingskopf (Bleistiftzeichnung)' (2:170f.) echo the later Rilke, while 'Die Cestius-Pyramide' (2:183-6) uses a motif found most significantly in August von Platen's 'Cestius-Pyramide'. Other poems deal with artistic works to create only conventional effects: 'Rembrandt (Drei Selbstbildnisse)' (2:190-2), 'Zwiesprache mit Shakespeares Bild' (2:205). More substantial works, despite the evident derivativeness, are 'Der Ikonenmaler' (2:194-8), which in particular echoes the 'Buch vom mönchischen Leben' from Rilke's 'Stundenbuch', and 'Der Maler Brouwer' (2:198-201), monologues presenting very different artistic lives as monk and roué, though united in their disapproval of life in towns.[27] They explore aspects of artistic inspiration and experience in the religious ecstasy of a monastic cell or in the midst of drunken revelry. The two extremes are

---

[27] In 'Der Maler Brouwer' this dislike leads to imagery that would not have been out of place in 'Blut und Boden' poetry:

> Güte wohnt nicht in den Städten.
> Bücke mich ins Feld, zu jäten,
> nah der Erde, schwarz und feucht,
> draus der Toten Odem räucht.

also linked in the five short poems of the cycle mentioned above, 'Der Regenbogen: Improvisationen über alte Musik'. These are loosely held together by variations on the image of the rainbow, progressing from 'Bogen' to 'Regenbogen', then to 'Lebensbrücke' and finally 'Brücke der Gnade'. They reflect the problems and aspirations of Christian artists who endure the tension between the sensual beauty of life and art and the awareness of its transience, a tension tempered but by no means resolved by Christian hope. Of overriding importance here is the composer Dietrich Buxtehude, who was later to function in Bobrowski's prose as a central figure of orientation, experiencing

> Erdenpfad und Zionsschimmer,
> draus mein Leben zählt.[28]

Two further poems, 'Europäische Ode' (2:192f.) and its partial retraction 'Europa' (2:203f.), clearly illustrate the lack of certainty of this period. These employ the myth of the rape of the classical Europa to reflect on the National Socialist 'rape' of Europe. In the 'Europäische Ode' Bobrowski could still claim half-optimistically

> Aber auch im Aschenstaub der Ruinen
> lebt deine Rühmung,

and could address Europa as 'Mutter du der Menschheit' and see European culture as ultimately victorious, in that the war against Hitler was fought in the name of European values. By 'Europa' this optimism is gone, and the poem confronts this 'sanfte Mär' with reality:

> [...] Auch vor unsern Augen
> geschah der Raub der Lieblichen. Und keine
> Sage wird das verklären: Unterm Würggriff
> das Ächzen aus dem eingerissenen
> blutigen Mund – Wir standen stumm, ertaubten
> Sinnes, wie Salz, und sahen sie hintaumeln
> zerwühlte Straßen; hinter ihr die Schergen,
> fahrigen Blickes, Trunkene, sich rühmend –

The image of 'Würgen' and the guilt of the 'Beobachter' recur in later poems, but without the classical background and imagery that here robs the self-criticism of its immediacy: the brute fact of personal guilt and

---

[28] 'Der Regenbogen' is analysed at length in Eberhard Haufe's 'Johannes Bobrowski und Dietrich Buxtehude', *SZNB* 189-236.

responsibility is aestheticised behind classical and Biblical ('wie Salz')
imagery.

In a very few surviving poems from these years Bobrowski turns to a
more specifically Eastern European subject-matter, reflecting primarily
his sorrow at the loss of his East Prussian homeland. The Sapphic 'Haff
und See' (2:217) ends a series of memories of the past with the stanza:

> Spürst es heut nach Jahren und schmeckst es nächtens
> oft im Traume. Weißt, wie du einst mit offnen
> Armen niederstürmtest den schmalen Steig, der
> See nur entgegen.

It was a tone that he soon utterly rejected.

Bobrowski sent 'Der Ikonenmaler' to Hans Ricke on March 27 1952,
but admitted that he already had 'kein Verhältnis' to it. In the same
letter he referred to a more recent poem:

> Das Neueste schicke ich Dir auch. Es hat bisher keine Überschrift, meint aber
> eine östliche Landschaft von 1942. Ich bin bereit, es für mein bestes Gedicht
> zu halten, zumal die ersten Versuche, es vor Hörern zu lesen, bestätigten, daß
> es wenigstens in den Bildern zwingend genug ist, um gewisse Vorstellungen
> zu erwecken. (*Marbach* 317)

This poem is 'Städte sah ich' (2:221). Like 'Der Ikonenmaler' its
origins are to be found, as Bobrowski here indicates, ten years before.
The thoughts that gave rise to the 'Ikonenmaler' have been identified in
the poem 'Christusbild des Polyeukt Nikiforow, 3. Sept. 1191' (2:35f.),
written 1943 and anticipating both some of the more striking imagery of
'Der Ikonenmaler' and also some comments Bobrowski wrote in an
explanatory note to the poem.[29] This 'Christusbild', which Bobrowski
had clearly just re-read before working on 'Der Ikonenmaler', is
contained in the '1943 Ausgabe letzter Hand'. Just a couple of pages
away from it in the 'Ausgabe' is to be found the short cycle 'Schmany'
(2:55f.), a weak alcaic cycle (4x3 stanzas) on the accelerated transience
of existence in wartime Russia.[30] It ends with images of comfort that in
part surprisingly anticipate 'Städte sah ich':

---

[29] Quoted in Eberhard Haufe's analysis in 'Zu einem Ikonengedicht Johannes Bobrowskis', *Wegweiser 3: Ein Almanach aus dem Union Verlag*, 1987, 83-94, pp.85f.

[30] The state of the booklet does not, however, allow one to claim that the poems were
always kept in the same order.

> Im Windlosen aber, im Durchlug da
> steht, einer Kerze gleichend, in schmalem Weiß
> ein Kirchenbau. Der hebt die Kuppel
> stumm wie ein Trost, den die Trän' verschattet.

These lines re-appear in 'Städe sah ich' altered but identifiable as: 'kauerte [...] ein Dorf, der Zigeunerin gleichend, der dunklen'. Elsewhere the lines from 'Schmany': 'Hütten stehn, [...] im angstvollen Land, ertrinkend' are also altered but not beyond recognition to become 'Städte. [...] Die versinken im Land'. Just as Bobrowski draws on 'Christusbild' for the 'Ikonenmaler', so in 'Städte sah ich' he appears to have adapted imagery from 'Schmany'. He also appears to have drawn some imagery from the 1952 poem 'Haff und See' (2:217). Here a village *anhebt* and 'Kiefern *kauern*'. In 'Städte sah ich' these images are inverted in the lines 'Draußen / *kauerte*, ehe der Wald / *anhob*, ein Dorf'.[31]

'Städte sah ich'/'Unter dem Nachtrand' is conventionally considered, together with 'Pruzzische Elegie', as marking the start of Bobrowski's 'Sarmatian' poetry. It presents the transience of towns within the Russian landscape, and by implication the destruction brought about by the German attack, by metamorphosing the relatively stable dwellings within this landscape into more transient habitations, tents and eventually boats. Within this shifting process the persona threatens a village which is compared to (and whose fate is hence associated with) one of the prime victims of National Socialist genocide, a gypsy woman. In contrast to the 'Schmany' poem, however, 'Städte sah ich' presents no comfort in view of a church illuminating the path like a burning candle. Instead the poem ends with reference to smoke, a reminder, in this context, of the fate of the victims in the crematoria. As with the development of a different, moral dimension of imagery between 'Die Kurische Nehrung' and 'Pruzzische Elegie', so in 'Städte sah ich' the reversal of imagery from the 'Schmany' cycle indicates the new direction towards the poems of Bobrowski's 'Sarmatischer Divan'. It

---

[31] An even earlier manuscript version of 'Städte sah ich', altered by Bobrowski, again allows a look into Bobrowski's poetic process. Initially the first line ran 'Städte sah ich im Osten / im stäubenden Wind'. In general the alterations aim to break up longer syntactical units, with (e.g.) 'vor [...] / Türen und rinnenden Brunnen' becoming 'vor [...] / Türen, an rinnenden Brunnen' and 'ein Dorf, den braunen / Zigeunern gleich' being altered to 'ein Dorf, der Zigeunerin / gleichend, der dunklen'.

marked the end of a contradictory and complex development, inspired, whatever its immediate cause,[32] by the re-reading of his Russian works of the early 1940s. It would appear that this re-reading propelled Bobrowski on the path to Sarmatia.

---

[32] Haufe suggests that it might have been the result of a period of introspection brought about through working on 'Der Ikonenmaler'.

3

SARMATIA: *SARMATISCHE ZEIT, SCHATTENLAND STRÖME*

Introduction

With two exceptions,[1] the poems included in *Sarmatische Zeit* and *Schattenland Ströme* were written between June 1953 and August 1961, between the East German Uprising and the building of the Berlin Wall. It was a period marked by considerable official cultural changes in the GDR: the last phase of the Stalinist anti-formalism campaign; a short period of relative cultural liberalism after 1953; the re-establishment of socialist realism as official aesthetic doctrine in the cultural freeze after the 1956 Hungarian Uprising; the first Bitterfeld Conference of 1959 with its appeal 'Greif zur Feder, Kumpel, die sozialistische National-kultur braucht dich!', and the international sense of crisis in early 1961. For much of this period Bobrowski was working at aspects of his 'Sarmatischer Divan'.[2]

In an important letter to Hans Ricke of October 9 1956 he explained his intention with unusual clarity:

> Ich will nicht schlechthin schöne Gedichte machen [...]. Ich will etwas *tun* mit meinen Versen, mühevoll und entsagungsvoll *tun*. [...] Ich will etwas tun, wozu ich durch Abstammung und Herkunft, durch Erziehung und Erfahrungen fähig geworden zu sein glaube. [...]
> Ich will [...] in einem großangelegten (wenigstens dem Umfang nach) Gedichtbuch gegenüberstellen: Russen, Polen, Aisten samt Pruzzen, Kuren, Litauern, Juden – meinen Deutschen. Dazu muß alles herhalten: Landschaft, Lebensart, Vorstellungsweise, Lieder, Märchen, Sagen, Mythologisches, Ge-schichte, die großen Repräsentanten in Kunst und Dichtung und Historie. Es muß aber sichtbar werden am meisten: die Rolle, die mein Volk dort bei den Völkern gespielt hat. Und so wird die Auseinandersetzung mit der jüngsten Zeit, für mich: der Krieg der Nazis, einen wesentlichen und sicher den gewichtigsten Teil ausmachen. So werde ich in den Gedichten stehen, uniformiert und durchaus kenntlich. Das will ich: eine große tragische Kon-stellation in der Geschichte auf meine Schultern nehmen, bescheiden und für mich, und das daran gestalten, was ich schaffe. Und das soll ein (unsichtbarer, vielleicht ganz nutzloser) Beitrag sein zur Tilgung einer unübersehbaren historischen Schuld meines Volkes, begangen eben an den Völkern des

---

[1] 'Unter dem Nachtrand' (1:124) and 'Pruzzische Elegie' (1:33-5.), both of which were completed in 1952. See previous chapter.

[2] His working title. The ironic respect for Goethe's 'West-Östlicher Diwan' is clear.

Ostens. [...]

Ich liebe die Landschaft, die Geschichte, die Menschen meiner Heimat. Und ich liebe die Deutschen. Aus solchem Grundgefühl soll das weite Land zwischen Weichsel und Wolga/Don sichtbar werden in Gedichten. (*Marbach* 320f.)

With this as framework he emphasised in the same letter: 'festzuhalten: jedes Gedicht [...] ist ein Teilstück, ein Mosaikstein. Alle zusammen werden einmal [...] ein einziges (freilich in sich vielschichtiges, kompliziertes) Bild abgeben'.

He appears to have abandoned such almost encyclopaedic intentions by, at the latest, April 30 1959, when he admitted to Karl Schwedhelm:

Eine ursprüngliche Absicht, mit meinen Gedichten zu einer Darstellung der Begegnung meines Volkes mit den Völkern des Ostens zu kommen, einer unglücklichen und schuldhaften Begegnung, ist aufgegeben. So nötig eine solche Bemühung wäre und so sehr mein Leben unter solchen Erfahrungen steht, scheint mir inzwischen eine 'lyrische Aufarbeitung' unmöglich. Es bleibt bei gelegentlichen Hervorbringungen, die von der Erinnerung genährt sind, von der unlösbaren Verwurzelung in einer Landschaft, die mit allem Recht verloren ist. (4:327)

Yet despite appearing to abandon these intentions, Bobrowski's claims concerning them became ever more precise in the 1960s: for Bender he refers to

die Deutschen und der europäische Osten. [...] Eine lange Geschichte aus Unglück und Verschuldung, [...] die meinem Volk zu Buch steht. Wohl nicht zu tilgen und zu sühnen, aber eine Hoffnung wert und einen redlichen Versuch in deutschen Gedichten. (4:335)

Elsewhere, in his application of November 16 1962 to join the East German Writers' Union, the 'Schriftstellerverband', he asserted almost dogmatically:

Hauptthema: Der Versuch, das unglückliche und schuldhafte Verhältnis des deutschen Volkes zu seinen östlichen Nachbarvölkern bis in die jüngste Vergangenheit zum Ausdruck zu bringen und damit zur Überwindung revanchistischer Tendenzen beizutragen. (*SZNB* 14)

The list of such claims could be continued.[3] They must, however, be

---

[3] See also *SZNB* 19 and *SZNB* 32. This confidence of purpose was not always reflected in private. In a letter of May 21 1959 to Jokostra he claimed:

Gedichte gehen nicht aufs Publikum, sie sind als Selbstaussagen (im weiteren seen in the historical context of the GDR, where his 'vielschichtiges, kompliziertes [...] Bild' was viewed with extreme suspicion. His later claims attempt to provide a justification for his poems, and he made these claims so breathtakingly simple that even the East German cultural authorities could both understand and approve. By this means he was able to live his poetic existence relatively untouched.

Certainly, the possibility of a complete misunderstanding was ever present, and a poem like 'Dryade' (1:83) with its evocation of the tree nymph might well be interpreted as close in spirit to the apolitical nature poetry of Lehmann and Loerke, whose works, despite occasional expressions of admiration, Bobrowski rejected. Even more problematical was the tenor of some earlier poems: out of the protecting context of a published volume, some of these ('Die Daubas', 'Kindheit', 'Die alte Heerstraße') appear as elegiac expressions of lament at the loss of East Prussia. This loss, the result of the shift of borders after 1945, was, however, a matter of grave political concern involving the Soviet Union, Poland, and East and West Germany, and with such a background such poetry could well be interpreted as 'revanchistisch', as giving support to the political and territorial aspirations of right-wing West German 'Heimatvertriebenenverbände'. It was an interpretation that made the writer Franz Fühmann admit:

> [...] daß ich anfangs [Bobrowskis] Lyrik schroff ablehnend gegenüber-
> gestanden bin, ja in ihr etwas Unerlaubtes gesehen habe: das Wachhalten,
> vielleicht sogar Wiedererwecken von Gefühlen, die aussterben mußten,
> Sentiments der Erinnerungen an die Nebelmorgen hinter der Weichsel und den
> süßen Ruf des [Pirols].[4]

Another misinterpretation possible within the GDR context was to see 'Sarmatien' as a semi-utopian 'Orplid', a politically suspect escape from the present. Such a suspicion was inevitably present but was aired publicly in an article by Adolf Endler in *Sonntag* a few months before Bobrowski's death. The effect of this article on Bobrowski's prose will be examined later. By emphasising in his public statements the element of guilt and attempted recompense, Bobrowski was able to ward off such criticism for some time.

Sinn) auch durchaus privater Natur. Die Teilnahme anderer ist Zufall, Glücksfall oder Irrtum. Im Grunde gehen sie nur den Erzeuger selbst an. (*Marbach* 428)

[4] *Zweiundzwanzig Tage oder die Hälfte des Lebens*, Rostock 1974, p.59. The 'Pirol' (golden oriole) plays an important part above all in Bobrowski's poem 'Kindheit'.

The contradiction, however, between the complexity of the works and the apparent simplicity of his objectives remained.[5] Even the word 'Sarmatien' requires explanation, so that when he read to the Gruppe 47 in Aschaffenburg in 1960 Bobrowski needed to introduce his subject-matter:

> Unter Sarmatien verstehe ich nach Ptolemäus das Gebiet zwischen Schwarzem Meer und Ostsee. Zwischen Weichsel und der Linie Don-Mittlere Wolga. Ein Gebiet, aus dem ich stamme und in dem ich herumgekommen bin. (*Marbach* 121f.)

The explanation highlights two elements: the historicity of the denotation, and Bobrowski's personal involvement in this area, as the place from whence he came and where he had 'herumgekommen' (a reference to his years as a soldier). 'Sarmatien' is a fortunate term, with no implications of cultural superiority or inferiority, while its historical remoteness allowed the illusion of a single geographical and cultural unit embracing the various post-Ptolemaic nation-states with their controversially shifting boundaries. It could, of course, be interpreted to imply the timelessness of mythical, ahistorical, 'escapist' poetry, but a number of poems point in their very titles to specific dates: 'Vogelstraßen 1957' (1:114f.), 'Der Ilmensee 1941' (1:53), 'Kaunas 1941' (1:60f.), 'Kathedrale 1941' (1:130f.) and 'Dorfkirche 1942' (1:132), while even the two poems 'Trauer um Jahnn' (1:36) and 'Gedächtnis für B.L.' (1:138) indicate a specific time, as they relate to the deaths of Hans Henny Jahnn (1959) and Boris Leonidovich Pasternak (1960). Such historical pointers, especially to years as significant as 1941 and 1942, are calculated to undermine the idea of Sarmatia as the timeless myth, and despite the presence throughout these poems of the mythological and other pre-rational elements to which Bobrowski had referred in his letter to Ricke ('Vorstellungsweise [...] Mythologisches') Sarmatia is a historical rather than a mythical landscape. This historical dimension is indicated by such historical markers, the individual mosaic stones, but it is also presented throughout the volumes in the develop-

---

[5] Two early attempts to solve the paradox are those by Renate von Heydebrand, 'Engagierte Esoterik: Die Gedichte Johannes Bobrowskis' in *Wissenschaft als Dialog: Studien zur Literatur und Kunst seit der Jahrhundertwende: Wolfgang Rasch zum 65 Geburtstag*, eds. Renate von Heydebrand and Klaus Günther Just, Stuttgart 1969, pp.386-450, and by Dagmar Deskau, *Der aufgelöste Widerspruch: 'Engagement' und 'Dunkelheit' in der Lyrik Johannes Bobrowskis*, Stuttgart 1975.

ment of a system of images drawn from nature that point as signs to historical developments.

Style

The poems of the Sarmatian volumes show considerable stylistic as well as thematic uniformity. They are almost without exception rhymeless and written in free rhythms that display considerable knowledge of odic forms.[6] They are characterised by a particular use of nature/landscape imagery and frequently display a distinctive movement from apparent evocation to reflection within the individual poem,[7] with a tripartite structure involving changes of tense, of perspective, involving indeed very different forms of expression.[8]

The poems often begin with short, sometimes verbless clusters of words, reminiscent of Trakl, rhythmically and often syntactically un-structured, with an implication, simply through lack of any tense indicators, of a time in the present:

> Wildnis. Gegen den Wind.
> Erstarrt. In den Sand
> eingesunken der Fluß.
> > 'Der Ilmensee 1941' (1:53)

> Holzbank, ein hartes meuble.
> Dort, zwischen Kiefernbäumen,
> die Schaukel – ein Brett, zwei geschälte
> Stangen.
> > 'Wiederkehr' (1:63)

> Heller Sand, Spuren,
> grün, und der fliegende Wald
> Finsternis.
> > 'Erzählung' (1:87)

> Kalt,
> die durchspeerte Luft,

---

[6] The volumes also contain two odes, 'Der Muschelbläser' (1:100) (alcaic), and 'Ode auf Thomas Chatterton' (1:103f.) (sapphic).

[7] See the title of an early critical work by Wolfram Mauser *Beschwörung und Reflexion*, Frankfurt/M. 1970.

[8] Bobrowski himself suggested a form of tripartite division in a letter of November 25 1960 to Max Hölzer, (quoted *Marbach* 350), when he referred to the 'Auseinander-trennung von Vorgang, Reflexion, Gedächtnis' in his 'Sommergeschrei' (1:85).

das Schwarz und das Weiß, Licht, redend
auf Vogelstraßen.
                              'Nachtschwalben' (1:108)

'Immer zu benennen' (1:143) gives a paradigmatic example of this
device, that of 'naming':

Immer zu benennen:
den Baum, den Vogel im Flug,
den rötlichen Fels, wo der Strom
zieht, grün, und den Fisch
im weißen Rauch, wenn es dunkelt
über die Wälder herab.

It is an act of evocation of which the specifically moral limitations are
immediately admitted:

Zeichen, Farben, es ist
ein Spiel, ich bin bedenklich,
es möchte nicht enden
gerecht.

Many of these poems then break out of this unsyntactical nominalism
into a phase of greater syntactical clarity, involving more epic elements,
often presented in the past tense and frequently including what appear to
be the poet's individual memories. In 'Immer zu benennen' this phase is
marked by the poet's awareness of his forgetfulness:

Und wer lehrt mich,
was ich vergaß: der Steine
Schlaf, den Schlaf
der Vögel im Flug, der Bäume
Schlaf, im Dunkel
geht ihre Rede – ?

In 'Die Memel' (1:67f.), for example, the memories are more specific:

Einmal mit dem Wind
gingen wir, stellten das Netz
in der Mündung des Wiesenbachs.
In den Erlen
hing die Laterne. Der Alte
nahm sie herab.
Das Schmugglerboot stieß auf den Sand.[9]

---

[9] This 'epic' element is also especially clear in 'Der Don' (1:121) and 'Wagenfahrt'

In almost all cases the poems present an overlapping of times, with apparent present evocation giving way to indications of tentative memories. Out of the tension of these contrasting elements arises the final section, grammatically in the present tense, but in reality often representing an overcoming of such dualism in a potential unity. This section often culminates in an appeal or a cry, or reference to an act of communication, or some literary or Biblical or religious allusion.

The pattern thus frequently, but not invariably, involves a shift from a verbless naming to past tense verbs to some conclusion in the present tense. Again 'Immer zu benennen' provides a clear example, even though the present tense is not used:

> Wär da ein Gott
> und im Fleisch,
> und könnte mich rufen, ich würd
> umhergehn, ich würd
> warten ein wenig.

'Holunderblüte' (1:94) is unusually direct in its concluding appeal:

> Leute, ihr redet: Vergessen [...]
> Leute, es möcht der Holunder
> sterben
> an eurer Vergeßlichkeit.

While, however, a basic tripartite structure is generally evident, the specific elements of this structure vary considerably. 'Die alte Heerstraße' (1:16f.) starts with syntactical completeness, if with unconventional word order: 'Seitab ist gezogen / auf der verfallenen Straße / der Korse, ein südlicher Kaiser', while 'Auf den jüdischen Händler A.S.' (1:15) starts: 'Ich bin aus Rasainen'. These are, however, the exceptions, and the basic development is clear if constantly varied. In her attempt to define it, Dagmar Deskau has emphasised the possible influence of the classical Pindaric ode, with its strophe, antistrophe and epode, but also referred, in explanation of Bobrowski's 'positive abrundende Haltung' to the Pindaric odes of Gryphius.[10] John Flores has succinctly called the three phases 'incantatory', 'narrative', and 'opta-

---

(1:18).

[10] '"Dunkelheit" und "Engagement": Zur Gestaltung des Geschichtsbezuges in der Lyrik Johannes Bobrowskis', unpublished doctoral dissertation, University of Mainz 1973, p.124.

tive',[11] while from a very different perspective Dorothee Sölle saw ('verallgemeinernd') a 'Bewegungskurve [...] aus dem mythischen Nennen, über dessen Zerstörung in der Geschichte, zum zitierten anklingenden biblischen Versprechen'.[12] More recently Oliver Schütze has analysed the possible influence of Hölderlin and tentatively suggested parallels between the three sections of Bobrowski's poems and Hölderlin's 'Wechsel der Töne': 'naiv', 'heroisch' and 'idealisch'.[13]

However useful such definitions may be, they can only approximate to the sense of a perceptible movement, from words without ordering principle, verbless, tenseless, context-less, to a situation where, in a number of different ways, order is created. The final phase of these poems frequently introduces some pre-existent verbal or metrical quotation as a specific form of pre-established order. These quotations function as points of poetic security, as the harbour reached safely at the end of the journey that is the poem. Several, as Sölle suggests and as is clear from the above, are derived from the Judaeo-Christian tradition. The ending of 'Holzhaus' ('ihre Stätte / kennt sie nicht mehr') uses Psalm 103: 16,[14] while the poem 'Ja, ich sprech in den Wind' (2:333f.) ends with the words: 'In der Welt habt ihr Angst' (John 16: 33).[15] Both poems end with quotations that mark the point of deepest darkness but also the turning point in the Biblical text, as both Biblical quotations move on immediately to express the writer's hope. For those 'who have ears to hear', these quotations act as signs, pointing to ultimate comfort in the divine ordering of the world. Other poems ending with evident Christian or Biblical resonances include 'Der Wachtelschlag' (1:76f.) ('Lobet Gott') 'An den Chassid Barkan' (1:95) with 'auszusäen mit

---

[11] John Flores, *Poetry in East Germany: Adjustments, Visions, and Provocations, 1945-1970*, New Haven and London 1971, pp.249-53.

[12] Dorothee Sölle, 'Für eine Zeit ohne Angst: Christliche Elemente in der Lyrik Johannes Bobrowskis', *Almanach für Literatur und Theologie*, 2 (1968), 143-66 (p.153).

[13] Oliver Schütze, *Natur und Geschichte im Blick des Wanderers: Zur lyrischen Situation bei Bobrowski und Hölderlin*, Würzburg 1990, pp.199-207.

[14] 'Ein Mensch ist in seinem Leben wie Gras, er blüht wie eine Blume auf dem Felde; wenn der Wind darüber geht, so ist sie nimmer da, und ihre Stätte kennet sie nicht mehr. Die Gnade aber des Herrn währt von Ewigkeit zu Ewigkeit über denen, die ihn fürchten.'

[15] 'In der Welt habt ihr Angst; aber seid getrost, ich habe die Welt überwunden.'

Tränen, / zu ernten fröhlich',[16] 'Nänie' (1:101) with the image of the rainbow and the concluding lines: 'Frieden / ist uns versprochen', and 'Ostern' (1:136) with 'Hosianna'.

Yet other poems are brought to a conclusion with quotations from literary or historical texts. 'Seestück' (1:102) ends with the word 'Schattengestalt', which Bobrowski agreed he had found in Herder, in the *Ideen* Book 8, ch.2.[17] A number of poems to individual writers or painters conclude not surprisingly with quotations from or recognisable references to their works: 'Ode auf Thomas Chatterton' (1:103f.), 'Hölderlin in Tübingen' (1:107), 'Hamann' (1:92), 'Gertrud Kolmar' (1:116) and 'An Nelly Sachs' (1:119f.). Yet others end with concealed quotations from other sources, and the poem 'Mickiewicz' (1:144f.), to which I will return at the end of this chapter, ends with a very obscure reference to a novel by H. W. Seidel. Other works conclude with pseudo-quotations or snatches of speech: 'Der Don' (1:121), 'Anruf' (1:3), 'Das Holzhaus über der Wilia' (1:19f.), 'Der Wanderer' (1:88), 'Gedächtnis für einen Flußfischer' (1:11), in which the miaouing of the cat appears onomatopoeically (but also as a concealed quotation, see 5:24) as 'Der Himmel stürzt ein!', 'Wagenfahrt' (1:18), 'Am Strom' (1:23), 'Villon' (1:37), 'Auf der Taurischen Straße' (1:49), 'Kaunas 1941' (1:60f.).

In addition to such verbal 'harbours', many of these poems end with a 'rhythmisches Leitmotiv' from the metrical 'vocabulary' of the classical ode.[18] Such echoes occur within the body of the poems, with, for example, a 'perfect elegiac distich' in 'Pruzzische Elegie',[19] but they most frequently occur in the concluding line. The two most common of these leitmotifs are the choriambus x--x and the adoneus x--x-, which, as the last line of the sapphic ode, carries with it a sense of completion and roundness that underpins the verbal resolution on the metrical level. The quality Bobrowski associated with this particular metrical structure is evident from his own sapphic ode 'Sappho' (2:292), where he

---

[16] See Psalm 126: 5.

[17] See *Sarmatische Zeit: Erinnerung und Zukunft, Johannes Bobrowski Colloquium 1989*, ed. Alfred Kelletat, Sankelmark 1991, p.37. Future references to this volume will occur in the text as *Sankelmark*.

[18] See Deskau, '"Dunkelheit" und "Engagement"', p.103.

[19] See Theodore Ziolkowski, *The Classical German Elegy, 1795-1950*, Princeton, N.J, Guildford 1980, p.281. The lines he refers to are 'Volk der schwarzen Wälder [...] Jagd'.

suggests that the line offers 'eine Zeit, ein Verweilen', before the reader is caught up in the 'Chaos' of his own life after a pause that lasts for the 'Zug eines Atems' (the adoneus).[20] In some poems the discovery of these 'quotations' adds considerably to what comfort the poem offers: 'Dorf' (1:5), 'Wagenfahrt' (1:18), 'Die Günderrode' (1:39) end in the choriambus; 'Nymphe' (1:8), 'Die Spur im Sand' (1:28), 'Der Wanderer' (1:88), 'Aleksis Kivi' (1:40f.) and 'Immer zu benennen' in the adoneus.

The poem 'Der Wanderer' complements the illustration above of this movement in 'Immer zu benennen', as its tripartite division is underlined by the coincidence of the three sections with the three stanzas and as the disjointed elements of the introduction are restated in the concluding stanza in a syntactically correct (if visionary and apparently unreal) form.

> Abends,
> der Strom ertönt,
> der schwere Atem der Wälder,
> Himmel, beflogen
> von schreienden Vögeln, Küsten
> der Finsternis, alt,
> darüber die Feuer der Sterne.
>
> Menschlich hab ich gelebt,
> zu zählen vergessen die Tore,
> die offenen. An die verschloßnen
> hab ich gepocht.
>
> Jedes Tor ist offen.
> Der Rufer steht mit gebreiteten
> Armen. So tritt an den Tisch.
> Rede: Die Wälder tönen,
> den eratmenden Strom
> durchfliegen die Fische, der Himmel
> zittert von Feuern.

The first stanza presents a syntactically disjointed evening scene of isolation. The landscape is inhospitable and, as in the early letter to Ina Seidel quoted above, appears to offer no hold for the eye, which is

---

[20] Compare the letter to Jokostra of March 4 1959: 'wir pflanzen auf das Chaos Blumen und ziehen uns mit einer Zeile Davids oder Deborahs ins Tageslicht,' quoted in Peter Jokostra, 'Celan ist bestenfalls eine Parfümfabrik', *Die Welt*, October 30 1971.

drawn ever upward to the comfortless stars. In the second stanza the wanderer/poet turns to an analysis of his own existence, echoing Matthew 7: 7 ('klopfet an, so wird euch aufgetan') and defining his own human existence in terms of its weaknesses, forgetfulness of past benefits on the one hand, and unnatural demands (that all gates be open) on the other.[21] These concerns are interrupted by the call of an unnamed but welcoming 'Rufer', who contradicts the gloomy assessment of reality and offers open hospitality.[22] In response to this, the wanderer's new 'Rede' restates the original scene of syntactical disorder as a vision that contains both considerable vitality and a harmonious interchange of natural characteristics ('den eratmenden Strom / durchfliegen die Fische') and that also shows syntactical order and a clear metrical structure.[23] 'Der Wanderer' thus moves towards some form of ordering (in its widest sense), not within rational categories but in terms of an irrationally interrelated whole, brought about by some epiphanic contact with the 'Rufer'. It is a poetic, not a rational resolution.

As well as this movement, the poems in general are characterised by their thorough-going use of imagery drawn from the Sarmatian landscape, whether in poems dealing with childhood, or love, or the effects of the German invasion of Poland and the Soviet Union, or in the poems to the various inhabitants of the area, or to other writers. The reader observes the experiences, memories and thoughts of a poetic persona steeped in the landscape, nature and history of Sarmatia, from its high culture to the various contradictory elements of its popular and local myths and customs, and hence participates in the partial re-creation of a self-referential Sarmatian whole. Within this poetic world the reader is the indirect, though evidently welcome, addressee, observing the creation of a poetic discourse as a stranger, one of the 'Fremden' to

---

[21] Such a combination is a recurrent image. In 'Giotto' (2:167-9) Bobrowski wrote: 'Du hast dich nur dem Einen übereignet: // ein Mensch zu sein, zu schlagen mit den Fäusten / an die verschlossnen Türen' while in the late 'Ankunft' (1:183f.) he uses the version: 'Hier wird sprechen, / der vor das Tor tritt, der / Lebendige, er wird sagen: // Wer des Wegs kommt, / trete herein'. See also 'Liebesgespräch' (2:348): 'Wer lebt, wird reden. / Und gehn vor das Tor. Es trete / herein, wer des Wegs kommt'.

[22] The echo of Trakl's, 'Ein Winterabend' is unmistakable: 'Vielen ist der Tisch bereitet / [...] / Wanderer tritt still herein'. In Trakl's poem, with its references to 'der Baum der Gnaden' and 'Brot und Wein', the religious dimension is more explicit.

[23] The last two lines are a triple amphibrac and an adoneus.

whom 'Anruf', the first poem of the cycle, refers in its almost Biblical
welcoming command: 'Heiß willkommen die Fremden. / Du wirst ein
Fremder sein. Bald' (1:3).

The imagery is of nature, more specifically of landscape, and it is a
landscape into which human history has passed. This dual existence – as
natural phenomenon and as a sign or indicator of historical events – runs
throughout the works and was developing in even earlier, pre-Sarmatian
poems. The link is particularly evident with natural/landscape images
implying destruction, which are occasionally directly linked with
historical events. In the war-poem 'Aufenthalt' (1:126), the 'Ich', ('ein
hölzerner Schatten, / beschlagen mit Eisen') is clearly a German soldier
in the 'Land um die Wolgaquelle'. This figure, however, 'stand auf
verschütteten Strömen', and this unreal image here of the breakdown of
natural order implies in this context the destruction brought about by his
presence. Similarly, in 'Der Ilmensee 1941' (1:53) a river is gone: 'In
den Sand / eingesunken der Fluß'. Meanwhile, in the same poem, a wolf
is itself unnaturally frightened by a 'Schattengesicht'. Again, natural
order is inverted. In 'Verlassene Ortschaft' (1:123) the market-place,
natural centre of life, is empty. The natural image of the thunderstorm
develops an almost apocalyptic dimension as a metaphoric expression of
these events in 'Abend der Fischerdörfer' (1:129) which is placed
immediately before the signposting 'Kathedrale 1941'. Here the indiscriminate destructiveness of the storm ('der im Geröll den Stein / trifft,
der schlägt eines Vogels / zuckenden Schatten im Sand') conveys the
indiscriminate destructiveness of invasion. In 'Wetterzeichen' (1:98f.)
the signs of this destruction in a landscape are particularly clear, as is
the obligation this imposes on the poet:

> Flamme, flieg,
> [...] zerbrochen
> die Lüfte dann, auf dem Sand
> reglos der Fluß
>
> und der Hügel getroffen,
> ich halt einen Baum, ich red noch:
> Wir sahen kommen die Zeichen
> und schwinden, her durch die Stille
> zwei Federn fielen herab.

Similarly in 'Windmühle' (1:45) the Sarmatian experience and Bobrowski's personal history are presented using the image of the storm. In
this poem the persona presents his previous existence before the storm

as a part of the Sarmatian community ('ich ging / mit den Schnittern'). The windmill, 'starr und alt', has its fixed position as a point of unchanging reference. With the breaking of the storm as a clear, almost allegorical image of war and destruction, the mill itself takes flight and leaves, accompanying the emigrating herons, as a shift to winter confirms:

> [...] Nun mit grauen
> Flügeln greift sie die Lüfte.
> Lautlos hebt sie sich auf überm Land.
>
> Mit den Reihern davon
> fährt sie, groß vor den weißen
> Himmeln. Wild aus der Ferne
> glänzt ihr das Auge
> des Winters nach.

In this continuing winter the persona establishes his home in the 'Höhlung' left by the mill and, identifying with the 'Eisvogel', the kingfisher, which, according to popular legend, breeds in winter, concentrates on rebuilding his existence:

> Eisvogel Herz,
> aus Gräten und Flossen
> bau dein Nest in der Höhlung,
> im flüsternden Blut.
>
> Bei den Kindern der Ebene, Töchtern und Söhnen,
> bleib, bei den kleinen Schatten
> aus Liedern und Tänzen, du
> halt ein Novembergras
> gegen den Schnee.[24]

What remains after this disaster are remnants ('Gräten und Flossen'), the new generation, the memories of lost folklore ('kleine Schatten / aus Liedern und Tänzen') and the slender, almost absurd hope of the last lines: 'halt ein Novembergras / gegen den Schnee'.

Other images for this destruction are derived from the world of animals: the wolf in 'Tod des Wolfs' (1:91) is killed by a wild boar

---

[24] Here too Bobrowski uses a direct address as well as a metrical quotation. The poem itself functions as this 'Novembergras', and its modicum of comfort is achieved by the establishment of such a relationship to a 'du' as well as the comforting awareness of tradition.

('tapferes / Schweinchen, dem Bösen hast / heimgezahlt'), but in other
poems it is the hawk ('Lettische Lieder'), occasionally contrasted with
the peaceful lark, or the 'räubrischer Fisch'. There is, however, no
mechanical allegorisation, and an image with potentially negative
connotations may function positively. In 'Kloster bei Nowgorod'
(1:134) the pike, a predatory fish, is presented with another quality, that
of movement, as a sign of returning life, of hope in a desolate landscape:

> [..] silberner steigt,
> flossenstarrend
> der Hecht aus dem Grund.

Similarly, crows, viewed conventionally as birds of death in
'Dorfmusik' (1:141) and 'Die alte Heerstraße' (1:16f.), function in
'Wintergeschrei' (1:90) as remnants of life in a frozen world:

> Krähen, Krähen,
> grünes Eis, Krähen
> über dem Strom [...]
> ein wenig Blut
> dein Herz
> mitten im Eis.

The significance of the image in this cycle generally depends on its
funtion within its poem and is not predetermined.

Not surprisingly the images with which Bobrowski most frequently
expressed the destruction of Sarmatia involve snow, ice, cold and winter
and the struggle against them. 'Windmühle' ends with the appeal 'du /
halt ein Novembergras / gegen den Schnee'; in 'Tod des Wolfs' the
sound of the 'Schweinchen' 'macht mir im Dunkel / warm'. In 'Die
Tomsker Straße' (1:135) the break with the idyll ('ein Land wie der
Himmel, / einen Sommer, aufschäumt' er / von Blumen') is completed
with the words: 'es kam / aber der Schnee'. In 'Winterlicht' (1:71f.) the
snow is linked directly to the destruction of the idyll, but also to another
important set of images of destruction, namely images of silence, which
accompany winter:[25]

> Unsrer Hütten dunkel
> redende Güte, ihr sanftes
> Wort ist verschneit.[26]

---

[25] Again this is not always the case. In 'Friedhof' (1:25) winter 'schreit [zurück]'.

[26] This line forms the starting point for Stefan Reichert's *Das verschneite Wort:*

In 'Der Don' (1:121) the river in winter is 'gefangen, Eishauch / wehte er, Stille finster / folgte ihm nach'. In 'Alter Hof in Wilna' (1:93) Bobrowski describes 'der Vater': 'er hat / gesungen gegen das Schweigen'; in 'Der Wachtelschlag' (1:76f.) he rejoices at hearing the call of the bird 'einfach / gerufen im Finsteren in / die Woge Schweigen, die aufrauscht, / Tiefe hinter sich, raumlos, / Leere'.[27] Again in 'Windmühle' one of the comforts against the winter is found in the 'Schatten aus *Liedern* und Tänzen'.

By contrast sound and attempts at communication form one of the most consistent positive sets of images of the two volumes. In 'Ebene' (1:80) the poet pleads: 'Lehr mich reden, Gras'. In other poems the 'Rede' can involve a 'Schrei', as in 'Die Memel' (1:67f.), where the lost childhood area is a 'Bild aus Schweigen' to be transformed into: 'Tafeln dem Künft'gen: mein Schrei', while in 'Französisches Dorf' (1:105) the poet's rescue from his Hölderlinian meditations ('wenn ich die Wetterfahn' / kreisen seh, die Zeit nach ihr zähl') is accomplished by an 'Angélique': 'aus dem höchsten / Fenster schrei mich ins Licht!' Such repeated images construct the framework within which the details of Sarmatia and its history are presented. They introduce a historical dimension, whether presenting aspects of the destruction of Sarmatia or forces opposing or reacting to this destruction. As in 'Pruzzische Elegie', the natural landscape 'speaks' of its history.

The context provided by the cyclical arrangement of his poems allows this landscape to evoke both the historical Sarmatia itself and the events leading up to Bobrowski's loss of physical contact with it. It constitutes an ironic (and possibly unconscious) rebuttal of Brecht's 'An die Nachgeborenen' that Bobrowski actually holds 'ein Gespräch über Bäume' which does *not* involve 'ein Schweigen über so viele Untaten'. On the contrary: the cyclical arrangement of the poems, wherein the individual poems are 'Mosaiksteine', as well as the inclusion of obvious pointers to personal or national historical guilt, create a context in which even individual poems whose content is apparently unrelated to these events gain an ethical dimension: even the apparently 'pure', non-

---

Untersuchungen zur Lyrik Johannes Bobrowskis, Bonn 1989. Reichert sees Bobrowski's aim as the uncovering and eventual recovery of this 'Wort'.

[27] In this context the 'Leere' is associated with silence. In 'Über dem Strom' (1:127f.) it is associated with snow: 'Schnee. // Der den Himmel füllt, / Schnee, und die Leere hinter / der Röte, hinter den Feuern, / die Leere'.

historical 'nature poem' presents an aspect of German historical guilt in the European East.

Cyclical Arrangement

As the letter to Ricke quoted above indicates, Bobrowski attached great importance to the arrangement of his poems into cycles, and *Sarmatische Zeit* and *Schattenland Ströme* are carefully arranged and interlinked. At the most superficial level this is evident in the organisation into sections, with three main numbered sections in each, but with both volumes also containing a motto and single introductory and concluding poems set apart from the rest. In this, *Schattenland Ströme* follows the pattern established by the West German publishers of *Sarmatische Zeit*.[28] The middle sections of both volumes are also similar in consisting largely of poems to or about writers, artists and musicians.

The volumes are linked through a series of correspondences between individual poems. The widest frame is produced by 'Anruf', the first poem of the first volume, and 'Mickiewicz', the last of the second, which although written several years apart, contain the same unusual combination of images. 'Anruf' begins with the evocation 'Wilna, Eiche / du', while the first stanza of 'Mickiewicz' links the images of 'Eichenwald' and 'Wilnaer Tor'. The images represent symbolically two reference points for some of the historical experiences underlying the cycle, with Wilna (Vilnius) a North European centre of Jewish culture until the Nazi invasion, and the oak recalling the tree-worship of the pre-Christian inhabitants of the area massacred by the Teutonic Knights. Both civilisations were destroyed as a result primarily of German violence.

This external bracket is further strengthened by two other poems from the extremities of the collection, with 'Nymphe' (1:8), the fourth poem of *Sarmatische Zeit*, written July 1955, and 'Die Furt' (1:139), the sixth from last poem from *Schattenland Ströme*, written May 1956, employing related images:

> Wege sind
> durch den Wald,

---

[28] Initially Bobrowski had had 'Pruzzische Elegie' in a separate section in *Sarmatische Zeit*. The poem was, however, rejected by the West German publishers and so the original arrangement was slightly modified.

> verborgne [...]
> Syrinx, dein Ach, ein Geklirr,
> fährt durch die Büsche.

and

> Durch die Wälder geschlungen,
> ihr weißen Wege [...]
> Schilfflöten
> tönten.[29]

There are other deliberately engineered parallels within the volumes, as, for example, parallel references to the late twelfth century Russian historical work the *Song of Igor* in the introductory poems to the two final sections: in 'Der Singschwan' (1:44) the reference is explicit: 'es tönt von der Heerfahrt / Igors das traurige Lied', while in 'Der Don' (1:121) the reference is to the call of the 'Diw', the bird that sang a warning to Prince Igor: 'Dort / singt der Diw, / im Turm'.[30] Such specific repetitions, as well as the constant repetition of a limited number of images and key words, hold the two volumes together into a single cycle.

Within each volume too there is a clear parallel development, as each follows a roughly biographical course. The first section of *Sarmatische Zeit* contains a number of poems that refer to Bobrowski's youth. Most deal with small discrete units, the village in 'Dorf' (1:5), the individually experienced childhood in 'Kindheit' (1:6f.), a fisherman in 'Gedächtnis für einen Flußfischer' (1:11), the Haff in 'Die Frauen der Nehrungsfischer' (1:13), a Jewish trader in 'Auf den jüdischen Händler A.S.' (1:15). Others are love poems: 'Liebesgedicht' (1:12), 'Fischerhafen' (1:14), 'Am Strom' (1:23). Throughout, elegiac tones predominate. The section ends with a summarizing poem 'Die Sarmatische Ebene' (1:30f.) which provides a wider context for the previous poems, and 'Gegenlicht' (1:32), a poem expressing alienation at the tensions brought about by this concern with the past, by breathing 'die andere Zeit, / die nicht mehr kommt'.

After the thematically central 'Pruzzische Elegie', the next section

---

[29] Syrinx, of course, is associated with the sound of 'Schilfflöten'.

[30] See *Altrussische Dichtung aus dem 11.-18. Jahrhundert*, ed. Helmut Grasshoff, Leipzig 1971, p.59: 'es erhob sich der Diw, schrie in den Wipfeln, hieß feindliches Land aufhorchen'. I acknowledge in passing that this is possibly an eighteenth century

presents poems to writers in whose fate Bobrowski had had some deep
personal interest or whose fate he felt he in some way shared. These
include 'Trauer um Jahnn' (1:36) and 'Aleksis Kivi' (1:40f.),whose
Seven Brothers Bobrowski once described as 'mir das schönste Buch
überhaupt' (*Marbach* 645). Within the autobiographical progression of
the volume, these first three sections – on his rural childhood, on the
Pruzzi and on these writers and others – point to the influences that most
affected Bobrowski: his childhood idyll, his knowledge of the history of
German invasions in the East, and the wide range of his reading.

In the concluding section to this first volume a number of poems
continue the theme of 'Gegenlicht' with images of alienation from the
present, which appears as a time of continuing, indeed continuous
winter, snow and cold: 'Windmühle', 'Lettische Lieder', 'Die Düna'
(1:58), 'Nachtweg' (1:59). One possible reason for this alienation is
indicated in the titles of the poems 'Kaunas 1941' (1:60f.), a poem of
self-reproach at Bobrowski's passivity at the time of the massacre of the
Jews of Kaunas during the German advance,[31] and 'Der Ilmensee 1941'
(1:53), which returns to Bobrowski's experiences in Russia. Many
poems from this section end either with images of the coming of winter
or with images suggesting how life within this winter would be possible,
presenting responses to the problem succinctly summarised in 'Steppe'
(1:52), where the knowledge both of the existence of a 'Glanz' and of
its distance stamps his life in exile:

> Dörfer,
> wie will ich leben
> noch? In der Ferne weiß ich
> endlos rinnender Himmel
> Glanz.

The imagery used in poems whose content is historically defined by
the title (especially 'Der Ilmensee 1941') affects interpretation of its use
in other poems, so that, as indicated above, the 'storm' and 'snow'
images of 'Windmühle' are influenced by the more specifically
historical references to the same images from poems with dates, while
the violent endings of 'Lettische Lieder' and 'Auf der Taurischen

---

forgery.

[31] The massacre has been well cocumented. For a recent account see, for example,
Daniel Goldhagen, *Hitler's Willing Executioners: Ordinary Germans and the Holocaust*
London 1996, pp.151, 191f.

Straße' (1:49), the latter concluding with an allusion to the mythical Enkidu, provide a wider historical backdrop for the more recent violence of 'Kaunas 1941'. Other effects can be achieved by this device, and the significance of the poems 'Aufenthalt' (1:126) and 'Abend der Fischerdörfer' (1:129) (original title 'Korostyn 1941') is clarified through their being placed between 'Nordrussische Stadt (Pustoschka 1941)' (1:125) and 'Kathedrale 1941' (1:130f.).

The volume ends with an 'Absage', in which Bobrowski appears to resign before the terrible sameness of history ('Neues hat nie begonnen'), faced with which only retreat into the family and a religiously inspired hope have any significance. The poem represented, however, as he admitted in a letter to Jokostra, a very limited resignation, and the second volume followed quickly, imitating the first in its structure. In the first section the poems deal with historically undefined themes relating to the poet's childhood experiences. The few exceptions ('Hamann' and 'Holunderblüte') evidently deal with writers of significance because of their importance even to the young Bobrowski. The second section repeats but varies the pattern of the third (second, if one leaves aside 'Pruzzische Elegie') section in *Sarmatische Zeit*. It opens with a poem, 'Der Muschelbläser', to a mysteriously inspiring 'Luftgeist' (1:100), but the next poem 'Nänie' (1:101), while showing elements of myth, is, as a note claims, 'gerichtet an Buxtehude'. The reference to Buxtehude recalls the poem 'Trauer um Jahnn' (1:36), from the earlier volume, where it had stood in almost precisely the same position, since Jahnn and Buxtehude were inextricably linked in Bobrowski's mind as he adapted material from Jahnn's works in his own interpretation of Buxtehude's biography.[32] The section then moves from the past to the present, with Chatterton, Brentano, Hölderlin, Bezruč and Saint John Perse appearing in roughly chronological order, before ending with three poems to Jewish writers, Gertrud Kolmar, Else Lasker-Schüler and Nelly Sachs, of whom the last was, at the time the poem was written, still alive. In the final section of this volume, Bobrowski turns to his own wider Russian experiences, to Russian culture and the invasion of the Soviet Union, and a number of titles contain the dates 1941, 1942. The section and the volume as a whole then end with a number of poems in which Bobrowski introduces the

---

[32] This point is considered in more detail in the later discussion of the short story 'D.B.H.'.

theme of death, in the form of a 'return' or 'Heimkehr'. At the very end
of the volume, as at the end of *Sarmatische Zeit*, Bobrowski appears to
view his own poetic productions with a new distance: in the poem
'Immer zu benennen' he indicated his awareness of the limitations of his
poetic style, while the concluding 'Mickiewicz' is a hermetic *tour de
force* to which I will return.

The final section of *Schattenland Ströme* is the most tightly organised of the whole cycle and represents a remarkable final summary of
Bobrowski's Sarmatian experience. The poems 'Der Don' and 'Ikone'
(1:122) with which the section starts present two poles of Russian
culture – the paganism of the 'Diw' and the specifically Eastern Christianity of the icon. The word 'Ebenen', which occurs in both, relates
them, and the two together reflect the 'double faith' ('dvoeverie')
occasionally seen as characteristic of Russian religiosity. These are
followed by a number of poems dealing almost exclusively with aspects
of the German invasion, from the ominous 'Verlassene Ortschaft'
(1:123) to the 'Bericht' (1:133) on the life and certain death of the
Polish Jewish partisan Bajla Gelblung, before ending with 'Kloster bei
Nowgorod' (1:134). The first four of these express with ever greater
intensity the awareness of complicity in guilt, climaxing in the poem
'Aufenthalt' (1:126) in the totally self-condemnatory:

> [...] ich stand
> auf verschütteten Strömen,
> hörte seufzen den Sand,
> ich war ein hölzerner Schatten,
> beschlagen mir Eisen, umflogen
> vom fallenden Licht.

Other poems in this section refer to the German soldier's sense of
alienation in this area, again using the 'Ebenen' of the first two poems
('Über dem Strom' – 1:127f.: 'ich seh die Ebenen / abgewandt, alt'),
until, in a number of poems, the effect of the invasion on Russian
ecclesiastical architecture is documented, from the dated 'Kathedrale
1941' (1:130f.) and 'Dorfkirche 1942' (1:132) to the less chronologically specific 'Kloster bei Nowgorod' (1:134). In the concluding
Russian poems Bobrowski touches on the history of internal exile in
Tsarist Russia in 'Die Tomsker Straße' (1:135) and the specific quality
of an Orthodox Easter in 'Ostern' (1:136), before turning to Russian
popular culture with 'Russische Lieder' (1:137) and Russian higher
culture in 'Gedächtnis für B.L.' i.e. Boris Leonidovich Pasternak

(1:138). Bobrowski's reflections on the death of this writer ('Dein Tod fragt meinem Leben nach') introduce the last phase of the Sarmatian cycle, that of homecoming, return, death itself. 'Die Furt', the short poem echoing the imagery of 'Nymphe' from *Sarmatische Zeit*, concludes 'kehr ich zurück', and the central lines of 'Holzhaus' (1:140) repeat 'So kehren / wir alle zurück', while the connection between this theme of return and death and the title of the poem 'Heimweg' (1:142) is self-evident. Death also remains central to the poem 'Dorfmusik' (1:141) which like 'Holzhaus' ends with signs of hope: 'Ich bin wo ich bin: im Sand / mit der Raute in der Hand'. Rue, the 'herb of grace' was traditionally placed in coffins at burial as a sign of grace. 'Heimweg' ends with similar images of death and existential hope, evoking the pagan Lethe, but also the concept of 'walking on the water' with its Christian association of hope and succour:

> Dämmrung. Die Fledermäuse
> fahren ums Haupt mir. Das Ruder
> zerbrochen, so werd ich nicht sinken, ich gehe
> über den Strom.

After 'Immer zu benennen', 'Mickiewicz' returns to the theme of homecoming and/or death: 'ich werd kommen'.

Such an arrangement of the poems creates a semi-autobiographical framework, leading through childhood to guilt to the mixed emotions of the exile, but within the loose autobiographical frame the poems touch on the significant areas of the Sarmatian landmass: Latvia, Lithuania, Russia, Finland, as well as rivers and the vast plain in 'Die Sarmatische Ebene' (1:30f.). The time-scale is equally vast, extending from the mythical time of Enkidu (1:49) and the mother-figure '– Ischtar oder anderen Namens –' (1:30f.) through the tumult of the Middle Ages ('Wilna' and the 'Pruzzische Elegie') and of the Napoleonic conflict ('Die alte Heerstraße') up to the destruction caused during the Second World War. Indeed, in the poem 'Vogelstraßen 1957' (1:114f.) Bobrowski looks beyond the end of this war to the dangers of post-war atomic testing.

Poetic Development

The organisation of these poems into cycles conceals considerable changes of emphasis over this period, and a number of poems from the 'Nachlaß' indicate the particular difficulty Bobrowski had with earlier

encyclopaedic intentions.[33] Of overriding significance in this development was a change of emphasis, away from elegiac tones, in which
Bobrowski guiltily, unhappily or uncertainly abandoned himself to the
enjoyment of his memories, and towards a greater distance and objec-
tivity. From its very title onwards, the 'Pruzzische Elegie' of July 1952
laments as an elegy the annihilation of the Pruzzi:

> Dir
> Ein Lied zu singen,
> hell von zorniger Liebe –
> dunkel aber, von Klage
> bitter
> [...]
> heut ein Gesang, vor Klage
> arm –

Another very early personal poem 'Die Daubas' (1:69f.), 'litauischer
Name für das linke Memelufer bei Ragnit' (1:287), enumerates fond
memories associated with a childhood spent in this area and is a poem
of lament, suggesting a passive involvement in this loss ('Wir ließen die
Dörfer dem Sande. / Kaum wie ein Flößerruf / zogen wir fort') and
concluding with an expression of longing which, although negated,
indicates the suffering involved in overcoming this yearning: 'So / sehn
ich mich nicht'. Other early poems adopt a smaller scale: 'Kindheit'
(November 14 1954) evokes rural childhood memories associated with
East Prussia under the shadow of their coming loss, a loss still keenly
felt as the poem ends not with a resolution but only a repetition of the
beginning:

> Kindheit –
> da hab ich den Pirol geliebt – (1:6f.)

Many of these poems echo the line from Goethe's 'Euphrosyne',
'Ach, wer ruft nicht so gern Unwiederbringliches an', as containing the
essence of the elegy. On the purely verbal level the link is clear: 'Anruf'
(September 25 1957), the introductory poem of *Sarmatische Zeit*, contains a central 'Ach' and itself 'ruft [...] Unwiederbringliches an':

---

[33] In particular, in a period in 1955/56 Bobrowski's intentions led to a number of long
but very shallow poems: 'Die Memel' (2:255-7); 'Auf einer Burg' (2:259-62); 'Flurgott'
(2:263f.); 'Flußgott' (2:264-6); 'Östlicher Reiter' (2:266-8), 'Der Rombinus' (2:270-3);
'Das griechische Lied (Kiew 986)' (2:275-7); the 'Städte 1941' cycle (2:294-8), and

> Ach, es ist der helle
> Glanz, das Sommergestirn,
> fortgeschenkt. (1:3)

At the end of the same volume 'Winterlicht' (December 23 1955, 1:71f.) refers to the destruction of Sarmatia in the memory of a 'hölzerner Eimer':

> [...] Wer kam?
> löste von rostender Kette ihn?
> ach, wer trank?

In 'Ode auf Thomas Chatterton' (April 9 1955) (1:103f.) the problem of a poetic appeal to the past is also raised, with sympathy for the attempt but also with implicit criticism: [Chatterton] 'rief die hingesunkne Zeit mit verblichnen Namen. / Ach, sie erwachte // nie doch'. In 'Die Frauen der Nehrungsfischer' (June 15 1955) the ambiguity of such a concern with a happier past is presented from another perspective as the harshness of the women's present life is contrasted with an easier past:

> Vor Zeiten, sagt man, umglänzte
> hundertschwärmig der Hering
> draußen die Meerbucht.

But this idyll is over (and the disappearance of some herring shoals from the Baltic coast is a historical fact): 'Und gering war der Fang', while the tale of this happier time is described as 'das alte Lied', narrated by a 'Närrin'. It may indeed once have been a reality, but what counts, for better or for worse, is the challenge, expressed here as poverty, of present and future.

By 1957 this 'Ach', the vocabulary of lament had almost completely passed out of the poems.[34] Instead, past and present are both increasingly viewed as elements of a single time continuum. 'Zeit' is increasingly replaced by 'Strom', with the title of the later volume *Schattenland Ströme* as a logical extension, and Bobrowski gives himself the poetic freedom to move back and forth within the new unity of this stream. His personal loss appears subsumed within such fluidity, and the

---

'Christburg' (2:299-301).

[34] But not always. See 'Das Holzhaus über der Wilia' (August 13 1957, 1:19f.) and 'Der Habicht' (July 1959, 1:62), 'Ach, emporgetragen / über den Baum / Dämmerung', and even the later 'Alter Hof in Wilna' (August 14 1960, 1:93).

elegiac element is reduced. The objects presented lose to a greater extent their personal significance as memories, and Bobrowski no longer presents directly his own process of the *overcoming* of his loss. Instead the later poems present the Sarmatian material within the broader context of the flow of time, within which the loss of Sarmatia is viewed with greater acceptance, as a natural metaphor for the passage of time itself.

Bobrowski still, however, clearly felt himself alien within his present, and a key concept in poems from the later 1950s is the word 'fremd'. In 'Das Holzhaus über der Wilia' and 'Anruf' (August 13 1957 and September 25 1957) this sense of feeling 'fremd' in the present is implicitly contrasted with the hospitality of the past:

> [...] Ehe der Winter
> kam, umflog uns der Fremde Schnee.
> [...]
> Um Neumond
> einmal
> stand der Fremde im Hof.
> 'Wie lebst du?' fragt' er. Alinka
> saß im Fenster. Sie schrie:
> 'Türriegellos!' (1:19f.)

> Heiß willkommen die Fremden.
> Du wirst ein Fremder sein. Bald. (1:3)

Repeated expressions of this sense of not belonging may be found in poems of the next few years. In 'Gegenlicht' (1:32) of December 10 1959 Bobrowski defines his position as

> den Mann mit geschlossenen Augen,
> [...]
> der in den Regen
> atmet die andere Zeit,
> die nicht mehr kommt, die andre,
> ungesagte [...]
> zornig.

In 'Windmühle', as suggested above, he represents his heart as a kingfisher, facing the challenge of living on in an age of ice surrounded by the pathetic remnants ('Gräten und Flossen') of a past completely destroyed.

By late 1960 expressions of personal loss and the difficulties of living 'in der Fremde' were being subordinated to more dispassionate presentations of other aspects of this past, in which the 'Erinnerungs-motive' referred to in a letter to Jokostra (December 19/20 1958) are gradually replaced.[35] The imagery of Sarmatia expresses increasingly the necessary transience of all things. Under such circumstances the relationship of the individual to his childhood experiences becomes increasingly secondary, compared with the more general theme of the passage of time.

In the very last phase of work at these Sarmatian volumes, poems turn increasingly to historical individuals: to Hölderlin (May 30 1961), Mickiewicz (May 7 1961), Nelly Sachs (June 19 1961), or Petr Bezruč (March 2 1961), or to Christian themes, in 'Ostern' (April 1961) and 'Der Wachtelschlag' (February 21 1961), or themes related to the war, in 'Bericht' (January 17 1961), 'Verlassene Ortschaft' (February 5 1961) or 'Aufenthalt' (March 17 1961), while in other poems the Sarmatian vocabulary remains but it is applied to ever less evidently Sarmatian themes. These include 'Dryade' (March 21 1961) and 'Erzählung' (April 10 1961). In place of the 'Trauerarbeit' at Sarmatia comes a new concern, emphasised by the positioning of the poems at the end of *Schattenland Ströme*, of home-coming in more traditionally Christian terms, as a return in death from the Christian pilgrimage of life. Such diversification anticipates the move to the new subject-matter and style of *Wetterzeichen*.

By the end of the second volume, the Sarmatian experience, as I will demonstrate, is being looked at from the viewpoint of complete reconciliation to this fate: the *process* of overcoming all too visible behind 'Die Daubas' has been completed, so that the volume as a whole can end with the acceptance of the words 'Es ist ganz leicht'.

A number of facets of this Sarmatian development may be observed with reference to individual poems dealing with aspects of the landscape.

'und Wege' (1:35)

The chronological development outlined above may be observed clearly in three poems whose subject-matter involves some of the roads of Sarmatia: 'Die alte Heerstraße' (1:16f.) of 1955 and the 1961 poems

---

[35] 'Ich bin bei meinen Ostvölkern eingekehrt, aber jetzt ohne Erinnerungsmotive. Es sind [...] in sprachlicher Hinsicht vielleicht nur Nuancen festzustellen, aber Du wirst es schon merken.' Quoted by Peter Jokostra in 'Celan ist bestenfalls eine Parfümfabrik'.

'Landstraße' (1:82) and 'Die Tomsker Straße' (1:135).

The road of 'Die alte Heerstraße' (October 27 1955) is the road used by Napoleon in his retreat from Moscow. It is initially presented in relation to the French Emperor:

> Seitab ist gezogen
> auf der verfallenen Straße
> der Korse, ein südlicher Kaiser.

It has clearly been the scene of much inhumanity ('Krähen [...] heilige Flüche [...] Wölfe') but despite this the poet's abiding memory of the area, his 'Heimat', is of its beauty:

> Doch der verblauende Herbst
> fährt um das Dorf und die Wolke
> auf. Wie Weinen ist eure
> Schönheit, Pfade der Heimat, nun.

The line at the centre of the poem runs: 'Und wir dürsten,' with a thirst unquenched by the present but met (though not sated) by memories of the homeland:

> So ist dein
> Herz ein Brunnen geworden
> uns [...]
> Heimat.

This is a source of succour absent from his current position, as he describes it, at 'fremden Tischen'.

The self-indulgence with such memories threatens to slide into sentimentality, but in its concluding lines the poem withdraws from any elegiac self-indulgence in an objectifying image that uses the figure of Orpheus who wept for his wife Eurydice and attempted to reverse the passage of time by retrieving her from the realm of the dead:

> Einst,
> vor Zeiten ist Orpheus
> hier gegangen am Hang
> dunkel. Es tönt herüber
> der Wald seine Klagen ewig.
>
> Ach, den Singenden narrte
> die Erde, die zahllose Stimme
> Eurydikes.

Orpheus's attempts are mocked as absurd by the reality of 'die Erde', and the nostalgia for this past is undermined by this image of the impossibility of a return. The poem as a whole thus plots the love and the painful sense of its pointlessness. Orpheus's laments are mentioned in order to be rejected, although, as the word 'Ach' again indicates, they are accorded considerable sympathy. The beauty and pull of the past is presented here as a threat, in process of being overcome.

'Landstraße' is a much more complex poem. It lacks the emotional immediacy of the address ('euch'), the vague but emotive 'schön', the elegiac 'Ach', the use of evocative, 'warm' words like 'Heimat', but also the negative 'fremd'. Here too an ich/wir is present, and the affection for this countryside is plain:

> Was wir hörten: die Unken,
> dunkel, der Wind
> ging auf dem Kalmusufer, ich war
> alt wie ein Rauch
> zwischen Morgen und Abend.

The road here too is a historical road.[36]

> Ich hab den Marmor gesehn,
> eine Tafel unter den Buchen,
> wir fuhren vorbei, die Pferde
> scheuten, ein Schuß hat den Stein
> getroffen.

But the element of the idyll is reduced through the references to rearing horses and the small detail of the shot. Instead the poem concentrates on an almost visionary experience of the passing of time moving along such a road, with the times of day ('Morgen', 'Mittag', 'Abend', 'abends') accompanying the persona and the road, and with a constant dynamisation of the natural phenomena around the people on the road, as a wood 'kam' and 'fiel zurück', day 'lief' and ferns 'wandern und holen uns ein'. The road itself simply 'geht'. It is thus not crystallised into a remembered section of past time to be longed for but, with a rhetorical 'Ach', not attained, nor is it apostrophised. It is instead a phenomenon combining space and time.

---

[36] See the exact geographical description, 5:86. It is a road between Schreitlaugken and Bittehnen, passing the mausoleum of the von Dreßler family, a plaque of which was damaged during the First World War.

At the end, the 'Landstraße' gives way to a new phenomenon evoking the passing of time, the 'Strom', and this new symbolic value is underlined as the river too is immediately given a temporal dimension: 'an den Berg / legt sich, er atmet von Lüften, / mit Flößen und *abends* dem Segel / der Blinde, der Strom'.[37] Within the landscape that Bobrowski presents in this 1961 poem, all things are in flux, and the flow of this motion continues, by extension to the present day. The 'Landstraße' itself gives way to a 'Strom'.

Compared with 'Die alte Heerstraße', 'Landstraße' presents considerably more specific detail. While, however, the details fit together to create a coherent whole, they are individually more fragmented, less emotionally laden. The experience of this road is more focused, but its reflection is less comforting. It presents an incident particular in place and time, but views this within the context of the flow of time, and the elegiac lament is reduced as the flow of time is accentuated.

A different process is presented in 'Die Tomsker Straße', where the road to Tomsk, a notorious destination for internal exiles in Tsarist Russia, is presented by a persona who is completely unaffected by it. The opening images of the poem echo but parody the Biblical imagery of Psalm 137 associated with exile:

> Schrei herüber, der Wind
> schlägt in die Harfenstricke
> – Tiergedärm, auf die Äste
> der Birke gewunden.[38]

The poetic voice has no personal vision of the road: 'ich seh / aber die Straße nicht'. Instead it presents it through its past description ('voreinst') by a persona Jelisaweta who described it as a place leading into exile but also as one giving others the opportunity to show human kindness. The central lines of the poem refer to the way in which exiles were treated by the local inhabitants and run:

> der Fremdling kam,
> schritt vorüber, keiner
> sagte 'Verbannter', 'unglücklich'
> hieß er.[39]

---

[37] The reference to 'der Blinde' echoes Hölderlin's 'blindness' of 'Der Rhein'.

[38] Bobrowski suggested that this was a common practice in the Urals (5:138).

[39] Bobrowski took this detail directly from a translation of a work by Alexander Herzen

This road too is presented as caught up in transience, with its passage linked first with summer ('So war die Straße [...] / sie ging / in ein Land wie der Himmel, / einen Sommer,') and then with winter, until Jelisaweta herself is drawn into these natural/historical events, apparently being herself forced into an exile from which she eventually returns: 'es kam / aber der Schnee, es kam / Jelisaweta nach Jahren'.

The Tomsk road is presented in its association with exile and the return from exile, but in the final stanza it too is caught up in time as Bobrowski, although avoiding any word for river, has Jelisaweta return to a scene 'am *Ufer*' where her grandchild 'warf *die Angel* ins Gras'. The river, image for the stream of time in which the road exists, is implicitly present although unmentioned, and the poem suggests even a future dimension with its reference to the grandchild. As with 'Landstraße' and the memorial 'unter den Buchen', the historical reality of the Tomsk road is introduced into the stream of time, with the road itself subordinate to time – 'Sommer', 'Schnee' and finally 'Strom'.

In both these poems from the last few months of the Sarmatian project the hopeless elegiac call, the 'Ach' of 'Die alte Heerstraße', is replaced by objectifying images of the passage of time, while the movement into a state of permanent winter or night seen already in 'Winterlicht', 'Der Singschwan' and 'Windmühle' is overtaken by images that bind Sarmatian memories into the wider context of an unending stream of time. Within such a context the historical and unique (the 'Tafel' in 'Landstraße', the fate of Jelisaweta in 'Die Tomsker Straße') is subsumed into the greater unity of this flow. Bobrowski presents the memory and overcomes its pain in one undivided movement.

'Berghänge' (1:35)

Apart from the earlier works, it is relatively rare for Bobrowski to leave more than one version of a poem. This in itself has made analysis of poetic development more problematic. In the case of the poem 'Der Judenberg' (1:109), two versions exist, and a comparison of these two versions makes the development away from the tone of melancholy visible with even greater clarity:

(*Byloe i dumy*, 1852-1868) in his library, *Erlebtes und Gedachtes*, Weimar 1953 p.132. He marked this passage in his copy of the book (5:138).

Der Judenberg

Spinnenreise,
weiß, mit rötlichem Sand
stäubte die Erde – Wald,
flechtenhaarig, Tierschrei,
stieß um die Wange ihm, Gras
stach seine Schläfe.

Spät, wenn der Uhu, Sausen
aus hundert Nächten, umherstrich
durch den Schlaf der Geniste,
hob er sich in der Grillen
Schwirrgesträuch, einen fahlen
Mondweg zu sehn, der heraufkam
an die seufzende Eiche, die Greisin, in ihrem
Wurzelgeflecht verging.

Über das Bruch sah er hin.
Jäh, undeutbar, Lichtschein
flog vorüber, diesen
Herzschlag lang ragte wüstes
Schaufelgeweih aus der Finsternis,
zottig, ein tränendes Haupt.

Unter die Hände gepreßt
Zeit, unbenannt: die Schwärme,
gelb, die dem Curragh
folgten, tönende Wolken
über der See, die Bienen
folgten dem frommen Vater,
er rührte die Ruder, er sagte:
Ich werd tot sein im grünen Tal.

Note: 'die letzte Strophe des Gedichts bezieht sich auf eine irische Legende'

Ignoring the title for a while, it is useful to attempt a 'naive' interpretation. The first word, 'Spinnenreise' suggests a number of interpretations: the journey of spiders, the journey accompanied by spiders, a journey to somewhere or something 'wo es spinnt'? With greater probability it reflects the apparent movement of strands from spiders' webs in the breeze in late summer.[40]

---

[40] The image may be related to the beginning of another poem on the other racial group annihilated by Nazi Germany, namely gypsies. Thus the poem 'Gedenkblatt' (1:97) begins 'Jahre, / Spinnenfäden, / die großen Spinnen, Jahre '.

The opening section of this poem is typical: the poet appears to be struggling to put the words together, with the 'Spinnenreise' and the 'weiß' syntactically unrelated to the actual main verb 'stäubte', as the poet tries to make a sentence (i.e. sense) of some memory or experience. The same halting, uncertain syntax is then immediately repeated, except that now the resolution is left even more unclear: 'Wald' appears to be the subject, with 'flechtenhaarig' as a post-positioned adjective and 'Tierschrei' in apposition. Then, third time lucky, the last image floods out in the typical adoneus.

The start suggests elements of a somehow threatening, ominous landscape, in which the 'er' (of lines 5/6) seems under attack. In the second stanza the same atmosphere of menace is continued through the image of the eagle owl ('Uhu') disturbing the sleep of the lesser mass of birds, their 'Geniste', their undifferentiated nests. The unidentified 'er' is now active, seems to belong more in this landscape: he rises in order to see – does not have to look for – the 'fahler Mondweg', which loses itself in the roots of the mysterious, anthropomorphic oak, and (in the third stanza) he remains the figure through whose eyes the landscape is further experienced. He is the one who saw something, and the climax of what he saw, in this mysterious light, for the beat of a heart, was an elk, ('wüstes Schaufelgeweih') near enough for him to see its eyes – 'ein tränendes Haupt'. The reader shares for a moment (*'diesen Herzschlag lang'*) this unforgettable experience. Despite this, the status of the 'er' remains unclear. It has human features ('Wange', 'Schläfe'), but no recognisable contour. It has eyes, presumably, and a beating heart that can respond with excitement to this chance meeting, but unlike the 'ich' of the war-poems, it is not obviously identifiable as Bobrowski himself. It is not, in the words of the 1956 letter to Ricke, 'uniformiert und durchaus kenntlich'.

The reference to the oak, one of the holy trees of pre-Christian Northern Europe, appeared to suggest a heathen landscape. The final stanza, however, is from a totally different area. It refers, as the word 'Legende' in the note suggests, to the tale of a saint, identified by Haufe (5:113) as the 'Mönch Dominik', and his legendary journey from Wales back to Ireland. He had been studying under St. David, and one of his duties there had been bee-keeping for the monastery. When he returned to Ireland to die, a swarm of his bees settled on his ship, and thus was apiculture introduced into Ireland. The link between this stanza and what had gone before is initially unclear but becomes clearer if we look at the earlier version of this poem.

'Der Judenberg' was first published in the second section of *Schattenland Ströme*. Its dating is surprisingly problematic. Bobrowski himself in his hand-written notes dated it as June 10 1955, and this date is taken over in the *Gesammelte Werke*. However, in a letter to Bobrowski of December 3 1960 (*Chronik* 57) Max Hölzer commented very positively: 'Der neue Schluß des "Judenberges" ist ergreifend', clearly referring to the conclusion of the poem as presented in *Schattenland Ströme*.

The rejected concluding stanza, to be found in Bobrowski's 'Nachlaß' and finally published in 5:112 ran as follows:

> In meine Hände
> gepreßt
> halt ich Schwärme von Tagen.
> Brichst mir die Finger, wehende
> Stunde aus Heimweh.
> So werd ich
> folgen auf deiner Fluchtspur
> mein Alter hinab.[41]

The meaning of this earlier conclusion is much clearer: 'swarms' of memories, of which the first stanzas offer an example, accompany the poet through life but remain suppressed, pressed under his hands – until, occasionally, in a 'wehende / Stunde aus Heimweh' they break out. The result of such pressure is such a poem. In view of this, the poet is resigned to his fate, the homesickness typical of the poems of the mid 1950s.

In the conclusion of the later version the 'Schwärme von Tagen' becomes 'Zeit, unbenannt' and a swarm of bees, and the memories have become productive, even though (this is implied in the fact that they are now bees) they can still cause pain. The resignation to a life of 'Heimweh' spent following their 'Fluchtspur' has also been replaced by the image of the saint rowing from Wales to Ireland, physically positioned so that he is looking backwards, the natural position for rowing, but through this very means propelling himself forward.

The two versions of the concluding stanza of this poem illustrate the

---

[41] Despite a number of other differences in the course of the whole poem, which might justify a textual editor in treating them as separate poems, it is clear that they represent two versions of the same poem.

change in Bobrowski's poetic re-working of his past. The emphasis of the 1955 version lay on resignation to the effects of an unproductive, painful 'Stunde aus Heimweh'. The 1960 poem saw instead a much more positive role for memories, directed productively towards the future and accepting without demur the inevitability of death. If we now consider the title, the significance of the poem becomes even clearer. 'Der Judenberg' is deceptive; it has been assumed, wrongly, that it is a mythical or imagined Mount Juda.[42] It is, in fact, a small wooded hill near Motzischken, a place Bobrowski regularly visited in his teens and beyond. It is thus the scene of childhood memories, in this case perhaps a memory experienced by an impressionable youth (the 'er' from whom the poet's 'ich' has distanced himself) who was enjoying the thrill and excitement of a visit, from 'civilised' Tilsit, to this pagan 'hostile' landscape. As such 'Der Judenberg' is a place personally experienced and now irretrievably lost, but bearing a name that reminds the poet of one of the reasons for that loss, the slaughter of the Jews in Hitler's 'Endlösung'. It is, as Bobrowski wrote in his statement for Schwedhelm, part of the 'Landschaft, die mit allem Recht verloren ist', with the happy childhood memories of the experience inextricably bound up with a geographical name that reminds of the reason for the loss.

The pain of the memory of this experience appears to remain; Bobrowski's poetic struggle, in these two versions, involves the attempt to create something positive out of it. This he succeeds in doing in the changed version of the last stanza.

'*Flüsse, glanzlos noch oft*' (1:35)

Within the vastness of Sarmatia, 'Der Judenberg' is a single 'Mosaikstein'. More significant for the landscape as a whole, and forming a significant focal point in these volumes, are rivers, and in his concentration on these, Bobrowski consciously continued the tradition of the river poem associated especially with Hölderlin ('Der Rhein', 'Der Ister', 'Der Main', 'Der Neckar'), a point on which critics have commented at considerable length.[43] For Hölderlin rivers had constituted a central

---

[42] See especially Werner Schulz in his otherwise very perceptive analysis of the poem in *Die aufgehobene Zeit: Zeitstruktur und Zeitelemente in der Lyrik Johannes Bobrowskis*, New York 1983, pp.154-61.

[43] In particular the 'Stromgedicht'. See Haufe's 'Zur Entwicklung der sarmatischen Lyrik Bobrowskis', p.57; Leistner's *Johannes Bobrowski* p.46 (who emphasises the

aspect of a poetic landscape formed by his search for signs and for
indications of signs of the divine guiding hand. His vision of rivers,
especially his interpretation of the courses of the Rhine and the Danube
(Ister) as signs pointing to the eventual arrival of the 'Göttertag', the
new day of fulfilled existence, is well known, and Bobrowski was fully
aware of this. The progress of these rivers in Hölderlin's works constitutes a positive sign of possible future harmony. Rivers flow into their
'Bruder Rhein', or 'freudig' to the ocean, to the 'stillerhabenen Rhein'
with its 'Städten' and 'lustigen Inseln', 'wo ihn in die Arme der Vater
aufnimmt'. The intention of these poems is to present the path to the all-
uniting 'Brautnacht' ('Der Rhein'), image for the new dawn, or, in
another poem, the 'Friedensfeier', the Romantic equivalent of the 1960s
'Age of Aquarius'. Hölderlin presents his poetic landscape with the
express aim 'Bestehendes gut zu deuten', as signs pointing to the future,
but his poetry itself helps point the way, by guiding in the process of
interpretation. Here as in all his works he intends to help recreate the
transformed glories of a fulfilled past existence in the present or near
future. For Hölderlin the greatest threat to this new flowering of the
human spirit lay in man's lack of awareness, and David Constantine
rightly emphasises his 'dread of insensibility' as a central feature.[44] For
Bobrowski not insensitivity but forgetfulness is the danger, and his rivers offer points of remembering, physical indicators of past events,
rather than signs of divine guidance and possible future harmony.

Repeating the pattern of 1944/45, Bobrowski moves between poems
to specific rivers, 'Die Jura' (December 15 1958), 'Die Düna' (March
24 1959), 'Die Memel' (June 16 1959) and 'Der Don' (August 3 1960),
and poems dedicated more to the 'principle' of the river: 'Am Strom'
(June 19 1958), 'Über dem Strom' (October 5 1960), and above all
'Stromgedicht' (May 11 1959). 'Die Jura' (1:9f.), the earliest of these
poems, is also one of the longest. It is a poem of remembrance and of
love for a beautiful, ever-changing and complex river, presenting its
flow through two strands: in a temporal strand images of summer
('sommers') give way to images of cold ('mit klammen Fingern') and
finally to the ice of winter, while in another strand Bobrowski follows

---

contrasts to Hölderlin); Schütze's *Natur und Geschichte* (passim) and Reichert's *Das
verschneite Wort* (passim).

[44] David Constantine, 'Saying and Not-Saying in Hölderlin's Works', in *Taboos in
German Literature*, ed. David Jackson, Oxford 1996, p.53.

the course of the river from its mythological origins as a 'sandige Spur' brought about by the god Perkun, to its end, subsumed in the river Nemona, the Memel.

The work echoes Hölderlin's use of myth in its evocation of the river as a 'schöner Bruder der Wälder' and in a reference to its possible divine origins: 'und die Quellen / schossen hervor, seiner Blicke / sandige Spur', which echo Hölderlin's reference in 'Der Rhein' to the origin of the river and its irritation: 'anklagt [...] den Donnerer, der ihn gezeuget'.[45] In clear contrast to Hölderlin's works, the union with the larger Nemona receives no special mention: there is no mythical embrace by brother, father or sister. Instead, the natural end of the Jura is accompanied by the 'Feuer' of autumn (storms or bright autumn foliage) and the advent of winter, in face of which the 'Strom', the Nemona (the Jura is a 'Fluß' and has now completely disappeared in the larger river) 'schreit aus breiten Lungen':

> Wer entzündet die späten
> Feuer des Jahrs, wo der Strom,
> Nemona, geht, aus breiten
> Lungen schreit vor dem Eis,
> das herabfällt? Aus offenen Himmeln
> stürzt es, es fährt ein gelber
> Rauch vor ihm her.

In these final images Bobrowski paradoxically combines fire and ice, indicating unnatural finality. He also presents the first part of the image in the form of a question with the human personal pronoun 'wer'. It is a development implying a human agent behind the cataclysmic event he is describing, the double death of the river. He thereby effects a transition from natural and mythological elements to images indicating human responsibility for the 'destruction' of the Jura and the Nemona, which is itself personalised and anthropomorphised through the image of 'breiten Lungen'. Both the course of the year and the course of the Jura, as a representative river of Sarmatia, coincide in an end in 'Eis', the stasis of winter. The poem has also moved away from myth ('ein großer / Gott der Fluren') to the issue of individual personal responsibility: 'Wer?'. In

---

[45] Friedrich Hölderlin, *Sämtliche Werke*, Stuttgart 1946, vol. 2, p.150. Elsewhere too the poem echoes Hölderlin: 'In der großen Stille / komm ich zu dir' reminds of Hölderlin's 'Der Archipelagus': 'Komm ich zu dir und grüß in deiner Stille dich, Alter' (vol. 2, p.107).

this it presents in more specific form the problem raised in 'Immer zu benennen' where 'Zeichen' and 'Farben' are rejected as leading to a potential injustice ('es möchte nicht enden / gerecht'). In 'Die Jura' the end (of the river, of the experience, of Sarmatia) has been 'ungerecht', and this is a human category. Although a 'landscape' poem, 'Die Jura' has introduced the dimension of human responsibility for the final demise: the myth is destroyed through historical reality.

Bobrowski knew the River Düna more from his time as a soldier stationed near Riga in 1944 than as a child. 'Die Düna' (1:58), written shortly before 'Stromgedicht', is another poem in which the beauty of the river is emphasised:

> Düna, Morgenfrühe
> immer um dich und der herrliche
> Wind der Ebnen.

This poem also presents both a chronological progression, from 'Morgenfrühe' to 'Mittag' to 'Nacht', (but later to 'Tags'), and, although not with as much detail as in 'Die Jura', a final progression to the sea:

> schweren Mundes gehst du,
> dunkel – die Möwen
> sprühn und die Wasser auf,
> schreiend empfängt dich das Meer –
> du gehst ihm entgegen.
>
> In seinem Schatten,
> vom Grund
> das alte Getier
> seufzt dir zu.

Here too the end of the river appears accompanied by elements of unnatural violence, though of a different order: the meeting between the beautiful Düna, which is apostrophised ('du') and anthropomorphised ('schweren Mundes'), and the Bay of Riga appears as a lascivious embrace by a de-individualised, sub-human 'alte[s] Getier'.

Both poems present then the movement of individual Sarmatian rivers towards an inappropriate, unnatural end. Despite their passing, the rivers still act as points of orientation or reference for the poet. In 'Die Jura':

> In der großen Stille
> komm ich zu dir [...]

> Mein Kahn
> folgt deinem Herzlaut.

In 'Die Düna':

> Müd
> um den Mittag
> bin ich gekommen [...]
> Ich will vom Atem der Ströme
> leben, vom Sprind
> trinken, das Irdische trinken.

Although the memories of these contacts, these points of orientation remain, the rivers have been lost. Bobrowski recreates them poetically within their Sarmatian frames of reference, alluding to their human contact (an old painter in 'Die Jura' or the adjoining town in 'Die Düna'), to their mythology, to their physical flowing. But in conclusion he emphasises their unnatural destruction as a destruction involving by extension that of Sarmatia itself, and, despite any superficial similarities, in contrast to Hölderlin's joyous if admittedly tense cycle of rebirth and harmony, Bobrowski presents a movement into oblivion. His own poems are directed against this oblivion.

With 'Stromgedicht' (1:54f.) Bobrowski turned away from individual rivers. This poem he saw, at least for a while, as one of his more significant achievements.[46] As the second poem from the 1950s with this title (see 'Stromgedicht' of June 20 1958, 2:318), it offers, as a dream, a vision of this river:

> Traum,
> jählings,
> aus Feuern der Habichtsnacht,
> Tieraug,
> Blitz unter reglosem Lid
> vor, Pfeilbündel Schilf,
> wo der Otter, ein Herzsprung,
> taucht.

---

[46] He described it in a letter to Jokostra (June 11 1959):

> Im Gedicht ging es nur um die Gestalt, sozusagen, eines ganzen Stromes – Größenordnung etwa zwischen Düna und Wolga. Daher die Länge. Und dann: Auf Einzelschönheiten, sozusagen, kam es nicht an. Ich bin entschlossen, es für den Höhepunkt der letzten Jahre zu halten, sonst kann ich nicht weiterschreiben. (5:62)

The poem then depicts, as in Hölderlin's works, the course of a river as an anthropomorphic development, although frequently overlaid with specific detail. It includes the heroic youth of the river ('er kommt / waffenlos, ein anderer / Held'), and the river itself displays a number of human characteristics ('Kindheit', 'Speise'), and when it dies it leaves a 'Spur seines Atems'. But the death is ignominious: 'auf dem Schlick / stirbt er'. The description of the river in general is indebted to Hölderlin's 'Der Rhein' in its vocabulary and its use of myth, but as with 'Die Jura' and 'Die Düna', the end of this river is viewed differently and is related to a wider destruction, here accompanied by remnants of human history:

> [...] Inseln,
> schwebend, Morast, gestürzte
> Tore, eingesunkene
> Bögen, Fahnen aus Vogelgeripp
> und Tang –
> auf dem Schlick
> stirbt er, auf den Watten
> noch Spur seines Atems, Möwen
> decken sie zu.

The settling gulls reinforce the finality of this end as they cover the river, and the whole stanza gives this death a sense of physical disintegration that distinguishes it from Hölderlin's timeless 'Vater Rhein'. Bobrowski's river, like Sarmatia, is a historical phenomenon, and there will be no rebirth.

In the penultimate stanza of the poem the dream ends and here Bobrowski relates this presentation of the river directly to Sarmatia as a sign:

> Zeichen an bläulicher Wand,
> gekratzt in den Mörtel
> mit dem Nagelrand, Bild,
> Abbild,
> sarmatisch.

The image itself – 'gekratzt mit dem Nagelrand' – is inadequate and inaccurate, a sign that is losing or has lost much detail, with the fear of forgetfulness again parallel to Hölderlin's fear of insensibility. As Haufe emphasised, it is a vision rather than a memory,[47] and at the end of the poem the poet admits his devotion to the river as providing a sense of direction to his existence and a mysterious beauty behind a bland exterior:

> lange
> folg ich dir,
> Strom,
> an Rändern der Wälder,
> ermattend
> leicht, im alten
> Zinn ein Geräusch.

With this last image Bobrowski, as in 'Der Judenberg', finds a form of objective correlative to his endeavour, in the idea of 'Zinngeschrei', the particular sound produced when tin is bent back and forth. The tin itself is thus, as Reichert comments (p.169) 'totes Gerät, das ihm [...] die ehemals lebendige Vergangenheit in seinen poetischen Träumen zu neuer Wirklichkeit erwecken half'.[48]

In all these poems the rivers function as 'Zeichen [...] / Bild, / Abbild' of Sarmatia. The poems belong to a period after that of direct expressions of loss and depict instead the end of these rivers with stark finality. They express no desire to return to this area. 'Die Memel' (1:67f.), written shortly after 'Stromgedicht', creates in this context an anachronistic impression. The Memel had been the defining river of Bobrowski's childhood, running past Tilsit and forming for part of its course the border between East Prussia and the Memelland. It was the subject of at least three poems, from the early ode in 'Zeit aus Schweigen', with its characteristic unstilled longing[49] to the January 15 1955 'Die Memel', (2:255-7) which was considerably reworked for the later (June 16 1959) and final 'Die Memel'. The 1955 poem had been

---

[47] In a short analysis of this poem Haufe summarizes its peculiarity:

> Was das Gedicht zu einem wirklichen, freilich auch schwierigen 'Höhepunkt' der sarmatischen Lyrik Bobrowskis macht, ist die völlige Tilgung des bisher vorherrschenden Erinnerungsgestus, ist die aufs äußerste gesteigerte poetisch-visionäre Gegenwärtigkeit seines Gegenstandes bei gleichzeitig größter Ferne von aller Realität. (*Sankelmark*, p.33)

[48] Haufe (5:63) refers also to the 1955 radio play *Zinngeschrei* by Günter Eich.

[49] 'Da die Fluten teilen und untertauchen / ganz in deine Heiterkeit, deiner Jugend / Märchen lauschen' (2:63).

one of the 'encyclopaedic' poems like 'Christburg' (2:299-301), which
presented a historical overview and which were later rejected. Using
vocabulary close to that of 'Der Judenberg' this early 'Die Memel' had
confronted the vague, uncomfortably alien elements of the countryside
('Getier der Vorzeit / stieg aus der Dämmerung so / leise, undeutbar')
with the arrival of Christian settlers who imposed their behaviour on the
land:

> [...] hoben
> alten Volkes Gesetz
> auf in den Armen, anstimmend
> Glockenlieder. Mauern
> fügend, wurden sie froh
> sandiger Wege.[50]

Before its final appeal (incorporated also in the later poem), the early
poem had ended with the approach of winter ('Schollengang dröhnt mit
den Nächten bald') and a 'Wolfzeit', images for the earlier destruction
of this Sarmatian life and the continuing destruction in the present.

Compared with this poem, the 1959 'Die Memel' reduces the
element of the historical struggle between Christians and pagans (the
'altes Volk') across the river, and concentrates instead on specific
childhood memories, roused by the call of a bird at the approach of
night. The sequence of memories concludes with one of night-fishing,
apparently interrupted by the arrival of smugglers. After an apostrophe
to the river, reminiscent again of Hölderlin ('Aus der Finsternis /
kommst du, mein Strom, / aus den Wolken') the Memel is addressed as
the centre of its landscape of 'Wege' and 'Flüsse', a natural means of
communication and commerce (the rafts floating downstream), but also
a barrier that requires a 'Fähre'.

Here, however, the atmosphere changes: 'Die Fähre / liegt auf dem
Sand'. The smugglers' easily crossed border has become more problematic, even closed, and with this change come images of a different order,
as the sky grows dark with armies of birds 'Vogel*heere*' (as in 'Wände
weiß', 2:315: '[es] kommen die Vogelheere, / tragen die Bläue fort')
and (as in 'Die Jura') with smoke ('Brunnenrauch, harziger Wälder
Rauch'). Under such circumstances the peaceful concluding scene of the
local women, some pregnant, and their children swimming or standing

---

[50] See 'Christburg': 'Galgen richtend, / wurden sie heimisch / im Bernsteinland' (2:301).
Haufe (5:344) sees these as Protestants expelled from Salzburg in 1731.

overlooking the river is sadly ironic.[51] They are the innocent, un-suspecting victims of an impending catastrophe, signified by the approaching dark.

The poem ends, like the 1955 'Die Memel', with the poet asserting his love for this river as all that is left, since he cannot visit or see it:

> Strom,
> alleine immer
> kann ich dich lieben
> nur.
> Bild aus Schweigen.
> Tafeln dem Künft'gen: mein Schrei.
> Der nie dich erhielt.
> Nun im Dunkel
> halt ich dich fest.

As in 'Stromgedicht', the summary of what has gone before is developed: here from a one-dimensional 'Bild aus Schweigen' through the suffering writer's 'Schrei' to a moral message ('Tafeln') directed at future generations that never experienced such events. In the current darkness ('Der Himmel dunkelt' has become a permanent feature 'Nun im Dunkel') the memory must be preserved.

The last of these river poems, 'Der Don' (1:121), written August 3 1960, differs significantly from the others, as indeed does the Don itself. The Memel and Jura were rivers from Bobrowski's childhood, while the Düna was a river physically close to East Prussia. Compared to these, the Don was a river that Bobrowski almost certainly only saw in the context of war and imprisonment. It is, therefore, not surprising, that it appears as the frozen, silent centre of a desolate landscape of captivity, echoing the emotions of the prisoner:

> [...] Aber
> der Strom gefangen, Eishauch
> wehte er, Stille finster
> folgte ihm nach.
>
> Weiß war der Strom.

Within this desolation, all poetic signs are negative. It is silent, cold

---

[51] The images were taken almost unchanged from the poem 'Der Rombinus (II)' (2:316f.)

and dark, and white is not a sign of light and innocence but of snow, cold and death. Even when the perspective widens beyond the immediate river, it meets not images of freedom, but, whatever their origin – Haufe suggests (5:125) a fata morgana – new images of incarceration:

> die Ufer drüben
> flogen davon, wir sahn
> [...] Mauern
> gegen den Himmel.

In such surroundings there is no comfort for the German, and with the river reflecting the poet's remembered emotions so accurately, the poem ends with a reference to the Diw, the mythological bird that had prophesied the destruction of Prince Igor's army:

> Dort
> singt der Diw,
> im Turm,
> er schreit an die Wolke, der Vogel
> ganz aus Unglück.

The very landscape is appalled by this invasion and unites, the natural and the dead, to join in battle against the invaders:

> Hügel, öffnet euch, sagt er,
> tretet hervor gerüstet,
> Tote, legt an den Helm.

In the winter of this poem the River Don runs no course. Instead, in complete accord with the circumstances in which Bobrowski experienced it, it is frozen and motionless, full of animosity and fear, a hostile strangeness in which the spirits of the past rise up against the present invaders. It is an appropriate poem with which to introduce, as Bobrowski did, the final and most explicitly self-accusatory section of the two volumes.

Novgorod

Bobrowski's poems on the ancient Russian city of Novgorod form a distinct group that merits particular attention. The town had symbolic significance far beyond its historical significance, as its inclusion in the introductory poem 'Anruf' indicated. As a symbolic representative of the beauty and destruction of European Russian civilisation, it stands in the published volumes for the many other towns and villages mentioned in earlier unpublished poems – Shelon, Welebizy, Pustoschka, Schmany, Majewo, Pskow, Opotschka – as well as being the town that Bobrowski most associated with the destruction of Russia which he witnessed and to which he contributed. It will become clear, however, that the two central Novgorod poems included in the Sarmatian volumes were written in conjunction with each other as carriers of one single message.

Novgorod had shared the vicissitudes of much of Sarmatia back to the earliest historical times. In the ninth century (then called Holmgård) it had been the residence of the Scandinavian Rurik. It later became one of the great Russian cities of late-medieval commerce, with contacts with German (later Hansa) and Scandinavian merchants and links as far as the White Sea. As a sovereign city it enjoyed considerable independence, until it was annexed 1475-1478 by Ivan III of Moscow. A century later it was ravaged by Ivan IV (the Terrible) and later still it fought unsuccessfully in an uprising against the Tsar Alexei (1650). By the early twentieth century much of its mediaeval splendour had been lost, but despite a very small population (around 30,000) it could boast over forty architecturally significant churches, including the St. Sophia Cathedral. This cathedral, which was largely destroyed during the German invasion,[52] formed a focal point for Bobrowski's works, and he wrote at least two poems on the destruction he experienced in Novgorod: 'Kloster bei Nowgorod' (1:134) (later than July 1958 – see 5:136) and 'Kathedrale 1941' (1:130f., May 1960 – see 5:131ff.). These two Novgorod poems are placed in *Schattenland Ströme* embracing two other poems on the war, 'Dorfkirche 1942' (1:132) and 'Bericht' (1:133).

'Kloster bei Nowgorod' is a later version of the rhyming 'Kloster bei Nowgorod' (2:226) and of two poems entitled 'Orthodoxes Kloster' which were also not included in the anthologies.[53] The poem refers probably to the monastery of St. Antonius (5:137):

---

[52] See *SZNB*, photograph opposite p.144.

[53] See Brian Keith-Smith, 'Bobrowski's poetic Nachlaß – Icons of Hope' in *Johannes Bobrowski 1917-1965*, ed. John P.Wieczorek, Reading 1996, pp.68f. See also 5:135ff. The production of so many versions of these poems indicates the importance Bobrowski attached to the subject-matter.

Kloster bei Nowgorod

Strom, schwer,
den die Lüfte umdrängen, alt,
Geister der tiefen
Ebene, redend im Regen
uferhinab. Der Hecht
steht unterm Schilf.

An dem weißen Gemäuer
Glockenschläge Licht,
über die Dächer sinkend
das Hungertuch Nacht, von verstummten
Vögeln durchstürzt.

Türen, leer, der steinerne
Pfad, auf verwachsener Stufe
der Greis mit dem weißen Scheitel,
wenn Gesang im ertönenden Bogen
aufsteht, Wind tritt ins erzene
Tor, silberner steigt,
flossenstarrend
der Hecht aus dem Grund.

The tripartite structure of the poem is clearly pronounced and corresponds to the three stanzas. The start is a typically stuttering evocation
of the natural, almost pagan scene surrounding the monastery ('Geister
[...] redend') with just a single syntactically complete sentence in the
first two stanzas, 'Der Hecht / steht unterm Schilf', an image of stasis,
immobility. This is followed by a stanza in which the fall of evening is
presented with images of confrontation between the light and sound of
the monastery and the dark and unnatural silence of night ('verstummten Vögeln'). The 'Glockenschläge Licht' are preceded by images of
heaviness ('schwer'), oppression ('umdrängten') and immobility ('Der
Hecht steht') and followed by images of dark ('Nacht'), starvation
('Hungertuch') and silence ('verstummt').

The concluding stanza links elements from the first stanza directly to
the monastery. It starts with a fragmentary evocation of the destruction
of this monastery, with 'Türen, leer' echoing phonetically the 'Strom,
schwer' of the beginning, occupied in its desolation by 'der Greis mit
dem weißen Scheitel', a faint echo of the bearded, white-haired old man
of naive Christian iconography, at mention of whom the poem undergoes a dizzy shift of mood to recapitulate the imagery of the first stanza,
but now under the aspect of hope: song 'aufsteht' (the echo of the

'Auferstehung' is deliberate); the oppressive 'Lüfte [...] umdrängen' gives way to a 'Wind' which, filling the 'leere Türen', 'tritt ins erzene Tor', while the pike, suddenly active and 'flossenstarrend' appears swept up in the same movement, and the word 'silberner' contradicts the earlier darkness, as 'Gesang' replaces the initial prosaic 'redend'.

The poem uses syntactically incomplete phrases and clauses almost throughout, and in key images, including the synaesthesic 'Glockenschläge Licht' and the surprisingly apt 'Hungertuch',[54] it creates a vision of moods, from the bleak stasis of the beginning with its echo of the pagan past, to the end, where these 'Lüfte' have been sanitized to a 'Wind' and welcomed 'ins erzene Tor' and the whole of nature responds with a growth of movement, musicality and activity.

'Kathedrale 1941' deals with the fate of St. Sophia:

> Die wir sahn
> über dem Winterstrom,
> über der Wasser reißender
> Schwärze, Sophia, klingendes
> Herz der verdüsterten Nowgorod –
>
> Finster wars schon voreinst.
> Doch mit schäumenden, heitren
> Delphinen vorübergezogen
> kam die Zeit, Fruchtgärten
> brannten die Wange dir, oft
> hinter den Zäunen hielten
> Pilger nassen Gesichts
> in deiner Kuppeln goldnem Geschrei.
>
> Und deine Nacht, die Mondschlucht,
> tödlich blaß, es erglänzte
> der halkyonische Vogel
> im Eisenist.
>
> Rauch hat dir die Wände

---

[54] Alfred Behrmann in his interpretation of this poem refers to the specific significance of the word 'Hungertuch' as an altar cloth created to remind the congregation of starvation overcome. See Alfred Behrmann, *Facetten: Untersuchungen zum Werk Johannes Bobrowskis*, Stuttgart 1977, p.58. The poem has been analysed by a number of critics, including Wolfram Mauser, *Beschwörung und Reflexion*, p.63, Sigfrid Hoefert, *West-Östliches in der Lyrik Johannes Bobrowskis* (Munich 1968) p.42, and Alfred Kelletat in the essay 'Zur lyrischen Sangart Johannes Bobrowskis' in *Seminar* 8 (1972), pp.117-36.

geschwärzt, deine Türen zerbrach
Feuer, wie wird sein
das Licht deinen Fensterhöhlen?
Alles an unsrem Leben
wars getan, der Schrei
wie das Schweigen, wir sahn
steigen über die Ebene,
weiß, dein Gesicht.

Damals
in den Mooren,
draußen, ging auf
der Zorn.
Zorn, eine schwere Saat.
Wie will ich rufen
einmal
das Aug mir noch
hell?

This poem too has a tripartite structure: a halting start, here expressed through the initial anacoluthon, followed by a more flowing set of images evoking the history of the cathedral, while at the end the poet turns to the consequences of the destruction, to which he was a reluctant contributor, and insists, in an almost Biblical tone, on the need to contribute personally ('Wie will *ich* rufen') to the process of atonement and reconciliation ('das Aug mir noch / hell').

Bobrowski traces in outline the history of St. Sophia, which was built in 988, rebuilt in 1045-52 and restored in 1893-1900. The initial impression of the 'wir', German soldiers observing it over the River Wolkow, is one of darkness ('Schwärze'), and Novgorod itself is 'verdüstert'. That such physical darkness involves also a historical dimension is clear from the next stanza: 'Finster wars schon voreinst'. The physical and the historical 'night' coexist in the poem.

The second stanza emphasises the long success of the town and its cathedral, using a mixture of mythical and anthropomorphic images, with the 'Delphinen' as the creatures that attended journeys by the sea and river gods, and with the church itself having 'Wangen' and a 'Geschrei'. It is an evocation of a time of plenty ('Fruchtgärten') which echoes Hölderlin in its combination of the real, the metaphorical and the mythical. Compared to these earlier confident sounds ('deiner Kuppeln goldne[s] Geschrei') the cathedral appears reduced now to a mere 'klingendes Herz'.[55]

In the next stanza, the cathedral is presented as surviving as an 'Eisvogel' ('erglänzte') even in the most fatal ('tödlich blaß') of times. The image of the 'Eisvogel', as in 'Windmühle', is one of reduced activity but still of life, of memory overcoming ice, death and forgetfulness. It is a 'Vogel gegen das Eis'.[56] At this point (stanza 4) the poem returns to the more immediate past, the final destruction of this cathedral by the invaders, a destruction, the final consequences of which ('wie wird sein [...]?') are still unclear. The vocabulary used to describe the cathedral shifts for a while from the anthropomorphic to the architectural ('Wände', 'Türen', 'Fensterhöhlen'), while the new man-produced blackening ('Rauch hat [...] geschwärzt') marks both a new dimension of darkness in the poem compared with the river's natural 'reißende Schwärze', and also a new human violence compared to the metaphorical 'Wangen gebrannt'. The images mark an unnatural reversal of the earlier images as the poet finally admits his own indirect responsibility for the destruction ('Schrei') and its aftermath ('Schweigen'): 'alles an unsrem Leben / wars getan'. The poem then ends, typically, with Biblical allusions: to the famous passages on sowing and reaping (e.g. 'Wer Unrecht sät, der wird Unglück ernten'; 'sie säen Wind und werden Sturm ernten') and (with the opposite of 'hell' being *trübe*) to the less obvious Lamentations 5: 16f.: 'O weh, daß wir so gesündigt haben! Darum ist auch unser Herz krank, und unsere Augen sind *trübe* geworden'.[57] The image 'ging auf [...] Saat' also echoes and in part repeats a short passage from the *Song of Igor*, which, in German translation and referring to a previous conflict, reads: 'Die schwarze Erde unter den Hufen war mit Knochen besät und mit Blut getränkt, und die Saat ging als Kummer auf im russischen Land'.[58]

The poem evokes both the immediate past of 1941 and the long history of the cathedral, and it ends with its 'Gesicht', its 'face' but also

---

[55] See 'Pruzzische Elegie': 'So von tiefen / Glocken bleibt, die zersprungen, / Schellengeklingel'.

[56] Deskau, '"Dunkelheit" und "Engagement"', p.275.

[57] In Psalm 6 the two words occur in relative proximity:

2: Ach Herr, strafe mich nicht in deinem *Zorn*;

8: Mein Auge ist *trübe* geworden vor Gram...

See also 'Aufenthalt' (1:126): 'mit trüben Augen Hunde / sahen uns laufen hinab'.

[58] *Altrussische Dichtung aus dem 11.-18. Jahrhundert*, p.62.

its vision, rising up above the plains. It is a surprising reversal: as if in atonement for this destruction, the poem itself resurrects the cathedral whose destruction it describes: the crepuscular, static imagery of the first stanza ('Die wir sahn / über dem Winterstrom, / über der Wasser reißender *Schwärze, Sophia*') is replaced by dynamic movement and brightness ('wir sahn / steigen über die Ebene, / *weiß, dein Gesicht*'), while the cathedral, following or replacing (or preserving the memory of) the earlier pilgrims, now itself possesses the ultimate human feature, the face. The dynamic movement counteracts on a poetic level the destruction depicted and anticipates an answer to the final question. The poem itself contains the germ of something that might counter the heavy harvest of 'Zorn'.

A link between the two poems indicates what this germ might be, an element whose importance underlies Bobrowski's entire Sarmatian oeuvre: 'Kathedrale 1941' refers to the cathedral as a '*klingendes* Herz'; in 'Kloster bei Nowgorod' one finds, almost juxtaposed, the phrases 'im *ertönenden* Bogen' and '*erzene* Tor'. Separately these phrases have little significance. Together, a mosaic within a mosaic, they produce the famous passage from 1 Corinthians 13: 1: 'Wenn ich mit Menschen- und mit Engelzungen redete und hätte der Liebe nicht, so wäre ich ein *tönend Erz* oder eine *klingende* Schelle'. The quotation recurs more recognisably in 'Das Word Mensch' ('Wo Liebe nicht ist, / sprich das Wort nicht aus'), but its presence in these poems on the ruined cathedrals recalls the love Bobrowski emphasised in his October 1956 letter to Ricke, and the moral imperative he associated with it: to think of the past in order to help prevent similar disasters in the future.

'unter ihnen allen die Judenheit' (4:335)

Bobrowski's Sarmatian frame of reference includes not just the history and geography of Sarmatia but also the inhabitants, in particular the Jews, to whom he referred when he described the Memelland as a place where 'Polen, Litauer, Russen, Deutsche miteinander lebten, unter ihnen allen die Judenheit' (4:335). Bobrowski carefully and deliberately scattered poems to or about Jews throughout these two volumes, as a symbolic illustration of their omnipresence in Sarmatia, and their presence is occasionally decisive, even where neither title nor subject-matter emphasises them.[59] Poems dedicated to Jews, historical or

---

[59] Thus in 'Kindheit' (1:6f.), the third poem in *Sarmatische Zeit*, Bobrowski remembers

fictional, almost always concentrate on their innocent but by no means idyllicised life in Eastern Europe: the Chassidism in 'An den Chassid Barkan' (1:95); the life of the wandering Jewish merchant in 'Auf den jüdischen Händler A.S.' (1:15); the joys and occasional complications of life in the *shtetl* as in 'Wagenfahrt' (1:18) or 'Die Heimat des Malers Chagall' (1:56); the more general theme of persecution and the Diaspora in 'Die Spur im Sand' (1:28).[60] They generally avoid as unnecessary direct reference to the subsequent fate of the Jews under National Socialism, and only in 'Bericht' (1:133), an untypical poem, and the highly personal 'Kaunas 1941' (1:60f.) does Bobrowski concentrate on this suffering.[61]

Bobrowski's respect for Jews and Jewish culture is well documented. On August 25 1960 he wrote to Christoph Meckel: 'du weißt, für mich entscheidet sich der Wert eines Menschen an seiner Stellung zu den Juden' (*Marbach* 437), while he wrote to Peter Jokostra on February 6 1959, 'Jeder Jude ist mir das unbegreifliche Wunder, ohne das ich nicht leben kann,' and on January 12 1960 he commented 'Ich bin da fromm: Jeder Jude ist mir ein Beweis göttlicher Weltordnung'.[62] Despite this, the poems do not glorify Jews but present them instead as possible models for existence in forms of exile, and the two poems 'Auf den jüdischen Händler A.S.' of June 1954 and 'An den Chassid Barkan' of June 1960 show paradigmatically the extent to which they provided points for self-orientation. In the earlier poem the trader A.S. represents one possible ideal of life in exile. He remains aware of his indebtedness to previous generations, 'Alles haben wir, jede / Zeit aus den Händen

---

as an important part of his childhood: 'mit seinem / Wägelchen zog der graue / Jude vorbei'. The simple reference mutes the idyll of the other memories and provides an anticipatory justification for the loss at the end. I have looked at the significance of the title 'Der Judenberg' above.

[60] In a letter to Jokostra of May 21 1959 Bobrowski claimed that this poem (written August 12 1954) was 'von Celan beeindruckt' (5:35).

[61] 'Holunderblüte' (1:94) draws on the description of a *Russian* pogrom in the work 'The Story of my Dovecote' by Isaak Babel (1894-1941).

[62] The words are derived from Hamann's letter of January 1 1780 to Herder: 'Ein Wunder aller Wunder der göttl. Vorsehung, Regierung und Staatskunst – mehr als Noahs Kasten und Loths Weib u Moses brennender Busch ist für mich jeder Jude'. *Johann Georg Hamann: Briefwechsel*, ed. Walther Ziesemer and Arthur Henkel, Wiesbaden 1955ff., vol.4, p.147. The context of these comments is Bobrowski's struggle for recognition by the Jewish writer Paul Celan, a point of reference to which I

der Väter', and of their continuing presence in everyday life: 'Ihr über-
sterntes Gefürcht / glänzt im Gezweig unsrer Rede'.[63] This concern is
shown leading not to the self-destructive melancholy of which Bobrowski was all too aware, but to a paradoxical combination of attachment to
the lost home and an acceptance of homelessness as a way of life. The
poem ends:

> Immer geht einer davon,
> schaut nicht zurück, kein Winken
> folgt ihm. Doch hält ihn der Alten
> Spruch an den Pfosten des Tores
> über dem Meer noch. Fern
> weckt ihn der Birkenwege
> wehe tönendes Saitenspiel.

Although set in a clearly Jewish context, the poem here avoids specifically Jewish pointers. The *mezuzah* is generalised to become 'der
Alten Spruch' (echoing, incidentally, 'der Väter Rede' from the
introductory 'Anruf') and the initial Jewish 'Ich [...] aus Rasainen' is
transformed into a generalised 'einer', whose sleep is still disturbed by
memories of his past home but who 'schaut nicht zurück'.

In this 1954 poem the pains of memory are sublimated through the
reference to the fate of the Jewish trader whose whole tradition is built
upon this loss of homeland, but who retains a clear sense of identity. In
the later 'An den Chassid Barkan' Bobrowski draws on his knowledge
of the Chassidic life that had interested him since, at the latest, his
acquisition of Martin Buber's *Erzählungen der Chassidim* in 1956. In
particular he links their observance of religious rites to their joy at life:

> [...] So kamen immer
> eure Männer, umwachsen
> wie mit den Bärten eisern
> mit ihren Namen, aber
> die Locke leicht und die Füße
> heiter, im Tanz, vom brennenden
> Dornbusch, von einem Strom
> (an den Weiden hingen die Harfen).

The significant Biblical references here are to Exodus 3, where God

---

will return in chapter 4.

[63] Another version of the recurrent linking of language and twigs/branches, as in
'Pruzzische Elegie': 'wie hing Gerücht im Geäst ihr!'.

spoke to Moses in exile and made His presence known in the burning bush as the traditional Yahweh of the Jews – 'ich bin der Gott [...] Abrahams, der Gott Isaaks und der Gott Jakobs',[64] and to Psalm 137, where the Jews exiled in Babylon refused to sing for their captors. The wandering Chassidim too live in and for the present despite a full awareness of the past. The last stanza then emphasises the poet's hope to learn from them:

> Geh nicht fort. Die Zeit
> kommt auf, deine Pfade zu lieben, [...]
> auszusäen mit Tränen,
> zu ernten fröhlich.

In the typical turn to direct speech at the end of a poem, communicating here with the Chassidim, the poet recognises the need to 'deine Pfade lieben', meaning in this context to accept fully the life of homelessness ('Pfade'), and to respect the life-affirming way in which the Chassidim cope with this. The last lines then incorporate another Biblical quotation, from the end of the 'Wallfahrtslied' Psalm 126, in which the Psalmist expresses his conviction that the prisoners of Zion will eventually be released and that the sorrows of the present will be overcome: 'Die mit Tränen säen, werden mit Freuden ernten'.

In these two poems Bobrowski emphasised what he can learn from his Jewish fellow-Sarmatians. In 'Die Spur im Sand' he associated himself with them through 'deiner Väter Gott', the shared Judaeo-Christian God, who will 'uns noch die Jahre / [...] heller färben'. It is a certainty that gives him the ability to share Jewish exile and hope:

> Und gehe.
> Und deine Ferne
> trag ich, dein Erwarten
> auf meiner Schulter.

A more problematic aspect with which to identify presents itself in the poem 'Die Heimat des Malers Chagall' (1:56). Here the area around Vitebsk, where Chagall was born, is seen apparently in a state of final dissolution. It is initially presented as enjoying an endangered ('Noch') normality:

---

[64] Pascal started his 'Testament' with a reference to this passage, and Bobrowski kept it on a sheet of paper before him.

Noch um die Häuser
der Wälder trockener Duft,
Rauschbeere und Erdmoos.

The 'Rauschbeere' indicate coming celebrations, which are related to an
event from Chagall's life: 'der Ahn / lugte vom Dach / in den Hoch-
zeitstag'. The whole of Vitebsk seems fatally unaware ('Und wir hingen
in Träumen') of gathering dusk and a threatening storm, so that,
deceived by the apparent security of the 'Verläßliches / um unsrer Väter
Heimatgestirne [...] / [...] Engel [...] // [...] Nähe des Künftigen', they do
not see the gathering flood 'da es dunkelt, die Stadt / schwimmt durchs
Gewölk, / rot'. Behind the dense set of allusions to Chagall's life and
paintings (see 5:63ff.) stands a threat to which the Jews in this poem
seem oblivious. They 'hingen in Träumen' and failed to see the
impending disaster implied in the images of the 'brennender Hörner-
schall', the gathering darkness and the final word of the poem 'rot'.

These poems present a group with which Bobrowski, as a
'Sarmatian' now himself experiencing a form of exile, identifies: in the
shared Judaeo-Christian religious background; in the shared aim for the
exile to retain an identity while looking to the present and future, but
also – and more controversially – in the sense of the shared responsibility of the Sarmatian who failed to react to the signals of impending
doom and by so doing contributed passively to the final catastrophe.

'Anrufe an Sternbilder'

Bobrowski's poems to or about Jews are almost always concerned with
identification and self-orientation. So too are poems about other named
individuals, normally fellow artists in the widest sense. Comments in a
letter to Max Hölzer concerning a proposal to publish several of these
poems are revealing:

> Ellermann hat angeboten, 1961 einen Band mit meinen Gedichten an Personen
> [...] zu machen; 'Bildnis des Dichters' nennt er das und zeigt so das aller-
> blankste Hinterteil seines Unverstandes. Ich hab [...] ihn bloß darauf hinge-
> wiesen, daß das keine Porträts sind sondern Anrufe an Sternbilder, nach denen
> der alte Sarmate die Himmelsrichtung peilt. (April 12 1960, *Marbach* 347)

Christoph Meckel offers an alternative, more poetic interpretation:

> Es sind nicht Portraits der Gerufenen [...]. Bobrowski hat sich ihrer Namen
> bemächtigt, ihrer Sprachen, Epochen und Biografien, und sie in das Sarma-
> tische Reich entführt, im unzeitlichen eigenen Weltteil untergebracht,

poetisches Kidnapping großen Stils. Er holte sich, die ihn bestätigten, Mickiewicz und Klopstock, und brachte auf seine Seite, was ihm fehlte – zum Beispiel die Poeme von Saint John Perse, sein atlantisches Licht, die offene reiche Geschichtlichkeit seiner Eklogen. Er holte die Welt nach Sarmatien und in sein Haus. (*Marbach* 525)

With so many possible 'Sternbilder'/kidnap victims (up to forty in the published volumes, depending on one's definition) it is dangerous to single out any one individual as a uniquely important lodestar, and just as *Sarmatische Zeit* began with the poem 'Anruf' to two such different towns as Vilnius and Novgorod, so these 'Anrufe' collectively constitute a multiple process of self-orientation. The process also involves occasional partial rejection, following a star for a while before going in a different direction. The poems are sign-posts indicating possible directions, not poetic pen-portraits.

Bobrowski had written such poems since at the latest 'Der Maler Keßler' (2:133-7) from his period in captivity. With the cycle 'Der Regenbogen' (autumn 1952) these works achieved a new level of maturity, and in April 1955 he wrote the 'Ode auf Thomas Chatterton' (1:103f.), which was indeed included in the Sarmatian volumes. It was, however, written in an untypical odic form and with a pronounced elegiac element ('Ach!...'), and so it is a poem to Joseph Conrad of 3 July 1956 that introduced into such portrait poems the new style of the Sarmatian cycles.[65] The subjects of the poems in these volumes range in time from the late medieval French poet François Villon to a number of Bobrowski's contemporaries, including Hans Henny Jahnn, Boris Pasternak and Nelly Sachs. In general the points of orientation involve people who, in different ways, had to live with the consequences of forms of exile (Conrad, Villon, Mickiewicz) or sense of failure (Chatterton) or persecution or deep psychological trauma or sense of rejection (alcoholism, homosexuality in a homophobic or male-dominated world).

---

[65] Eberhard Haufe summarized the changes in 'Joseph Conrad' compared to earlier poems as follows:

> Neu war, abgesehen von Sprache und Rhythmus, die lyrische Verarbeitung konkreter biographischer, sozialer, auch betont fremdländischer Details. Was 1952 verfließende innere Biographie [...] war, [a reference to the 'Regenbogen' cycle] gewann nun die Präzision unverwechselbaren und paradigmatischen Menschenschicksals. (*SZNB* 2012)

Two very different poems 'Joseph Conrad' and 'Mickiewicz' illustrate both the continuity and the development of these works, with 'Joseph Conrad' as the earliest mature 'Anruf' and 'Mickiewicz' occupying a vital position at the end of the volume, marking Bobrowski's point of leave-taking from the Sarmatian oeuvre. Together the two poems also illustrate the increasing allusiveness of detail that characterises the volumes.

Joseph Conrad

Linien,
über der Kimmung,
leicht, falbes Gebirg. Der Streifen
Weiß. Dort geht
zu Ende die Flut. Der Küste
Fiebergrün scheint herauf.

Und der Wind
fährt, ein Sprung in der Wölbung
aus Licht, bleiernem Licht. Das Schiff
aber ist da. Hier steh ich. Ich hab in den Lungen
die unaufhörliche Ferne.
Und sag deinen Namen,
mein Schiff.

Einmal, im hellen Abend,
wie der Habicht der Berge um Tschernigow,
blick ich hinaus, weißblühende
Städtchen, am Dnjestr gesungen,
hör ich, ich rufe den polnischen
Zimmermann. Dort,
sag ich, die Boote sind schwarz.
Das hab ich vergessen.

Himmel über uns, Ferne
bis unter die Segel, dunkelnd.
Und, inmitten, die brennende
Treue der Männer, gekommen
über die Meerflut. (1:42)[66]

Bobrowski had known and admired the works of Joseph Conrad

---

[66] The poem has been analysed by Brigitte Bischof, who sees the work – wrongly, I believe – as a lyrical portrait and from this perspective criticises it for its occasional lacunae and lack of detail: 'Der polnische Zimmermann: Zu dem Gedicht "Joseph

since the war years, and in 1952/3 he had prepared a summary of his biography, together with others (Barlach, Brust, Buxtehude etc.). His knowledge of Conrad's background is reflected in some of the detail of the poem. Conrad's *The Mirror of the Sea* he particularly admired (*Chronik* 73). The two writers shared the sense of the epigone: Conrad looked back in almost metaphysical awe at the beauty of sailing boats and the loyalty, for him a key concept, of their crews; Bobrowski looked back to the beauty and the ideal of multi-ethnic tolerance from the Memelland. Both had lost their homeland: Conrad's 'Poland' was divided and strictly speaking did not exist, as did Bobrowski's East Prussia and Memelland. There was also the additional personal link that Conrad's mother had been born a Bobrowski and Bobrowski felt familial affection for him as his 'sagenhafter Urgroßonkel' (*SZNB* 64).

The poem shows the typical stuttering, disorientating, verbless beginning, which gradually gains shape in the last lines of the first stanza, as the mariner recognises the signs of danger – the 'Streifen Weiß' (breakers) and the more insidiously dangerous 'Fiebergrün' of the coast. The atmosphere surrounding the ship is oppressive, with the light itself presented as 'bleiern', and the whole is disturbed but not broken by a breath of wind. The image is that of a ship half-becalmed off a doubly hostile coast. Then, however, in the middle of the second stanza, the focus changes. In a series of staccato statements attention turns from the surroundings to the mariner himself and to his ship, whose presence stands out in stark simplicity: 'Das Schiff / aber ist da. Hier steh ich'. The words constitute a solemn form of self-positioning, emphasising Conrad's attachment to ships and echoing Luther's apocryphal response at Worms in 1521. The next few lines also appear to be lines of self-definition. This figure is full of 'die unaufhörliche Ferne', the continuing influence of his distant home which fills his lungs as a precondition for his existence. He can still only repeat, almost as a form of mantra, the name of his ship. As an expression of the indivisibility of this existence, the 'unaufhörliche Ferne' and the name of the ship are not separated by 'aber' but linked by 'und'.

In the third stanza elements of this past reassert themselves in a comparison,[67] while a synaesthesic image indicates that some song he is

---

Conrad" von Johannes Bobrowski', in *Neophilologicus* 59 (1975), 579-91.

[67] Chernigov was the place of Conrad's father's exile from January 1863 to 1868, and the Dniestr had been one of the rivers of his earliest childhood.

listening to reminds him of his youth. For a moment he is completely immersed in this past, but by the end of the stanza, the distance to this past has re-established itself: the only Pole present is the carpenter and they exchange a few words about the past, culminating in an unfocussed amnesia: 'das hab ich vergessen'. The poem returns in the last stanza to the situation at the beginning, with its contrast between the encroaching and darkening 'Ferne' on the one hand and the community, with its life-preserving 'brennende / Treue der Männer', on the other.

This is a poem on the unresolved tensions of life for someone who has 'in den Lungen / die unaufhörliche Ferne' but who, despite this burden, is attempting to become part of a new community in face of the stresses and dangers of the present. With this intention it evokes an unspecified incident from the adventurous sea-life of Conrad, who remembered and felt drawn to his divided lost homeland and who revisited in on two occasions, in 1893 and in 1914, before establishing himself in England with a new family and circle of friends, and a new-found existential certainty ('Hier steh ich').

As one of the earliest 'Anrufe', 'Joseph Conrad' is a relatively simple poem. 'Mickiewicz' (1:144f.), the concluding poem to *Schatten-land Ströme,* is much more complex. As the final piece laid in the Sarmatian mosaic it also presents a surprising summary of Bobrowski's intentions.

Mickiewiecz

Vor dem Eichenwald bin ich, das Schloß
stumm, eine Kerze
stellte die Mutter
unter das Bild im Wilnaer Tor, auf dem Strom
flogen Segel, im Rauch,
der Habicht fuhr
über die Bläue, ein roter
Abend ist ihm gefolgt

und eine Zeit der Städte
und eine der Straßen, der Felssturz
Krim, vor dem Meer
Wegstaub erhob sich, der Wagen
kam durch die Steppe von Akkerman –

Ich gewöhn mich ins Glück,
ich sage, es ist ganz leicht,

ich denk, meine Stimme trägt,
ich trink einen Regen, zurück
leg ich den Kopf auf die Mauer
Paris, ich trinke den Himmel
wie einen Mund, ich seh,
den die Lüfte erheben, den Habicht
über dem Eichwald, der Strom
führt einen Bogen hinab
in die Ebenen, fort,
unter den Schwalbenlüften
fort, aus der rieselnden Frühe,
über die Dörfer gespannt
und die Wälder: der Tag,
glänzend vom Zorn, einer Rüstung –

Ich werd kommen, vom Singsang
müd, vom Gered, nur den Flug
einer Etüde über dem Ohr, ich werd stehn
auf den Hängen, hören
nach einem Ruf und den Ton
suchen mit zitterndem Mund,
sagen: es ist ganz leicht.

The poem is post-dated in the Sarmatian volumes by 'Hölderlin in Tübingen' (1:107) and 'An Nelly Sachs' (1:119f.). Its position at the end of the volume indicates, however, its significance and indeed that of Adam Mickiewicz (1798-1855) for Bobrowski.[68] As well as his famous epic *Pan Tadeusz* (1834) Mickiewicz wrote a number of other significant works, in particular the *Crimean Sonnets* (1826) and the Byronic *Konrad Wallenrod* (1828). After studying at Vilnius and starting to work in Kaunas he was arrested (1823) for plotting against the Tsar and then exiled (1824) to Central Russia. In 1829 following an erotically and poetically fruitful period he left Russia and after moving about Europe finally settled in Paris, where he stayed for almost all the

---

[68] It has been interpreted by Jacek Buras in 'Johannes Bobrowskis "Mickiewicz": Eine Interpretation' in *Weimarer Beiträge* 16 (1970) vol.1, pp.212-6 who saw it (p.216) as a programmatical poem, a 'lyrisches Testament, das einem neuen Verhältnis zwischen Deutschen und Polen gilt', and by Sigfrid Hoefert, 'Johannes Bobrowski und Adam Mickiewicz: Zu einem Gedicht auf den polnischen Nationaldichter' in *Mickiewicz-Blätter* 43 (1970) 1-4 for whom 'das Gedicht [...] unser Mitgefühl für das Schicksal des Dichters im Exil [erweckt]' (p.4). Most recently Eva Adelsbach has devoted a short chapter to it in *Bobrowskis Widmungstexte an Dichter und Künstler des 18. Jahrhunderts: Dialogizität und Intertextualität*, St. Ingbert 1990, pp.155-8.

rest of his life. Here he confirmed his literary reputation with *Pan Tadeusz* before virtually giving up literature for journalistic and other activities. To the end of his life he hoped to liberate Poland, and when he died in Constantinople, he was attempting to raise a Polish Legion to fight the Tsar.

'Mickiewicz' rounds off the volume *Schattenland Ströme*, but the writer's presence, as I have indicated above, frames the volume as a whole. Mickiewicz was also named in *Sarmatische Zeit* in the poem 'Wilna' (1:21f.) ('Es hat / Mickiewicz besungen der wilder / leuchtenden Tage Glanz'), while Pan Tadeusz is mentioned in the introductory poem to *Schattenland Ströme* 'Der Wachtelschlag' (1:76f.). He clearly, therefore, played a significant role in Bobrowski's Sarmatian world, and in his first letter to Jokostra, Bobrowski had insisted on a direct and personal link: 'Ich bin vom Lande, vom allerplattesten, aus dem äußersten Winkel der ehemals deutschen Ostgebiete, wo man mehr litauisch sprach und wo Mickiewicz herstammt' (*Marbach* 449). Both writers shared a similar form of patriotism, which could allow Mickiewicz, an ardent Polish patriot who wrote in Polish, to be passionately attached to the mixed culture of his region and to accept, apparently with no sense of divided loyalties, its Lithuanian historical tradition and White Ruthenian folklore.[69] Indeed, so strong was this attachment, especially in exile, that he could start *Pan Tadeusz* with a hymn of praise not to Poland but to Lithuania:

> O Lithuania, my country, thou
> Art like good health; I never knew till now
> How precious, till I lost thee.[70]

The same complexity runs through the works of the German poet Bobrowski who could start *Sarmatische Zeit* with his 'Anruf' to Vilnius and Novgorod.

There is little direct evidence of poetic influence. What unites both writers is the fact of distance from their Central European homelands, but both also, in admittedly completely different ways, experienced a life-long sense of guilt at voluntary/involuntary actions from their

---

[69] See *Adam Mickiewicz in World Literature*, Waclaw Lednicki (ed.), Berkeley and Los Angeles 1956, pp.589f.

[70] *Pan Tadeusz or The Last Foray in Lithuania*, tr. Kenneth Mackenzie, London 1966, p.2.

earlier life. For Mickiewicz this had been his failure to hurry back from Italy to Poland to involve himself in the 1830 Polish Uprising, even though he believed this had been at least in part inspired by his own *Konrad Wallenrod*. For Bobrowski it was his involvement in the German invasion of the East.

The poem 'Mickiewicz' draws from a number of sources, primarily Mickiewicz's life and works, but also includes completely discrete material from elsewhere. It starts with an apparently definitive statement of present position, followed by a flurry of undeveloped images, now in the past tense, drawn from Mickiewicz's childhood and youth. The 'Schloß' is in Novogrodek (near Mickiewicz's birthplace) and contains a miraculous image of the Virgin Mary, but clearly one that did not respond ('stumm') to appeals when Mickiewicz suffered serious illness as a child, since his mother went to pray for his recovery at the 'Bild im Wilnaer Tor', the famous Ostra Brama in Vilnius.[71] The material for this is taken from the first lines of *Pan Tadeusz*.

The next few images are not found in Mickiewicz's writings but are common in Bobrowski's Sarmatian works. Although unclear in detail the sense of the scene as a whole is clear, with Bobrowski's recurrent negative images 'Rauch', a rising 'Habicht' and 'rot' apparently triumphant over the flying (scattered?) 'Segel', as, in a more clichéd metaphor, the winds of fate scattered Mickiewicz and his youthful conspirators. With the enjambement leading to the next stanza, the images appear as the precursor to the period of Mickiewicz's exile in Russia and beyond, the 'Zeit der Städte [...] und der Straßen'.

From the initial period of exile in Russia Bobrowski refers specifically, through the mention of Akkerman, to the period spent in the Crimea and the *Crimean Sonnets*, in the first of which Mickiewicz sees himself travelling through the plains of Akkerman and concludes:

> We halt. How still! [...]
> I hear
> The butterfly that rocks the grass.
> [...]
> So still it is, a voice might reach my ear

---

[71] See 'Am Strom': 'Du kamst / den Mondweg, von Ostra Brama / kamst du herab, von des alten / Bildes Glanz' (1:23) and Bobrowski's note: 'Ostra Brama – Tor in Wilna, alter Wallfahrtsort mit wundertätigem Marienbild' (1:286).

from Lithuania – Onward! No one calls.[72]

The next stanza is the longest of the poem. It brings a new tone, with constant repetition of the 'ich', and a change in tense, back to the present, and indicates that the previous two stanzas were in fact memories viewed from the poetic present, which is evidently the time spent in Paris. Here Mickiewicz consolidated his international reputation as an émigré Polish writer but suffered increasingly from his inability to return to his homeland. This questionable success is expressed in the first line through the unusual construction: 'ich gewöhn mich INS Glück,' with its implication that it is only through becoming inured to his exile that he may find happiness, an interpretation underlined by the claim, expressed with false conviction, that 'es ist ganz leicht'. Buras (p.215) sees the phrase, repeated at the end of the work, as conveying 'eher [...] ein[en] Vorwurf als eine Feststellung', as being 'selbstironisch, pejorativ'.

Beyond all doubt is the extent to which Mickiewicz hoped that his voice would be heard in his homeland, and his longing is expressed in the sensual image of the middle lines of the poem, the image of drinking the rain and the sky – reminders of his distant homeland, things common to Paris and to Poland – 'wie einen Mund'.[73] Under such circumstances Paris becomes for Mickiewicz 'eine Mauer', an image of his sense of imprisonment and exclusion from wider spaces.[74] The stanza as a whole echoes Bobrowski's own conviction that he would 'hier in Berlin [...] nicht anwurzeln' (1:xlvi).

The image of this current 'prison' leads naturally to its opposite: the dream of flowing freedom 'fort [...] fort', as Mickiewicz escapes in spirit into the 'Ebenen [...] Dörfer [...] Wälder'.[75] As the use of the plural

---

[72] *Adam Mickiewicz 1798-1855: Selected Poetry and Prose*, ed. S. Helsztynski, Warsaw 1955, p.65.

[73] This imagery may be related to lines from the 'Epilogue' to *Pan Tadeusz*:

To think of such things in a Paris street,
Where on my ears the city's noises beat. (p.283)

[74] It is, of course, possible that this is a reference to the support Mickiewicz is reputed to have received in Paris from Freemasons. It goes without saying that Bobrowski wrote this poem *before* the building of the wall through Berlin.

[75] This passage too could relate to the 'Epilogue' of *Pan Tadeusz:*

I longed to fly, a bird of feeble flight,

here indicates, these are no longer individual geographical entities but constitute an image of the whole of Sarmatia. The poetic persona still, however, sees the hawk hovering, a threat underlined in an oblique reference to a potential victim (*'Schwalben*lüften').[76] The vision re-activates the image of the 'Strom' from the beginning of the poem and re-establishes the temporal progression suggested earlier by the reference to a 'roter Abend' (presumably followed by the 'night' of exile), in references to a 'rieselnde Frühe' and a 'Tag, / glänzend vom Zorn, einer Rüstung'. Such apocalyptic imagery (*'Dies irae'*!) clearly reflects Mickiewicz's in part religiously inspired longing for the violent over-throw of the Russian occupation.

Borne along by this vision, the persona anticipates its possible return to this landscape, but replaces the image of wrath and armour with a vision of a poet returning, exhausted by the superficial 'Singsang'[77] and 'Gered' of Paris, waiting for an unspecified 'Ruf' and searching for its own answering 'Ton'.[78] The words 'es ist ganz leicht', which accompanied the sense of resignation in Paris, are repeated in apparent acceptance of this new situation.

The significance of these words, like the form of this return, is not clear.[79] The imagery of a 'Ruf' and a potential reply is, however,

---

Beyond the thunder and the stormy zone,
And seek the sunshine and the shade alone,
The homely plot and endless childhood days. (loc. cit.)

[76] In fact there is an element of ambiguity here, in that the 'den' ('ich seh, / *den* die Lüfte erheben, den Habicht / über dem Eichwald') could apply equally to the bird and the poet. The 'Schwalbenlüfte' imply, however, hawk as threat rather than as an image of the poet himself.

[77] The reference to the étude is probably to the works of Chopin, especially the 'Revolutionary Étude' (C minor, opus 10 No. 12). Mickiewicz met him in Paris.

[78] It is tempting to link the 'call' directly to Christian images of death as the end of life's pilgrimage, as in the section 'Die pilgernde Gemeinde' from the Protestant *Glaubensstimme*. Gerhard Tersteegen's 'Kommt Kinder, laßt uns gehen' expressly states: 'Wir kennen ja den Treuen, der uns gerufen hat,' while Paul Gerhardt's hymn: 'Ich bin ein Gast auf Erden' implies the call ('Ach komm, mein Gott, und löse mein Herz, wenn dein Herz will') and self-confidently declares that, in death, 'da will ich herrlich singen'. Bobrowski's figure is more modest and will only 'den Ton suchen'.

[79] Dorothee Sölle in 'Für eine Zeit ohne Angst' (p.162) sees the words as suggesting the possibility of 'ein menschliches Lebenkönnen [...] eine Hoffnung'. Buras sees them as expressing 'die Möglichkeit einer anderen und stilleren Rückkehr in seine Heimat: als Dienst an ihr durch dichterische Vergegenwärtigung', with Mickiewicz and Bobrowski

common in Bobrowski's poetry. In the last stanza of the previous poem 'Immer zu benennen' (1:143) one finds the claim: 'Wär da ein Gott / und im Fleisch, / und könnte mich rufen, ich würd / umhergehn'. More immediately relevant is the first poem in *Schattenland Ströme* 'Der Wachtelschlag', with its Mickiewicz reference, where the poetic 'Ich' links a call and a response with the claim: 'Wachtel, ich hörte gern / deinen Ruf, / einfach, [...] "Lobet / Gott"', and then continues: '"Lobet Gott" / sag ich'. What is clear is the extent to which a 'Ruf', whether anticipated or interpreted or posited brings with it the possibility of an answer. The combination functions in its bare essentials as an expression of hope fulfilled. In this hope the waiting for a call forms a clear contrast with the historical Mickiewicz's experiences on the plain of Akkerman, where, he wrote, 'No one calls'.

The poem evidently presents, from the point of view of exile in Paris, an imagined life of Mickiewicz, following three biographical phases: childhood, Russian exile, Parisian exile. These are followed by a dream of a return to Poland/Lithuania. The persona is seen thinking of his past experiences, summarising his ambivalent present happiness, and looking into the future. It is, however, as the last stanza makes clear, no 'objective' portrait, but instead uses elements of Mickiewicz's biography to illustrate an experience of exile[80] and the longing for some form of return. The stanza, however, alters the reality of the life of Mickiewicz. His hatred of the Russians, his attempts to overthrow them by violence, above all his own later rejection of poetry – all these constitutive elements of his life are played down, and Bobrowski's Mickiewicz appears thus not as a portrait but as a point of personal orientation, to be used, but then abandoned.

The final gnomic words of the poem – and of Bobrowski's entire Sarmatian oeuvre – have remain unexplained, and it is tempting to assume that they constitute a quotation from some work by Mickiewicz. There is, however, no source for them there. They do, however, occur at an important point in the novel *Krüsemann: Ein Roman aus der Zeit*

---

finding their way home, 'indem sie eine untergehende oder schon untergegangene Welt im Wort aufbewahrten' (p.215). The words 'es ist ganz leicht' then are an expression of their 'Bewußtsein heroischer Bescheidung' (p.216).

[80] Schütze correctly comments (*Natur und Geschichte*, p.70) on the last stanza: 'Das lyrische Ich des Gedichts beschreibt zwar den porträtierten polnischen Exildichter aus der Innenperspektive, erscheint aber kaum anders als in anderen, nicht porträtierenden Gedichten'.

nach dem Kriege[81] by Heinrich Wolfgang Seidel (1876-1945), and, almost more significantly, they are words that are emphasised and heavily glossed in a review of this novel, a copy of which was contained in Bobrowski's library. In the novel they occur as the dying words of the hero Ottokar Krüsemann:

> 'Ich ruhe ja', sagte er, 'nie war es so gut, niemals.' [...] Dann senkten sich seine Lider, als suche er etwas, das er gesehen, im Innersten zu bewältigen, sie [a witness to his death] hörte ihn flüstern: 'Es ist – ganz – leicht!' und dann verharrte er in einem unbeweglichen Schweigen, und sie wußte, daß alles zu Ende war. (p.259)

It is a strange novel, in which Krüsemann, a retired merchant, saves Segewold, a Latvian student, from starvation and provides him with a roof and sufficient money to continue his studies. It is inevitably a fragile relationship and despite (or because of) Krüsemann's fatherly solicitude the two drift apart. The novel's loose plot provided Seidel with opportunities to criticise recent historical developments and to satirise some of the artistic and cultural trends of the Weimar Republic, trends for which Krüsemann evidently had no understanding. Krüsemann's quiet undramatic dying words express his resignation and the manner in which he lived his entire life and accepted the inevitability of death.

The poem evidently ends in a quiet acceptance of death very different from that of Mickiewicz in Constantinople. It is then a work in which Bobrowski follows his respected Mickiewicz but quietly replaces his wrathful longing for an armed and triumphant homecoming ('Zorn', 'Rüstung') with an acquiescence in a form of homecoming (as in 'Heimweg', 1:142) in death at the end of life's pilgrimage, with the words 'es ist ganz leicht' sealing this acceptance.

There is no further reference to *Krüsemann* in the poem, and it is legitimate to ask how much Bobrowski actually knew of the work. He had corresponded with Ina Seidel, the author's wife, since September 1942 (*Marbach* 278), and this may have played some part in the choice of this particular quotation. That these are Krüsemann's dying words may also explain in part their position at the end of this poem. It is not, however, clear from their position in the novel how they relate to the whole Sarmatian oeuvre that is being brought to an end. An answer is to

---

[81] Published Berlin 1935.

be found in the review mentioned above. This is an unpaginated, undated publisher's note, distributed in spring 1936 by the publishers G. Grote, a copy of a long review of *Krüsemann* written in 1935 by Ernst Wiechert (1887-1950). Here Wiechert praises *Krüsemann* for its quiet tone against the background of 'das Getöse der Lautsprecher' (i.e. National Socialism) and quotes Raabe: 'Unbemerkt kommt alles, was Dauer haben wird in dieser wechselnden, lärmvollen Welt voll falschen Heldentums, falschen Glücks und unechter Schönheit'. Then he comments on Krüsemann's dying words:

> [Krüsemann] geht [...] still aus einer Welt, die er nie verstanden hat, aber aus der zu scheiden nun doch mit den friedlichen Worten gelingt: 'Es – ist – ganz – leicht.'
> Und was könnte einer Dichtung Größeres gelingen, als daß sie uns aus den Schmerzen, Wirrnissen und Schauern ihrer Welt mit diesem selben Bewußtsein entläßt: 'Es war ganz leicht'? Dann ist etwas geschehen, was zu der Kunst der Erschütterung eine größere Kunst fügt: die der Versöhnung. [...]
> 'Es ist ganz leicht...'
> *Wo aber lebte mehr Liebe als in den Büchern, deren Geschehen in einem solchen Wort endet?* [my italics]

With his positioning of this poem Bobrowski announces his withdrawal from his Sarmatian world. The reason for this is, I believe, clear. He had created precisely the work of love to which Wiechert's words applied. As he had informed Ricke in October 1956: 'Ich liebe die Landschaft, die Geschichte, die Menschen meiner Heimat. Und ich liebe die Deutschen'. By choosing to finish this work with Krüsemann's dying words, he confirms, with Wiechert, that he has overcome the 'Schmerzen, Wirrnisse und Schauern' of his experience, that he has reached the end of this particular poetic world. Unlike Mickiewicz, who continued his struggle to the end, Bobrowski has also achieved the 'größere Kunst' to which Wiechert here refers, namely that of 'Versöhnung'.

'Mickiewicz' is a poem whose points of reference include centuries of conflict between Russians, Poles and the Baltic states. Even the reference to Akkerman constitutes a historical pointer – to the Treaty of Akkerman whose failure led to the Russian-Turkish War of 1828.[82] It is an act of self-orientation making free use of a figure with whom Bob-

---

[82] Akkerman itself, incidentally, suffered the fate of much of 'Sarmatia', having at different times been part of different nations.

rowski shared a number of experiences, but using a completely different figure of orientation at the end. Above all, however, 'Mickiewicz' constitutes a private declaration of love for and leave-taking from the poetic world to which Bobrowski had devoted so many years of his productive life. He could indeed claim a few weeks later in a letter of June 29 1961 to Max Hölzer (*SZNB* 117): 'mit [*Schattenland Ströme*] ist die Bestandsaufnahme meiner östlichen Vergangenheit [...] abgeschlossen'.

4

ORIENTATIONS: HAMANN, KLOPSTOCK, CELAN

Within Bobrowski's Sarmatian world the two figures of Conrad and Mickiewicz were ideally suited for the role of victims of 'poetic kidnapping'. Bobrowski could use and distort their biography at will and credit Mickiewicz, as demonstrated above, with some words of Krüsemann that flatly contradicted the historical figure. Of a different order of significance for him were three other figures, two of whom accompanied him from his school days, and one of whom provoked, irritated, in part fascinated him from the mid-1950s onward. The first two are Johann Georg Hamann and Friedrich Gottlieb Klopstock. The last is the Rumanian German Jewish writer Paul Celan. Each provided a stimulus for some aspect of his later works, both during and after the Sarmatian phase.

The character and works of Hamann provided Bobrowski with a model of existence whose significance can hardly be overstated. Bobrowski wrote at least three poems to or about him, 'Hamann' (1:92), 'Epilog auf Hamann' (1:232) and 'J.G.Hamann' (2:222), and had him appear as a positive figure of orientation in the early short story 'Epitaph für Pinnau'.[1] Hamann quotations occur unacknowledged, above all in the last novel *Litauische Claviere*. Outside his literary works, he once referred to his determination to write a life history of

---

[1] These works have individually or collectively been subjected to a number of analyses. See in particular Brigitte Bischoff, 'Bobrowski und Hamann', *Zeitschrift für deutsche Philologie* 94 (1975), pp.553-82; Bernhard Gajek, 'Autor – Gedicht – Leser: Zu Johannes Bobrowskis Hamann-Gedicht' in *Literatur und Geistesgeschichte: Festschrift für Heinz Otto Burger*, ed. R.Grimm and C.Wiedemann, W.Berlin 1968, pp.308-24; Alfred Kelletat, 'Griechisches Triptychon aus deutschen Gedichten: Peter Huchel – Johannes Bobrowski – Joachim Uhlmann', in *Festschrift für Konstantinos J. Merentitis*, Athens 1972, pp.182-94; Eberhard Haufe, 'Der Moralist und die Welt der Geschichte: Studie zu Johannes Bobrowskis Erzählung "Epitaph für Pinnau"', *Neue Zeit* September 2 1970; Bernd Leistner, *Johannes Bobrowski: Studien und Interpretationen*, pp.25ff. The poem 'Steh. Sprich. Die Stimme' (2:349f.) has been subjected to an interpretation as a poem totally infused with the spirit of and quotations from Hamann by Jürgen Henkys, in 'Bobrowskis Jona-Strophe: Hinweise zur Interpretation eines Nachlaß-gedichtes' (*SZNB* 167-88). Tgahrt provides an illuminating vision of the complexities of the poem 'Hamann' in the chapter 'Ein paar Fäden aus einem Gedicht', *Marbach* 379-408.

him and shed some light on a mysterious time that Hamann spent in London, where he experienced a shattering religious conversion. As Lektor at the Union Verlag Bobrowski also helped Martin Seils produce the edition of Hamann's works *Entkleidung und Verklärung* (1963), and, as a review of a small selection of Hamann's works from the 1950s demonstrates, he was a cognoscente of the minutiae of Hamann's life and times (4:367-9). His 'Nachlaß' is saturated with transcriptions from Hamann's works, short excerpts from them and copies of quotations, and his library contained a significant collection of Hamann editions, old and valuable, new and scholarly. This was a figure whose personal fascination for Bobrowski is self-evident.

This fascination drew on a number of factors. The most significant was the fact that both were Christians, living in a society dominated by aspects of a dogmatic 'victorious' rationalism. Hamann dedicated his life's work to a struggle against this form of rationalism, which he castigated for its theological, anthropological, but also aesthetic and linguistic shortcomings. The many works in which he did this provided Bobrowski with a number of different stimuli in all these areas of his existence. But for Bobrowski the fascination was almost certainly also brought about by his sense of closeness, specifically to Hamann and not Kant, during his youth in Königsberg. Hamann was the half-forgotten local hero, and from his youth onwards Bobrowski's interest in the byways of German intellectual history drove him nearer to the forgotten, the outsider, rather than the established.

In her article 'Bobrowski und Hamann' Brigitte Bischof sensibly concludes with a series of questions which reveal her own interpretation of the relationship:

> War es das aufrechte Christentum Hamanns, der auch in einer glaubensfeindlichen Umwelt von seinem Gott Zeugnis ablegte? War es der Mut, mit dem er das Einzelne, Individuelle und Geschichtlich-Konkrete vor allumfassenden Systemen und Abstraktionen zu retten suchte? War es der Umstand, daß Hamann das Gefühl gegen das nur Vernünftige setzte, daß er die Verwirklichung des ganzen Menschen auf seine Fahne schrieb? Oder war es die Skepsis, mit der Hamann der optimistischen Selbstüberschätzung seiner aufgeklärten Zeitgenossen gegenüberstand, und die Demut, mit der er sich dem göttlichen Willen beugte? (p.582)

Other critics have concentrated more on the possible effect of Hamann's statements on language and poetry, and Dagmar Deskau relates Bobrowski's poetic complexity to these:

> Bobrowski geht [...] von einem säkularisierten 'Sündenfall' des Menschen
> aus, von der 'Geschichte aus Unglück und Verschuldung [...] die meinem
> Volk zu Buch steht.' [...] – Und er drückt dies durch 'dunkle' Naturzeichen
> aus, die – im Sinne Hamanns – der 'Spiegel' sind, durch den hindurch
> Historisches nur gebrochen und undeutlich erkennbar wird.[2]

Bernd Leistner also emphasises the relation between the darkness of
Hamann's prose and Bobrowski's poetry, and David Scrase suggests a
shared congeniality with the cabala but also with a 'Rousseauesque
glorification of the primitive, folk, pagan'.[3]

In view of the central importance of the unselfish love and resignation that I perceive, in 'Mickiewicz' especially and in the Novgorod
poems, as underlying the Sarmatian project, it is not surprising to find
one aspect of Hamann's theology, the centrality of the love of God, also
suggested, above all by Leistner, as a possible point of orientation, and
he quotes with approval some comments by Walter Leibrecht:

> Ohne Gottesliebe und ohne Menschenliebe ist keine wahre Erkenntnis des
> Wirklichen möglich; denn alles Wirkliche ist vom Geist der Liebe geschaffen
> und kann nur von der Liebe erkannt werden.[4]

That the Sarmatian cycles were a work of love has always been clear.
The extent to which this love underpinned them is now even clearer.
This link between knowledge and love is another of the threads linking
Bobrowski to Hamann.

Bobrowski's relation to Hamann is evidently existential, rather than
simply intellectual, let alone narrowly literary, and attempts to establish
direct influence on Bobrowski's works, especially on his poetry, have
rarely carried complete conviction. Hamann was a philosopher and
theologian, Bobrowski was a poet, and for the poet the two figures
Klopstock and Celan provided other forms of orientation. For both
writers, one long dead and the other still alive when Bobrowski lived,
Bobrowski felt a respect that would allow no biographical distortion.
They do not appear as material for poems but as the addressees of
poems, whether stated, in the case of Klopstock, or unstated with Celan.
The length of the period during which they featured as issues within his

---

[2] *Der aufgelöste Widerspruch*, p.61.

[3] *Understanding Johannes Bobrowski*, S.Carolina 1995, pp.10ff.

[4] *Gott und Mensch bei Johann Georg Hamann*, Gütersloh 1958, p.141.

works is, as with Hamann, an indication of their significance, but Bobrowski saw them as standing at opposite ends of a poetical spectrum encompassing life and death. Ironically in this context he saw the dead poet as more living than the living one.

An examination of some of the traces left by these two figures and their confrontation here sheds light on Bobrowski's poetic antipathies and inclinations. In his own confrontation with them Bobrowski, a writer with little patience for theorising about his works, found himself forced to construct a conceptual framework within which his works fitted. They constituted two main markers in his self-orientation in the later years of Sarmatia and the years beyond. This self-orientation also helped him produce a defence against a number of critical attacks, as will become clear.

For much of the time he had been working at his Sarmatian 'Bestandsaufnahme' Bobrowski had been a virtually unrecognised minor poet. With the publication of *Sarmatische Zeit* came 'ein kleiner Ruhm' (1:161) together with its inevitable accompaniment: public criticism. This was particularly pronounced at a reading of January 26 1961 in Klaus Völker's 'Keller' in front of, among others, a number of Walter Höllerer's students (*Marbach* 168). Christoph Meckel has summarised the criticism that Bobrowski met here: that his language was 'alt', 'verbraucht' and 'nicht mehr plausibel', his subject-matter 'provinziell', and that all that he offered was 'eine gewisse dumpfe Exotik'.[5] In a letter to Helmut Bartuschek written shortly afterwards (February 2 1961) Bobrowski showed his concern: 'Ich hab neulich vor Höllerers Studenten gelesen und eine ganze Phalanx beredter junger Leute gegen mich gehabt. Was heißt das schon? Man tut, was man kann, und das so redlich wie möglich' (*Marbach* 168). This word 'redlich' was to play a vital role in his poetic self-justification.

On February 4 1961 two days after this letter Bobrowski completed 'Immer zu benennen'. Unsurprisingly in view of the criticism, it shows considerable reticence. It does not justify his poetic devices and aims but frankly admits (in the language just described as 'alt' and 'provinziell') his own 'Bedenken' concerning their moral and poetic adequacy. His justification, such as it is, is *ex negativo*: that with circumstances as they are, this is all that is possible; there is no divine 'call' to provide another language, but there is no time apart from the present, so no

---

[5] Christoph Meckel, *Erinnerung an Johannes Bobrowski*, Frankfurt/M.1981, pp.9ff.

sense in waiting.

Almost exactly a year later on 5 February 1962, Bobrowski wrote 'An Klopstock' (1:161), one of the key poems of his posthumous volume *Wetterzeichen*. This was followed at sporadic intervals by a number of other poems in which he reflected explicitly on aspects of his poetry, including the gnomic 'Sprache' (1:177), but especially 'Wiedererweckung' (1:203f.) and 'Mit Liedern Sapphos' (1:206). Taken together these poems indicate a growing confidence in language, and specifically the German language, and in his own use of it. The same confidence is reflected in the more positive outlook on life occasionally expressed in other poems from the volume, as indeed for the poet Bobrowski existential and poetological confidence were interrelated.

Central to this process was the consideration of Klopstock and Celan. Individually, Bobrowski's relations to these writers, and especially the former, have been widely recognised.[6] What has not been adequately appreciated, largely as a result of the incomplete publication of Bobrowski's correspondence, is the extent to which Bobrowski saw them as opposites.

Bobrowski's acquaintance with Klopstock was, of course, the longer. He read him while still at school in Königsberg and admitted his significance in the post-war years. On 8 January 1952 he could refer in a letter to Hans Ricke to the 'ganz großen Einfluß Hölderlins, Klopstocks, Rilkes, Hofmillers, Barlachs, Brittings, Stifters und unzähliger anderer' (*Chronik* 31). As, however, the very mixed list indicates, Klopstock at the time appears to have been just one influence out of many, and his position in the list after Hölderlin is significant. In a later letter to Ricke (29 December 1957) Bobrowski commented on the modernity of Klopstock: 'Ich bilde die Landschaften meiner Jugend ab. / Ich les wieder Mörike und Eichendorff, und Klopstock scheint mir moderner als das meiste Zeitgenössische' (*Chronik* 40). In January 1961, with, for

---

[6] See Anni Carlsson, 'Johannes Bobrowski und Klopstock' in *Neue Zürcher Zeitung* January 16 1966, p.21; Manfred Seidler, 'Bobrowski, Klopstock und der antike Vers', in *Lebende Antike: Symposium für Rudolf Sühnel*, ed. Horst Meller and Hans-Joachim Zimmermann, Berlin 1967, pp.542-54. The works by Minde, Rittig and Schütze have analysed and emphasised rather the differences between Bobrowski and Klopstock. For an interpretation of the poem 'An Klopstock', see in particular Alfred Kelletat, '"An Klopstock": Bemerkungen zu Johannes Bobrowskis Widmungsgedicht' in *Lyrik von allen Seiten: Gedichte und Aufsätze des ersten Lyrikertreffens in Münster*, ed. Lothar Jordan, Axel Marquardt and Winfried Woesler, Frankfurt/M. 1981, pp.412-28.

him, unusual academic distance, Bobrowski wrote to Hubert Gersch answering questions on aspects of his poetry and using Klopstock as a particular point of reference:

> Besser hält man sich wohl an eine Klopstocksche Behandlung der Sprache und kommt wie Hölderlin über die antiken Metren zur freien Wirtschaft mit dem Wort wie mit dem Syntax. [...] Bei uns fallen, von Klopstock bis Voß zum absoluten Gesetz erhoben, natürliche Betonung und Versrhythmus zusammen.[7]

In an interview with Irma Reblitz of late March 1965 he admits his debt to his 'Meister – Klopstock' and continues:

> Darüber müßte ich einen ganzen Vortrag halten, was ich an Klopstock sehe: Verlebendigung der Sprache, ein Ausnutzen der sprachlichen Möglichkeiten, Neufassung der Metrik. [...] Das ist für mich ein Meister, der, ich bin sicher, in seiner Wirkung in Deutschland alles überholen wird, was nachher gekommen ist. (4:488)

Other significant comments on Klopstock are passed in 1959 to Jokostra, and their particular significance, as will become clear, lies in their context: as part of an on-going indirect debate with Celan.

The actual poem 'An Klopstock' (1:161) was written a week after the important letter to Max Hölzer in which he lamented the building of the Berlin Wall and the fact that he was now cut off from friends, but in which he also emphasised his faith: 'und doch mit einer geradezu eschatologischen Hoffnung, die mich mit einer Ruhe und Sicherheit erfüllt, für die ich die Gründe nicht mehr beibringen kann' (*Sankelmark* 41f.).

An Klopstock

Wenn ich das Wirkliche nicht
wollte, dieses: ich sag
Strom und Wald,
ich hab in die Sinne aber
gebunden die Finsternis,
Stimme des eilenden Vogels, den Pfeilstoß
Licht um den Abhang

und die tönenden Wasser –
wie wollt ich

---

[7] Quoted by Renate von Heydebrand in 'Engagierte Esoterik', p.526.

sagen deinen Namen,
wenn mich ein kleiner Ruhm
fände – ich hab
aufgehoben, dran ich vorüberging,
Schattenfabel von den Verschuldungen
und der Sühnung:
so als den Taten
trau ich – du führtest sie – trau ich
der Vergeßlichen Sprache,
sag ich hinab in die Winter
ungeflügelt, aus Röhricht
ihr Wort.

Haufe relates the poem to the 'Einwände anderer' (5:168), to which he interprets it as a form of answer. If this is the case, then it is a complex answer, since 'An Klopstock' initially emphasises the considerable discrepancy between words ('ich sag') and the reality to which they refer and which Bobrowski has 'in die Sinne [...] gebunden'. In view of this discrepancy the saying of Klopstock's name might involve, he appears to suggest, a case of lèse-majesté. He finds comfort, however, so the poem implies, in his faith in language, *despite* this apparent discrepancy between it and reality.

Bobrowski's most significant recent public naming of Klopstock had been in the note he wrote shortly before 17 July 1961 for Hans Bender's *Widerspiel – Deutsche Lyrik seit 1945*, which referred to Germany's 'lange Geschichte aus Unglück und Verschuldung [...] nicht zu [...] sühnen, aber eine Hoffnung wert und einen redlichen Versuch in deutschen Gedichten'. Four years before the interview with Reblitz, this note had ended with the words: 'Zu Hilfe habe ich einen Zuchtmeister: Klopstock' (4:335). 'An Klopstock' appears to have been written with these ideas in mind. As well as the reference to Klopstock himself, the note's reference to 'Verschuldung' and 'Sühnung' recurs as the 'Schattenfabel von den *Verschuldungen* / und der *Sühnung*', and the 'Hoffnung [...] und einen redlichen Versuch' is implied in the words 'trau ich [...] trau ich [...]', while the specific phrase 'in deutschen Gedichten' is also implied in the poem in 'der Vergeßlichen Sprache', a reference to what Bobrowski elsewhere, quoting Hamann, called the 'Land, [...] wo man nichts nichts nichts gedenkt' (1:232).

Like 'Joseph Conrad' and 'Mickiewicz' this poem is an 'Anruf an ein Sternbild', but here Bobrowski addresses his subject directly in order to evaluate his own aims and achievements. Bobrowski himself is central, as is clear from the fact that the first person forms the subject of nine out of eleven verbs and is the direct object of a tenth. Only once does the addressee function as subject, in a clause which, though parenthetical, is fundamental to Bobrowski's faith in his language: 'du führtest sie'.

Bobrowski still appears, as in 'Immer zu benennen', to accept the possible inadequacy of the vocabulary and poetic means criticised by the Höllerer group. Here, however, the poem ends in a more balanced statement of faith in language: 'trau ich der Vergeßlichen Sprache'. This faith in language is bound up with Bobrowski's admiration for Klopstock, and forms, as will become clear, a significant aspect of his dispute with Celan. Although writing principally about himself, he partly echoes themes and phrases from works by Klopstock, by this means indicating areas of comparison between himself and Klopstock. These include the famous first few words of Klopstock's epic *Messias*, 'Sing, unsterbliche Seele, der sündigen Menschen Erlösung', which recurs in 'An Klopstock' as the 'Schattenfabel[8] von den Verschuldungen / und der Sühnung', but where for Klopstock the guilt is expiated by Christ, for Bobrowski both guilt and atonement remain a human concern. In order to attempt this atonement with his own 'redlicher Versuch', Bobrowski needs a faith in language – both in the *German* language so misused by the Nazis, and in his own particular *poetic* language misunderstood and condemned by Höllerer, and in justifying this faith Bobrowski again refers indirectly to Klopstock, this time to the minor ode 'Fragen'.[9] Here Klopstock had praised the use of the German language in words that clearly anticipate 'An Klopstock'.

'Fragen' opens with a few stanzas castigating Germans who only wish to imitate the French or English, but concludes positively:

> Zwar, werther Hermanns, hat die bestäubte Schlacht
> Uns oft gekrönet! hat sich des Jünglings Blick
> Entflammt! hat laut sein Herz geschlagen,
> Brennend nach kühnerer That gedurstet!
>
> Deß Zeug' ist Höchsted, dort, wo die dunkle Schlacht
> Noch donnert, wo mit edlen Britanniern,

---

[8] The actual word 'Schattenfabel' probably derives from the beginning of Herder's poem 'Mein Schicksal' (1770): 'Meines Lebens verworrene / Schattenfabel! o früh, frühe begann sie schon / dunkel'.

[9] Klopstock, *Sämmtliche Werke*, Leipzig 1823, vol.1, pp.97f.

Gleich würdig ihrer großen Väter,
Deutsche dem Gallier Flucht geboten!

Das Werk des Meisters, welches von hohem Geist
Geflügelt hinschwebt, ist, wie des Helden That,
Unsterblich! wird, gleich ihr, den Lorbeer
Männlich verdienen, und niedersehen!

The equation of 'des Helden Tat' and 'Werk des Meisters' (of deed and language) is common to both poems and Klopstock's verses constitute the background for Bobrowski's sense of faith ('trau ich') and hope. But in the concluding lines of 'An Klopstock' Bobrowski goes his own way and demonstrates the differences between himself and his master. Where in Klopstock's 'Fragen' the 'Werk des Meisters' is 'geflügelt', Bobrowski's 'Wort' is 'ungeflügelt'; for Klopstock it will be 'unsterblich'; for Bobrowski it is written in 'der Vergeßlichen Sprache'. Similarly, Klopstock claims that this work 'hinschwebt', while Bobrowski speaks it instead 'hinab in die Winter'.

Even more all-pervasive as a means of self-definition is the syntax of the poem. Klopstock insisted in his essay 'Von der Darstellung' that '[der Dichter] muß [...] den Zuhörer so oft er kann, hinreißen, und nicht hinleiten'. Bobrowski, on the other hand, wrote of the possible effects of art: 'Und wenn Kunst nicht geeignet ist, Massenbewegungen hervorzurufen, – zu befragen und dringlich zu befragen, dazu sollte sie geeignet sein' (4:448). The halting, ambiguous syntax of the poem attempts just this. It does not 'hinreißen', it 'befragt', and it achieves this using an ironic reversal of one of Klopstock's most characteristic syntactical constructions, the extended 'wenn'-clause. As used by Klopstock in poems such as 'An Fanny' ('Wenn einst ich tot bin') and 'Thuiskon' ('Wenn die Strahlen vor der Dämmrung') this construction creates an intensity of emotion which 'hinreißt'. Making use in this poem of an apparently similar construction, Bobrowski creates the very different effect of a retarding syntactical dislocation, ('wenn ich [...] wie wollt ich [...] wenn mich [...]') and the poem's very structure thereby presents an aspect of his self-definition.

The poem thus offers an exposition of the poetic reality (the aspects Bobrowski has 'in die Sinne gebunden') behind his saying of Klopstock's name. It is a considerable act of poetic justification for naming him, but also for saying the words 'Strom und Wald'. Such simple words are still, despite Höllerer's criticism, appropriate for post-war German poetry, and despite all the differences between his own poetry and Klopstock's poetic flights, Bobrowski is justified in using Klopstock's name, in claiming himself to be in the tradition of Klopstock, in claiming that he wanted 'das Wirkliche' and yet wrote as he did.

The ending of 'Immer zu benennen' implied a defence *ex negativo* in the absence of any unambiguous, absolute divinity. 'An Klopstock' indicates greater confidence in the power of poetry. It justifies the use of the same nature imagery to which Höllerer's students objected by referring to Klopstock's own confidence in the emotive power of language, but also justifies his use of Klopstock's name in his statement to Bender by pointing to common elements between the two of them, *while continuing to emphasise the differences.* It is an irony lost on most commentators on Bobrowski's relation to Klopstock that the one work dedicated to Klopstock is one that emphasises these differences.

If 'An Klopstock' is addressed to a writer whom Bobrowski praised as the originator of a living tradition of German poetry, the later poem 'Wiedererweckung' marks a point in a different and much more strained relationship with a living poet. Paul Celan (1920-1970) was a writer engaged, so Bobrowski believed, in the destruction of language. He probably first confronted Celan's name in the anthology *Ergriffenes Dasein* in April 1954 and appears to have been impressed by him.[10] In Celan and in other poets from the anthology he found, as he wrote to Fritz Schaumann (April 26 1954), 'eine Bestätigung meiner, hier notwendig sinnlos erscheinenden, Vorstellungen von den Möglichkeiten dichterischer Erfassung' (*Marbach* 302), convincing him that he should not have doubt in his works while 'dies und jenes "in der Luft liegt"'. His slightly later poetic response of August 12 1954 was the poem 'Die Spur im Sand' (1:28).[11]

Celan's poetry does not feature again in published correspondence until the correspondence with Jokostra. In late 1958 Bobrowski's interest was roused through his attempt to invite Celan to attend a conference of the Evangelische Akademie Berlin-Weißensee on Russian

---

[10] *Ergriffenes Dasein: Deutsche Lyrik 1900-1950*, ed. H.E.Holthusen and Friedhelm Kemp, Ebenhausen bei München 1953.

[11] Embarrassingly direct was the influence on Bobrowski's 1954 poem 'Heimat', an early version of which (*Marbach* 313) contained the line: 'Dir ward ein Grab in den Lüften'. The corresponding words in Celan's 'Todesfuge' run 'wir schaufeln ein Grab in den Lüften'.

literature (*Marbach* 422-4) and also through a letter by Jokostra implying that Celan, as Bobrowski reported to Fonrobert in a letter of December 19 1958 'an einigem Zeug von mir Geschmack gefunden [hat]' (*Marbach* 424). It was the kind of confirmation that Bobrowski, with his difficulties finding publishers at the time, desperately sought. For a long time he appears to have known few of Celan's works apart from the 1953 *Mohn und Gedächtnis*, and a letter of May 5 1959 indicates a certain distance: '[ich] werd [...] nie ganz den Eindruck los, daß [Celan] alles recht praktikabel sagt, soll heißen: melodisch, mit edlem Parfüm [...] und gängigem Sentiment.' He felt, however, something approaching guilt at this partial rejection: 'Verzeih, wenn das zu bösartig klingt. Ich mein es nicht so', or 'Bitte, steck mir ein Licht auf, ich möcht dem Celan nicht unrecht tun' (May 10 1959). Through 1959 and 1960 he attempted to come to terms with these works, especially with the *Sprachgitter*, which he started to read in early May 1959, and to which the comments given above refer. His letters indicate his frustration, as he initially finds the volume 'belanglos und armselig'. On the other hand he proudly drops Celan's name as one of the 'Zelebritäten der Lyrik' who have acknowledged his existence,[12] and he is overwhelmed by Celan's present to him in November 1959 of his translation of works by Osip Mandelshtam and the greetings that accompanied it, greetings that forced the East German 'Lyrikant' Erich Arendt to recognise Bobrowski himself as a poet.[13] Being accepted by Celan gave Bobrowski a sense of legitimacy for his poetry.[14]

For most of 1959, however, he remained critical of Celan's works.[15] The criticism is located especially in the letters to Jokostra of May 10 1959 and May 21 1959, and one point of comparison is significant.

---

[12] In a letter of March 31 1959 (*Marbach* 14) to his cousin Georg Bobrowski.

[13] See letter to Peter Hamm of November 19 1959 (*Marbach* 28f.).

[14] Thus in Bobrowski's first letter to Celan (November 19 1959) he interprets Celan's greetings and the gesture of friendship as 'eine Stärkung, eine Aufforderung, bei einem Tun zu bleiben, gegen dessen mögliche Auswirkung immer mehr zu sprechen scheint,' and sees Celan's reply of November 24 1959 as 'ein Ausweis, einer, der gilt' (*Marbach* 426). In a letter of August 12 1960 he is explicit: 'legitimieren müßte mich wohl erst einmal die Zustimmung der Betroffenen'. The reference is to Celan and Sachs.

[15] To Jokostra he wrote (October 5 1959):
Noch einmal: Celan ist nichts, bestenfalls eine Parfümfabrik, die jetzt Juchten liefert und früher Veilchen. Aber das sag ich, ohne den Beweis anzutreten. Ich hab nur das gleiche Magenweh bei ihm wie bei Rilke. (*Marbach* 428-30).

While writing the first of these letters, Bobrowski was reading not only Celan's *Sprachgitter* but also *Das schwere Land,* a volume of works by the minor contemporary poet Klaus Demus. After admitting his total inability to understand Celan, he criticises aspects of Demus's volume but also praises him:

> Der Demus [...] schmeckt mir sehr. Besonders sein Pathos. Ein paar Dinge geraten ihm zwar ins Ungefähre, soll heißen: werden undeutlich, aber das liegt wohl daran, daß er ein paar Hölderlin-Vokabeln und ein bißchen Trakl geerbt hat.

In the letter of May 21 1959 he effectively contrasts the two. Of Celan's works he comments:

> dazu fehlt das Entscheidende. Die Gedichte sind undynamisch. Sie fassen sich an wie sehr kostbares altes Papier. Es gibt wohl keine Genialität, die sich steril, wenn Du willst: trocken, asketisch äußerte.

He then immediately turns to Demus, whom he places in a wider context:

> Der Demus ist viel jünger (im Geist), er hat nicht die heiligen Erfahrungen eines alten Volkes, gegen das gestellt wir alle Barbaren sind. Aber es gibt bei ihm Dinge [...], die in ihrer Kraft an die einmalige Gewalt Klopstockscher Strophen gemahnen, bei dem mir immer mehr zum Bewußtsein kommt, daß er das größte Ereignis der deutschen Literatur ist. Wo sonst hat einer mit seinem Gedicht gleich eine ganz neue Sprache geschaffen?

Bobrowski here, as in the interview with Reblitz quoted above, associates Klopstock's poetry with life and dynamism, while here additionally condemning Celan's as precious and lifeless. This echoes the substance of a letter written two months earlier, in which he comforted an evidently despondent Jokostra and quoted and commented on lines from Celan's 'Nächtlich geschürzt':[16] 'Wort – eine Leiche, das stimmt für Dich nicht; wer das sagt und auch nur einen Satz nachfolgen läßt, treibt Reliquienkult' (March 4 1959). This evocative phrase is just one element in a long process of coming to terms with Celan, but it confirms Bobrowski's association of Celan's language with a lack of vitality.[17] It

---

[16] Paul Celan, *Gesammelte Werke*, Frankfurt/M. 1983, vol.1, pp.125f.

[17] The association is, incidentally, shared by Theodor Adorno, who commented:

> [Celans] Lyrik ist durchdrungen von der Scham der Kunst angesichts des wie der Erfahrung so der Sublimierung sich entziehenden Leids. Celans Gedichte wollen

is in the same letter that Bobrowski expresses his own personal faith in
poetry, however reduced: 'ich hab schon ein Vierteljahr nichts mehr
geschrieben [...] aber ich hab ein ungebrochenes Vertrauen zur Wirk-
samkeit des Gedichts – vielleicht nicht des *Gedichts*, sondern des
Verses'.

In August 1960 Bobrowski's interest in Celan was again roused by
news of Celan's poem 'Zürich, zum Storchen' (*Werke*, vol.1, pp.214f.)
dedicated to Nelly Sachs, which Jokostra sent him later that month,
together with an essay he had himself published in *Eckart*.[18] Then in
December 1961 Bobrowski was flattered to find his own poem 'An
Nelly Sachs' (1:119f.) placed beside Celan's in the Suhrkamp volume
dedicated to Nelly Sachs.[19] After this his attention only turned seriously
to Celan again in early 1964 with *Die Niemandsrose* and news of
scandals. To this period belongs the poem 'Wiedererweckung' (1:203f.),
originally dedicated to Celan, but also intended, like 'An Klopstock', as
a form of self-definition through indirect comparison.

Wiedererweckung

Das
Land
leer,
durch ausgebreitete Tücher
heraufgrünt das andre, darunter-
gelegte, das ein Verdacht
war
früher. Es kommt
aus der Pestzeit, weiß
von Knochen, Rippen, Wirbeln,
Speichen, vom Kalk.

Zähl
die Gräser

---

das äußerste Entsetzen durch Verschweigen sagen. [...] Sie ahmen eine Sprache
unterhalb der hilflosen der Menschen, ja aller organischen nach, die des Toten von
Stein und Stern. Beseitigt werden die letzten Rudimente des Organischen. [...] Die
Sprache des Leblosen wird zum letzten Trost über den jeglichen Sinnes ver-
lustigen Tod. (*Ästhetische Theorie*, ed. G.Adorno and R.Tiedemann, Frankfurt/M.
1977, p.477.)

[18] 'Zeit und Unzeit in der Dichtung Paul Celans', *Eckart-Jahrbuch*, 29 (1960), pp.162-
74.

[19] *Nelly Sachs zu Ehren: Gedichte, Prosa, Beiträge*, Frankfurt/M. 1961.

und zähl
Fäden aus Regenwasser,
und Licht, die Blättchen
zähl, und zeichne ein
deine Schritte, Wildspuren,
und Stimmen, beleb
mit Worten
das Blut in den Bäumen und
den Lungen, den Rost
schlag von Wänden
und Stufen,
an deinen Händen
bleibt er, dort mag er sich
nähren
mit deinen Nägeln.

Es ist nicht die Zeit, ihn zu fragen.
Es ist die Zeit für das Wasser
an Halmen, für die erneute
Fügung der Blätter, und Augen
öffne das Laub.[20]

Although written in the shadow of the reading of Celan's *Die Niemandsrose*, 'Wiedererweckung' has little direct reference to this volume. The 'Pestzeit' echoes the *envoi* of Celan's 'Eine Gauner- und Ganovenweise' (*Werke*, vol.1, p.229f.) and the link between cold and resurrection distantly echoes 'Das Eis wird auferstehen' from 'Eis. Eden' (*Werke*, vol.1, p.224). The first few lines also distantly echo a phrase from 'Eis. Eden': 'Es ist ein Land Verloren'. The 'Gras', 'grün' and 'Spuren' recur in 'Engführung' (*Werke*, vol.1, pp.195-204), a poem for which Bobrowski certainly showed some respect. The repeated 'Zähl' reminds, of course, of a similar repetition in 'Zähle die Mandeln' (*Werke*, vol.1, p.78). Instead 'Wiedererweckung' appears to draw on the poems of *Von Schwelle zu Schwelle* that had earlier roused Bobrowski's irritation: 'Kalk ist und Kreide. / Und Kiesel. / Schnee. Und mehr noch des Weißen' ('Flügelnacht', *Werke*, vol.1, p.128) anticipates the white of the central line, while 'Es ist die Zeit' repeats almost exactly the line

---

[20] The poem has been analysed exhaustively by Reichert (pp.21-58) with specific reference to Bobrowski's understanding of nature and history, as well as with reference to Jews, Celan himself and the works of Hamann. He too sees it as a combination of criticism and appeal.

'Es ist Zeit' from 'Corona' (*Werke*, vol.1, p.37).[21]

'Wiedererweckung' presents a vision of a spring re-awakening, in which nature and mankind but above all language participate. The process of re-awakening leads to an interchange of characteristics on a number of levels, as the language of the poem itself creates its own links: the ambiguity of the 'weiß', which could imply either knowledge or the paleness of infection; the sharing of 'Blut' by trees and lungs; and fingernails, like iron nails, eaten by rust. At the end of the poem the new foliage opens its eyes. The poem itself progresses on the page from the empty white of the first three lines to the comparatively long lines in the last stanza.

As in 'An Klopstock', the form of the poem underlines the content. Here an initial undynamic scene of complete stasis undergoes a progressive dynamisation, and the poem moves, with a number of echoes of Celan's stylistic idiosyncrasies accompanying the verbal echoes, to a human involvement through the life-giving power of words ('beleb / *mit Worten*'). With such an awakening the poet is not simply an observer ('Zähl') but also a participant who registers his own marks in the landscape: 'zeichne ein [...]'. Finally the whole of nature begins to awaken and the poet turns at the end from addressing the 'du', that is himself or his fellow word-smith, to a direct address to nature itself which he has through his work helped revivify.

In its expression of optimistic hope of a new beginning, to which language itself contributes dynamically, 'Wiedererweckung' stands diametrically opposed to the key idea Bobrowski drew from Celan of 'Ein Wort [...] eine Leiche'. It presents instead images of nature undergoing a natural regeneration through time, the 'Pestzeit', to emerge tainted but also possibly enriched by what it has experienced. The poet's task is to leave his mark ('Schritte'), to register what he sees and hears ('Wildspuren, / und Stimmen'), but also to contribute to this regeneration through his own words. The unstated but implied argument is that Celan has been failing to do this.

As well as these few direct links to Celan's poetry, 'Wiedererweckung' contains a striking echo of the speech Celan delivered when he accepted the Bremen Literaturpreis on January 26 1958. Speaking here inevitably about language, Celan comments on what is left after its

---

[21] Behind this lie, of course, Rilke's 'Herbsttag' ('Herr, es ist Zeit') and beyond that the Biblical phrase from Psalm 102: 14 and Ecclesiastes 3: 1: 'Ein jegliches hat seine Zeit'.

distortions in recent history:

> Sie, die Sprache, blieb unverloren, ja, trotz allem. Aber sie mußte nun hin-
> durchgehen durch ihre eigenen Antwortlosigkeiten, hindurchgehen durch
> furchtbares Verstummen, hindurchgehen durch die tausend Finsternisse tod-
> bringender Rede. [...] [Sie] ging hindurch und durfte wieder zutage treten,
> 'angereichert' von all dem. (*Werke*, vol.3, pp.185f.)

In 'Wiedererweckung' the reference to this other 'Land' that resur-
faces and (is) 'weiß von der Pestzeit' activates the latent imagery of
Celan's ironic 'durfte wieder zutage treten, "angereichert" von all dem'.
Bobrowski's punning 'weiß' takes this up. Where, however, Celan's
'Wort' remains, in his *poem*, 'eine Leiche', Bobrowski appears to see it
green, in the colour of spring, and his poem, addressed to Celan,
involves a direct appeal for a confidence in the power of language that
he evidently felt Celan lacked. Bobrowski confronts here his own image
of Celan and rejects its implications, presenting in this poem a poetic
landscape and a language that are in process of rebirth. The German
language may know of death, as Celan implies in his speech, but this
does not in itself make of it a 'Leiche'.

Reference back to 'An Klopstock' makes the direction of 'Wiedererweckung' clear: Bobrowski uses the eighteenth-century poet's devices
and implies some poetic empathy, but is determined to control the
emotional outpourings in the name of moderation. He uses Celan's
devices and imagery with considerably more distance and then subverts
them completely, appealing to a latent vitality which, he thought, Celan
could never have. Like 'An Klopstock', 'Wiedererweckung' involves a
distancing from a fellow poet. Here, however, this distancing is more
extreme: Bobrowski accepted Klopstock as his 'Zuchtmeister', despite
the differences, but Celan's ideas on the German language (or what
Bobrowski *thought* were his ideas) were anathema to him. Together
with Celan's concentration on poetic techniques that made writing, as
Bobrowski wrote to Jokostra on May 21 1959, 'die Konstruktion von
Spezialgeräten oder -formen für Hochspezialisierte' (*Marbach* 428) this
sense of their essential lifelessness contributed to Bobrowski's sense of
frustration and guilt.

This is not the last reference to Celan's 'Nächtlich geschürzt' in
Wetterzeichen, and a few weeks later Bobrowski wrote 'Mit Liedern
Sapphos' (1:206), another declaration of faith in language, commencing
arguably with a statement of self-distancing from Celan. The poem
starts with a reference to Sappho and a partial quotation from one of her

surviving poetic fragments. It concludes with reference to an anecdote according to which Solon, who lived at about the same time as Sappho (600BC), longed to learn a song of Sappho and then die.[22]

> Aufgeschürzt die haarige
> Lippe, von der Insel
> schrie wie der Maulesel schreit
> die magere Kleine:
>
> > einen peplos,
> > safranfarbenen, kränze,
> > phrygische, purpur
>
> Solon
> vor dem Haus,
> wo die Luft umhergeht:
> Singt es noch einmal, sagt er,
>
> daß ich erlerne das
> Inselgeschrei, die Rufe
> über der Erde dicht,
> die im verbrannten Kraut,
>
> es erlerne, daß ich
> sterb darüber, Worte
> hab und Worte, das Sausen,
> den Luftzug hinter dem Haupt und,
> Worte, über der Brust.

The choice of Sappho to illustrate a poem on the power of words is not surprising. In July 1956 Bobrowski had written one poem 'Sappho' (2:292) which evoked her works with the imagery of lasting beauty as 'goldne Nägel' and as promising some respite: 'Gönnst dem Länder-fremden an deines Verses / Stufe eine Zeit, ein Verweilen'. The reference is more personal than it might appear: Bobrowski was himself a 'Länderfremder' near Lake Ilmen when he turned to Sapphic metres for his own poetry.

The contrast between Celan's 'Nächtlich geschürzt' and the imagery

---

[22] The poem has been well analysed by Ernst Günther Schmidt in 'Die Sappho-Gedichte Johannes Bobrowskis' in *Das Altertum* 18 (1972), pp.49-61. He points to Bobrowski's possession of an edition of Sappho's poetry (*Sappho, griechisch und deutsch*, ed. Max Treu, Munich 1963), which itself contains both the original for Bobrowski's Sapphic fragment and the details of the anecdote with Solon.

of the first few lines is evident. 'Nächtlich geschürzt', i.e. 'closed', (the reference in Celan is to flowers at night) is opened at the beginning of Bobrowski's poem to lips which are 'Aufgeschürzt', the first essential for communication. In addition, Celan's 'Inselhin' (the section of the volume *Von Schwelle zu Schwelle* introduced by 'Nächtlich geschürzt') is reversed: 'von der Insel / schrie'. Beyond these verbal echoes 'Mit Liedern Sapphos' emphasises not separation, as in 'Nächtlich geschürzt' ('Sie stehen getrennt in der Welt, / ein jeglicher bei seiner Nacht') but openness for communication, for words despite the distance between Solon in Athens and Sappho on Lesbos. It is not the words that are dead ('Leiche') at the end of this poem but, if anything, the recipient Solon, who is over-burdened by the sensuality of language: '[daß ich] es erlerne, daß ich / sterb darüber, Worte / hab und Worte'.

Bobrowski uses here an apocryphal comment of praise for Sappho by Solon, as well as a quotation from Sappho's verse that has survived the centuries. Their collective coincidental survival appears to demonstrate the possible physical continuation of the poetic word, in the same way that the words of Solon emphasise their potential influence. The contrast here with Celan's hesitancy is striking and deliberate. For all his personal respect for Celan, Bobrowski implies a distance to his poetic tenets which ensured that, unlike Hamann and Klopstock, Celan's direct influence on his poetry was strictly limited. If the first two accompanied Bobrowski, as they did, throughout his mature life, then Celan, despite his contemporaneity, remained a relatively peripheral figure.

5

BEYOND SARMATIA: *WETTERZEICHEN*

Introduction

The volume *Wetterzeichen* was published in East Germany in 1966 (Union Verlag) and in West Germany in 1967 (Verlag Klaus Wagenbach) after Bobrowski's unexpected death in September 1965. With the exception of 'Zu Christoph Meckels Graphiken' (1:215) and 'Das Wort Mensch' (1:217), added by the posthumous editor, Bobrowski had himself selected the poems for inclusion, but had not arranged them into the sort of cycle that characterised the previous two volumes. Most of the poems were written after the final division of Berlin with the building of the Berlin Wall. This was an event disturbing enough for someone like Bobrowski whose office was situated directly on the border, but it brought with it restrictions on movement and communication that severely disrupted his affectionate contact with friends in West Berlin and beyond. The collection reflects this traumatic experience and alludes to the building of the Wall itself and the restrictions it brought about.

Despite his continued poetical 'kidnapping' in this volume, Bobrowski saw these poems as representing a distinct post-Sarmatian phase. He occasionally referred in letters to his innovations and plans: 'Ich hab, denk ich, Neues angefangen mit den letzten Gedichten' (May 20 1963 to Michael Hamburger, quoted in *Marbach* 343), or (to Manfred Peter Hein, October 22 1964): 'Mir scheint, alles bisherige waren Vorstufen, das Eigentliche, was ich zu sagen habe, kommt erst noch' (1:lxxviii). Despite this emphasis on a new beginning, however, a number of works continue to refer to aspects of the wider Sarmatian theme, including 'Der lettische Herbst' (1:156), 'Die Ebene bei Shmany' (1:164), 'Das Dorf Tolmingkehmen' (1:165), 'Die Wolgastädte' (1:169), 'Auszug der Götter' (1:176), and 'Namen für den Verfolgten' (1:191), which incorporates Old Prussian vocabulary. Other late poems which were not included in *Wetterzeichen*, such as 'Der Opferstein' (2:347, August 21 1962) and 'Die Sokaiter Fähre' (2:351, December 23 1964) also continue the Sarmatian cycle in subject-matter and vocabulary. The elegiac 'Ach', however, which played such a significant role in earlier poems, no longer occurs, and fewer poems appear concerned with acceptance of the loss of the past in the stream of transience. Instead, a number of poems indicate completely new developments. *Wetterzeichen* also contains some weaker short poems such as 'Vorsorge' (1:209) and 'Entfremdung' (1:214) which do little other than flesh out an individual image. The use of abstractions in these titles is symptomatic, and 'Vorsorge' significantly starts: 'Anfälle von Trunksucht. / Sie kommen / wie das Schweigen / kommt' (1:209).

This last volume muddies the conveniently clear image of Bobrowski as the 'Sarmatian' poet.[1] More than in the earlier works he draws on imagery from his immediate contemporary experiences, either in direct reference (in titles) to areas of his new homeland of the German Democratic Republic, 'Krypta/Dom zu Brandenburg' (1:197) and 'Märkisches Museum' (1:195), or to new and younger acquaintances: G. B. Fuchs, in 'Anthropomorphe Landschaft' (1:187) and Christoph Meckel in 'Zu Christoph Meckels Graphiken' (1:215), or to areas outside his new 'home' that he had recently visited: 'Alter Hof in Häme' (1:208), 'Humlegård' (1:212). Other poems continue the line of 'Hölderlin in Tübingen' but with East German geographical reference: 'Jakub Bart in *Ralbitz*' (1:182) and 'Barlach in *Güstrow*' (1:188), while in 'Die Ostseestädte' (1:173) the title introduces not, as might have been expected, a Sarmatian perspective on the towns against a background of 'Ebenen' and 'Ströme', but a very different landscape. To this poem I will return.

The surface subject-matter of many of these poems thus draws ever closer to the immediate present. In yet other poems apparently 'Sarmatian' images are used with direct reference to contemporary events, with one of the earliest poems of the volume, 'Mitternachtsdorf' (1:155) particularly striking for its highly esoteric denunciation of the building of the Berlin Wall a few days before. The poem 'Stadt' (1:198) appears to involve direct criticism both of events that were taking place on the Berlin border almost below Bobrowski's office window, and also of the lies with which they were justified. The development towards direct confrontation with the problems that faced him in the present in East Berlin is clear.

The poems to or about individuals continue the development ob-

---

[1] This is a view that is still surprisingly common. See Walter Hindebrandt, 'Leiden und Widerhall: Die Sarmatische Herausforderung Johannes Bobrowskis und Herta Müllers' in *deutsche studien* 119, 30 (Sept 1993) 195-207: 'Fest steht, daß es Bobrowski bis zu seinem Tode nicht gelang, sich vom sarmatischen Thema freizuschwimmen' (p.205).

served in *Sarmatische Zeit* and *Schattenland Ströme*. *Wetterzeichen*
contains poems dedicated to literary figures of the past as far back as
Solon and Sappho (1:206), as I indicate in the previous chapter, but also
poems dedicated to the lives and works of much more contemporary
figures, such as Calder, Jawlensky and Bobrowski's friend Meckel.
Other poems may be read as attempts at a dialogue with living writers,
with 'Wiedererweckung', as also suggested in the previous chapter,
marking an attempt at a dialogue with Paul Celan, and 'Antwort'
(1:185) 'answering' Walter Groß's poem 'Aus den Wäldern' (*Chronik*
77). Bobrowski's Christian beliefs continue to inform his poetry, but in
Wetterzeichen may be seen references to epiphanies beyond the theme
of exile and home-coming characteristic of the late works in *Schattenland Ströme*.

Accompanying these changes of emphasis in subject-matter are
changes in style, with the development of an occasional lighter tone, as
the elegiac 'ach' is superseded by the occasional use of the word
'heiter'. The 'Anthropomorphe Landschaft' is even whimsical in its first
three stanzas, with their reference to 'Eine promovierte / Herbstzeit-
lose', and in 'Haus' (1:201f.) this less solemn tone allows deliberately
trite rhymes: 'Da fährt das Licht übers Dach / und will den Amseln
nach'. Other poems display a similar lightness of touch, and
'Märkisches Museum' (1:195) contains the lines 'Sand / geht auf
Händen, es dreht sich / die heitere Luft', as though the whole of creation
is taking part in an aerial acrobatic display.[2] Such changes represent
movements away from the Sarmatian bedrock and towards an encounter
with more directly contemporary developments, building on ideas or
images anticipated in the earlier volumes, rather than creating completely new forms.

The most thorough-going new development is the shift from the
concern with his past, his 'Thema', to a new concern for the present and
the dimension of hope that he discovers about him. One indication of
this change of direction is to be found in the imagery of night, snow, ice
and winter that informed the scenery of the earlier poems: in
Sarmatische Zeit and *Schattenland Ströme* was to be found hardly a
single poem that ended in an intimation of something beyond winter.
More typical, as we have seen, were poems ending in visions of the

---

[2] A similar image is to be found in 'Zu Christoph Meckels Graphiken': 'Ging auf
Händen oder / stand auf der Richtstatt'.

approach of winter or night. In *Wetterzeichen* this is not inevitably the case, and a number of poems indicate the possibility of a time when the snows may be retreating. In 'Uferweg' (1:166) Bobrowski refers in a complex, distanced image to the 'Fluchtweg des Schnees', and more clearly in 'Wiedererweckung', as we have seen, he implies the possibility of a time beyond that of winter and perpetual snow. Such images convey a sense of greater hope for the present.

Towards the Present: Towns

One aspect of this development may be seen in a series of poems whose titles refer to towns. Named Eastern European towns had constituted essential markers on Bobrowski's earlier Sarmatian map, with Vilnius, Novgorod, Kaunas and 'Nordrussische Stadt (Pustoschka 1941)' featuring in individual poems, while throughout one finds references to 'die kleinen / Städte im Wind' mentioned in 'Unter dem Nachtrand'. *Wetterzeichen* too includes a Novgorod poem, 'Nowgorod (Ankunft der Heiligen)' (1:158f.) but significantly this poem lacks the earlier emphasis on the German destruction of the town. It presents instead legends concerning the miraculous arrival of local icons and the need to remember and respect them.[3] The development away from Sarmatia is evident in three related poems: 'Die Wolgastädte' (1:169, June 2 1962), 'Ostseestädte' (1:173, September 4 1962) and 'Stadt' (1:198, November 13 1963). 'Wolgastädte', especially bearing in mind the Volga Germans, continues the theme of the 'lange Geschichte aus Unglück und Verschuldung'; 'Ostseestädte' uses the present tense almost throughout and appears to lack any historical dimension, while 'Stadt' must be seen in the context of the immediate present, with the 'Polonäse / der Lampen kahlhäuptig' as a striking image of the lighting along the Berlin Wall and the 'Todesstreifen', the 'Wunde' through Berlin.

> Die Wolgastädte
>
> Der Mauerstrich.
> Türme. Die Stufe des Ufers. Einst,
> die hölzerne Brücke zerriß. Über die Weite fuhren
> Tatarenfeuer. Mit strähnigem Bart
> Nacht, ein Wandermönch, kam
> redend. Die Morgen

---

[3] See G. Wolf, *Beschreibung eines Zimmers* pp.84ff.

schossen herauf, die Zisternen
standen im Blut.

Geh umher auf dem Stein.
Hier im gläsernen Mittag
über die Augen hob
Minin die Hand. Dann Geschrei
stob herauf, den Wassern entgegen, Stjenkas
Ankunft – Es gehn auf dem Ufer
bis an die Hüften im Unterholz
Sibiriaken, ihre
Wälder ziehn ihnen nach.

Dort
einen Menschenmund
hörte ich rufen:
Komm in dein Haus
durch die vermauerte Tür,
die Fenster schlag auf
gegen das Lichtmeer.

The first two stanzas combine in a single compound image a multi-plicity of strands of the history of this area, focusing on what is typical of these towns, but also using precise historical detail. The 'Holzbrücke' that 'zerriß' suggests the destruction of the pontoon bridges once typical of the upper reaches (e.g. in Tver); the 'Mauerstrich' and 'Türme' could well be Kazan, which as described in the 1889 *Meyers Konversations-Lexikon* has a fortification with 'eine mit fünf Türmen geschmückte Mauer' (article 'Kasan'), or Bolgary, a ruined town also once possessing walls and towers.[4] The 'Tatarenfeuer' evoke the mass destruction of the area in the wake of early Tatar invasions, when Nizhniy Novgorod and Kazan were repeatedly attacked and burned. Minin and Stenka are popular Russian folk-heroes: Minin (Kuz'ma Minin) was a Russian merchant from Nizhniy Novgorod who in 1612 helped free Moscow from Polish control; Stenka (i.e. Stepan Razin) was a popuiar Cossack leader who laid waste to towns on the Volga in the late 1660s. Before his death (he was executed in 1671) he had attacked the Volga towns of Simbirsk and Saratov. The apparently obscure image of 'Sibiriaken' walking along in the undergrowth followed by their 'Wälder' may well

---

[4] Haufe (5:175) suggests Nizhniy Novgorod.

refer to the trade in wood carried on to the present day along the Volga.[5]

Although the figures mentioned are relatively minor historical figures, the events associated with them are of crucial historical importance: the lifting of the Tatar yoke (1479-1481), the arrival of the first Romanov Tsar (1613), which was to lead to the Europeanisation of Russia, and the final destruction of Cossack power in 1671, and there is a reminder even of the earlier Christianisation of Russia in the reference to the 'Wandermönch'. The poem thus mentions or implies or evokes the existence of many of the tribes and races whose influence on this area has been felt: Greeks, Russians, Poles, Tatars, Cossacks, Siberians, and views them against all the violent history of the area.

It opens with images of walled defences and violence: 'zerriss', 'schossen', 'Blut'. Yet despite this, the first two stanzas present an objective, distanced work, with, in this panoramic view, no sense of personal involvement.[6] Instead Bobrowski addresses only an unnamed 'Du', although this persona's dramatic placing on a viewpoint 'auf dem Stein' suggests the inhospitable nature of the landscape. After this visionary summary of violent history and exploitation of nature, in the last stanza the poetic persona remembers a call he heard here. The words used ('Menschenmund [...] rufen') recall those of Daniel (Daniel 8: 16) after his vision: 'ich hörte eine Menschenstimme rufen', and with this echo the message communicated gains in weight and implies a complete break with what had gone before. The imagery itself in part repeats that of the first stanza ('Mauerstrich' – 'vermauert') which it retracts. Central to this call is the suggested need for a new openness, with the poetic 'ich' commanded to enter his own barricaded property and throw it open to the 'sea of light'. In this admittedly unclear image, the poem appears to imply an ideal of interpersonal openness after a period of non-communication. In this it continues the Sarmatian concern with remembering the many-facetted 'Schuld' of the past, while proposing a new openness as a means to overcome it. Despite lacking an evident German historical dimension in the first two stanzas, implicit in the last stanza is a reminder of German presence in this area,

---

[5] 'Uferweg' (1:166), written six weeks before, refers to walking along the river-bank 'das Holz vom Ufer zu stoßen'.

[6] In fact, Bobrowski had spent time near the Volga at least twice: in 1943 (see 'Aufenthalt') he had been somewhere near its source, while, more significantly, in 1949 he had spent several months near Nizhniy Novgorod on an 'antifa' course.

Bobrowski's theme of 'die Deutschen und der europäische Osten'.

Such a need for openness does not, of course refer simply to historical events involving Germans and Russians. It also includes relations between the Germans themselves, and the concluding plea for a greater openness contributes to the great theme, which runs through this last volume, of the need to oppose 'Vermauerung', whether it be internal or external, as something that contains the danger of ossification.

In its Sarmatian imagery, 'Die Wolgastädte' still echoes the earlier volumes, but is noticeably more distant: the material is drawn not from experience but from extensive reading of its history and geography. By contrast, the poem 'Die Ostseestädte' (September 4 1962) moves far from this wide Sarmatian world towards places nearer home, and the important historical dimension of 'Die Wolgastädte' plays a less significant role.

> Das Licht ohne Aufgang und Niedergang.
> Das Wasser, das sich am Tod der Falter belebt.
> Regen ist Regen.
> Der Wind, der unter der Wolke
> in Hadern daherkommt,
> hat den Sand der Flüsse gestrählt, eine Düne
> geführt über die See.
>
> Licht
> kommt zurück
> über das Wasser. Regen
> findet den Weg
> den Vögeln nach. Bunte Tafeln
> sind aufgeschlagen
> in den zerbröckelnden hohen
> Gemäuern landauf, landab.
> Dort steht zu lesen:
> Es wuchs das Gras.

The poem opens with the evocation of a dreary, rainy day, with diffused light but no visible movement of the sun, which is concealed behind clouds. The end-stopped 'Regen ist Regen' confirms the petrification of the scene, and the only sign of life is produced paradoxically by drowning moths. What movement finally occurs, brought about by the wind, is either pettily truculent ('Hader' – a word with strong Biblical connotations) or senseless, as the wind 'combs' the river-sand or leads a dune across the sea.

In the second stanza these images of inactivity or senselessness or destruction are revoked. The light of the sun ('das Licht') is replaced by a more general light ('Licht'), and with it movement. As light returns, the rain is freed from its immobility and 'findet den Weg / den Vögeln nach'. The birds act as counterpart to the dying moths of the first stanza and present a new element of life, anticipating through their movement a concluding set of images of openness and freedom and (as in 'Wieder-erweckung') of new life.

At the end of the poem Bobrowski constructs a contrast between the 'bunte Tafeln' and the 'zerbröckelnde hohe Gemäuer' that stand 'land-auf, landab', with the walls' crumbling apparently related to the opening of these 'Tafeln'. Together, this movement, the bright colours and the crumbling walls constitute an unambiguous sign of hope with immediate personal relevance, especially when seen against the background of Bobrowski's own recent poetic success in publication, with its ensuing visit (July 17 1962) to Vienna and with the prospect of a visit to Berlin-Wannsee in October as guest of the Gruppe 47. Both cases involved visits beyond the confines of the GDR, beyond the 'hohen Gemäuern landauf, landab', and with this prospect even the period of dreary rain is seen as beneficial, by causing the grass to grow.[7] The image clearly suggests a breakthrough after the stagnation of 'Regen ist Regen'.

'Die Ostseestädte' does not function as a sign pointing to historical events, as in 'Die alte Heerstraße' or in 'Die Wolgastädte'. Instead it marks the almost arbitrary setting for an example of hope overcoming despair. The poem itself functions as the 'Tafel' it concludes with, looking to the present and future, rather than the past.

The last of these three poems, written over a year later in November 1963, indicates an even more direct turn to contemporary events.

Stadt

Sie sehn, die dein Blut
forderten, sie sehen:
die Wunde eitert nicht aus.
Um die scharfen Ränder
legen sich Nebel. Es geht

---

[7] The Biblical dimension of 'Tafeln' is strengthened as the poem echoes the lines from 2 Samuel 23: 1-3, where the effects of God's favour to David are described: 'Und ist wie das Licht des Morgens, wenn die Sonne aufgeht am Morgen ohne Wolken, da vom Glanz nach dem Regen das Gras auf der Erde wächst'.

an die Polonäse
der Lampen kahlhäuptig. Auch kommt
auf der Schnee.

Hier
springen die Steine, gemalte
Wände, die Treppe
bricht, um die Taubenkadaver
– ihre Standarten –
stellen sich die Rattenheere auf.

Hier wird,
sagt man,
grünen ein Baum
und den Himmel halten,
sagt man,
auf Zweigen und Blättern.

Compared to the relatively optimistic situation in which 'Die Ostseestädte' were written, 'Stadt' was composed towards the end of a year of
considerable personal bitterness for Bobrowski. It was the year that had
seen the break with Peter Huchel,[8] the difficulties put in the way of his
attending the 1963 Gruppe 47 meeting in Saulgau, above all his
problems with the East German CDU, which led to new depths of disillusionment. The town of the title is identifiable as a Berlin characterised by the rows of floodlights along the border, the wound, and by the
disintegration that has left standing 'gemalte Wände' (which separate)
but has destroyed 'die Treppe' (which might link). Within such a landscape it is not surprising to see not 'bunte Tafeln' but the anticipated
advent of winter. Signs of life are reduced to 'Rattenheere' bearing the
cadavers of doves as their standards, while the plural 'Heere' embraces
both armies lined up across Berlin.

The last stanza repeats but alters imagery from the earlier 'Die Tomsker Straße' (1:135), where stood the lines:

[...] ein Land wie der Himmel,
einen Sommer, aufschäumt' er
von Blumen, die riesigen Bäume
trugen den Himmel.

---

[8] Bobrowski himself recognised that his behaviour towards Peter Huchel had been
reprehensible. See *Bobrowski/Huchel Briefwechsel*, pp.26-31.

The similarity is evident, but the differences predominate: in 'Die Tomsker Straße' the image is introduced by an identified individual, 'Jelisaweta', whom the poetic voice treats with respect; in 'Stadt' it is introduced by an anonymous 'man'. The image of the 'Himmel' being carried aloft is, in the earlier poem, a reference to a past state, while in 'Stadt' it is something promised for the future, together with the new promise of the 'Grünen eines Baumes'.[9]

These are, however, false promises from false prophets. The repetition of the words 'sagt man' can only make the words more questionable, as does the description of the trees. It may indeed be conceivable that the 'riesige Bäume' of 'Die Tomsker Straße' hold the sky/heaven, but this is hardly the case for the 'Zweige und Blätter' of 'Stadt'. Instead the second meaning of 'Blätter' suggests itself, i.e. sheets of paper, with the implication that this is a heaven based on paper theories. This poem thus concludes with direct reference to the present and a condemnation of the organised dishonesty of those whose promises were so vain.[10]

Although not concerned directly with towns, the last poem of *Wetterzeichen*, 'Das Wort Mensch' (1:217), focuses on a clearly important town where natural elements have been carefully (i.e. unnaturally) introduced:

Die Stadt
alt und neu,
schön belebt, mit Bäumen
auch
und Fahrzeugen, hier

hör ich das Wort, die Vokabel
hör ich hier häufig, ich kann
aufzählen von wem, ich kann
anfangen damit.[11]

---

[9] The image has Biblical origins, in the Old Testament, where God makes Aaron's rod 'grünen' (Numbers 17: 16ff.), then it becomes an image of a promise made by God to Israel (Isaiah 27: 6), and then more generally to the righteous (Psalm 92: 13).

[10] Different approaches to this poem have been taken by Stefan Reichert in *Das verschneite Wort* (pp.59-65) and Bernd Leistner, *Johannes Bobrowski: Studien und Interpretationen*, p.212. Leistner relates it directly to the 'seinerzeit von Bobrowski unmittelbar beobachteten [...] Peter-Fechter Vorfall von 1962'. Peter Fechter was an East German shot by border guards at the Berlin Wall and left to die (August 17, 1962).

[11] In an earlier version of the poem Bobrowski had enumerated these: 'von Soziologen, /

The last stanza of the poem is apodictic:

> Wo Liebe nicht ist,
> Sprich das Wort nicht aus.

The last lines combine elements of two Biblical passages: the famous 1 Corinthians 13: 1: 'Wenn ich mit Menschen- und mit Engelzungen redete und hätte der Liebe nicht, so wäre ich ein tönend Erz oder eine klingende Schelle'[12] and Exodus 20: 7, the commandment: 'Du sollst den Namen des Herrn, deines Gottes nicht unnütz führen'. This particular verse was quoted by Bobrowski in his lecture on 'Lyrik der DDR' (4:423-42). In an atheistic East Germany for which, in theory, 'der Mensch' is the ultimate authority, Bobrowski's imprecation involves a clear warning against its over-use.[13]

Towards the Present: 'Mitternachtsdorf'

In these four poems where the word 'Stadt' plays a significant role may be seen a development away from Sarmatia towards expression of more immediate experiences. In the last two poems Bobrowski also turns away from the vocabulary of Sarmatia, while in 'Stadt' he uses it only with an ironic echo of the imagery of 'Die Tomsker Straße'. In 'Mitternachtsdorf' (1:155), a much earlier poem from *Wetterzeichen*, Bobrowski applies Sarmatian imagery directly in order to comment critically on contemporary events. 'Stadt' had concentrated on the destructiveness of the wall and on the dishonesty of those who protected themselves behind it with promises of a better future. 'Mitternachtsdorf' expresses the shock Bobrowski experienced in August 1961. It was written less than a week after the unexpected building of the Berlin Wall and represents an early reaction to this considerable personal disaster.

The period immediately before August 13 1961 had been one of considerable poetic productivity and success. The Sarmatian project had been completed, and Bobrowski was establishing his reputation in the

---

Bühnenleuten, Turnlehrern / Zeitungsleuten Zahnärzten' (5:217).

[12] See the analysis of the earlier Novgorod poems above.

[13] See the similar warning in Günter Kunert's poem 'Was ist denn in dir' (*Verkündigung des Wetters*, 1966) where he describes the word as 'verachtet, veraltet, verlogen' (but still 'abwaschbar'). Bernd Leistner sees 'Das Wort Mensch' as a lyrical retraction of the poem 'Stadt' (see above). In view of the criticism it implies, this is unlikely to have been the case.

West and developing personal contacts with Western writers. The division posed a serious threat to these contacts and visits, and since he worked at the offices of the Union Verlag in Charlottenstraße, close to the centre of Berlin, he experienced daily, both in his personal and in his professional life, the consequences of its construction. Later, as reflected in 'Stadt', he was also to experience at first hand the brutality associated with it.

Immediately after August 13 Bobrowski's poetic output dropped significantly, with less than half a dozen poems known to have been completed in the rest of the year, and even as late as January 30 1962 he commented to Max Hölzer on this lack of productivity and on his sense of isolation: 'Seit Monaten nichts geschrieben, in einer Dürre lebend [...] – getrennt von den Freunden, auch den hiesigen'. 'Mitternachtsdorf' (written August 19 1961) responds to the all too concrete beginning of this 'Dürre' and contains very specific criticism of the circumstances that brought it about.

Mitternachtsdorf

Im verwinkelten Himmel
mit schwerem Fuß
tappt durch den Schatten Saturn
und pfeift seinen Monden.

Aus dem zerbrochnen Dach
wär es zu sehen, aber
das Haus ganz voll von Schlaf
wie von Wäldern
rührt sich im Schlaf,
auf seinem Atem mit offenen
Flügeln schlafen die Vögel.

Laß uns schlafen einer
des andern Schlaf und hören
nicht die Sterne und alle
Stimmen im Finstren, das Blut
nur wie es fällt und zurücksinkt
mit rotgeränderten, schwärzlichen
Blättern unter das Herz.

Morgen magst du verstreun
Asche über den Himmel,
vor die näherkommenden
Schritte Saturns.

A first reading of this poem finds no relation to the turbulence of the

previous week and would appear to confirm the cliché of Bobrowski as
the backward-looking Sarmatian. It is symmetrically constructed, with
stanzas 1 and 4 dominated by the approach of Saturn, while stanzas 2
and 3 present the 'Mitternachtsdorf' of the title. The poem as a whole is
dominated by sleep – of nature in stanza 2 and of the lovers in stanza 3.
Nothing takes cognisance of this advent, and the lovers in particular turn
to each other ('schlafen einer / des andern Schlaf') and to themselves
('das Blut').[14] Ominously, both stanzas are themselves framed by
references to decay, with the damaged roof reflected in the images of
autumnal decay used to describe the lovers' blood. While there may be a
circular movement to the lovers' sleep, the movement of the flow of
blood is downwards, and at the end of the poem the 'du' is left alone
with its mourning ('Asche verstreun'). Saturn itself poses a threat that
becomes more direct and personal in the progression from a non-
directional 'tappt' (first line) to the 'näherkommend' of the end. 'Mitternachtsdorf' appears to be a love poem in which the lovers, in the
timeless 'Sarmatian' world of the midnight village, postpone the need to
face this figure by turning to one another in intimacy and love.

The figure of Saturn here is central. Traditionally he has had three
aspects. The 'days of Saturn', the Roman Saturnalia, were a period of
celebration, rejoicing and orgiastic activity, and Saturn was linked with
the advent of the Golden Age. He had also, however, more negative
associations with the Greek god Chronos who consumed his own
children. The third association, of greater apparent relevance to Bobrowski, was that famously celebrated in Holst's *Planets*: the 'Bringer of
Old Age'. The issue of ageing concerned Bobrowski and he had written
to Hölzer on April 25 1961, a few months before writing this poem, of
'die Entdeckung, daß die sogenannte Lebenshöhe überschritten ist [...]
eine Entdeckung von der Heftigkeit eines Schocks' (*Chronik* 59). Such
associations would indeed explain the generally autumnal atmosphere of
the poem.[15]

---

[14] The image of 'schlafen einer / des andern Schlaf' is taken from Bobrowski's at that
time unpublished poem 'Zeit der Erwartung' (2:247).

[15] This image of Saturn as the Bringer of Old Age is present in Günter Grass's 'Saturn'
(*Gleisdreieck*, 1960), a poem with which Bobrowski may well have been familiar. Grass
too had linked Saturn and ashes, ending:

als ich meiner Zigarette
die Asche abklopfte.

There is, however, another interpretation of Saturn's significance, of which Bobrowski, with his interest in the German Baroque, must have been aware.[16] This is the image of Saturn presented in the 'Planetenkinderbilder' of the late Middle Ages and the Baroque. Günther Weydt has pointed out with reference to the engraving of Saturn in the *Planetenkinderbilder* of Georg Pencz (1531) that 'hier wie durchgängig in den astrologischen Zeugnissen die *Gefangenschaft* in mehreren Formen zu erkennen [ist]',[17] while Grimmelshausen, collating many disparate images from this rich tradition, writes in his *Ewigwährender Kalender:*

> Saturnus [...] ein Verderber und Feind der Natur / gifftig / von Natur kalt und trocken [...] er ist Mannlichs Geschlecht / graw und bleichfarb / mit einem dunckelenschein; [...] ist böß / der menschlichen Natur sehr schädlich [...] die grosse Infortuna genant; sein Bild ist gleich einen alten Mann / welcher sich an einen Stab leinet.
> [Er] regieret über [...] alte Leuth die in Herrschafft sitzen [...] bawen / Bawmeister [...] Maurer / Steinmetzen. [Er] bedeut Gefängnuß.[18]

Saturn here is the patron of wall-builders, symbol of prisons, and protector and ruler of 'old men in power',[19] and faced with this 'grosse Infortuna' it is not surprising that Bobrowski's lovers respond by turning away in resignation and sorrow. Behind the Saturn of Old Age, there moves a threatening Saturn of startling political actuality in the

---

Nachts kommt Saturn
und hält seine Hand auf.
Mit meiner Asche
putzt seine Zähne Saturn.
In seinen Rachen
werden wir steigen.

[16] The unpublished early poem 'Gryphius' (2:233) is not relevant here, but the short story 'Von nachgelassenen Poesien' (4:17-22), which is set in the Königsberg of Simon Dach, had been completed in mid-July 1961, just a few weeks before 'Mitternachtsdorf'. I will return to this later. Earlier still Bobrowski had referred directly to a lost 'planetary' suite by Buxtehude: 'der die Planeten rief / mit einer alten Qual' (1:149).

[17] Günther Weydt, *Nachahmung und Schöpfung im Barock: Studien um Grimmelshausen*, Bern 1968, p.257. My italics.

[18] Ibid. pp.325f.

[19] Comments on the advanced age of the East German leadership (Wolf Biermann's 'verdorbene Greise') belonged to the stock-in-trade of critical voices in the GDR.

days immediately after August 13 1961.[20]

Epiphanies

In contrast to these poems, which point, I suggest, increasingly to
contemporary events, stand others which present images of meetings,
contacts and experiences of epiphany, adumbrating forms of spiritual
transcendence. 'Krypta/Dom zu Brandenburg' (1:197, written October
18. 1963) continues the line of poems devoted to religious buildings, but
where in *Sarmatische Zeit* and *Schattenland Ströme* the churches and
cathedrals had been almost exclusively those of Russia during the war
years, and the dominant images had been of destruction, this poem has
as its starting point the experience of a visit to the crypt of a relatively
local fourteenth-century Gothic cathedral in the company of Jürgen
Henkys on the previous day. At the time of Bobrowski's visit the
entrance to the crypt was being restored (*Chronik* 39).

The poem belies the second part of its title in that it presents no
image of the cathedral, no reference to any recognisable architectural
feature apart from the crypt. Instead it evokes the complex emotional
experience of the visit, showing the dramatic shifts of mood that
accompany it. The focal point is situated below ground level in the
crypt, described as a 'Gefäß für die Finsternis'. Above are the trees 'mit
kahlem Haupt', an indication of the autumnal mood (the visit took place
mid-October). In the rest of the poem the poet addresses a 'du' who

---

[20] For a different interpretation of this poem see the discussion of 'Mitternachtsdorf' in
Stefan Reichert's *Das verschneite Wort*, pp.270-9. Reichert ignores the tradition to
which I refer and suggests a link between Saturn and the USSR, with the moons as
Soviet satellites: 'die DDR baute die Mauer durch Berlin im Auftrag der Sowjetunion
und der übrigen Staaten des Warschauer Paktes, also des kommunistischen Mutter-
staates und seiner Satellitenstaaten' (p.276). He also suggests a link between Saturn and
the Soviet hammer and sickle (*via* Kronos as god of harvest), and between the words
'laß uns schlafen einer des andern Schlaf' and the date August 13 *via* 'Zeit der
Erwartung' (2:247), which refers to the goddess Diana, whose functions included that of
protectress of slaves and whose public holiday occurred on August 13. In his review of
Reichert's monograph in *Zeitschrift für Germanistik* 11 (1990), pp.747-9, Bernd
Leistner disputes this and claims that it is only 'die als äußerst bedrohlich empfundene
Kriegsgefahr' which the persona fears, suggesting that the poem involves no 'kritisch-
politische Auseinandersetzung, die Bezug auf den Kommunismus nähme'. Instead, he
suggests, the Saturn complex signifies 'nichts anderes als ein heranziehendes großes
Unheil' (p.749). Reichert sees the possibility of contemporary allusion but, I believe,
fails to take account of Bobrowski's cultural points of reference.

appears confronted with the reality of its own death. In stanza 2 this prospect leads to a cry of anguish at the inevitability of final passive helplessness ('wer trägt mir die Haare?'). Stanzas 3 and 4, on the other hand, confront at greater length the 'evening', the approach of death before the final 'Finsternis':

> Daß der Abend, sagst du,
> nicht käme – er kommt mit dem Rauch
> auf dem Wasser, er nennt
> vom andern Ufer herüber
> seinen Namen ohne Laut –
>
> daß er nicht käme, du schlag
> den Stein an den Glockenrand: so
> wird erschallen erzen
> die Heldin, auf ihrem Ruf
> flügellos
> werden die Lüfte
> stehn und werden umhergehn
> unbeschuht.

This approaching evening is characterised by the paradoxical evocation of silence ('er nennt [...] / seinen Namen ohne Laut') and the visual obliteration brought about by the 'Rauch / auf dem Wasser', but the approach is to be brought to a standstill, as the last stanza makes clear, by the sound of a 'heroic' church bell: 'erzen / die Heldin'.

In the allusive final image the effects of this sound are described with an echo from the passage from the Gospels where the disciples lose their nerve in a tempest (Matthew 8: 23-7) and wake the sleeping Christ, begging Him to still the wind (here the 'Lüfte'). The last word, 'unbeschuht', obscure but evocative, implies, in contrast to the violence of a poem like the 'Auszug der Götter' (1:176) ('Stimme / schwarz, die das Ufer / mit Schuhen zertritt') the lack of any threat (wearing no shoes is hardly a martial characteristic), but it also echoes God's calling Moses from the burning bush, stopping him from getting too close and ordered him to remove his shoes as a sign of respect:

> Tritt nicht herzu, zieh deine Schuhe von deinen Füßen; denn der Ort, darauf du stehst ist heiliges Land! [...] Ich bin der Gott deines Vaters, der Gott Abrahams, der Gott Isaaks und der Gott Jakobs. (Exodus 3: 2-6)

Faced with the physical horror of death, the poet still finds hope and comfort in the awareness that this crypt too is 'heiliges Land'.

Such expressions of hope (there is no certainty – the verb remains in
the future) are repeated in other forms and in other poems. In
'Krypta/Dom zu Brandenburg' it is the evident holiness of the place and
the tolling of the bell that bring about the shift of mood. The later 'Alter
Hof in Häme' (1:208) presents a similar experience of a change of
mood. Like 'Krypta' it was written shortly after the experience it
describes, the visit with a number of other writers to Mukkula (Finland)
to attend a writers' seminar (*Chronik* 86f.). The visit included an
excursion (led by Manfred Peter Hein) to an old estate, now tourist
attraction, Urajärvi. The area was within Bobrowski's wider Sarmatian
world, and he anticipated with relish the visit in a letter of June 4 1964
to Michael Hamburger (*Marbach* 234). He drew great satisfaction from
it, as subsequent letters (e.g. July 2 1964) and an interview for *Neue Zeit*
(4:467-9) demonstrated. His selective name-dropping (James Baldwin,
Pinter etc.) to friends indicated his sense of pride at the acceptance the
contacts offered.

The poem starts:

> Schöllkraut. Zum Geschrei
> der Kuckucke.
> Voll Staub
> Klette und Nessel.
>
> Die Bretterstufen am Haus.
> Aus der Tür
> treten die Hölzer.

It presents a derelict and overrun old farmyard. Despite the flora and
fauna and a number of spots of colour, the impression is ultimately one
of decay, and the poem approaches its conclusion with images of lack of
communication:

> [...] Eingeschlafen
> der künstliche Schwan.
> Tote Stimme.
>
> Wie im Gras der Engel
> mit zerfressener Hüfte, hölzern, die Spur
> Mehl hinter sich,
> taub, ohne Rede. Der Rufer
> hat noch gewartet, die Hand
> erhoben, an leerer Scheune
> lange.
> Dort steht der Holunder.

In this situation the worm-eaten figure of a wooden angel is as useless as the artificial swan, and the poem appears to be moving towards silence. It ends, however, with the image of the 'Rufer' by an empty barn. A similar 'Rufer' had occurred in 'Der Wanderer', where its context had given it clear Christian connotations. In 'Alter Hof in Häme' the weeds, decay and silence are unexpectedly counterbalanced by this calling, beckoning figure in front of an empty 'Scheune', the waiting barn in which the Lord will 'sammeln seinen Weizen' (Matthew 3: 12). The identity of the 'Rufer' is unclear, but its appearance here – like that of the 'Heldin' in 'Krypta' – abruptly reverses the poem's previous direction. From examples of the unproductive 'tares' of the beginning, the poem turns to the gathering of the harvest.

At the end of 'Alter Hof' stands, however, the 'Holunder', the elder, a tree without pronounced Christian significance, but with important pagan connotations as a protector of home and hearth:

> Der Holunder stand bei den alten Germanen in hohem Ansehen, in dem Baum wohnt der gute Geist des Hofes und Gehöftes, die Hollermutter, Frau Ellhorn, daher schützt der Baum das Haus vor Feuersgefahr, das Vieh vor Seuchen.[21]

The poem ends thus with a combination of Christian and pagan images that promise or imply comfort, protection and succour. The combination from the Germanic and Christian cultures of Northern Europe presents less an exclusively Christian hope than an existential attitude that finds solace in the recognition of disparate signs of security from different cultures. Like the short story 'Roter Stein' (3:79-84) where the old woman Lina's pagan rites appear ultimately acceptable to the deity, the poem ends with indications of respect for both Christian and pagan observances.

These are not Christian poems in any conventional sense, and confirm Bobrowski's claim (4:455) that he was 'nur sehr bedingt' 'ein christlicher Schriftsteller'. They are, however, poems which Bobrowski described in his talk on the 'Lyrik der DDR' as poems 'aus christlicher Haltung, aus einem christlichen Lebensgrund heraus' (4:442). Another but more ambiguous example of such poetry is 'Der Blitz' (1:194). In

---

[21] *Meyers Großes Konversations-Lexikon*, 6th ed., Leipzig & Vienna 1903ff., article 'Sambucus'.

his lecture on the 'Lyrik der DDR' Bobrowski had spoken of his inability to use the name of Christ in his poems:

> Christus [...] ist für den Christen niemals bloß ein Wort. Christus 'bedeutet'.
> Diese 'Bedeutung' kann man immer neu sagen, wiederholen, aber man kann
> sie nicht zum Material für Dichtung benutzen. Damit würde man sie
> degradieren. (4:442)

'Der Blitz' demonstrates a different possibility:

> Der Blitz
>
> Der mich zuwirft
> dem Sand
> oder allein der Muschel,
> dem Baum
> oder der Schnecke
> am schwingenden Blatt,
> ich stürz in die Heuschreckenzüge,
> nah vorüber
> geh ich dem Vogelflug,
>
> der gibt mir auch
> einen Schlaf wie in Feuern,
> einen Atem aus Schnee,
> der zeigt einen Hohlweg
> die Lüfte hinab.
>
> Heiter fahr ich
> über den Wäldern, einsilbig.
> Ich hör nicht,
> der Redende hört nicht.
> Reicht mir ein Wasser herauf,
> sagt er,
> ich brenne.

Minde comments:

> Auch in seiner Natur [i.e. nature as presented in this poem] verbinden sich
> magische [...] und allzu anthropomorphische Züge [...] zu harmloser Dämonie.
> Wie in ['Märkisches Museum'] wird die 'Heiterkeit' auch explizit genannt.[22]

As the title indicates, it is about lightning, and it is tempting to agree
with Minde. One sees the anthropomorphic elements, the 'Schlaf', the
'Atem', indeed the whole idea of the lightning as a persona ('ich'). The

---

[22] *Johannes Bobrowskis Lyrik und die Tradition*, p.204.

poem suggests, however, significantly more than just a description of lightning and its course. The repetition of 'oder' as well as the parenthetical three lines at the end of the first stanza suggest not a single fate but various alternative fates and, more importantly, an acquiescence in these fates – with the lightning/'ich' content to let what happens happen. These possible alternative fates are not, however, the result of chance but are described as the results of an action by a 'Der', this being the first word of the poem as a whole and of the second stanza. While this 'der' is unnamed, it is he who controls and directs the lightning and it is to the will of this 'he' that the lightning, apparently willingly, submits. It is only in the last stanza that the lightning appears to have reached a sort of independence, the result of what has gone before. It becomes 'heiter' and, we are told, does not listen to something, and neither does the 'Redende', which, in context, is the longer sound of the thunder that follows the monosyllabic ('einsilbig') flash.

Bobrowski underlines this growing independence in his positioning of the words of the poem, using the simplest means to suggest a gradual growth in distance. The first stanza starts with 'Der mich' and has these two key elements of the poem in closest proximity as subject and direct object; stanza two has them slightly more distant, a word apart, as subject and indirect object, while in stanza three, after an apparent liberation, the 'ich' becomes syntactically entirely separate from the 'er'; they do not occur in the same sentence.[23]

The mood of this last stanza is, however, more complex than one of unalloyed joy. The 'Heiterkeit' of the lightning is ambiguous, as it leads to a headstrong failure to listen to attempted communication. Indeed, with the 'er' of the end of the poem identical with the 'der' of the beginning, the poem conveys an impression of ingratitude alongside this sense of liberation. The ambiguity is not, however, surprising, as the first chapter of *Levins Mühle* (3:10) demonstrates:

> Man soll sich den klaren Blick durch Sachkenntnis nicht trüben lassen, werden die Leute sagen, denen es gleich ist, woher ihre Urteile kommen, und das hat schon etwas für sich, die Kunst zum Beispiel wäre ohne dieses Prinzip nicht so heiter, wie Schiller sich das denkt, aber wir werden doch lieber Sach-kenntnis aufwenden und genau sein, d.h. also, uns den klaren Blick trüben.

---

[23] The lines starting 'ich stürz' are deceptive. They describe exclusively the result of the 'zuwerfen', to which they are subordinate.

In the novel the narrator rejects 'Heiterkeit' in favour of historical accuracy, and this rejection is echoed in the poem's implied criticism of those elements that do not hear: the lightning itself and its accompanying thunder.

One may well read the poem as a self-reflecting illustration of the theme of the poet and his own product, the poem, the work of art that becomes independent, that takes on a life of its own and loses its moral value in its artistic 'Heiterkeit'. This was, after all, a recurrent theme of Bobrowski's criticism of other writers.[24] Another dimension to the poem, however, demands attention. It is evident that in the last stanza mood and imagery change. We read exactly what it is that the lightning and thunder do not hear: the voice of someone above, an 'er', asking to be passed up some water. It is not possible to read this without thinking of the words from the cross 'mich dürstet' followed immediately by the vinegar and Christ's death (John 19: 29-30), and this Biblical reference is anticipated by other images in the poem. The word 'Heuschreckenzüge' is not biblical, but references to 'plagues of locusts' (i.e. 'Heuschrecken') are. Equally, the image of thunder and lightning being directed along a path is a recurrent one, with Job commenting on God: 'als er dem Regen ein Gesetz gegeben hat und dem Blitz und Donner den Weg' (Job 28: 26; similarly 38: 25).[25] In the same context (37: 10f.) Job links breath and frost, and God's directing of lightning and storms: 'aus der Wolke kommt sein Blitz'.

The poem has lightning as its subject-matter, but it is held together by allusions, at the beginning, to the omnipotent deity, the unnameable Yahweh of the Old Testament, and, at the end, to the suffering and thirsting Son of God of the New Testament. A further revealing comment beyond these quotations and semi-quotations is offered in *Peake's Commentary*.[26] This suggests four widely accepted etymologies of the Old Testament Yahweh. Relevant for an interpretation of this poem is the first one:

> The original meaning of the root letters is 'to fall' or 'to blow'. Yahweh is thus 'he who falls' or, causative, 'he who causes (the Lightning) to fall'. (p.212)

---

[24] See especially 4:446.

[25] The fact that this Biblical 'Weg' becomes a 'Hohlweg' in the poem is an example of Bobrowski's preference for tactile, non-abstract imagery.

[26] *Peake's Commentary on the Bible*, London and Edinburgh, 1962.

'Der Blitz' is thus not a poem of 'harmlose Dämonie' but a poem of considerable moral seriousness. As in 'Immer zu benennen' (1:143) ('Zeichen, Farben, es ist / ein Spiel, ich bin bedenklich, / es möchte nicht enden / gerecht') it expresses concern at a possible loss of moral direction, at the danger for the artist or human being who loses his way. It is not the expression of 'Heiterkeit' that we see here, but an expression of the danger of such 'Heiterkeit'.

A new Language

These thematic developments were accompanied by developments in Bobrowski's poetic language. 'Stadt' and 'Das Wort Mensch' leave the vocabulary of Sarmatia almost entirely behind, as do such poems as 'Zu Christoph Meckels Graphiken' and 'Mobile von Calder'. A development may also be observed within the actual vocabulary of nature that had been characteristic of Sarmatia. One aspect of this is the introduction of a freer, indeed whimsical imagery of 'Heiterkeit', as the occurrence of the word 'heiter' in 'Märkisches Museum' has indicated. Another is an increasing emphasis on the world, on reality itself as being a reality of language. This involves more than just the verbal interchange between human and natural elements observed above, as in the concluding lines of 'Wiedererweckung': 'und Augen öffne das Laub'. 'Feuerstelle' (1:180) has the poet claim: 'Wir hörten / die Münder im Laub', but in a further development the persona of the poet disappears and the possibility of simple human projection is diminished as these 'Münder im Laub' begin to communicate between themselves, 'talking' reality into existence. Several of Bobrowski's later poems follow this creative process.

Such a development implies considerable faith in language as a creative power and appears to present an area where the existential influence of Hamann affects more directly Bobrowski's poetic production. Bobrowski's interest in Hamann had indeed been life-long, but in 1962/3 it was raised yet again as he worked with Martin Seils at the Union Verlag's anthology of Hamann's works.[27] Central is Hamann's belief in reality as the spoken Word of God, and Bobrowski's new emphasis on language as reality must be seen against the background of Hamann's apodictic statement in 'Aesthetica in nuce' on this relation:

---

[27] *Johann Georg Hamann: Entkleidung und Verklärung*, ed. Martin Seils, Berlin 1963.

> Rede, daß ich Dich sehe! – – Dieser Wunsch wurde durch die Schöpfung er-
> füllt, die eine Rede an die Kreatur durch die Kreatur ist; denn ein Tag sagts
> dem andern, und eine Nacht thuts kund der andern.[28]

Hamann's aphorism is an expression of a religious conviction. Bobrowski, however, uses the idea underlying this as a poetically productive
myth, of reality as a spoken and hence living, vibrant, changing phenomenon.

'Kolnoer Tanz' (1:199) presents the linguistic formation of reality in
almost paradigmatic form.[29] As the title indicates, it depicts a dance,
apparently expressing extremes of emotion, but with a *basso continuo* of
tears concealed behind a mask (here 'Leintuch') of laughter. The
process of verbalisation begins in the second stanza:

> [...] der Stieglitz
> pfeift an den Balken hinauf,
> rot und blau die Stockrosen
> sagen über den Zaun:
> Es kommt ein Regen, bald,
> der wird für uns weinen.

If the goldfinch 'pfeift [...] hinauf', as though attempting to communicate, the hollyhocks actually talk 'sagen über den Zaun', and the content
of their conversation – the impending arrival of rain – is given as a
statement in direct speech. The stanza ends then with a repetition of the
tears motif, but here transferred to the flowers talking about the rain. In
the next short stanza, the process of verbalisation is extended beyond
the animal and vegetable to embrace the bitter-sweet emotions of the
dance:

> Warum weinen, fragt das Gelächter.
> Warum lachen, fragen die Tränen.

In the last two lines of the poem, the verbalisation becomes so complete
that the poetic voice can address the dance directly with the command:
'sprich doch' before concluding, in order to express that it is ended,

---

[28] Hamann, *Sämtliche Werke*, ed. J.Nadler, Vienna 1949, vol. 2, p.198. Hamann draws
here in part from Psalm 19: 3: 'Ein Tag sagt's dem andern, und eine Nacht tut's kund
der andern'. 'Rede, daß ich dich sehe' occurs also in *Litauische Claviere* (3:312).

[29] Kolno is a Polish town on the River Pisa, just south of the East Prussia border. It is
possible that the advance of the German armies in 1939 took Bobrowski through here.

with the words 'Nun spricht er nicht mehr'. In the course of the poem the dance itself has become a 'Sprechen', and with the end of the poem the dance too stops (and *vice versa*).

The two part poem 'Haus' (1:201f.) shows similar characteristics. The first part picks out individual elements of the house: the roof, the wall, the flower-bed, and subjects them to a growing anthropomorphisation and verbalisation:

> Da fährt das Licht übers Dach
> und will den Amseln nach.
> Holunder verwischt auf der Wand
> die Linien einer Hand.
> Im Rundbeet der Rittersporn
> hat aus dem Ohr mich verlorn.
> Nun schreibt an das Firstholz der Regen:
> Hier werd ich mich niederlegen.

That the light 'will den Amseln nach' already suggests volition, and by the third image, that of the 'Rittersporn', the delphinium is epitomised by its 'Ohr', a well-observed image of the shape of the flower, but also, and here primarily, a stage in the process of verbalisation, as the relation between 'mich' and flower is aural. That the image is drawn from the standard German idiom 'jemanden aus den *Augen* verlieren' only underlines the change. In the next couplet especially the fall and settling of rain is presented as a linguistic phenomenon.

The second part of the poem then presents a whimsical vision of dawn, using as its central image the departing shadows. These too are verbalised into monologues concerned with what they will turn out to be in the light of the day:

> An der Wand die Schatten
> reden mit Stimmen:
> Wie werden wir uns kleiden
> für den Tag?
>
> Eine Zitterblume
> ins Haar, eine grüne
> Ranke über die Augen,
> ein Dreiblatt an die Brust.[30]

---

[30] I interpret the question 'Wie werden wir uns kleiden / für den Tag?' as a reference to the shadowy, grey shapes of night gaining colour, clarity of outline and a third dimension with the arrival of light.

The poet joins in and encourages them in their turn to help create the new dawn:

> Schatten, tretet hervor,
> das Licht will beginnen mit kleinen
> Schritten, zeigt ihm
> den Weg.

The rest of the poem evokes the interplay of light and shadow and sound as the dawn ('Feuergeschrei / der Hähne über die Dächer') arrives. As in 'Kolnoer Tanz' ('sprich doch') here too in the last stanza the poet seeks verbal communication, addressing the shadows themselves: 'Schatten, ich will's / hören, Schatten, sprecht: / Du wirst hier bleiben / eine Zeit'.

Reality itself is occasionally presented as a form of language. In 'Das Wasser' (1:174) the poet addresses water, which has 'heard' the wind itself create a landscape of words: 'Du hörtest ihn [den Wind] sagen: Hier sind die Weiden, / hier ist das Eulenhaus', while in 'Ankunft' (1:183f.) the colours of the landscape, the white of the cottage walls and the grass of the river-bank, are dissolved into language, 'Rufe' and 'Stimmen':

> [...] die weißen Rufe
> flogen der Dörfer, die grüne
> Stimme des Ufers.

Similarly in 'An Runge' (1:175) 'der Feldberg [kommt] und redet / in Vogelsprüchen'. In such poems the landscape reflects on itself, indeed creates itself in language, with the whole of reality caught up in this process of creation: 'Dunkel, / sprich mit den Händen. / Wassergeräusch baut Nester / in die gefiederte Stille' ('Undine', 1:210); 'Gegenstände, Flöte und Uhr, / flogen, hingen / an Wolke und Regen, hatten / Hände gekehrt und Stimmen / nach der Erde ' ('Zu Christoph Meckels Graphiken', 1:215); 'Die Bäume treten / aus ihren Wasserschuhen, es wird / hörbar Gelb, eine Sprache der Steine, Sand / geht auf Händen' ('Märkisches Museum', 1:195).

Such imagery may occasionally appear whimsical in its naiveté, but its intention in these later poems is paradoxically serious. In the Sarmatian poems the landscape and the human vocabulary attached to it preserve memories of the historical past, a landscape where 'Namen reden von dir / zertretenes Volk / Flüsse, glanzlos noch oft', and Bobrowski provides this language with a context that will remind of the German 'lange Geschichte aus Unglück und Verschuldung'. The later poems now point to and implicitly defend a more fundamental language of reality. Between a Celan for whom the German language was 'eine Leiche' (again, it is Bobrowski's own perception that matters here) and an official East German language that Bobrowski considered atrophying and dying, his works attempt to present a language that is creative and vibrant, the language, as he saw it, that is the bedrock of reality.

Such thoughts may draw from Hamann's substance, but as with Hamann himself they are not to be construed as wilfully anti-rational. In his 1956 review of *Johann Georg Hamanns Hauptschriften erklärt* (vols. 1 and 7) Bobrowski refers to Hamann as a member of the Enlightenment, a 'seltsamer Aufklärer' (4:368). It is a surprising description for a writer normally associated with irrational sentiments opposed to the Enlightenment, but it is a view confirmed in *Entkleidung und Verklärung*. In the afterword to this volume Bobrowski will have read:

> Hamann hat dem Rationalismus, der Vernunftgläubigkeit dieses Jahrhunderts, sehr entschieden und sehr konsequent den Anspruch auf absolute Geltung bestritten. Doch hat er das keineswegs getan, um nun der Unvernunft das Wort zu reden. Er war kein Irrationalist. Er wollte vielmehr auch die Vernunft einbetten in die lebendige Ganzheit eines vollen Menschseins. (p.508)

Bobrowski too is concerned with this 'lebendige Ganzheit', with the reminder that man's own reality is more than just the product of reason and calculation, and indeed the early work 'Kentauren' (2:132f.) had pleaded for a less divisive interpretation of human existence.[31] The works of *Wetterzeichen* appear to remind of this potential unity through their hints at a uniting language beyond the divisive logic and materialistic dogma that surrounded him.

---

[31]   Ach, ich lasse mir den Glauben
        [...]
        daß mir Hand, Gehör, Gesicht,

        Seel, Geist – alles gleichermaßen
        teilhaft ist und zugetan,
        daß ich mit der Seele fassen,
        mit den Händen fühlen kann.
        [...]
        Oh Kentauren! Fabelwesen,
        Bilder jener bessern Zeit
        da man weniger gelesen,
        aber mehr gelebt als heut.

Bobrowski's poems in this last volume attempt to preserve this sense of the totality of existence that he saw as increasingly threatened. In a letter of April 23 1963, he complained of this threat and of the impoverishment of human existence that it brought with it:

> Vor Zeiten, sagen die alten Inder, war das Denkvermögen schön über den ganzen Korpus verteilt, das Rückenmark hinunter, also von der Schwanz-wurzel bis zum Schädel reichend. Aber es hat sich immer mehr hinauf-geschoben, oder besser: die Leut haben sich angewöhnt, nur noch mit dem letzten, dicksten Ende vom Gehirn, oben im Dachstübchen sozusagen, zu denken. Da wird dann alles dünn, abstrahiert, hin und her reflektiert: Riechen, Hören, Schmecken, Sehen. (*Marbach* 413)

Against the threat of such abstractions, these poems hold up the unique concrete word of nature.

In these years the GDR was isolating itself externally through its policy of 'Abgrenzung' and through its physical separation from the West. Within its own boundaries it was producing a society of compla-cent opportunists who saw themselves and their socialist dogma as the undisputed victors of history, from which no new lessons may be learnt. If the Sarmatian volumes remind of the richness of a complex past and this past bears witness to the complexities of ever more distant pasts, then in the poems of *Wetterzeichen* Bobrowski appears to be reminding of the complexities of reality itself, to which reason provides no adequate explanation. In his references to crumbling and collapsing walls he looks to a political world without such divisions; in his insistence on epiphanies in the middle of daily life he counters his atheist state's insistence on the one materialistic path to absolute truth and knowledge; in his presentation of a 'language' of nature he looks back to an earlier sense of the magical unity of reality. The later poems remind of the complexity and many-sidedness of existence, but beyond this also of the validity of other, earlier experiences increasingly (he felt) marginalised and denigrated in his contemporary life. To abandon these would be to betray his own version of humanity.

'Mickiewicz', the poem with which Bobrowski chose to conclude the Sarmatian volumes, involves, as I have demonstrated, a confession of love for 'Sarmatia' and of reconciliation at its loss. It is uncertain whether Bobrowski would have chosen to conclude his *Wetterzeichen* volume with the poem 'Das Wort Mensch', which was only placed there posthumously by his editor. It remains, however, a fortunate coincidence that the poem with which the volume ends involves another statement of love, not now for Sarmatia but for the new object of concern towards which, I have suggested, this last volume increasingly turns: 'Das Wort Mensch [...] Wo Liebe nicht ist, / sprich das Wort nicht aus'.

6

THE TURN TO PROSE: THE SHORT STORIES

Introduction

Bobrowski's poetry may be seen as a double expression of love, for the Eastern European continuum he called Sarmatia, and for the wider concern of human totality. Sarmatia, the object of the one, no longer existed. The threat to a totality of human existence was something he saw coming from the exaggerated insistance on distinctions and on rationality that he experienced within his own country. In opposing this the poems in *Wetterzeichen* presented a wider range of subject-matter, and, as I have indicated, developed away from Sarmatia and towards his East German present. They continued, however, with the process of kidnapping started in the earlier volumes.

Similar developments may be observed in the prose to which Bobrowski began increasingly to devote himself after 1960, and indeed, the poetic kidnapping was developed to new heights. Initially he drew on his 'Sarmatian' material to present episodes or individuals with limited direct relevance for his present. By late 1963, after completing *Levins Mühle* and himself experiencing a period of considerable tension with the GDR authorities, his short stories begin to address critically issues of direct relevance to his own relations with his state: the problem of the alienated artist as well as the problem of living in a society governed by ideology and complacency. A more critical treatment by journalists in the last few months of his life may also be seen to have had an effect on at least one of his last short prose works.

Like his other works, the stories were published in East and West, though exceptionally in different forms. In October 1964 Bobrowski collected his texts for publication by the Union Verlag in the single volume *Boehlendorff und Mäusefest*. He later added to this collection 'In eine Hauptstadt verschlagen', and the entire volume appeared shortly after his death in September 1965. For publication in the West the collection was split up, with *Mäusefest und andere Erzählungen* published by the Verlag Klaus Wagenbach in May 1965, and *Boehlendorff und andere: Erzählungen* published by the Deutsche Verlags-Anstalt in August 1965. With few exceptions these volumes contained everything that Bobrowski had written between 1959 and 1964. The short stories written in 1965, together with these other texts, then appeared in the volume *Der Mahner,* published in 1967 (Union Verlag) and 1968 (Klaus Wagenbach Verlag).

Prose-writing was a task that Bobrowski initially found uncongenial, and his letters are peppered with expressions of irritation or frustration. On June 29 1961 he wrote to Max Hölzer: 'Und jetzt probiere ich Prosa. Das ist ein bittres Geschäft. Weil ich erst lernen muß zu arbeiten. Bisher hat mich mein Thema getragen' (*Marbach* 639). To Jokostra (March 22 1962) he complained: 'Ich laborier langsam an Prosa, kurzen Geschichten' (ibid.) and a letter to Christoph Meckel (September 17 1963) referred to a 'Prosa-Krise' (*SZNB* 408). It was, however, a crisis brought about by his own determination to *experiment,* and as such it was a productive crisis. By contrast, Bobrowski's *public* pronouncements in interviews and speeches show increasing confidence, and in March 1965 he could claim: 'Im Augenblick bin ich [...] der Meinung, daß ich einigermaßen gut Geschichten erzähle. Vor zwei Jahren dachte ich, daß ich eigentlich Gedichte schreiben sollte' (4:479).

Although never attaining the status of a coherent theory, Bobrowski's utterances on prose identify a number of repeated factors. Most significantly, he saw his works within an oral tradition and looked back in part to certain 'Volksbücher'. This was a spoken tradition that differed greatly from the literary tradition of the GDR, and his adherence to it is related to a sense of intense disquiet with the language he found around him:

> Ich habe die Volksbücher gern gelesen, und ich mag vor allem dieses Eulen-spiegel-Buch. Aber das ist es nicht allein. Ich habe ganz bestimmte Befürch-tungen für den Zustand der Sprache. Ich fürchte eine gewisse Stagnation in der Entwicklung, wenn wir in dem bisherigen Literaturdeutsch bleiben. Und ich habe mich also bemüht, volkstümliche Redewendungen, sehr handliche Redewendungen, eben volkstümliches Sprechen bis zum Jargon, mit einzube-ziehen, um einfach die Sprache ein bißchen lockerer, ein bißchen farbiger und lebendiger zu halten. Außerdem geht das auch auf die Syntax. Ich bemühe mich da um verkürzte Satzformen, um im Deutschen nicht sehr gebräuchliche Konstruktionen, die alle etwas Handliches haben. Ich muß das gut lesen und sprechen können, was ich da geschrieben habe. (4:472)

In tandem with this opposition to the stultifying written language came a clear rejection of all conventional demands for a formal plot, and Bobrowski on a number of occasions stressed the 'openness' of his prose. He directed his criticism against East German conventional language, but also against any 'Stehenbleiben auf künstlerischen Techniken der Realisten des 19. Jahrhunderts, wie es manchmal von

Kritikern empfohlen worden ist' (4:453). Elsewhere he expresses his preference for the 'offene Form' and tactically defends his use of it with a reference to Flaubert's letters:

> Ich versuche für meine Person, ein bißchen vom Zwang zur Fabel wegzu-
> kommen, wie er vor einem Jahrhundert etabliert worden ist [...]. Aber da kann
> ich mich auch auf einen Mann aus dem vorigen Jahrhundert berufen, auf
> Flaubert, der das schon theoretisch in den Briefen ausführt. Ich glaube schon,
> daß das ein Nutzen wäre, besonders für die Kurzgeschichte, also für eine, wie
> ich sie auffasse, offene Form. (4:498)

In an earlier interview he had referred to his very abstract compositional technique, and specifically of the early text 'Mäusefest' (4:47-9) he commented:

> Das fing an, so wie die Geschichten bei mir alle anfangen: ohne Plan und ohne
> Überlegung, einfach mit solch einem Spiel von Licht und Schatten [...]. Ich
> pflege Geschichten immer so anzufangen, ohne daß ich eine Handlung vor mir
> habe. (4:481)

Later he played with the idea – really only thinking out loud in an interview – that his stories might unconsciously follow musical forms:

> Man könnte sagen, es gibt Formen, die etwa eine Suite wären oder so der Typ
> der alten Ouvertüre, die einen Introduktionssatz hat und dann – dadurch vor-
> bereitet, aber nicht immer – verschiedene, gegeneinandergesetzte Partien-
> typen. Und ich meine, auch zur Ouvertüre des 19. Jahrhunderts besteht
> vielleicht eine Beziehung. (4:498)

Such narrative games are characteristic, as we shall see, both of the short stories and the longer prose.

Within such an open structure the role of the author/narrator (Bob-rowski did not always make the distinction clear) is central (4:475), and Bobrowski emphasises his 'Hausrecht [...] nicht nur der Sprache gegen-über, sondern auch den Fakten gegenüber' (4:476). This 'Hausrecht' could take many forms, but involved above all the selection (and indeed distortion) of historical material for the story-telling (4:475). Bobrowski adds, deducts, alters material at will. As he emphasised: when a story is told it does not recapitulate history but instead 'es entsteht etwas Neues' (4:481).

The comments show little theoretical interest in the differences be-tween his prose and his poetry, and when comparing the two Bobrowski rather blurs the distinction. He is unworried by accusations of writing 'poetic' prose. He does, however, see one major difference between prose and poetry, which may explain the difficulties he encountered writing it:

> Das mehr summierende oder mehr grundsätzliche Gedicht [...] kann ganz be-stimmte Sachverhalte nicht vermitteln. Dazu bedarf es des Details, [...] der deutlicheren Ausarbeitung der Szenerie [...] Das ist für mich nur möglich in der Erzählung. (4:464)

This involved work.

Such considerations do not show a high level of artistic awareness, and indeed Bobrowski's thoughts hardly extend beyond the platitudi-nous. It is hardly original to state 'daß man gerade für die Prosa sehr genaue, sehr präzise Sachverhalte braucht, daß man die Erfahrung braucht, die Wirklichkeit, wenn man etwas tatsächlich wahr darstellen will' (4:464f.). Only in a small number of comments does he indicate specific characteristics, and it is significant for the level of his interest that he does not formulate them *ex cathedra* but only in response to questions. Such characteristics include a preference for long introduc-tions to some stories, a characteristic that he recognises as related to the form of the overture (4:498), and a preference for shock tactics:

> Ich bringe mit Vorliebe den Spaß herein in diese ernsthaften Geschichten und will damit so eine kleine Art Schocktherapie. Ich möchte den Hörer und den Leser zu einem Gelächter kriegen und möchte dann durch den Fakt, den ich dahintersetze, bewirken, daß ihm das Lachen im Hals steckenbleibt. (4:499)

It is impossible either from his random comments or from the texts themselves to establish the precise origins of Bobrowski's narrative style. In the context of his concern at the stagnation of East German prose he admitted, as seen above, the possible influence of 'Volks-bücher', and it is in the nature of such a tradition that named influences are difficult to establish. Critics have suggested other sources, such as the Russian *skaz*[1] used in the nineteenth century by Gogol and Leskov,[2] and also by the twentieth-century writer Isaak Babel,[3] while others have referred to Robert Walser,[4] and Scholem Alechem.[5] Apart from the

---

[1] See Bernd Leistner, 'Der Erzähler', *SZNB* 323-39.

[2] Bobrowski knew the works of Leskov, ('den russischsten unter den großen russischen Erzählern des 19. Jahrhunderts') as is clear from his review of the translation *Herren und Knechte* (4:376f.).

[3] See the poem 'Holunderblüte' (1:94).

[4] Günter Jäckel, 'Die Behandlung der Kurzgeschichte bei Johannes Bobrowski', *SZNB*

'Volksbücher', Bobrowski himself at various times and for various reasons related his prose *privately* to Babel, Sudermann, Robert Walser, Arno Schmidt, Dickens, Gomringer and Laurence Sterne, but *publicly* to Babel, Joseph Conrad and, nonsensically, 'den ganz späten Mörike' (4:488).

The link with Sudermann, the late nineteenth-century East Prussian writer to whom he initially dedicated *Levins Mühle*, is clearest, in particular to his *Litauische Geschichten*.[6] Apart from the self-evident coincidences of geographical background, with Tilsit, Königsberg and Heydekrug, the Haff and references to villages along the Memel, the two writers offer similar references to local folklore, often with some form of explanatory comment; they both use a narrator who comments both on his own story-telling and on the events of the story, and they both generally use the present tense. Throughout Bobrowski's prose one finds plot elements or phrases which could be drawn from Sudermann but also from their shared background: arson for insurance purposes, the potential difficulty with 'Altensitzer' ('Jons und Erdme'), and so on. Where Bobrowski in 'Begebenheit' presents the scandal of the christening of an illegitimate child and refers to the priest's refusal to help the suffering mother, Sudermann, in 'Die Magd', presents an unpleasant scene at Marinke's wedding reception and regrets the absence of the priest who might have been able to prevent it. The temporary rescue of the policeman Krolikowski in *Levins Mühle* (he is being sucked down into the moor when he is fortunate enough to find a firm footing on a submerged tree stump) is anticipated more cheerfully in the efforts by Jons and Erdme to produce a firm foundation for their chimney. The similarities remain, however, at these superficial stylistic and topographical levels.

Robert Walser's influence is also arguable. Bobrowski had marked a number of stories in his edition of Walser's works,[7] including 'Kleist in Thun' and 'Brentano I and II', and the influence of such works has been

---

247, and Günter Hartung, 'Bobrowskis Boehlendorff', *SZNB* 268f.

[5] Peter Albert, *Die Deutschen und der europäische Osten – 'Vergangenheitsbewältigung' als Historismuskritik im Erzählwerk Johannes Bobrowskis*, Erlangen 1990, p.169, quoting a letter by Eberhard Haufe.

[6] In a letter to Christopher Middleton Bobrowski could refer to parts of *Levins Mühle* being written 'im Stil Sudermanns' (*Marbach* 683).

[7] *Robert Walser: Prosa*, ed. Walther Höllerer, Frankfurt/M. 1960.

suggested in the later 'Künstlergeschichten'. In other areas too Bobrowski may have found some confirmation for his own works. Walser's use of 'genreless' prose forms (sketches, anecdotes, descriptions of paintings) was followed by Bobrowski, as was his provincial subject-matter. Both also cultivated an occasional imbalance between topographical description and narrative action, as in Walser's 'Büren'.

Wherever it was drawn from, this prose style, the 'interrumpierende Erzählhaltung'[8] constituted a rejection of the monologistic style of prevailing East German prose. After the anti-formalism campaign of the early 1950s had curtailed interest in the techniques of the stream of consciousness or experimental prose associated with Joyce and Döblin, East German fictional prose had been largely characterised by its subordination of literary quality to artistic didacticism. The officially sanctioned dogma of socialist realism dictated the need for a clear narrative perspective, infused with socialist ideals, and with emphasis on the narrative aim of telling a closed, completed story. Following the arguments of Lukács, whose political fall from grace in 1956 did not immediately affect the influence of his aesthetic ideas, key elements in the cultural argument had centred on concepts like 'totality', the need to recognise the achievements of nineteenth-century prose writers, avoidance of experiment etc. It remained a basic tenet of East German criticism that the work of literature should be reasonable accessible to a fictitious 'average reader'. Such works had almost completely avoided unconventional literary language and any techniques that played with the notion of narrative. More immediately for Bobrowski's mature prose the period directly before 1959 had been distinguished by official emphasis on the need to deal with contemporary subject-matter, and from 1959 these interests were focused, through the so-called Bitterfeld Movement, on the productive union of the writer and the workplace.[9] In view of the almost 'formalist' comments Bobrowski made of his own work, it is not surprising that he nowhere refers to any influence by an East German prose writer.

---

[8] See Horst Bienek and Michael Hamburger, 'In Memoriam Johannes Bobrowski' in *Merkur* 20 (1966), vol. 2, 131-7 (p.136).

[9] Bobrowski's attitude to Bitterfeld is clear from his lecture 'Lyrik der DDR', where he refers to '[jene] Konferenz, die die Parole "Kumpel, greif zur Feder" ausgab. Seither gibt es schon eine ganze Anzahl dichtende Arbeiter, Förster und Bauern' (4:438).

Early Prose

In an interview of late March 1965 Bobrowski linked prose with the very beginning of his writing: 'Ich wollte, und das ist der Anfang meiner Schreiberei, damals [...] die russische Landschaft festlegen [...] Ich habe es mit Zeichnen und dann mit Prosa probiert' (4:480). None of these early attempts appear to have survived,[10] and Bobrowski quickly turned to the classical ode. The earliest surviving stories stem from his period of captivity and the first years in East Berlin. They show few indications of his future style. The four sketches, 'Zu einem Totentanz' (4:177-9), completed in 1947, almost all intensify the directness of the horror through the use of the present tense, like the later works. The same motif of the dance of death recurs in the 1951 sketch 'Der Schauspieler' (4:192f.), which places death in a modern setting. It is memorable for the grotesqueness of its central image – that of death as stripping away the roles, the 'Masken [...] aus [...] Papier' to reveal the facelessness of the actor X, who has 'nur eine formlose, teigige Masse' onto which his wig slowly settles, 'ein wenig verklebt von dem weißen Brei' (4:192).

Two longer texts from 1951 illustrate the early lack of an individual voice. The autobiographical 'Im Gefangenenlager' (4:180-7) at least anticipates aspects of his future 'Thema', but despite the realistic frame-work of a camp for German prisoners of war, the story consists of little more than an extended anecdote concerning the death, foretold by his batman, of the character A.[11] Quoting Gryphius's poem 'Vanitas! Vanitatum Vanitas' it ends with a turn away from such musings on the past towards the uncertain future: 'Was künftig, wessen wird es sein?'.[12]

In two respects at least the story anticipates characteristics of later works. It is narrated in the present tense, and it starts with an unusually long and symbolic topographical setting which anticipates 'Rainfarn' (1964) and 'Der Mahner' (1965). It also develops a narration orientated in part towards dialogue with the reader, addressing him ('Leser, halte

---

[10] It is conceivable that Bobrowski, with his chronic lack of interest in dates, is referring here to the start of the prose piece 'Im Gefangenenlager' (4:180-7) of 1950/51, which does indeed attempt to describe a Russian landscape.

[11] See the analysis by Eberhard Haufe, 'Zu Bobrowskis Erzählung "Im Gefangenen-lager"', *Sinn und Form* 34 (1982) 620-2. Bobrowski offered the text for publication in October 1960 to Felix Berner at the Deutsche Verlags-Anstalt.

[12] See the poem 'Gryphius' (2:233).

dich heran, dir ist eine Geschichte versprochen!') or encouraging him to become critically active: 'Leser [...] frage, um was es geht, und vor allem, um wen!'. The setting, an extended description of the Russian plain around the camp, is all too clearly functional. Geological and other changes leave the observer, we are told, with the impression of an unfinished landscape, 'im Stich gelassen', 'nicht fertiggeworden', 'nicht fertiggestellt', a 'Landschaft von mächtiger Gestaltlosigkeit' whose inhabitants have not tamed it but have 'selber in ihrer Lebensart das Wesen der Ebene angenommen' (4:180f.). The narrative voice remains, however, a disembodied 'wir' and the result is tired and second-hand. In one incident at least the narrative anticipates what was to become one of Bobrowski's most effective narrative characteristics – the shift into the speech or thought processes of the protagonists: in face of the destruction they see around them 'sie [the German prisoners] hören, daß sie zu dieser Zerstörung beigetragen haben, ja, daß sie die Urheber sind. Sie sind in dieses Land gekommen; ungerufen, das ist vielleicht wahr, aber wer will das alles begreifen?' (4:181). It is an example of the devious self-justification of the guilty who hide from their guilt by refusing to understand it.

The other story from 1951, 'Der Soldat an der Birke' (4:188-91) sets the topos of refusing to allow a burial against the background of the Thirty Years War. It is also narrated in the present tense but develops a completely different narrative technique with few narrative intrusions. It presents the story of a soldier who is brought back to humanity through his love for a recently widowed woman: left to guard the hanging corpse of a would-be deserter, he prefers to spend the night with her and discovers in the morning that the body has been taken down and buried. Instead of the expected fear, he recognises that it was his duty too to bury the soldier:

> «Sie haben ihn begraben», sagt er ganz laut vor Staunen. Und langsamer: «Hätt's auch tun können. Hätt' Zeit gehabt.» Und er spürt, wie ein Lachen in ihm aufwacht, richtig breit, und ihn ganz ausfüllt bis in die Arme und die Schenkel hinein. (4:191)

He then sensibly deserts with the woman and they head for the relative safety of the woods.

These two totally different stories, with their different narrative techniques and different, though war-oriented subject matters, demonstrate the uncertainty of these early years. Other early prose texts move away from the narrative altogether, and from this period stems a collection of prose 'Bemerkungen' (4:195-209), aphoristic observations on art, life and religion, which illustrate the extent of Bobrowski's disillusionment with ideology, ideologues and all attempted systematisations.[13] Several of these aphorisms were incorporated in a further text, 'Daten zum Lebenswandel des Herrn S.' (4:210-213), which was apparently intended to form a framework to present them.

Apart from minor pieces ('Über Kunstwerte', 'Kulturdünger') satirising exaggerated respect for the past and for art, Bobrowski only returned to prose in 1959, with 'Es war eigentlich aus', before turning to it much more intensely after 1961. The collected works show the growing production: 1959: 1 story; 1960: 1 story; 1961: 3 stories; 1962: 7/8 stories; 1963: 5/6 stories; 1964: 10 stories; 1965 (first six months, before he was taken ill): 8 stories.

The earliest published stories:
'Es war eigentlich aus', 'Begebenheit'

Bobrowski's first mature prose works written with publication in mind were 'Es war eigentlich aus' (4:9-11), from Autumn 1959, set in contemporary Berlin, and 'Begebenheit' (4:12-16), from December 1960, set in East Prussia or the Memelland in the first third of the century. These are slight stories in which may be seen some of the influences to which Bobrowski was exposed, and he himself wrote of the second:

> da kam so eine Mischung aus Arno Schmidt und Sudermann raus. Und dabei hatte ich eine Mischung aus Dickens und Gomringer, also Tristram Shandy, vor. Es kommt eben immer totaliter aliter. (*Marbach* 651)

Although anticipating later works, these are, almost uniquely, past tense narratives. In setting and atmosphere, 'Es war eigentlich aus', which was written for an anthology of stories on city life planned by Günter Bruno Fuchs, shows the influence of the new friendship with Fuchs and

---

[13] The title of these aphorisms refers to Lichtenberg, whose aphorisms originally bore the title *Bemerkungen vermischten Inhalts*. Bobrowski eventually distanced himself from this type of writing for anything other than private consumption: 'Schluß mit einer gewissen Art von Bemerkungen, Maximen oder sonstwas, auf die ich mir zu gewissen Zeiten etwas eingebildet habe. Selbstverständigung – meinetwegen auch mal ein paar hübsche Formulierungen – das mag bleiben' (4:209).

Robert Wolfgang Schnell. The work is autobiographical, reflecting Bobrowski's move from the Altberliner Verlag Lucie Groszer to his more prestigious post at the Union Verlag in September 1959. Continuing the thematic interest in time from the poems, it emphasises, as the title indicates, the painless loosening of ties with one's past. The narrator accepts this in full and looks back on the past he had evidently enjoyed without nostalgia or melancholy.

This imperceptible passage of time ('Und jetzt weiß ich gar nicht, wann das alles aufhörte. Es ist einfach vergangen' – 4:10) has brought the narrator from a slightly seedy but attractively bohemian milieu to a new career and 'ein anderes Leben' in which he is obliged to pay more attention to 'Schneideranzügen [...] Haferflocken, Tee, Zigarren und einer Flasche Wein am Abend' (4:9). In the concluding paragraph he brings his readers up to the narrative present and indicates his own concluding attitude:

> Der Wirt soll gestorben sein. Helene – da weiß ich wirklich nichts. Und wollte ich mich jetzt noch erkundigen, es wäre alles zu spät. (4:11)

Compared to later works it is very much, in Bobrowski's own words, 'eine ganz kleine Sache [...] mit Großstadtromantik' (*Marbach* 657). It has an urban setting and characters, but its core situation is typical of some of the early poems, with a period of naive and uncritical enjoyment of life followed by a change and the acceptance of the need to adjust to the new situation. The story even contains verbal echoes of the 1954 'Die Daubas' (1:69f.), which had expressed the separation from this area with the stanza:

> Das ist vergangen.
> Wir ließen die Dörfer dem Sande.
> Kaum wie ein Flößerruf
> *zogen* wir *fort*. [my italics]

while then ending with the lines

> [...] – so
> sehn ich mich nicht,

In 'Es war eigentlich aus' the change is expressed with the words: 'Das seh ich nicht mehr. Ich bin *fortgezogen*' (4:9), and at the end of the same paragraph the new attitude is expressed with the words: 'es stimmte wohl gar *nicht*, wenn ich sagte, ich *sehne mich* zurück nach jener Zeit'. The work would thus appear to be a text, in which elements of the earlier Sarmatian emotional experience are translated to an urban setting. Later versions of this theme can be seen in 'Das Käuzchen' and 'Im Verfolg städtebaulicher Erwägungen'.

'Begebenheit' shows all too clearly the influence of Sudermann's atmosphere, but the turn to this geographical area also opens a fruitful development for the future. The title refers to the christening party of the illegitimate child of Lene Dewischeit and a Herr Meyer, but Lene's individual disgrace is of secondary importance compared with other events. An uninvited guest uses the party as an opportunity to buy some poison to remove his 'Altenteiler' parents. Another arranges for his own farm to burn down while he is away. For all these incidents Bobrowski unobtrusively indicates economic causes: the absent father of the child is introduced as 'der Herr Meyer' (4:16), suggesting sexual exploitation by a (German) social superior, the arson is 'wegen der Versicherung', and the planned murder is a consequence of the material difficulties of running a farm with dependent relatives: 'Die können einen Hof zugrunde richten, die Altenteiler. [...] Jeden Tag fünfzehn Eier, drei Pfund Butter [...] Aber es steht ja im Kontrakt' (4:15). Despite local colour and the evident sympathy for Lene the accumulation of such aspects is excessive, and the story runs the danger of appearing simply to illustrate the socialist theme of the economic dependence of morality.

Although of limited intrinsic interest, these two works mark the starting points for Bobrowski's 'Stadtgeschichten', where the town forms the backdrop to efforts at self-orientation in the present, and 'Dorfgeschichten' loosely in the tradition of Sudermann. To these two types came the 'Künstlergeschichten', to which I have referred briefly above.

'Stadtgeschichten':
'Das Käuzchen', 'Im Verfolg städtebaulicher Erwägungen'

A number of Bobrowski's texts are set in the present, including the satirical, and not very convincing, 'In Fingals Haus', 'Ein Herz für den Hund' and 'Das Stück', while in 'Dunkel und wenig Licht' he turns to a West German milieu similar to that of 'Es war eigentlich aus'. In 'Das Käuzchen' (4:77f.) and 'Im Verfolg städtebaulicher Erwägungen' (4:170f.), however, the function of the town as backdrop to a considera- tion of urgent personal issues is clear. The texts also illustrate, as in *Wetterzeichen*, Bobrowski's shift away from Sarmatian material, as the two texts treat the theme of the relationship between past and present in very different ways. The earlier 'Das Käuzchen' treats it as a personal problem of self-definition of the individual caught between an urban present and a rural past. It implies the existential superiority of the past. In 'Im Verfolg städtebaulicher Erwägungen' any reference to a superior rural past is studiously avoided. A consideration of the dates of composition of the two stories indicates a possible reason for this change. Together they show the development of a much more self-consciously defensive style, with an almost carefree element in 'Das Käuzchen' giving way to a statement of poetic position in the later text calculated to prevent a specific misinterpretation. Together, as texts from 1963 and 1965, they demonstrate a developing dialogue with the East German authorities. Despite the differences, however, both texts are parabolic, close in form to the late medieval *exemplum*, with a long illustration of a problem followed by a single paragraph that appears to point the moral.

'Das Käuzchen' presents the effect on the narrator of unexpectedly hearing a tawny owl call. The text falls into two parts. A first, longer section presents the particular situation of a full, committed life 'in der Stadt' being interrupted by this call in such a way that the day seem 'verschlafen', the narrator's existence there only a dream: 'das Käuzchen [...] schreit [...] Und wir kommen uns vor, als seien wir jetzt aufgewacht. [...] Wir sind aufgewacht' (4:77). Such an interruption leads to the inevitable question: 'Wie leben wir hier?', a question provided with a particular bias through a quotation from Büchner's *Dantons Tod*: 'Nimmt man das Vaterland an den Schuhsohlen mit?' with its implication that it is impossible to shake off one's 'fatherland', that one will never be free of its influence.

A possible answer to the question 'wie leben wir hier?' is provided in the second, much shorter section of the text contained in the last paragraph, in an image derived from the rural landscape to which the narrator's and his wife's dreams return. The scene is that of Bobrowski's childhood memories along the Memel. It is the image of a 'Sandweg' between 'Wiesen', as opposed to the sunken 'Hohlweg' found in other works, and the initial question is replaced by another, which remains unanswered:

> Wie breit ist [der Sandweg], kann man das sagen? Er geht über in die Wiese. Oder die Wiese hört auf. Oder geht über in einen Weg. Wie ist das genau? Es gibt keine Grenze. Der Weg ist nicht zuende. Und die Wiese fängt nicht an. Das ist nicht ausdrückbar. Und ist der Ort, wo wir leben. (4:78)

Despite the areas of greenery referred to in the story the town is predominantly a sphere of practical activity ('Fabrik', 'S-Bahn', 'Schulhof' and 'Friedhof'). It is also characterised by clear delineation, in particular the line between 'Straße' and 'kleine Gärten'. Within such a regulated context the blurring of distinctions brought about by the call of the owl presents a disturbing challenge. Present and past, waking and sleeping, practical activity and dreams, 'Sandweg' and 'Wiese' flow into one another and run counter to a town life based on the topographical equivalent of a division of labour. Bobrowski's experiences contradict this urban compartmentalisation, for which the word 'Grenze' is of such central significance. Only the rural past, the other part of his existence, suggests an answer, an image for the natural flow of the 'Ort, wo wir leben'. In this text it is the premise of the necessity for compartmentalisation, the premise providing the impetus for the initial question, that is false, and such implied divisions between the various aspects of human existence represent a challenge to be overcome.

The text 'Im Verfolg städtebaulicher Erwägungen' was completed in May 1965, shortly before Bobrowski began work on *Litauische Claviere* and at a time of considerable unease. The narrator here observes the demolition of a row of houses built in the late nineteenth century and sees how their inhabitants constantly move one house further down the street in order to avoid the demolition. The houses get ever more crowded, as they also get smaller, and the narrator concludes with a reference to the inevitability of the coffin:

> Wie werden die Leute da alle herausschauen können?
> Es findet sich ja noch immer ein Haus, vielleicht eins mit zwei Fenstern, das ist wenigstens etwas. Denn das letzte, denke ich, hat keines mehr. (4:171)

For most of its length the text can be interpreted as exposing the absurdity of attempting to resist the passing of time by clinging to the past. The last paragraph turns, however, against a completely different attitude, that expressed by the town-planner without interest in the past:

> Es können ja neue Häuser an die Stelle der alten gesetzt werden; alles neu, ein neuer Name für die Straße, neue Bewohner, man hat präzise, ausreichend detaillierte Vorstellungen, wenn es um die Zukunft geht. Aber wie das mit dem Alten, Früheren, dem Vergangenen gewesen ist, da bleibt man auf Vermutungen angewiesen. Das ist gewesen, und ist vergangen, Zeit, und verlorene Zeit. Wie Geschwätz. (4:171)

The first part of this conclusion may be read as uncritical narrative comment. The rest makes it clear that such an attitude may involve losing the opportunity to learn from history, turning time into 'verlorene Zeit'. The last words of the story, 'Wie Geschwätz', raise the criticism to a different level. They are drawn from Psalm 90: 8f., where the psalmist laments the passage of time and suggests a reason:

> Denn unsere Missetaten stellst du vor dich,
> unsere unerkannte Sünde ins Licht vor deinem Angesicht.
> Darum fahren alle unsre Tage dahin durch deinen Zorn,
> wir bringen unsre Jahre zu *wie ein Geschwätz.*

Through the word 'Geschwätz' Bobrowski raises the spectre of man's 'unerkannte Sünde', for him the failure to recognise past guilt, to pay appropriate attention to the past and hence to learn from history. It is this failure that makes time 'verloren, [...] Geschwätz'. Between the two extremes of clinging to the past and ignoring it completely the narrator implicitly indicates a third possibility, one that recognises the need to consider the possible significance of the past for the future, without in any way denying the importance of the present: 'wir werden hinübergehen müssen [...] uns [...] erkundigen [...] Wir müssen doch vielleicht wissen'. Haltingly and modestly, Bobrowski sets out here images of his own position between the extremes.

Both stories are set in Bobrowski's contemporary Berlin, although 'Das Käuzchen' still shows the influence of the Sarmatian past, with the rural image explaining 'wie man hier lebt' drawn from the memories of the past which, from the point of view of an urban and compartmentalised present, cause the problem in the first place. The text implicitly criticises the present for the unreality of its demands: despite such claims, the past continues to make itself felt, is still 'present'. Most of 'Im Verfolg' appears to point in the opposite direction, against those who stubbornly resist change, and only a single paragraph concerns the future-besotted city planners. Here, however, Bobrowski deliberately makes no reference to the specific Sarmatian rural past that he had touched on in 'Das Käuzchen' through the 'litauische Lieder' and the 'Sandweg' and that might have contained a corrective to the rationalists and planners. Instead he evokes the older literary tradition of the Psalms to express his concern: the need for a more receptive attitude to the past. It may be 'vergangen', but it need not be 'verloren', indeed it must not be 'verloren'.

The difference in emphasis between the two stories reflects the change in Bobrowski's own position when he wrote them, with the later work more defensive, directed against misinterpretations of his intentions by the East German cultural authorities which concerned and irritated him in the last year of his life. Anticipating *Litauische Claviere,* it marks an important stage in his justification of his works, and the severity with which he satirised those who cling to the past underlines his determination to distance himself from accusations that he is doing the same himself. By avoiding (unlike in 'Das Käuzchen') any implication that there is a Sarmatian ideal, he indicates the depth of this concern.[14]

Early 'Künstlergeschichten':
'Von nachgelassenen Poesien', 'Epitaph für Pinnau'

The work on the novel *Levins Mühle* that took up much of early 1963 led to a reduction in the number of short stories written in that year, before a new productive phase started again in later 1963 and 1964. Most of the short prose pieces completed before the break continued to reflect Bobrowski's Sarmatian theme, either directly, in that they deal with aspects of the German presence in the East, or more indirectly, in that they study the mentality of the inhabitants of these border areas. In some an individual is confronted with a local elite, with the confrontation leading to or threatening the destruction of that individual. In this confrontation may be seen the seeds of Bobrowski's later mature 'Künstlergeschichten' considered below. Particularly important in anticipating these is 'Von nachgelassenen Poesien' (4:17-22), a story, written in July 1961, on the anonymous 'M.', a 'Secretarius' and dilettante writer living in seventeenth-century Königsberg. Told largely as an interior monologue by M. himself, the story presents an evening in which he completes a poem, expresses his frustration at his own situation, gets drunk and experiences dreams or hallucinations in which he is greeted by his lover Katerina and by a bishop who had been walled up alive in Königsberg Cathedral.

The story can be placed chronologically by M's references to a number of his Königsberg acquaintances, especially the writers Adersbach (1610-1660) and Simon Dach (1605-1658) and other luminaries:

---

[14] Further details of the events leading to Bobrowski's concern are given in the chapter *Litauische Claviere.*

Valentin Thilo (1607-1662), the Brandenburgischer Kurfürst, Georg Wilhelm, (whose stay in Königsberg 1635-1640 offers a precise dating, as does the reference to the plague, which affected Königsberg badly in 1639), Heinrich Albert (1604-1651) and a poet Stobäus (1580-1648). 'M.' himself is an alienated 'Old Prussian', in the sense that although his family originated from this area he has lost all interest in the Old Prussian past or his roots. He claims to be descended from one of the peasants betrayed and executed in the local Peasants' Revolt in 1525 (see *Litauische Claviere*, 3:275f. and the poem 'Der Samländische Aufstand 1525' – 2:301f.). Despite this he has no knowledge of contemporary 'Prussian' or pagan culture ('ich müßt es doch wissen, aber ich weiß es nicht [...] die heidnischen Lieder [...].Von denen ich nichts weiß'). Instead he worries about the acceptability in his poem of a word like 'Alkgebirge' with its associations of pagan rites and revolt, and can only justify it, ignoring the difference between conventional classical and Old Prussian-Lithuanian paganism, by reference to Simon Dach's use of 'solche Namen auch, Phöbus ist bei ihm daheime'.

The density of historical allusion, especially to the fate of Bishop Johannes at the end of the text, is, however, illusory, since here as throughout his prose-works Bobrowski adapts elements from a number of different areas to create only a deceptive fiction of reality: the motto 'Sante Catarine sta uns bi un lat uns nit vorderven,' (4:21) associated here with the Cathedral belongs in a completely different church; the Hochmeister responsible for killing M.'s ancestor was Albrecht, not Albertus; the story of the Bishop, walled-up by the 'Hochmeister des Ordens, der nicht wollte, daß du die Kirche hier befestigst', and who ate his own arms conflates the fates of two very different bishops, Johannes Clare and Dieterich von Cuba.[15]

This local colour, geographical, cultural, historical, mythological does not then create a self-contained story from a past world but presents instead a composite picture of the suffering inflicted on this area for centuries by the 'Deutscher Orden' and its direct and indirect successors, the smugly superior, condescending German burghers of Königsberg. M.'s return to his small, unheated room is linked with the betrayal of his ancestors and with the fate of the Bishop, – but also with that of an 'armen, totgeschlagenen Bären, den sie von irgendwoher bis in die Roßgärten gejagt haben' (4:18) and of an old dog which '[sich]

---

[15] See further details in 6:273 and Leistner, *Johannes Bobrowski*, pp.98-108.

unter die Fleischbänke verkrochen [hatte]' (4:21). All are displaced,
homeless, and facing death directly (M. already sees his poems as
'nachgelassen') and for M. himself the only short comfort comes from
his drunken contact with Lithuanians, 'Lustige Leute, die viel reden',
but people whom he leaves as soon as he has found a suitable beginning
for the poem he is writing: 'Gehabt euch wohl. Ich hab einen Anfang für
mein Gedicht' (4:19).

'M.' has lost contact with his culture without establishing a new
intellectual or cultural home, and in keeping with his role as an anonymous writer of nondescript poetry he lacks identity and orientation. This
makes of him a surprisingly negative figure, offering no positive
orientation. The search for this orientation is to become a recurrent
theme in Bobrowski's 'Künstlergeschichten', and while in 'M.' he finds
nothing, in another early (pre-*Levins Mühle*) work 'Epitaph für Pinnau'
(4:53-7) he finds a more positive model. 'Epitaph für Pinnau' draws its
material from the works of Hamann and from biographies of Kant to
produce an intense and convincing image of a meal that in reality could
never have taken place. Later 'Künstlergeschichten' were to make
constant use of the technique of collecting and re-combining realistic
historical detail in order to produce texts with a similarly wide breadth
of reference. This story deals again with outsiders, with the response of
Enlightenment luminaries at a lunch party to news of the suicide of a
young man Pinnau. It criticises the lack of insight they display into the
sense of frustration that could lead a young man like Pinnau to commit
suicide. The news of Pinnau's suicide causes some consternation and
leads to a lively discussion, but to nothing else:

> Ein lebhaftes Gespräch. Das die Docken, Kegel, Rhomben, selbst die
> Pyramide Schulz in geradezu ausgelassene Bewegung bringt. Obwohl doch
> alles auf seinen Stühlen bleibt. Man müßte schwerhörig sein: dann könnte man
> es ganz genießen wie auf einer Redoute. (4:57)

Despite the lack of comprehension by these worthies, the narrator's
response to the suicide is sympathetic. The story ends with an incanta-
tion of grace by the Oberhofprediger Schulz and the turn to the waiting
meal: 'versammelst uns täglich um deine Gabe, versammle uns, Herr,
um deinen Thron' (4:57). The grace does, however, serve as a reminder
of a Christian security which Pinnau denied himself, and in a further
development from 'Von nachgelassenen Poesien' Bobrowski does at
least present here a more positive character in the person of Hamann,

who is able to understand Pinnau's frustrations, but who, clearly more than Pinnau, is able to live with the pressures they involved.[16] Bobrowski's later works deal with the theme of such pressures in other ways.

Dorfgeschichten:
'Brief aus Amerika', 'Idylle für alte Männer', 'Roter Stein',
'Lobellerwäldchen', 'De homine publico tractatus'

A number of other works develop aspects of the early 'Begebenheit' and are 'Dorfgeschichten', tales set in village or rural surroundings. These include from the period before the completion of *Levins Mühle* 'Brief aus Amerika' (1961) and 'Idylle für alte Männer' (1962). After *Levins Mühle* they include 'Roter Stein' (1963), 'Lobellerwäldchen' (1964), 'De homine publico tractatus' (1964) and 'Stiller Sommer; zugleich etwas über Wachteln' (1965), all set in the area that Bobrowski knew from his childhood and later holidays. References to characters buying a gramophone (4:128), a car (4:35) and to the introduction of a radio service (4:137f.) indicate the first few decades of the twentieth century, while the absence of specific reference to National Socialism might indicate a period before 1933.

Texts from both before and after work on *Levins Mühle* draw on intimate personal knowledge of an area. In 'Lobellerwäldchen' this embraces minute topographical and social distinctions as well as the detail of the local form of children's swing (4:128f.); in 'Stiller Sommer' it is the list of popular local names (4:157) for the quail; in 'Roter Stein' the reference to the 'Heidenstein [...] Gustabalde' (4:82) and the description of a magical concoction.[17] Here too a development may be observed, from more simple genre pictures, dedicated to memories of this lost past, to more consciously created models of behaviour and attitudes that apply well beyond the specific rural

---

[16] In reality Hamann reacted with complete insensitivity towards the suicide, and in a further distortion of historical truth, Bobrowski has *Kant* repeat words actually written by Hamann: Kant's 'Cavalirement, wie er gelebt' (4:56) is based on Hamann's letter to Christian Kraus of April 17 1779: 'Den 12 huj. Vormittags erschoß sich Buchhalter Pynnow cavalierement, wie er gelebt'. *Briefwechsel*, vol.4, p.72.

[17] The reference to Gustabalde may be in inaccurate memory of two standing stones 'Bartel und Justebalde' in Bartenstein. See 6:339f. and *Ostpreußen, Westpreußen, Danzig, Memel: Unvergessene Heimat*, Rudolf Naujoks and Georg Hermanowski, Würzburg, n.d., illustr. 106.

surroundings in which they are set. Both 'Brief aus Amerika' (4:24-6) and 'Idylle für alte Männer' (4:30-40) incline more towards the sympathetic miniature, presenting elderly people confronted with their own weakness and mortality. In the former Erdmuthe Gauptate receives a letter from her son in America, informing her that he has decided not to visit her. She realises that they will never meet again. In the latter the oldest man on an agricultural estate, Klapschies, after an active morning in which he has had too much to drink, becomes aware of his own frailty and closeness to death and 'schläft schmerzlich bewegt ein' (4:39). In both cases Bobrowski sympathetically emphasises the simple continuing vitality of his characters, facing their own existence un-sentimentally and unheroically. In 'Brief aus Amerika' he upturns the expectation that such a letter always involves good news. The economic success of Erdmuthe's son (but for how long on the eve, perhaps, of an economic slump?) is bought at the price of isolation from his family and his cultural background, and the story ends with Erdmuthe using photographs of her son and daughter-in-law to light a fire for her milk. The names and part of the plot may be taken from Sudermann's 'Jons und Erdme' (6:277). In writing her own name, the names of the couple and their relationship on the backs of the photos Erdmuthe associates herself with them and gives this action an almost magical dimension – as though she is consigning her family (like herself – the story opens with her singing 'Brenn mich, brenn mich, brenn mich' – 4:24) to the protection of the pagan divinity of fire. Through this symbolic act she puts this part of her life behind her and starts afresh. There is no sentimentality from her, as there is none from her capitalist American son, who, with some help from his wife, is not allowing his own past and his awareness of the beauty of his home-country to interfere with his search for financial security. Clearly, however, in the text Bobrow-ski's sympathies lie with Erdmuthe as the living and loving mother and not with the calculating son.

'Idylle für alte Männer' follows Klapschies's morning activities, with the narrative voice oscillating between his and an external narrator, who occasionally adds explanatory comments: 'Alwast, so heißt nämlich der Bäcker in Laswehlen, für den gesagt, der es nicht wissen kann' (4:33) before summarising the events of the day and, as with Erdmuthe, using them in order to generalise on the human condition in the face of death:

Große Dinge, [...] das Leben, das die Leute miteinander treiben. [...] Wenn der Tod kommt, nimmt er die Mütze ab und sagt: Nun dreh dich man nicht zur Wand. Und der Tischler Thetmeyer kommt hinterher und nimmt Maß.
Da ist es schon besser, man hat seinen Sarg auf dem Dachboden, wie es sich gehört, und die Wäsche parat im Schrank und die Raute im Topf auf dem Fenster. (4:39f.)

These two stories provide pen-portraits of characters from Bobrowski's more immediately experienced Sarmatian past. Although written in the present tense, they look back to 'Begebenheit' in their inclination towards the genre picture and the anecdotal. A number of 'Dorfgeschichten' written after *Levins Mühle* have greater evident applicability to the present, with greater development of the idea of the 'model' illustrating a particular East German issue. In 'Roter Stein' (4:79-84) the model is one of greater tolerance, despite the brutality of the background. Here the reader is presented with a view of rural life characterised by robbery and violence. The background to events is a sickness affecting the cows of the neighbourhood for which only the old woman Lina Warszus has a form of cure. This consists of a mixture of sympathetic magic (use of snake poison to drive out poison) and pagan spells ('die Wörterchen', 4:83), but part of the preparation for the spell involves using the 'roter Stein' of the story's title, a Christian gravestone that Lina Warszus drags over from a local graveyard. The stone is described as 'ein Kreuz, aber doch mehr ein Block, weil die Arme nur eben angedeutet sind' (4:80), but the colour, the red of the title, is that of the heathen 'Gustabalde': 'Sie steht am Weg nach Sommerau, [...] ein Heidenstein. Der ist von ganz früher' (4:82).[18] This pagan productivity is, however, surrounded by direct and indirect expressions of the narrator's faith in divine benevolence: at the end of the story Lina decides to give up magic for fear of 'Die Sünde, die Sünde. Die mich einklagt beim himmlischen Vater' (4:83) and starts to drag the stone back to the graveyard. The narrator uses the same naive expression of the 'himmlischer Vater' for his own different conclusion:

Da kann der himmlische Vater hinuntersehen, wenn er meint, oder hinunterhören [...].
Laß ihn doch liegen, den Stein, sagt da vielleicht der himmlische Vater, der hinuntersehen kann, wenn er meint. Was wirst dich viel quälen, in deinem Alter. (4:83f.)

---

[18] See previous footnote, where the stone illustrated is described as 'rötlich'.

That Lina then dies, symbolically half lying on the Cross, is an almost
superfluous statement of Bobrowski's sympathies.

As in the relatively insignificant 'Stiller Sommer; zugleich etwas
über Wachteln' Bobrowski expresses within his narrative space a sense
of religious security. 'Roter Stein' is, however, particularly striking for
its lack of Christian dogmatism. Lina's syncretic religiosity, her mixture
of Christian and pagan elements, is treated sympathetically and
presented positively, because motivated by consideration for her
fellows. As in the poem 'Alter Hof in Häme', this understated combination of Christian and pagan may be read as an act of unstated protest
against any form of dogmatism, Christian or otherwise. The Christian
writer Bobrowski may be writing here of the love of the 'himmlischer
Vater', but the tolerance this divinity expresses for those whose
religiosity is more syncretic, less dogmatic, may be seen as a pattern for
the secular authorities who (the text was written in October 1963) had
been pursuing him since the beginning of the year.

In two further 'Dorfgeschichten' from 1964, 'Lobellerwäldchen'
(4:127-34) and 'De homine publico tractatus' (4:135-9) Bobrowski
develops the form as a means of social comment. 'Lobellerwäldchen'
(the title refers to an inn situated near the village of Lobellen), a story
dealing with adultery and murder, shows like the other stories detailed
geographical knowledge of the area in which it is set – on the south
bank of the River Szeszupe – and ironically anticipates readers who are
themselves acquainted with the area, people for whom the River
Szeszupe flows into the Memel 'bekanntlich erst hinter Lenkeningken
und bei Lobellen noch längst nicht' (4:128, my italics). This fiction of
the knowledgeable reader is presented from the very beginning of the
story, as the title 'Lobellerwäldchen' is met immediately in the first
lines of the story's text by a fictional reader's failure to differentiate
between inn and village: 'Also Lobellen'. This is then rejected in a
scrappy dialogue between narrator and reader. The story thus starts:

Lobellerwäldchen

Also Lobellen.
    Nein, Lobellen gar nicht.
    Aber na ja doch.
    Aber na nein.

Only then does the narrator get a grip on his story and explain: 'Da muß man erklären, daß Lobellen ein Dorf ist [...] und Lobellerwäldchen eine Gartenwirtschaft'. This device, where the story spills over from the text into the title, like a picture extended into its frame, provides an open structure that allows the narrator naturally to intervene throughout, guiding, commenting or explaining or, at the end, turning away from the scene with an eloquent lack of comment. The ignorance displayed in the anticipated reader's initial response is an essential part of the story-telling, forcing the narrator to explain and warning the reader against hasty conclusions or generalisations. The narrative thrust is hence towards accuracy, and in the text the narrative provides examples of the need for this: lists of terms to describe the inn Lobellerwäldchen: 'eine Gastwirtschaft, ein Gartenlokal, ein Etablissement und ganz gehörig abgelegen von Lobellen'; lists of the titles and nicknames of Herr Tesche: 'Zollbichs, Zoller, Zöllner, Zolloberwachtmeister oder wie sich das nennt' (4:127). The schnaps they drink also requires explanation: 'Schnaps also. Eine besondere Sorte Korn, genannt Kornus, mancher sagt, aber unterschiedlos auf allen Schnaps, Branntwein, wir sagen besser Kartoffelsprit' (4:130). All three lists lead to greater clarity: the word 'gehörig' confirms ironically the social divide, while the 'wie sich das nennt' reflects the ambiguous social standing of the tax collector and the final 'Kartoffelsprit' indicates the more mundane reality of the drink just eulogised.

'Lobellerwäldchen', like the later 'Rainfarn' and 'Der Mahner', starts with a long introductory description of a landscape, the background to the hostelry attended by the carriage-owning classes of the village of Lobellen. As in 'Stiller Sommer' Bobrowski is at pains to produce initially the illusion of an idyllic scene:

> Hier ist man so schön im Wald. [...] Da denkt man, daß es hier ein Land ist wie Musik. [...] Sonntag heißt Sonntag, weil da die Sonne scheint. Es ist so gut hier, daß einem nichts Vernünftigeres einfällt. (4:127-9)

This is, however, a very fragile idyll, since by the end of the story the sordid truth has been revealed: Tesche's wife has just had a child, Marthe, by the horse-trader Heinrich, and after a long drunken discussion on compensation, Tesche is overwhelmed by the sight of the money Heinrich has in his wallet, kills him and (presumably) disposes of the body. The actual murder is presented as a surmise concerning Heinrich's last words:

> Was wird er auch schon gesagt haben? [...]
> Und Heinrich will sich aufrichten: Tesche, laß sein, hör auf, Tesche.
> Da ist nun schon alles erzählt. (4:133).

The body remains undiscovered, and after a short change of perspective in which Bobrowski looks into the future of the child, he summarises discussions on Heinrich's disappearance. The publican Ambrassat comments to Tesche on the danger from 'Gesindel [...] hier an der Grenze' (ibid.), a phrase which could be taken to refer to the customs-officer Tesche, whose duties take him to the border, but this appears to be the full extent of their interest, and life at the inn quickly returns to normality, indicated with a short coda that repeats phrases from the text as though nothing had happened:

> Ambrassats Grammophon. Ambrassats Schaukel. Ambrassats siebenfarbiger Kornus. Hier ist man so schön im Wald. Ihr sauft auch wie die Löcher, sagt die Bussatsche. Der Kaiser, sag ich euch, sagt Herr Bussat, der saß und saß. (4:134)

In view of the significance that Bobrowski attaches to detail in this story, it is quite appropriate that Heinrich should be killed as a result of his own ignorance: after the drinking session when they discussed compensation he and Tesche fall asleep in the wood. He is awakened when licked by a stag and wakes Tesche to tell him. Although the narrator explains that the stag is not white at all but 'grau, etwas dunkler als Isländisch Moos', Heinrich insists on describing it as a 'weißer Hirsch', adding 'Das bringt, wer weiß, Glück?' (4:134). It is a totally inappropriate conclusion, since in Lithuanian folklore the colour white can also be a colour of death or misfortune (6:392), but it is this word 'Glück', so inappropriately used, that Tesche hears and that leads to his murdering Heinrich. Heinrich dies as a result of his own ignorance of local lore.

In 'Lobellerwäldchen' Bobrowski circumvents the 'Zwang zur Fabel' with a narrative form that immediately involves the reader as partner in a dialogue. In 'De homine publico tractatus' (4:135-9) he develops, as in 'Das Käuzchen', a version of the *exemplum*. From the title onwards the work introduces an ironic note as it illustrates the qualities required of the 'homo publicus', the 'public servant'. In the first paragraph the narrator indicates an independent, potentially intellectual perspective through his comments on the discoveries of 'Bayer aus Wien' and a quotation from Neander's hymn 'Lobe den

Herrn', although he also undermines his position as an intellectual through his references to 'Faunen und Floren oder Florenfaunen oder umgekehrt'. He argues idealistically that man needs more than his instinctual physical nature in order to survive in the 'Lebenskampf': 'Es ist ein angenehmes Gefühl [...] aber das reicht nicht' (4:135). Man needs social qualities and above all an awareness of moral responsibilities, 'die man fühlt. Im Innern'. The rest of the text then illustrates this through the figure of Petrat, the lowly postal official who exhibits the prime virtues: 'Einhaltung der Dienststunden,' 'Einhaltung der Kompetenzen,' the willingness 'sich als ein Diener der Gesellschaft zu betrachten' and 'Menschenkenntnis' (4:135-8).

The work combines details of everyday life in an unnamed small village just south of Königsberg with the form of the 'tractatus', and the use of four numbered sections to illustrate these virtues sustains just this fiction. But despite all the wealth of detail, the narrator claims not to know where Petrat worked as 'Posthalter', even though he links his behaviour to the very specific social background of the small village: 'In Abschwangen oder sonstwo, aber nicht in Uderwangen, Uderwangen ist größer' (4:135). He occasionally also widens the reference through his own comments:

> 3) Der Beamte hat sich als ein Diener der Gesellschaft zu betrachten.
> Man sagt leicht statt Gesellschaft Staat, ich erwähne das nur. Er hat sich zu betrachten, steht da, wir setzen hinzu: und entsprechend zu handeln. (4:137)

Finally the narrator emphasises the importance of the new concept of 'Gefühl':

> Man hat so etwas alles im Gefühl. Vielleicht sind Gefühle etwas Unsicheres, aber es hilft nichts, man muß sich schon auf sie verlassen. Wenn man alles erst genau und selber sehen wollte, was richtete man an. (4:139)

This final rhetorical question flies in the face of dogmatic or one-sided interpretations of reality that 'know', and presents as a counterbalance a perception of life that includes and accepts the unclear and uncertain. The significance of this within a dogmatic East Germany is self-evident, like that of the 'irrational' elements increasingly visible in *Wetterzeichen*. Such a lack of dogmatic clarity is essential if the individual is to fulfil his social duties, and, as Bobrowski indicates with a short reference to a couple 'in Allenburg oder auch nicht in Allenburg' it is also essential for a fulfilled human existence:

> In Allenburg oder auch nicht in Allenburg gab es ein Ehepaar, er schielte, sie
> schielte, die beiden haben sich im Leben nie gesehen. Sind zusammen-
> geblieben, über die bösen Zeiten vierzehn/achtzehn hinweg, und zusammen
> gestorben, vierundzwanzig.
> Das meine ich. (4:139)

Bobrowski parodies in the text elements of a rhetorically constructed argument: a hypothesis ('Man ist auf das Leben nicht eingerichtet') is followed by a counter-argument, based on statements of authority (Bayer and Neander). This is then qualified and illustrated with references to Petrat, before the conclusion is stated at the end of the story as a general rule and provided with a further last exemplification. This last section, the 'epimythium', does not, however, present the conventional abstract summary of the 'exemplum' but instead takes the form of a second image illuminating, on a different level, the same general moral: the possibility of a fulfilled existence not based on (ideological) clarity of vision, indeed the sense that ideological clarity might lead to a loss of humanity.

'Mäusefest'

In the interview with Irma Reblitz of May 1965 Bobrowski commented in passing on the possibility that musical forms underlay his works. Such words apply in very different ways to a number of stories that look back to the advent of National Socialism and the first few days of the Second World War: 'Rainfarn', written before August 1964, and 'Der Mahner', written January 1965, place the events of the 1930s in Bobrowski's 'Vaterstadt' Tilsit and in Königsberg. The early (March 1 1962) 'Lipmanns Leib' (4:27-31) presents an incident of casual murder, chilling in its pointlessness.[19] In 'Mäusefest' (September/October 1962) and the later 'Der Tänzer Malige' (March 11 1965) two relatively minor incidents from the first days of the German invasion of the East are presented. The full horror of the 'Endlösung' is left to the time after the story. The opera, in Bobrowski's image, is not played, but the themes are present.

'Lipmanns Leib' concerns the accidental drowning by some nationalistic Germans of a deranged Jew near the Memel village of Bittehnen.

---

[19] See Bobrowski's letter to Felix Berner of April 30 1962: 'Es lag mir daran, ein sozusagen durchschnittliches Verhalten zu zeigen: Achtlosigkeit im Umgang mit dem Nächsten — also keine Verbrecher' (6:279).

It and 'Mäusefest' were written before *Levins Mühle*. In 'Der Tänzer Malige' Bobrowski illustrates the cruelty of some German soldiers towards Jews in the first few days of the war, but also the possibility of artistic response to such cruelties. The most impressive of these stories is 'Mäusefest' (4:47-9), chosen as title for one of the collections. It is the merest incident, a 'Spiel von Licht und Schatten' from the first days of the war. A German soldier visits the shop of an elderly Jew Moise Trumpeter one night shortly after the invasion of Poland. The undramatic confrontation of the two protagonists is moderated by the moon, and the event demonstrates the strengths and weakness of both characters. The German is presented with all his naive condescension and his inability to recognise the individual: 'Mal sehen, wie das Judenvolk haust, wird er sich draußen gedacht haben' (4:48). His attitude to Poland is equally closed: 'Das Land heißt Polen. Es ist ganz flach und sandig. Die Straßen sind schlecht, und es gibt viele Kinder hier [...] und dieses Polen ist ganz polnisch' (4:48f.). Poverty, children and Catholicism; the cliché is complete. In contrast, the Jewish Moise Trumpeter shows an almost self-destructive preparedness to make distinctions when confronted with this boy soldier, and the moon has to warn him that these are irrelevant in his situation:

> Das war ein Deutscher, sagt der Mond, du weißt doch, was mit diesen Deutschen ist. [...] Das war ein Deutscher [...]. Sag mir bloß nicht, der Junge ist keiner, oder jedenfalls kein schlimmer. Das macht jetzt keinen Unterschied mehr. Wenn sie über Polen gekommen sind, wie wird es mit deinen Leuten gehn? (4:49)

The moon thus attempts to warn Moise of the impending danger. The narrator warns him too, though more indirectly, as he refers to the mice and their ability, emphasised three times in the text, to disappear:

> Nur die Mäuse [...] sind fort und so schnell, daß man nicht sagen kann, wohin sie gelaufen sind. [...] Die Mäuse laufen davon, man weiß gar nicht, wohin sie alle so schnell verschwinden können. [...] Die Mäuse sind fort, verschwunden. (4:48f.)

In implied contrast to Moise, the narrator here continues: 'Mäuse können das'. In a situation of threatening starvation (Moise's shop, we are told, is 'leer') as an event at the beginning of the Second World War this 'Mäusefest, in kleinem Rahmen [ist] nichts Besonderes, aber auch nicht ganz alltäglich' (4:48). It contains no violence, just the blinkered generalisations of youth, with all their anticipated consequences. These are, however, hinted at as the German decides to leave without saying 'Aufwiedersehn' – ordinary courtesy has become impossible in awareness of the possible circumstances of this next meeting. Moise himself appears at the end to become ever more one with the wall that he is leaning against, 'ganz weiß' (again the association of white with death, as in 'Lobellerwäldchen'), and the story ends with his understating: 'ich werd Ärger kriegen mit meinem Gott'. This could perhaps refer to the 'Ärger' he will have from the Nazis for being Jewish; it could also refer to a possible 'Ärger' with his Jewish God, because of his failure to react against the German as he could have done, even if only by hating him. In Psalm 139: 19-21 one finds the claim, made to curry favour with the divinity: 'Ich hasse ja, Herr, die dich hassen [...] Ich hasse sie in rechtem Ernst'. It is this that Moise, with his awareness of the young soldier's shared humanity, is unable to do,[20] and the story, although clearly anticipating the mass horrors of the coming 'Endlösung', contains only an atmosphere of threat and the implication of future suffering.

The guilty conscience:
'Rainfarn', 'Der Mahner'

This same atmosphere of threat is to be found in 'Rainfarn' and 'Der Mahner', to which the other aspect of Bobrowski's comment on the overture applies: the typical form of the long 'Introduktion', a passage *leading into* the (understated) culminating events, and in both cases this 'Introduktion' takes a similar form as the narrator describes at length the town in which the events later take place. 'Rainfarn' in particular shows the influence of Robert Walser, as it uses Walser's frequently repeated situation of the 'Spaziergang' (the title of one of his longer stories) and also the disturbing exaggerated idyllicism through which Walser both conceals and exposes his nightmares.

---

[20] While the notion of such hatred may appear perverse, in essence it is not illogical. Peake comments on this Psalm:

> If we hesitate to make [verse] 21 our own, we should nevertheless recognise that for the Psalmist the experience of communion with God was not an escape from life in this world. He knew that there is a conflict between good and evil, that God is not neutral in that struggle, and that we are not called upon to be neutral either. (p.442)

The story is set in Tilsit, in an unspecified period before the annexation of the Memelland.[21] It uses the folklore belief that wearing a sprig of tansy (*tanacetum vulgare*) on 'Johannistag' (June 24) can make the wearer invisible, and the narrator imagines the uses to which this could be put during a walk from one end of the town, the nudist camp Sonnenbad, to the other, the Königin-Luisen-Brücke marking the border to the Memelland. The walk takes the narrator from a scene of dubious childhood pleasure to a place of definite historical guilt at the failure to help the victims of Nazism, and this state of invisibility is viewed increasingly critically as a form of existence preventing involvement in historical events. Wearing the tansy one is 'allein', then 'weit fort', metaphorically even 'gestorben'. Unable to participate, the wearer functions outside the nudist colony as a mere voyeur and politically as an impotent observer, and 'der Beobachter sieht nichts' (4:116).

A number of devices prevent even the possibility that the early parts of this work could be misinterpreted as reconstructing an idyll. The narrator quibbles over the distinction between 'Wald' and 'Wäldchen' ('was nennt man nicht alles Wald'), deliberately evoking memories of an infamous 'Buchenwald'. He presents a botanically detailed description of the tansy, with a touch of parody, here of Ernst Jünger, whose faithful observations of the beauty of nature blinded him to the reality of combat he was involved in. In describing Tilsit itself he avoids pathos through ironic or deflating comments and episodes, and the story has a particular personal dimension as he appears in such comments to be retracting his own 1946 poem 'Die Vaterstadt':

> [...] Ohne Maßen
> geliebte Stadt, so alt und schön geworden. (2:83)

This poem refers to the 'Luisendenkmal', a famous local statue, in the following terms:

> [...] Und aus dem schön gedrängten
> Buschwerk steigt auf das Mal der schmerzbeengten
> geliebten Königin –

---

[21] For a fuller analysis see Werner Zimmermann, 'Johannes Bobrowski: "Rainfarn"' in *Deutsche Prosadichtungen unseres Jahrhunderts: Interpretationen für Lehrende und Lernende* , Düsseldorf 1969, vol.2, pp.355-62.

In 'Rainfarn' this is reduced to the 'Denkmal der preußischen Luise [...] der großfüßigen Landesmutter'. The 'Deutsche Kirche' (known as the 'Deutschordenskirche' and the 'Stadtkirche') is likewise presented with diminished respect. The 1946 poem had stressed the poet's emotional attachment:

> Am Ufer kniet seit vielen hundert Jahren
> der Kirchenbau, ergraut längst und gestillt.
> Und wer noch je den Strom dahin gefahren,
> dem griff ins Herz des heitern Turmes Bild:
> Auf Kugeln ruhend, aufgeschnellt und mild
> in Schwüngen wachsend und in Bögen schwillt
> er auf mit Lauben, lichten, wunderbaren. (2:82)

The story emphasises instead an anecdote from the church's history: 'die deutsche Kirche: getreppter Turm, viergeschossig, mit kupfernem Helm und doppelter Galerie, sehr schön, der Napoleon hat ihn mit-nehmen wollen' (4:116).[22]

With the tansy in one's hat it is possible to walk unseen through the town from one end to the other, but:

> Muß man das andere Ende finden?
> [...] mit dem Rainfarn [...] wohl nicht. Ungesehen, also allein – da gelangt man ans Ende nicht. [...] Da ist man weit fort. (4:115)

The bridge at the other end of the town marks the border, the end of National Socialist Germany, and 'auf die Brücke zu gehen ein paar Familien, Väter, Mütter, Kinder, mit ein paar Taschen und Körben und können erst wieder stehn bleiben und atmen, wo Deutschland zuende ist' (4:116). By wearing the tansy, the narrator chooses non-participation.[23] At the end of the story he finally accepts the need to

---

[22] Together with the reference to music at Jakobsruhe, this anecdote echoes Suder-mann's story 'Die Reise nach Tilsit': 'In Tilsit ist ein Kirchturm [...] der ruht auf acht Kugeln, und darum hat ihn der Napoleon immer nach Frankreich mitnehmen wollen'. Hermann Sudermann, *Litauische Geschichten*, ed. B.J.Kenworthy, Walton on Thames 1971, p.57.

[23] This fern also removes the wearer from the dictates of time, and the narrator recognises a priest Connor, who has already died, and sees an incident described in Wilhelm Storost's *Ein Nachlaß schlichter litauischer Menschen* (1948) in which a gust of wind blows some notes from his balcony table. The same book is used in *Litauische Claviere* as the source of the Budras incident.

throw away the tansy and help the victims of Nazism, but admits that it is too late: 'aber wir haben das ja nicht getan' (4:117).

'Rainfarn' thus presents a 'Spaziergang' through Tilsit, and follows as it does the pattern of Bobrowski's own life, from childhood innocence through the missed opportunity to resist, vague or pointless as this might have been, to the sense of guilt from which he suffered in maturity, a sense of guilt personalised but also broadened in a shift from 'man' to 'wir' in the text. As in the poem 'Der Blitz' of the same period, 'Rainfarn' too creates an underlying 'Heiterkeit' which paradoxically emphasises the seriousness of his literary intentions, with the 'Sonnenbad' and the magic of tansy eventually rejected and replaced by the guilty observation of the spectacle of the refugees and reflections on what might have been.

In 'Der Mahner' Bobrowski turns to Königsberg and the fate of a deranged Lithuanian preacher shortly before the Nazi takeover. Here too the work concentrates on the personal guilt of omission in a historically decisive situation. Like 'Rainfarn' it begins with a long topographical introduction. Here too Bobrowski takes considerable measures to maintain distance, as the first few paragraphs concentrate on the peripheral element of the nicknames of towns and on the justification for calling Königsberg 'Pregel-Rom'. As in 'Rainfarn' the narrator also maintains distance through his play with words – not here the distinction between 'Wald' and 'Wäldchen' but concerning 'hoch' and 'Oberteich':

> Am höchsten allerdings ist der Oberteich, [...] und er fängt gleich an, wo die Bodenerhebung ihre volle Höhe erreicht hat und nun so weitergeht, nordwärts, als eine Art Hochebene, aber so hoch denn doch wieder nicht, so ganz wohl nicht.
> Auf jeden Fall trifft die Bezeichnung Oberteich zu, er ist oben und ist ein richtiger Teich [...].
> Also der Oberteich macht sich oben breit und tiefer, nach Süden, der Schloßteich. Aber der macht sich eher schmal als breit. (4:146)

Again as in 'Rainfarn' he draws attention to himself through a shift from a disembodied voice talking through the neutral third-person 'man' to a 'wir' with actual physical presence: 'Man kann, wie gesagt, hinaufsteigen, aber wir tun es nicht, wir stellen uns vor den Turm [...], lehnen uns meinetwegen an die Turmwand' (4:147).

Although the narrative concerns, as the title indicates, the fate of the Lithuanian 'Mahner', the narrator finds himself constantly diverted away from him by 'Skurrilitäten'. He does not follow him ('wir gehn ihm, denke ich, nicht nach, wir kennen ihn ja nun') or obey his command 'Haltet Gottes Gebote'. Instead he digresses to narrate the story of 'Adelgreiff und Schmalkilimundis oder Schmalkallaldis' (4:147), a historical predecessor for such a preacher, and then narrates a long anecdote (4:148f.) about a drunkard whose story he arbitrarily and quite unfairly conflates with that of the Lithuanian. Only too late the narrator recognises that such self-indulgent narrative diversions deprive him of the opportunity to follow this Lithuanian: 'Wir wollten dann aber doch noch dem Mann nachgehn, viel zu spät leider'. Instead he is confronted with marching Nazis. For these the narrator has only contempt: 'ein ganzer Zug, braun in braun, bis auf die Augen, die blau sein sollten, nach Möglichkeit. Aber wir kommen um die Skurrilitäten, oder wie man es nennen will, nicht herum' (4:149). Anecdotal 'Skurrilitäten' have given way to real history, and Bobrowski brings his story to a speedy end which again anticipates in an understatement the immediate horrific future: using a complicated coda he twice lists many of the characters he has introduced in the story: the 'stiller Litauer', the 'Saufkopp', the 'Dompfarrer' and 'Pfarrer'. Initially he sees them in their relation to a 'Straßenflötist Preuß', whom they fail to help distinguish between Communists and Nazis. Then he sees them in their future role as victims of the Nazis – 'Staatsfeind oder Volksfeind', 'asoziales Element', 'geistig minderwertig' (4:149f.). The double recapitulation of these persons, first as sharing guilt and then as victims, ends when Bobrowski focuses on the final confrontation between the 'Mahner' and the Nazis: 'Haltet Gottes Gebote, ruft er ihnen entgegen, als sie kommen. Aber das tun sie nicht' (4:150).

The narrator's own sense of moral failure is overwhelming: his selfindulgence, his joy at 'Skurrilitäten' and anecdotes, his literary play with echoes of Thomas Mann's novel *Doktor Faustus* have made him lose sight of the guilt such 'Heiterkeit' brings with it. As in 'Rainfarn' Bobrowski implies through his narrator that his own response to historical events was belated and inadequate. Beyond that, however, the stories illustrate Bobrowski's concern, evident from interviews, that works of literature may lose contact with the reality they draw on. It is the criticism of 'Heiterkeit' that occurs in 'Der Blitz' and in *Levins Mühle*, but also in such asides as his comment on passages from Günter Grass's *Hundejahre* which he experienced at the 1962 Gruppe 47 meeting:

> Hier verselbständigt sich der Anlaß, das Motiv, das Thema, indem es sich als Kunstwert, als literarisches Experiment entdeckt. [...] Zum Schluß hat sich der Anlaß verflüchtigt, das Kunstwerk hat sich ausschließlich als Kunstprodukt an die Stelle des vorhanden gewesenen Anliegens gesetzt. (4:446)

Later Künstlergeschichten:
'Junger Herr am Fenster', 'D.B.H.', 'Boehlendorff'

In 'Rainfarn' and 'Der Mahner' Bobrowski's attention was directed against his own sense of guilt, the issue of artistic responsibility with which he felt constantly confronted. Other works intend self-orientation with reference to his more immediate surroundings, and these constitute the most productive type of short story in these volumes. In a series of 'Künstlergeschichten' written after *Levins Mühle* Bobrowski presented what he described in an interview of November 1964 as 'Geschichten, die sich mit dem Widerspruch revolutionärer Personen und Persönlichkeiten, historischer Persönlichkeiten, mit ihrer Gesellschaft befassen' (4:474). Bobrowski refers here explicitly to 'Boehlendorff' (4:97-112), but other texts that he clearly had in mind included 'Junger Herr am Fenster' (i.e. Arthur Schopenhauer) (4:73-6) and 'D.B.H.' (i.e. Dietrich Buxtehude) (4:68-72), both probably written immediately after the completion of *Levins Mühle* in August/September 1963.

At a time when his relations with the East German authorities were at their most difficult, his works present models of behaviour in difficult situations, especially in situations which involved, as with himself, forms of cultural or physical exile. He concentrates still on the outsider, but unlike 'M.' in 'Von nachgelassenen Poesien' or Pinnau in 'Epitaph für Pinnau' the outsider is now presented not as a passive victim but in the endeavour to attain a satisfactory existence. The turning point in the search for more positive role models had been, I suggested, 'Epitaph für Pinnau', where Pinnau's despair and suicide were counterbalanced by Hamann's active and positive response to this society. Hamann remained, however, peripheral, a sign for the reader to interpret rather than a figure to relate to, and indeed, the significance of this sign is easily lost as the story satirises the successful but insensitive. With one major exception the protagonists in the later works turn away from self-destructive tendencies, and with Schopenhauer and Buxtehude this orientation involves acceptance of their (very different) forms of exile as a way of life. For all the differences, in this resilience they follow Hamann, not 'M.' or Pinnau.

'Junger Herr am Fenster' takes the form of an interior monologue by
the young Arthur Schopenhauer who is presented surveying the spot
where his father hanged himself.[24] His identity is never explicitly stated,
but it is clear from the reference to his mother as 'die geborene
Trosiener' (4:74) and to the gifted sister Adele that this is Schopenhauer, whose father did indeed die under strange, possibly suicidal
circumstances.[25] In the monologue he recalls his almost sadistic
presentation of details of his father's suicide to his mother and sister,
whom he holds partly responsible. He also, however, comes to terms
with his inevitable loss of home (which is identified through the street-
name Jopengasse as Danzig) as he sees that he will have to accompany
his mother and sister into virtual exile. The story maintains the fiction of
authenticity, with convincing use of realistic details of time and place,
but also alters significant details of Schopenhauer's own life, as well as
introducing elements from a work of fiction, Thomas Mann's *Budden-
brooks*.

Schopenhauer's character is presented in all its ambiguity, reflecting
the well-known contradiction that the historical Schopenhauer combined
a theoretical contempt for life with a pronounced desire for self-
preservation: his fascination here with his father's suicide does not
obscure his orientation towards life, while despite his sense that his
mother and sister have behaved disgracefully, (indeed he fantasises that
they are killed in revenge) he feels constantly drawn to follow them and
be in their presence.[26] The parallel to Bobrowski with his ambiguous
feelings towards his fellow-Germans is clear.

The text begins with a few lines presenting the difficulties and life of
a Johann Rosenmüller (1619-1684), using as introduction his choral
piece 'Welt ade, ich bin dein müde'. This is, however, instantly rejected
by the narrator: 'Das soll man hier gar nicht sagen' (4:73), before the
contradiction between Rosenmüller's work and his long and successful

---

[24] The text has been well analysed by Renate von Heydebrand in 'Überlegungen zur
Schreibweise Johannes Bobrowskis: Am Beispiel des Prosastücks "Junger Herr am
Fenster"', in *Der Deutschunterricht*, 21 (1960), no.5, 100-25.

[25] By drowning in Hamburg, not hanging in Danzig.

[26] Historically, after leaving the north, Schopenhauer's mother enjoyed a life of
considerable elegance in Weimar and rejected her son's 'Lamentiren über die dumme
Welt und das menschliche Elend', as she called it, refusing to let him interfere with her
socialising (quoted by Heydebrand, p.117).

life is revealed. Already in these first paragraphs the main theme of the story, the tension between theoretical pessimism and the need for practical optimism is anticipated before being developed in the main body of the work. This is a specific 'promythium', anticipating the main story not through an abstract moral but by introductory exemplification. As such it inverts the method used in 'De homine publico tractatus' and in 'Das Käuzchen', whereby the problem of the main story is explained or summarised by another shorter incident or image set at the end, the 'epimythium'.

Using the figure of Schopenhauer contemplating the suicide of his father, Bobrowski almost immediately gives the incident wider – if also highly personal – significance:

> Warum sollte ich überhaupt reden, mit euch [...]? Nur weil ich nicht leben kann ohne euch, ohne eure Hände und eure Stimmen? Ohne das Blut daran, ohne den Rost? (4:73)

The combination of blood, hands and rust is significant in other works: in 'Gertrud Kolmar' (1:116) occur the lines 'umher / geht meine Sprache und ist / rostig von Blut', while in 'Die Daubas II' one may read:

> Aber ich hör ja,
> der ich vergeßlich bin:
> sie reden im Schatten,
> immer sind sie's, es ist
> meine Sprache, nah
> und rostig von Blut. (2:311)

Above all in 'Wiedererweckung' it is associated with the German guilt of the 'Endlösung', and the image thus links the unhappy 'junger Herr' directly with Bobrowski himself, who was appalled by much that his fellow Germans had done but also inevitably drawn to them. For Schopenhauer in this story, the guilty people are his family, whose behaviour has driven his father to suicide:

> jetzt wo es sich herumskandalt durch die Stadt: die geborene Trosiener sei so schuldlos nicht an dem Vorfall, dem Suicid [...]. Ihr ewiges Gerede hat man doch noch im Ohr, das vom conflict, den Konventionen und diesen Passionen, diesen Trosienerschen, die also mit den Konventionen im Streit lägen – das war wohl der Ausdruck. (4:74f.)

He concludes, however, as he began, with his admission of dependence on them:

Nur fortgehn, euch nachgehn, euch meine Sätze zum Zählen überlassen, hören
auf euer Geschwätz mit verteilten Rollen, nicht erwarten, daß ihr sie singt.
Nur weil ich ohne eure Stimmen nicht leben kann? Weil ich ohne eure Hände
nicht leben kann? (4:76)

'D.B.H.' presents the problems of exile and artistry from a very different perspective. It too takes the form of an interior monologue, whose
protagonist Dietrich Buxtehude (1637-1707) is seen here in Lübeck on
the day on which he first meets the youth Nicolaus Bruhns, who
(historically) was soon to become his favourite pupil.[27] This first
decisive meeting is, however, presented almost incidentally through a
heavy mesh of allusion and cross-reference, as Buxtehude's character,
his doubts and fears as well as their partial overcoming, appear through
repeated images of 'Licht' and 'Libanon' and references to his choral
works 'Herr, ich lasse dich nicht, du segnest mich denn' and 'Liebster
meine Seele saget'. Buxtehude is shown (historically incorrectly) as
seeing himself in exile from his native Helsingör, from which, however,
as with Bobrowski and Sarmatia, he draws his inspiration.

The choice of Buxtehude as a form of model is not surprising.
Bobrowski had learnt to play the organ in Königsberg and had shown
interest in the composer since at the latest the early 1950s. In 1952,
possibly under the immediate influence of reading Stahl's biography of
Buxtehude,[28] he had written 'Dietrich Buxtehude' as part of his 'Regenbogen' cycle (2:206).[29] He also possessed the bibliophile edition of

---

[27] The short story has been analysed, with different conclusions, by, among others,
Eberhard Haufe, 'Johannes Bobrowski und Dietrich Buxtehude' in *SZNB* 189-236 and
Alfred Behrmann in *Facetten: Untersuchungen zum Werk Johannes Bobrowskis*,
Stuttgart 1977, pp.27-45, both of whom provide details of the musical background. See
also the comments by Bernd Leistner in *Johannes Bobrowski*, pp.95ff.

[28] Wilhelm Stahl, *Dietrich Buxtehude*, Kassel 1937.

[29] Later a version of the poem 'J.S.Bach' (June 25 1958) referred to him indirectly:

Daß er [i.e. Bach] die Meerbucht sah –
einen [i.e. Buxtehude] dort, der herging
hinter Feuern unsichtbar,
der die Planeten rief
mit einer alten Qual. (1:149)

The later poem 'Nänie' (October 11 1960) is annotated as dedicated to Buxtehude and
presents him as subject to very pagan desires, influences ('der mich gerufen hat') and
inspiration (expressed in the imagery of the 'mörderische concentus der Welt' and the

Buxtehude's works published by the 'Glaubensgemeinde Ugrino' between 1925 and 1937 and he admired the work of Hans Henny Jahnn, who had founded the fellowship, had helped initiate the edition, and had written of Buxtehude in his own novel *Fluß ohne Ufer*.[30]

Here too Bobrowski presents the fiction of realistic detail but arbitrarily changes biographies, and while drawing much of his documentary detail from Stahl's work, the figure he depicts relies in important aspects on the character presented in *Fluß ohne Ufer*. In Jahnn's novel Buxtehude's life before he moved to Lübeck is characterised as 'von Landesverrat und Sodomie befleckt' (quoted by Haufe in *SZNB* 405, FN 38), and the novel emphasised the physical, almost pagan dimension to his productivity, in particular his composition of a lost suite of seven planet sonatas. Echoes of the *fictional* Buxtehude's past – his apparent flight: 'dieses Licht, [...] das hinter mir her war, auf der Flucht hier herunter ins Nebelland' (4:70); his erotic associations with Bruhns: 'Du wirst über den Orgeln liegen wie über Weibern, dich aufrichten über den Orgeln wie über Weibern' (4:72); the distinctly pre-Christian situation of a work like 'Herr, ich lasse dich nicht, du segnest mich denn'[31] run through the text.

Buxtehude here is an artist who draws from two potentially contradictory traditions: the pagan tradition of the cosmic music of the planets, and the Christian North German tradition of the church cantata. This combination and the concomitant tension infuse the text, and the tension itself reaches its climax in a moment of self-doubt concerning the experiences that underlie his works:

> Und soll ich jetzt sagen: Es ist alles vorüber, es zählt nicht?
> Gut: Es ist alles vorüber, es zählt nicht.
> Du findest es auf, und es ist vorüber.
> Du findest es auf, und es zählt nicht.

But these doubts are immediately overcome:

> Da ist es gesagt.
> Und wird zurückgenommen. (4:71)

---

god Helios), but at the same time secure in a Christian belief that held out the promise of a peace which his secular life did not know: 'Frieden / ist uns versprochen'.

[30] *Fluß ohne Ufer*, Munich 1950.

[31] The reference is to Jacob's wrestling at Peniel (Genesis 32: 23ff.).

These doubts are not substantiated in biographies of Buxtehude and constitute an evidently personal experience of Bobrowski (aged forty-six and already ailing when he wrote the text), who uses the meeting with Bruhns to confront Buxtehude (aged, at the time, forty-four) with the need to review his life and work and reconsider his attitude to the source of his inspiration. The speed with which the doubts appear overcome is a sign of his own confidence, as he experiences the memory of light and composes in a total synthesis:

> Weit zurück, über der Bucht, das Geleucht. Nicht das Licht selber, ich weiß: der Widerschein. Oder das Echowerk: draußen über der Bucht. Wie in Helsingör: es erlischt. Erst noch Flöte und Terz, Gedackt und Krummhorn eine Weile, dann Gemshorn allein, am Ende nur: über dem Sund der Wind. (4:71)

After this creative activity Buxtehude's thoughts turn for a while to his one possible physical link with this source of his inspiration, which runs through his pupils, and especially through Bruhns: 'Einer von euch Libanesen wird hingehn. Für mich. Wird sehen [...]. Sehen das Licht [...]. Bruhns, du wirst das tun' (4:71f.). It is an attitude of selfless hope, not anticipating a renewal of contact, and as with 'Es war eigentlich aus' the link to the earliest 'Sarmatian' poems resurrects itself. Here too the rejection of longing is complete; the withdrawal even from the process of overcoming this longing appears irrevocable:

> Und wiederkehren wirst du [i.e. Bruhns, who is to return to the source of Buxtehude's inspiration but not come back to tell Buxtehude about it] nicht. Ich werde dich nicht fragen können. Warum auch? E war der erste Ton, zu Erden man mich führet.
> Aber was ich gesehen habe und nicht mehr sehen werde: sieh du es für mich. Noch eh ich steig vom E ins H. (4:72)

In this conclusion two lines of Buxtehude's thoughts assert themselves contrapunctally: the selfless desire that his pupils should experience the sensual inspiration that he had experienced and that filled his spiritual works, and the Christian certainty surrounding his own death and salvation. At the beginning of the work stood a motto that varied some lines from the 'Trauergedicht' written after Buxtehude's death. Here at the end the Buxtehude figure itself, still very much alive, quotes from the same work. It is, in context, an anachronism, but its existence above time lifts this hope too beyond the story and into Bobrowski's present.

Bobrowski's longest short story 'Boehlendorff' was written between April and July 1964 and deals with the last years of the minor Baltic writer Kasimir Ulrich Boehlendorff (1775-1825), who had been marginally involved in the short-lived Swiss Revolution of 1797/8 and had also been an acquaintance of Hölderlin.[32] After being touched by these political and cultural events, Böhlendorff had returned to the Courland area in 1803 where, after a period working as a private tutor, he went insane and finally committed suicide. The story is clearly related to Bobrowski's 'Generalthema' in that it deals with events peculiar to a part of the German East, the German-speaking land-owning gentry of Latvia (the 'German Barons') under Tsarist Russian rule at the beginning of the nineteenth century.

Bobrowski's attention was drawn to this figure when Bernd Jentzsch gave him a copy of *Das Baltische Dichterbuch* for his 47th birthday in April 1964.[33] Within a few days, he had started to write a story, as he wrote to Jentzsch, 'über den Poeten Kasimir Anton Ulrich Boehlendorff' (*SZNB* 129). The plot, such as it is, is relatively simple and comprises episodes from the life of Boehlendorff during the period of madness leading up to his suicide. These show him in his dealings with members of the German land-owning classes of the area and with the 'Volk' surrounding them. A recurrent theme is the close co-operation between land-owners and the church, both ironically in the intimation of an affair between the Baron von Campenhausen and Pfarrer Giese's wife (4:98) and more seriously in the accusation by the priest Marienfeld that Boehlendorff's influence on the poor of the area is leading to 'Abgabeverweigerungen [...] Unwillen bis vor die Kirchen-tür' (4:109). It is after hearing these accusations that Boehlendorff kills himself.

The material on Boehlendorff from the *Baltisches Dichterbuch* was very sketchy, but Bobrowski made little evident use of other readily available sources. His interest in Boehlendorff as a historical individual

---

[32] A number of critics have commented on aspects of this story: Bernd Jentzsch, 'Schöne Erde Vaterland', in *Johannes Bobrowski: Selbstzeugnisse und Beiträge über sein Werk*, p.129; Mechthild Dehn and Wilhelm Dehn, *Johannes Bobrowski: Prosa*, Munich 1972, pp.11-17; Horst Nalewski, 'Metaphernstruktur in Johannes Bobrowskis Erzählung "Boehlendorff"', in *Weimarer Beiträge*, 19 (1973), no.4, 103-18; Günter Hartung, 'Bobrowskis Boehlendorff', in *SZNB* 261-92. More recent is an 'Exkurs' by Schütze in his *Natur und Geschichte* (pp.158-71).

[33] *Das baltische Dichterbuch*, ed. Freiherr von Grotthuß, Reval 1895 (2nd. ed.).

was not great. Instead, as elsewhere, he presents a mixture of factual detail and deliberate, almost arbitrary invention or distortion. Apart from the name, Bobrowski altered details of Boehlendorff's publications, while the starting point of the story, an appeal in a journal for a 'Kreditbrief', though factual, was made in number 104 of the journal concerned, not 24. The story's conclusion, Boehlendorff's suicide, took place on April 10 1825, not in late April as in the text. Instead of attempting to attain factual accuracy Bobrowski assimilates material from the life and works of Hölderlin, especially transferring some of Hölderlin's friends to Boehlendorff's circle of acquaintances. Here too he alters, and, for example, the reference to Hölderlin's revolutionary friend Sinclair as a 'Seeoffizier' is not biographically justified. Of much greater significance, however, is the attribution to Boehlendorff of a question taken from the 'Ältestes Programm des deutschen Idealismus', a work conventionally accepted to have been written at least in part by Hölderlin: 'Wie muß eine Welt für ein moralisches Wesen beschaffen sein?'[34] It is a question that plays a central part in the story as a whole.

The starting point for the story is another question: 'Was weiß man von Boehlendorff?' (4:97), with, as in 'Epitaph für Pinnau', what people 'know' differing considerably according to their social standing.[35] The story as a whole forms an answer of sorts, before, at the end, the results are summarized:

> Guter Mensch. Was noch?
> Das ist, womöglich, schon etwas, und, womöglich, ist es unnötig, mehr über Boehlendorff zu wissen. (4:112)

What lies between is a depiction of a character tortured by frustration at his own impotence to right the wrongs he sees about him.

---

[34] The use of such details from the life and works of another writer is not unique: in 'Epitaph für Pinnau' Bobrowski puts words historically written by Hamann into Kant's mouth, while in *Litauische Claviere* (3:313) he fills out his life of Donelaitis with a letter actually written by Hamann.

[35] With 'Pinnau' 'Boehlendorff' also shares the fact that the titular hero commits suicide in face of the misery of his surroundings; of both it could be said: 'er hat gewollt, was nicht möglich ist'. In both too the main character is commented upon primarily by the very people who drove him to suicide (the wealthy bourgeoisie of Kant's lunch and the landed German gentry of Latvia), while more positive comments by the 'Volk' are reduced to a minimum and are stereotyped. The cook comments in 'Epitaph' on Pinnau and his family: 'Gute Menschen [...] Hübscher Mensch mit schwarze Haare' (4:55),

The story is remarkable for the vivid presentation, through 'erlebte Rede' and interior monologue, of Boehlendorff's growing madness, symptomatic for which are 'signs' he is convinced he can read in the marks of beetle holes in wood and of human hands on fence-posts, so that he can claim: 'Alles aufgeschrieben. Im Buch der Geschichte auf den Scheunentoren. In den Wäldern zu lesen, auf den abgehauenen Stämmen, und auf der Erde'. By the end he is himself contributing to the signs as he scratches them into stone slabs. As a further recurrent image, here of his sense of provincial claustrophobia, he experiences imaginary 'Zäune [...] hoch und weißgewaschen' (4:101) and has apocalyptic visions of a mighty flood that will sweep everything away, all the local villages: 'Galtern, Strasden, Rittelsdorf, Walgalen, Birsch' (4:99). In anticipation of this flood, he tramps the roads and treads down the soil. Like the mad beggar Morkus in 'Litauische Geschichte' (4:41f.), who threw money he collected into a lake, hoping it would rise and drown the 'Zarengeneral', his actions were futile, undertaken in the insane hope that a single individual could somehow affect historical progress. As with Morkus, however, they were actions undertaken in a spirit and with a hope of which the 'Volk' and Bobrowski himself could approve.

Boehlendorff, like Morkus, is rewarded with limited posthumous fame, even though his descriptions of the social revolution he has already experienced are met with horror by the 'Volk':

> Was sagen die Leute?
> Sitzen und schlagen die Hände vors Gesicht, seufzen zwischen den Fingern hindurch: Gräßlich. Mit geschlossenen Augen. (4:104)

After his suicide, his sparsely attended funeral provides the opportunity for reflection on the character but also on the choice of such a character as subject for a story. Then the sky floods the very area that he had been preparing, not with a destructive flood but with light:

> Der Lichtschein hat sich dem finsteren Himmel über das Haupt geworfen, ganz hoch steht er, und beginnt zu stürzen, jetzt, zu sinken, und breitet sich von oben her über die ganze Verfinsterung aus, über den harten Himmel, an dem der Sturm aufkommt und dieses Knirschen umherführt, von der Bucht heran, landeinwärts über Galtern, Strasden, Rittelsdorf, Walgalen, Birsch, über das Tal hin, tiefer nun, um den Ginster, aber dann wieder hinaus auf die Bucht, eine weiße Straße legt sich weithin über das Wasser. (4:111f.)

---

while of Boehlendorff the repeated refrain is 'guter Mensch' (4:111f.).

In 'Litauische Geschichte' Morkus achieved nothing, and 'der Himmel' finally kills his enemy with smallpox.[36] Similarly, Boehlendorff contributes nothing to any all-destroying flood, which is replaced here by the image of a flood of light. Where, however, Boehlendorff's fury only allows him to seek signs of a flood in response to his sense of moral outrage, the narrator suggests in this image an alternative, as the light counteracts the darkness and its attendant 'Knirschen', the 'gnashing of teeth' beloved of writers of the Old Testament, and provides a miraculous path over the water. As the whole story unites both Bobrowski's 'Gesamtthema' of the Germans and the European East and the theme of the suffering alienated individual, so this last image oscillates in its reference between the prophecy of historical change and the hope for individual redemption. Such an ambiguous ending does not confirm the fulfilment of Boehlendorff's hopes and aspirations, but neither does it denigrate their failure in his lifetime. It is an indication of the important fact that 'Boehlendorff' is not an 'expression of hopelessness' but a 'warning of how history was coming close to repeating itself'.[37]

This warning to the present is made specific in a central and evidently repeated episode in the story, when Boehlendorff utters the question that accompanies him wherever he goes: 'Wie muß eine Welt für ein moralisches Wesen beschaffen sein?' The question, born of his own experiences in the more revolutionary Western Europe, reflects his sense of the inadequacies of social structures in his homeland. Not surprisingly, it remains unanswered, met only by expressions of cynicism or lethargy or a destructive quibbling:

> Moralisches Wesen, ach du lieber Gott. Das ist jeder selber, meint jeder selber, da kann er hinkommen, wo er will, der Boehlendorff. Moralisches Wesen.

---

[36] After Morkus and the 'Zarengeneral' have both died the historical change that does occur takes a totally different form, coming not in a flood but in fire:

> Der Eiserne ist irgendwann umgekommen, in seinem Bett, weil ihm der Himmel die Blattern angehängt hat. [...] Und nach ihm ist es auch bald aus gewesen mit dem Zaren.
> In dem Jahr hat es Feuer gegeben in Škuodas , und wer sich zu fürchten hatte, hat sich gefürchtet und ist davongelaufen. (4:41f.)

[37] Dennis Tate, 'Unexpected affinities: Johannes Bobrowski's "Boehlendorff" and Franz Fühmann's "Barlach in Güstrow" as landmarks in the early evolution of GDR literature', in John Wieczorek (ed.) *Johannes Bobrowski (1917-1965)*, p.47.

Und eine Welt?
Das uns zur Prüfung auferlegte Jammertal?
In dem es sich übrigens ordnet.
Und beschaffen sein?
Und muß?
Wir hatten alle mal Ideen, sagt Pastor Beer. Und, wie man sagt: Wasser ver-
läuft sich. (4:103)

Against this background of collective moral cynicism ('Moralisches Wesen [...] Das ist jeder selber'), as well as anticipated historical and social stagnation and opportunism ('es ordnet sich, es bequemt sich' – 4:102) the question provides a stimulus to look beyond the individual and the existent towards an alternative which is presented in the story only as the apocalyptic negation of what Boehlendorff considers wrong. His own contributions to this apocalypse, both physical, as he tramples down the ground, and intellectual, in this question, have no effect, and it is only Boehlendorff's presence itself, as a thorn in the flesh of this specific form of complacency, that creates disharmony, that upsets the social stagnation of the area.

The question itself may be addressed to the ruling German upper class in Latvia. It contains, however, a challenge to every society, and it reverberates timelessly to Bobrowski's own present, the GDR recovering and stabilising after the trauma of 1961, and itself now threatened by new dangers of opportunism and complacency.[38] By pointing here to the individual, the 'moralisches Wesen', as an end in itself, indeed as the end of all history, and not as a means to an end, Bobrowski was writing against any society that did not place the self-fulfilment of the individual, as a unique being, at its centre. Here too its significance within the GDR is evident, and 'Boehlendorff', as Dennis Tate has argued, 'inspired the production of other texts which implied a close parallel between the alienated intellectuals of the Goethe period [...] and their GDR counterparts'.[39] The texts Tate refers to dealt with the past. The inspiration of Bobrowski's short story can, however, also be seen in other texts dealing more directly with East German reality, and Christa Wolf, a writer with very different subject-matter and very different

---

[38] Bobrowski appears to have been uncomfortably aware of this dimension. See the letter to Fischer of October 20 1964: 'Figur und Umstände sind historisch, so gut es geht' (6:355).

[39] 'Unexpected affinities', p.38.

views on social development, quotes with complete approval this very
sentence:

> 'Wie muß die [sic.] Welt für ein moralisches Wesen beschaffen sein?' Bob-
> rowskis Frage ist und bleibt stimulierend, weil sie hilft, die Welt einer
> menschenwürdigen Moral und nicht die Moral der Menschen einer noch
> wenig menschenwürdigen Welt anzupassen: Das wäre auch der physische Tod
> der Menschheit.[40]

Wolf's own novel *Nachdenken über Christa T.* (1968) – despite all
differences of setting and outlook – closely follows the pattern of
'Boehlendorff'. In its narrative style it develops the questioning,
investigative mode observed above, as it uncovers the life of Christa T.
from her writings and from memories of her. It also echoes
'Boehlendorff' in its content, with its criticism of a society whose smug
satisfaction at its own achievements indirectly led to the death of the
individual who dared question it. In one episode, Wolf's character
Dölling reveals a disastrous complacency, as the unnamed narrator
proposes a possible explanation for Christa T.'s 'Meer von Traurigkeit'
– 'Weil sie nicht so sein konnte, wie wir sie wollten' – and receives the
response:

> Wollten? [...] Wollten? [...] Waren wir nicht gezwungen, das Nächstliegende
> zu tun, so gut wie möglich, und es zu verlangen, immer wieder? Ist nicht Er-
> staunliches daraus geworden? Oder könnte es uns heute bessergehen?[41]

Christa T., by contrast, looks at the incompleteness of the world and
applies her own versions of Boehlendorff's question: 'Was braucht die
Welt zu ihrer Vollkommenheit?' (p.54) and 'Was fehlt der Welt zu ihrer
Vollkommenheit?' (p.61). In a central passage she meets one of her ex-
pupils, now a doctor, who almost explicitly rejects the question placed
in Boehlendorff's mouth:

> Was könnte denn, vom ärztlichen Standpunkt, aus einer Programmierung der
> Jugend mit einer hochgestochenen Moral, aus dem Zusammenstoß dieser
> Moral mit den Realitäten des Lebens, die *immer* stärker sind, glauben Sie mir;
> was kann also aus solchem Konflikt herauskommen? Komplexe bestenfalls.
> Die deutschen Erzieher haben schon immer an den Realitäten rütteln wollen,
> immer vergebens. (p.109)

---

[40] *Die Dimension des Autors: Aufsätze, Essays, Gespräche, Reden*, Berlin and Weimar
1986, vol.2, pp.348f.

[41] *Nachdenken über Christa T.*, Neuwied and Berlin 1978, p.50.

Bobrowski's Boehlendorff, we must remember, was just such a German 'Erzieher'.

Within a few years Bobrowski had moved on from the slight and derivative 'Es war eigentlich aus' and 'Begebenheit' to develop an open narrative style breaking entirely with socialist realism. He developed a language drawing productively from oral traditions, and a subject matter which, in various ways, contradicted the simplistic certainties of official GDR discourse. The Sarmatian background, where it still occurred, lost in this development much of its historical specificity. It was never an area of retreat, either historical or mythical, from the problems of the day. Instead it functioned in these stories as a geo-temporal complex allowing distanced observation and consideration of problems directly relevant to Bobrowski's own present. While doing this, he continued the process of poetic 'kidnapping' to which Meckel refers, not in order to produce 'objective' pen-portraits of historical and cultural individuals or events, but in order to provide points of orientation for himself and for his readers. Bobrowski's position 'zwischen allen Stühlen' has him attempting his own 'middle way', indulging his personal penchant for artistic play, intense allusion and love of the past, whilst arguing with himself and increasingly his own society over its concerns. Such self-orientation involve warnings against the temptations of despair, negatively in 'Von nachgelassenen Poesien' and 'Epitaph für Pinnau', more positively in 'Junger Herr am Fenster' and 'D.B.H.'. Increasingly, this orientation involves figures who live full and artistically productive lives, lived outside but in contact with the self-perpetuating certainties of their societies.

Such a sense of the importance of living outside certainties arises out of Bobrowski's own emphasis on the value of this position 'zwischen allen Stühlen', for which he provides so many examples: Lina Warszus's syncretic religiosity; the productive tension between Buxtehude's sensuality and his religious devotion; Schopenhauer's hesitating between love and rejection of family. In 'Rainfarn' and 'Der Mahner' the narrative voice itself is caught between the desire for artistic freedom of expression and its sense of the need for responsibility. In 'Lobellerwäldchen' the tension is resolved as the idyll is exposed. On a completely different level the humble postal official Petrat demonstrates his own ability to combine adherence to the letter of public service with a sense of his own value, to combine obedience to social rules with a sense of the importance of something as intangible or irrational as 'Gefühl'. Such sympathetic images of non-ideological humanity function as understating correctives to any society or institution claiming absolute truth, claiming for itself the victorious moral high-ground of history, and it is entirely appropriate that 'Boehlendorff', the longest and most famous of these short stories, should focus on a question for which no answer is provided – by Boehlendorff himself, by Bobrowski, or indeed by reality: 'Wie muß eine Welt für ein moralisches Wesen beschaffen sein?'

7

LEVINS MÜHLE

The novel *Levins Mühle* was first published in 1964 and was Bobrowski's first longer prose work since the unpublished 1950 'Bericht über
die ersten Jahre der Gefangenschaft' (4:264-317). Together with
Litauische Claviere it represents Bobrowski's most consistent attempt to
combine his treatment of his 'Eastern' theme with response to the actual
political and social situation in which he found himself. The novel is set
in 1874 largely in the village of Neumühl and in the towns of Briesen
and Strasburg in West Prussia, and presents a story, told by an 'Enkel',
of how his fictional 'Großvater' attempted to escape the consequences
of criminally destroying the water-mill of the title. This had been built
by a Jewish settler Levin whose commercial acumen represented a
threat to the Grandfather's long-established but economically backward
milling monopoly. After destroying Levin's mill by damming up the
stream and releasing the water to sweep it away the Grandfather uses his
contacts with fellow Protestants, the so-called 'Malkener Union'
between his own Baptists and members of the Evangelical Church who
lived in nearby Malken, to have Levin's legal action against him
thwarted. He also attempts to drive Levin's supporters out of the area
and, in a further criminal act, burns down an empty hut they have
occupied. In doing this, however, he loses much of his authority as
church elder and is made the object of public ridicule. A number of
incidents contribute to this. During a circus performance gypsies and
other social 'undesirables' publicly expose his guilt with a song, forcing
him to retreat in frustrated anger; while relieving himself in his outside
privy he is struck from below with a plank inserted in the 'Menschenkuhdreck' (3:155); and he is physically humiliated during a brawl that
he himself provoked with his anti-Polish comments. Unable to contain
his arrogance and sense of self-importance, he even finds himself
officially criticised by the commander of a platoon of Prussian soldiers
stationed in the village to keep the peace. At the end of the novel he has
sold his mill and moved to the provincial town of Briesen, where he
finds himself pursued by his children, who want their share of the pro-
ceeds of the sale of the mill, and by the Baptist priest Feller, who wants
a contribution to a new font in the Neumühl chapel. He is also

tormented by the local painter and 'lustige Person' (3:212) Philippi, whom he has alienated through his self-confessed anti-Semitism.

The Grandfather's supporters include the affluent and nationalistic local German land-owners and others (priests, policemen) who hope to benefit from his generosity. His opponents include, as well as Levin and the gypsies, a number of the less affluent or integrated Germans, especially women (Tante Huse, Josepha Feller, even his own wife Christina), and many local Poles.

The novel is based on a true incident from the 1870s. According to a chronicle of events prepared by Wilhelm Friedrich Ludwig Jahnke (1864-1936) a certain Johann Bobrowski had used flood-water from his millpond to destroy a mill belonging to a Jew called Lewin. He had, however, been taken to court, financially ruined and eventually forced to emigrate to America with his family. Details of these events were sent to Bobrowski by the West German family historian Georg Bobrowski, on May 8 1961 (*Marbach* 683-9).

The historical events depicted in the chronicle demonstrated the impartiality of the Prussian courts, since the guilty party was punished, even though the victims were Jews.[1] The chronicle showed, however, the considerable potential for misunderstanding present in its occasional condemnation of the (wronged) Jews:

> Die Juden [hatten] in der damaligen Zeit die Geschäfte ganz in ihren Händen. [...] Die Juden nahmen keine Rücksicht, es half kein Bitten und Flehen [...]. So wohlweislich hatten die Juden gesorgt, daß die ganze Familie Bobrowski als Bettler aus dem Grundstück wegziehen mußten. (*Marbach* 688f.)

Georg Bobrowski's covering letter itself referred to the 'tragische[s] Ende der Malker Linie der Bobrowski'. Bobrowski thanked him (June 19 1961) for the information ('unvergeßlich und fast ein Romanstoff nach der Art St. Reymonts') but felt that it could hardly be used 'für diese, für unsere Zeit [...], weil solch ein Buch gleich mit vordergründigen Ressentiments behängt werden würde' (*Marbach* 684). On the same day, however, he wrote to Felix Berner, indicating his interest in this 'Romanstoff aus der Familiengeschichte', and by early August 1961, just before the political and personal crisis brought about by the erection of the Berlin wall on August 13, he was making enquiries about

---

[1] Admittedly, these were not wandering Jews like the fictional Levin. They came from a well established East Prussian Jewish family. In the same way, the historical Jewish

the mechanics of water-mills. After August 13 other matters presented themselves, so that by November 1961 not even the frame of a plot had been completed. From autumn 1962 he was referring again to his intentions to write a novel, while finally on October 11 of the same year he wrote to Edith Klatt that he had started on one – 'wahrscheinlich aus Verzweiflung' (*Marbach* 681). Letters written in the first half of 1963 indicate steady progress, but also show how uncertain he was as to how long it would take to complete. The work was suddenly completed in mid-July 1963, after a few weeks hectic activity. It was published in September 1964 by the Union Verlag and the West German S. Fischer Verlag.[2]

As is already clear, Bobrowski used his main source very freely and with significant, indeed crucial alterations, especially in the ending. In historical reality Johann Bobrowski and family had been ruined; in *Levins Mühle* they retain their prosperity and the Grandfather can look forward to a financially secure, if by no means untroubled, retirement. On the other hand the historical Lewin was successful in his court-case, while the Levin of the novel is left penniless. Instead of having the court provide some justice, Bobrowski introduced in its stead a wide range of outsiders whose cumulative pressure forces the Grandfather out of Neumühl. For the continued persecution of the Grandfather in Briesen, Philippi, though based on Bobrowski's friend Günter Bruno Fuchs, was pure invention.

The plot is uncomplicated, but its progress is obscured through the oblique and indirect narrative style and through the inclusion of a number of digressions, as the narrator consistently refuses to provide a conventionally clear narrative. In the novel's sub-title *34 Sätze über meinen Großvater* he presents the fiction that he intends to tell his story in thirty-four sentences; he reflects on his own concerns and worries in telling this story, admitting, among other things, at the beginning of the story that he does not know whether it is a good thing to tell the story at all; he allows himself to be side-tracked into digressions concerning details. He also – in a manner designed to mislead his readers – insists: 'so ist es [...] auch gewesen' (3:10), but admits confusingly to the

---

settlement at Briesen was fully integrated, not as presented in the novel.

[2] For fuller details see 6:14-25 and Eberhard Haufe, 'Bobrowskis Weg zum Roman: Zur Vor- und Entstehungsgeschichte von *Levins Mühle*', in *Weimarer Beiträge*, 16 (1970), no.1, 163-77.

fictionality of the work as a whole. The clarity of the plot is further
obscured by the fact that he only refers to the Grandfather's criminal
activities obliquely. There are, as he comments, 'nirgends Beweise in
dieser ganzen Geschichte' (3:146).

The narrative voice also throughout draws attention towards itself
and away from the actual plot. The narrator as a figure constantly makes
his presence felt, appealing to his readers to remind them of things they
might rather forget, but also entering into conversation with the
characters, warning or instructing, explaining matters to them, occasionally expressing concern or despair, criticising them directly or indirectly, and commenting on their actions. He occasionally highlights the
point of introduction of new characters into his text by introducing them
clumsily or by hesitantly asking whether they need to be introduced at
all. A local official is thus introduced as follows:

> Der Herr Nolte, Friedrich Nolte, Amtsvorsteher in Neumühl, ist ein alter
> Mann. Wir haben ihn noch nicht erwähnt, weil er die ganze Zeit, von der wir
> hier geredet haben, bettlägerig war, aber wir bemühen ihn jetzt doch. (3:149)[3]

A further complicating characteristic of the text, as in the short stories, is that narrator and characters speak a similar language in a single
flow, uninterrupted by quotation marks. Bobrowski had had to work at
this language: it is a balanced, non-naturalistic colloquial German,
which does not attempt to imitate West Prussian *phonetically*, either for
the speech of the characters or for the narrator's own voice. It does, however, attempt to emulate the cadences and the (occasionally wayward)
syntax of the dialect.[4] In a letter to Gertrud Mentz, the widow of his
Königsberg headmaster, Bobrowski concedes that his work is

---

[3] Philippi is introduced similarly, with the words: 'Aber gerade jetzt, in diesem leidigen
Geschäft jetzt, führen wir eine neue Person daher: diesen Künstler, und das muß einen
Grund haben, der Grund heißt: Es ist nämlich Herbst' (3:212).

[4] Earlier textual alterations show the final intention: to replace, where possible, clearly
literary expressions with more colloquial ones, and to limit the number of West Prussian
expressions, while not attempting to eradicate them altogether. From the first chapter:
'Alle Leute haben nichts so gern wie feste Urteile' > 'Feste Urteile hat man schon gern';
'heißt es zwar' > 'werden die Leute sagen'; 'Immerhin könnte es sein' > 'Und es könnte
ja sein'. Further alterations reduced the number of intrusively moralising comments and
questions (*Marbach* 714). See also *Wegzeichen: Ein Almanach aus dem Union Verlag*, 3
(1987), 70-80, where G. Wirth quotes at length from an earlier version of the beginning
of Chapter 9 (pp.76f.) and 6:61.

auch sprachlich ein bißchen problematisch. Zwar ganz leicht verständlich aber doch ungewöhnlich: in der Hereinnahme von Umgangssprache, Dialekt, Jargon usw. Und zwar so, daß diese volkstümlichen Elemente ohne Übergänge ineinandergebracht werden mit der in der deutschen Erzählertradition entwickelten stilisierten Erzählhaltung. (*Marbach* 709)

Of particular significance for the development of this style, as with the short stories, was Hermann Sudermann. Bobrowski had initially dedicated the novel to him (*Marbach* 653), while to Christopher Middleton (June 11 1963) he wrote: 'Ich hab in der letzten Woche ein 25-Seiten-Kapitel für meinen Roman im Stil Sudermanns geschrieben' (*Marbach* 683). The influence shows in the use of the present tense, the occasional use of a single dialect word, (sometimes with explanation), and, arguably too in an episode describing the fate of Krolikowski in the swamp (3:151f.). Evident too is the influence of Laurence Sterne's *Tristram Shandy* in the narrative interruptions, extended asides, the use of a pause in the plot to tell part of another story – with many of the devices contributing to the effect of comic association or juxtaposition.

The novel begins with an obscure reference to one of Bobrowski's 'Sternzeichen', Joseph Conrad, as the narrator expresses his concern at the possible repercussions of the story he intends to narrate on his family:

Es ist vielleicht falsch, wenn ich jetzt erzähle, wie mein Großvater die Mühle weggeschwemmt hat, aber vielleicht ist es auch nicht falsch. Auch wenn es auf die Familie zurückfällt. Ob etwas unanständig ist oder anständig, das kommt darauf an, wo man sich befindet. (3:9)

In their apparent lack of conviction and certainty the opening words set the tone for the work as a whole. They also constitute a loose adaptation of a passage from a book well known to Bobrowski, the autobiographical *A Personal Record*, in which Conrad presents events concerning his 'grand-uncle Nicholas B. [...] Knight of the Legion of Honour' during Napoleon's retreat from Moscow, when hunger forced him to eat a dog. Conrad comments:

At this very day [...] I ask myself whether I am right in disclosing to a cold and fastidious world that awful episode in the family history. I ask myself – is it right? [...] But upon the whole, [...] I think that to cover it up by silence would be an exaggeration of literary restraint. Let the truth stand here.[5]

---

[5] Joseph Conrad, *The Mirror of the Sea* and *A Personal Record*, ed. Zdzislaw Najder,

Although not part of Bobrowski's immediate family history, the allusion further illustrates the 'family' engagement in the East, since the character Nicholas B. (i.e. Mikolaj *Bobrowski*, 1792-1864) had been a Pole fighting at the time for the French against the Tsarist Russians and their allies. It is a further incident in the complex interrelation between Bobrowski's here very extended 'family' and the 'lange Geschichte aus Unglück und Verschuldung' of which he wrote, though in this case the struggle is more general: between Western Europe and Russia, not between 'die Deutschen und ihre östlichen Nachbarn'.

As well as alluding to this link, the implied question ('Is it wrong to tell this story?') also opens a dialogue with the reader which is closed only at the very end of the novel when the question is answered indirectly but clearly in the 'Nein!' of the last 'Satz', with which Philippi refuses to leave the Grandfather in peace to forget his crime. Such a dialogue continues throughout, with greater or lesser intensity, and, for example, at the beginning of Chapter 9 Bobrowski addresses his reader directly:

> Der fünfzehnte Satz gehört nicht zur Handlung. Wenn auch zu uns, er heißt, nicht ganz genau: Die Sünden der Väter werden heimgesucht an den Kindern bis ins dritte und vierte Glied.
> Da reden wir also über die Väter oder Großväter und [...] finden [...] Schuldige über Schuldige und halten uns über sie auf und nehmen uns unterdessen vielleicht stillschweigend aus.
> Obwohl doch z.B. die ganze Geschichte hier unsertwegen erzählt wird. (3:126)

This uncertainty of the beginning is given substance in the next few paragraphs as Bobrowski proposes his first 'Satz' and immediately rejects it as open to misunderstandings. This 'Satz', 'Die Drewenz ist ein Nebenfluß in Polen' (3:9), taken in conjunction with the earlier reference to the Grandfather, evokes, as in 'Lobellerwäldchen', an immediate response from the fictitious reader: 'Also war dein Großvater ein Pole' (3:9). It is a logical but false conclusion, one that also conveniently eliminates the problem of specifically German responsibility,

---

Oxford 1988, p.32. The complexity of allusion in these first few sentences is not limited to Conrad. Robert Musil's *Der Mann ohne Eigenschaften* begins with a comment: 'Die Überschätzung der Frage, *wo man sich befinde*, [my italics] stammt aus der Hordenzeit, wo man die Futterplätze merken mußte', while Uwe Johnson's *Das dritte Buch über Achim* begins with a short consideration of the difficulties of the first two 'Sätze'. Such density of allusion imposes a careful reading-pattern on the reader.

and acknowledging this the narrator rewrites the 'erste Satz' into a new introductory sentence with the easy-going long-windedness of the nineteenth century realist novel in the manner of Theodor Fontane:

> Am Unterlauf der Weichsel, an einem ihrer kleinen Nebenflüsse, gab es in den siebziger Jahren des vorigen Jahrhunderts ein überwiegend von Deutschen bewohntes Dorf. (3:9)

The introduction creates the fiction of a lack of narrative confidence, a concern that any statement is open to misleading or false interpretations, so that even an apparently objective geographical statement carries unwanted implications. The narrator reinforces this lesson on the complexities of this area with two further statements. The first runs 'Nun müßte man aber dazusetzen, daß es ein blühendes Dorf war mit großen Scheunen und festen Ställen und [...] die dicksten Bauern waren Deutsche, die Polen im Dorf waren ärmer' (3:9). This sentence, which would have emphasised the affluence of the Germans compared with the poverty of the surrounding Poles, may have been accurate, but it might also stoke prejudices of German superiority over the proverbial 'polnische Wirtschaft', and so it is rejected: 'Aber das sage ich nicht' (3:10). Instead the narrator proposes a statement undermining the very concepts 'German' and 'Pole':

> Ich sage statt dessen: Die Deutschen hießen Kaminski, Tomaschewski und Kossakowski und die Polen Lebrecht und Germann. Und so ist es nämlich auch gewesen. (3:10).

It is a confusion of names that threatens the one of the main foundations of nationalism – the assumed existence of distinct nationalities with distinct (linguistic) identities.[6] At this point Bobrowski summarises his concerns:

> Feste Urteile hat man schon gern, und vielleicht ist es manch einem egal, woher er sie bekommt, mir ist es jetzt nicht egal, deshalb werde ich die Geschichte auch erzählen. (3:10)

---

[6] Towards the end of the novel, the reports by the Prussian Oberwachtmeister Plontke underline this confusion: 'Es sind aber verflucht fröhliche Menschen, diese Polacken. Und so deutsch' (3:202), and 'diese Polen [sind] doch äußerst deutsch' (3:208). In this he shows more sensitivity than the German soldier in 'Mäusefest' for whom 'dieses Polen hier ist ganz polnisch' (4:49).

He contrasts the 'klarer Blick' of the ignorant with the complicating effects of the 'Sachkenntnis' that he intends to offer. Such detailed knowledge acts as an argument against ideologically-based convictions, and it is in such a spirit that *Levins Mühle* is composed: written against all attempts to reduce the complexities of actual existence to a single or simple order. Any attempt at such an ordering, as exemplified with the complex material of German-Polish relations, inevitably simplifies and leads to false conclusions, so that attempts physically to impose such an order on the 'durcheinanderen Zustände' (3:199) of the area lead inevitably to injustice.

The narrative structure of the work also emphasises this, as the narrator himself rejects 'Ordnung', even to the extent of claiming not to know how his work will continue: 'Wenn man ganz genau weiß, was man erzählen will und wieviel davon, das ist, denke ich, nicht in Ordnung' (3:9). The prolonged play with the number thirty-four then becomes an example of an ordering structure doomed to fail. The number 34 was almost certainly chosen as homage to Günter Bruno Fuchs, whose novel *Krümelnehmer: 34 Kapitel aus dem Leben des Tierstimmen-Imitators Ewald K.* appeared in 1963.[7] Beyond this personal reference it echoes, of course, a whole range of musical and literary references to the number thirty-four.[8] The logic of such an aim is, however, soon lost, as the narrative voice loses count, at one point introduces a new category of 'Nebensätze' (3:60), which undermines the whole ordering principle, extends his concept of 'Satz' to include, apparently, sections several pages long: 'Das ist also der zweite Satz. Ein bißchen lang, aber noch nicht einmal zuende' (3:13), while elsewhere defining a 'Satz' as being characterised by 'schlagende Kürze und, vor allem, Gefühl' (3:147). Finally, in an attempt to fulfil his self-

---

[7] *Levins Mühle* contains a number of verbal echoes of this work.

[8] See Gotthard Lerchner's 'Intertextualität als ästhetisches Potential: Bobrowskis "34 Sätze über meinen Großvater"', *Zeitschrift für Germanistik*, 3 (1988), 307-20, which studies the range of significance of the 'Prätext' thirty-four from medieval literature through Pachelbel, Buxtehude and Bach up to Thomas Mann's *Doktor Faustus*. In Bobrowski's more immediate ambience is Jean Paul's *Leben Fibels*, which contains just such a play with form (here with 'chapters') and ends with four very short 'Nachkapitel', to make a total of thirty-four. It is possible that Fuchs himself drew originally from this text. Bobrowski edited *Leben Fibels* and wrote an afterword for it (4:349-52) at the very time he was working on *Levins Mühle*.

imposed plan, the narrator quickly adds four more 'Sätze' at the end of
the novel in order to arrive at the arbitrarily chosen number. In an earlier
draft he had even written of abandoning the idea altogether:

> Wir kommen schon eine hübsche Weile ohne diese Sätze über meinen
> Großvater aus, es geht sogar ganz gut. Wahrscheinlich braucht man solche
> Dinge überhaupt nicht. Aber wenn es tatsächlich so sein sollte, dann kommt
> diese Einsicht jedenfalls spät. Da sagen wir uns: Soll es gehn wie es geht. [...]
> Soll es also weitergehn mit den Sätzen.[9]

These 'Sätze' do not then summarise or organise the material of the
novel. They function instead as an element in an elaborate literary game,
emphasising the fictionality of the work as they draw attention to themselves and to the narrative voice audible behind them. Not all are
significant, but where they are, this significance is increased by their
status as a 'Satz'. In particular the fifteenth 'Satz' quoted above (3:126)
is of central importance for the story as a whole, while the quick
sequence of 'Sätze' at the end, 'Komm, wir singen', 'In Gollub spielen
die Zigeuner', 'Wenn wir nicht singen, singen andere' and 'Nein'
(3:222) suggests the potential for continued artistic struggle against the
Grandfather and his successors up to the present.

The choice of thirty-four 'Sätze' presents then an aesthetic game, a
doomed attempt to order the material of the novel. In contrast to this, the
attempts to order the material of reality in the novel are much more
serious and have more far-reaching consequences. These are based on
'feste Urteile' (3:10), pre-judgements, ideological constructs, and as
with his own 'Sätze' Bobrowski shows the prejudices in order to defeat
them. Many such 'feste Urteile' are exemplified in the five dreams,
graced with the title 'Geistererscheinungen' which the Grandfather
experiences and which underpin his mentality. For these too Bobrowski
used material provided by Georg Bobrowski concerning his family,[10]
and in *Levins Mühle* may be seen a partial settling of accounts with his
own family.

Bobrowski makes no attempt to integrate these dreams smoothly but
draws attention to them by giving them headings and numbering them
(e.g. 3:169). They extend back into the family's distant past and
illuminate the role the Grandfather feels his family has played in Polish-

---

[9] Quoted by G. Wirth, in *Wegzeichen*, pp.76f. Also 6:61.

[10] See 'Zur Geschichte der Familie Bobrowski', 4:318-26.

German history. Each presents some aspect or other of the Grandfather's image of this history and contributes to his sense of justification
for his actions. The first and clearest dream concerns events of 1516,
when his ancestor Poleske is executed for his part, together with the
more famous Matern, in banditry directed against merchants from
Danzig.[11] Poleske sees it as his duty to defend Polish interests against
the 'Gesockse [...], das sich breit um die Bucht herumgesetzt hat und
den Hintern ausstreckt gegen die Republik' (3:28).[12] His justification for
this banditry, and this is the concept to which the Grandfather relates, is
summarized in the words 'Mein Recht' (3:25), which link Poleske's
belief in the justice of his attacks on Danzig merchants with the
Grandfather's conviction that his destruction of Levin's mill was
justified. It is an irony lost on the Grandfather that he is basing his claim
for his *German* 'Recht' on an ancestor who claims to be defending — if
anything — *Polish* 'Recht' against *German* merchants.

In this area too may be seen elements of a dialogue with the family: a
letter of December 8 1957 by Georg Bobrowski to Johannes congratu-
lates him on the birth of his first son with the words:

> Weshalb soll ich mich über den in der Sippe neu auftretenden Namen 'Justus'
> wundern! Ich finde ihn ganz in der Ordnung und vor allem auch am Platze in
> einer Sippe, die für das Recht zwischen Wolga und Elbe Wunden empfing und
> büssen mußte.[13]

In the Grandfather's second dream an ancestor commits suicide
rather than convert to Catholicism. This dream too identifies the Grandfather's ancestors as Polish. It concerns the period of the Counter-
Reformation, when the largely Protestant Polish nobility was caught up
(1606) in a Rokosz, an armed uprising against Zygmunt III Wasa and
his Jesuits. Bobrowski's family history refers to the uprising, in which
his ancestors clearly backed the wrong side, and suggests that this may
be the reason why a complete branch of the family disappeared. The
significance of the dream for 1874 is clear from its context: the Malken
agreement between the Baptist Grandfather and his Evangelical brother-

---

[11] It is the same Matern who ghosts through Grass's novel *Hundejahre*.

[12] Significantly, the same word is used by a German before the Grandfather's brawl and
defeat in the inn as Kossakowski joins his side with the words: 'Nun aber raus mit das
Gesocks!' (3:192).

[13] Quoted in Bernd Leistner, *Der Epiker Johannes Bobrowski*, p.141.

in-law to work together against the Jew Levin and the Polish Catholics. The Grandfather draws justification for this act from a family memory of Catholic persecution.

The incident behind the third dream is set very precisely in the novel on January 15 1853 but actually concerns a historical event from 1883, when a Michael Bobrowski was found 'nackt, mit vollständig verbrannter Kleidung auf der Straße in Zgnilloblatt (bei Tillitz-Zaroslo)'.[14] The ancestor in this dream, identified by the Grandfather with the word 'Vater', is rumoured to have been an 'Opfer der Geister' (3:94), though the situation indicates human involvement. Here too the immediate context of the Grandfather's very public humiliation at the hands of the gypsies in Rosinka's barn explains its significance, in that just as the victim, Michael Bobrowski, was seen as an 'Opfer der Geister', so the Grandfather sees himself becoming a victim of the 'Zigeunergeister' (3:94). These gypsies are, however, pursuing the Grandfather because of what he has just done to Levin, and it is impossible not to see what happened to his own father as revenge by unknown parties for some similar unspecified dishonesties of his own. The Grandfather, unsurprisingly, learns nothing from this confrontation too, and what should have been an *absolute* warning he interprets purely tactically, as the need to defend himself: 'Mit mir nicht!' (3:94, 95).

The fourth 'Geistererscheinung' takes place when the Grandfather dozes off on his privy. It centres on the discovery of a love-affair between a girl Ofka and a Christian hero Jastrzemb, an affair interrupted by the return of the girl's father and leading to the Jastrzemb figure ('der ganz anders geheißen hat als Jastrzemb, vielleicht Zbylut' – 3:158) being attacked. The confusion of the spirits, 'Sehr alte Geister diesmal. Und sehr verwirrte, die sich nicht auskennen zwischen den Namen, den Familien, den Stämmen [...] zwischen den bösen und guten Göttern und Gespenstern' (3:159), indicates the Grandfather's own confusion, as he mixes names and centuries. He does not know what generation he is dreaming of[15] but relates the dream to the need to defend himself against the chaos surrounding him. It is a conclusion from which he draws no good, as with the 'Menschenkuhdreck', into which his hand slips as he sleeps, and which he finds 'bißchen dünn geraten' (3:159).

---

[14] Letter by Georg Bobrowski of March 8 1961 (6:119).

[15] 'Diese Ofka Strzegonia [...], mit der es schon gewiß eine Geschichte gibt, aber dreihundert Jahre später' (3:158).

The obscurity of the fifth dream is even more complete. It takes place the night before the Grandfather leaves for Briesen to re-establish order after discovering that Oberwachtmeister Plontke's report has criticised him personally. While in Briesen he unexpectedly sells his mill. This dream echoes the first dream (Poleske) and the fourth (Jastrzemb), as the Grandfather links the two men, although they lived centuries apart. He is confronted with the ambiguity of the history of the Jastrzembs, who, according to Bobrowski's own record, were allowed to bear a horseshoe in their coat of arms because they introduced horse-shoes and enabled the Christian Lechiti to defeat the heathen Polani at Lysa Góra (A.D. 999), while the cross was a reminder that in the late eleventh century members of the same family had taken part in the murder of Bishop Stanislav of Cracow (4:319). The dream focuses on images of isolation and, at the end, of leave-taking, with Poleske leaving to do what he saw as his duty, 'einer, der nicht mehr wiedergekehrt ist' (3:208).

Together the five dreams demonstrate the selectiveness of the 'hohes Geschichtsbewußtsein' of the Grandfather as a representative inhabitant of the area, but also, especially in the last two, demonstrate his utter confusion, so that the proud general claim 'man kennt sich also mit seinen Voreltern und Ahnen' (3:25) is disproved. The Grandfather's main point of reference is Poleske, with the memory of whom he associates a vague notion of 'Mein Recht' together with the need to act before it is too late. With Krysztof he associates Catholic intolerance and draws only confirmation that his Malkener Union is justified. The memory of his father's death produces only violent self-defence, including striking his own wife in his sleep, rather than a reappraisal of his own possible responsibility. These dreams do not provide moral counterweights so much as instinctive confirmations of the justice of his actions, and the literary topos of the dream as a warning remains unfulfilled as the Grandfather learns nothing about his personal guilt and ignores the implications for his nationalism present in the complexity of his family history. The narrator rightly comments, after the fourth dream: 'Manchmal denkt man schon, diese Geister, ältere und neuere und sogar ganz alte, sollten sich um ihn nicht mehr bemühen [...]. Nein, es ist keine Freude mit solchen Großvätern' (3:159).

As well as undermining the nationalism practised by the Grandfather, the novel equally dismisses the ideologies of anti-Semitism and (though more indirectly) its opposite 'philosemitism'. In particular the religious strand of anti-Semitism is displayed in the comments of one of the other inmates of Habedank's cell in Briesen, whom the narrator criticises with unusual directness as 'einer von denen, die überhaupt wenig sagen, dafür aber auch lauter Mist' (3:132). He displays all the arrogance (and ignorance) which, for Bobrowski, characterise the anti-Semite, and Bobrowski uses the recurrent theme of implied criticism of 'feste Urteile' (3:10) based on ignorance to condemn him:

> Diese Juden, sagt er, haben Jesum ans Kreuz geschlagen, mit Nägeln, Achtzöller. Er weiß das. Jetzt laufen sie rum auf der ganzen Welt, sagt er, das Kainszeichen der Jesusmörder auf ihrer Stirn.
> Das ist alles schon so alt, daß es aussieht wie eine leibhaftige Wahrheit. (3:132)

With Bobrowski's respect for Jews such criticism is inevitable. The concern with philosemitism is more unexpected but constitutes an important part of the landscape of the novel. Levin, himself the victim of the Grandfather's attack, is by no means an entirely positive character. After losing his mill, he now appears to have lost all will-power. He seems to discourage the others from acting, so that they end up having to ignore him. He also received little support from his fellow-Jews: 'Wärst nicht gekrochen, wärst nicht versoffen [...]. Alles solche Reden' (3:71), and the advice given by the Jewish teacher Onkel Sally to the Jewish schoolchildren in Briesen in the event of an 'Unglück' is particularly inappropriate:

> Wenn Unglück ist, ihr lauft mir nicht dazu, ihr bleibt mir hübsch stehen und geht nicht ran. Aber schreit, schreit, was ihr könnt! Werden schon welche kommen, andere, die werden helfen.
> Also, da ist der Levin enttäuscht. (3:138)

He himself has experienced such an 'Unglück' with the Grandfather and received no aid from his relatives.

Instead, it is his gypsy girlfriend Marie who provides him with the inspiration and strength to continue the struggle at all, and Levin draws particular encouragement from the resilience of her pubic hair, which refuses to be flattened as they sit naked in the rain (3:123).[16] Levin's re-

---

[16] An earlier version had developed this image even more: 'man sieht solch einem Härchen richtig an, wie trotzig es sich fühlt, wie es gar nicht daran denkt, sich diesem Regen einfach so zu fügen. Da hebt es sich und streckt sich vor und trägt einen klaren runden Tropfen an der Spitze' (6:60).

latives' response to Marie, who has helped so much, is, however, almost completely negative, and his Tante Glickle is evidently disturbed that Marie is a gypsy:

> [Sie] faßt Marie ins Auge und sagt: Leochen, wer ist das?
> Dieses ist meine Braut Marie, sagt Levin.
> Uij uij. Die Tante erschrickt ein bißchen. [...]
> Uij uij, Kind, sagt die Tante. Aber ganz beruhigt ist sie nicht. Leochens Braut?
> Wäre ja nicht gut. (3:139)

In the lecture 'Benannte Schuld – gebannte Schuld?' Bobrowski wrote of the philosemite's Jew: 'Da wird [...] ein Idealtyp hergestellt, eine romantisierte Gestalt von abgeklärter Weisheit und unbegreiflicher Leidensfähigkeit' (4:445). In these sections of *Levins Mühle* he upturns these, presenting the 'unbegreifliche Leidensfähigkeit' as meek and apathetic acquiescence in suffering, while the 'abgeklärte Weisheit' is reduced to an intense but practically irrelevant knowledge of the Bible and Rabbinical literature: 'Onkel Dowid, der Kinderlehrer, schreibt mit seinem Stock Zeichen auf die Dielenbretter. Die wird niemand lesen' (3:203).[17] Alongside his determination to avoid conveying the actual historical reality of the economic and judicial strength of the Jews at the time, Bobrowski is also clearly distancing himself from the alternative, the 'romantisierte Gestalt'.

Apart from the outcome of the struggle, the most significant change to the novel's source concerns the Grandfather's opponents. In historical reality these had been the Jews, with the assistance of the Prussian courts. In the novel the Grandfather is faced by a motley crew of outsiders, characterised by their active and productive love of music and their refusal 'sich zufrieden zu geben' (3:173). It is a group presented with considerable sympathy as one diametrically opposed to the Grandfather's ideologically distorted dualism. If the Grandfather feels that he is 'deutsch wie der Kaiser in Berlin' (3:72) and shares the

---

[17] See 'Questioning Philosemitism: The Depiction of Jews in the Prose Works of Johannes Bobrowski', John Wieczorek, in *German Life and Letters* 44 (1991) 122-32. For a wider perspective, see Heidy Müller, *Die Judendarstellung in der deutschsprachigen Erzählprosa (1945-1981)*, Königstein/Ts. 1986. Karl August Horst adopts a more critical attitude: 'Die Geschichte [i.e. *Levins Mühle*] ist für eine lehrhafte Geschichte eigentlich zu schön, zu poetisch, und Levin, das Unschuldslamm, ist dem Autor ein bißchen zu weiß – das heißt blaß – geraten'. In 'Johannes Bobrowski und der epische Realismus', *Merkur* 18 (1964), 1082.

German contempt for the 'durcheinanderen Zustände', one of the leaders of his opponents is described in very different terms:

> Weiszmantel heißt er, jeder kennt ihn, er gehört nirgends hin, er redet Deutsch und Polnisch durcheinander, da geht er, die Beine mit Lappen umwickelt und beschnürt, über Kreuz, wie ein Litauer. Weiszmantel, der die Lieder weiß. (3:68)

This group rejects in various ways the hypocritical social mores of the settled Germans: Marie and Levin conduct a very public love affair; Willuhn is a (German) alcoholic ex-teacher, while the Polish labourers appear incorrigibly lazy; Josepha, the (also alcoholic) wife of the corrupt priest Feller, eventually commits suicide in despair at this behaviour (3:166f.). Apart from these the group includes gypsies and a Polish-Italian travelling circus. The one apparently settled bourgeois German in this group, Tante Huse, is characterised by her unusual humanity towards unmarried mothers, which has alienated her from her fellow-Germans. Bobrowski's affection for this group is undeniable.

The contribution by gypsies here is particularly significant, and Bobrowski emphasises this by having the 'German' party refer without differentiation to the whole group as 'Zigeuner', 'Zigahnchen' etc. In the context of the 'zweite oder dritte Nebensatz [...]: Richtige Zigeuner sind richtig schön' he uses specifically the example of gypsies to deliver his most prolonged warning against over-hasty generalisations and to relate the groups of the story to the events of the Nazi period:

> Richtige Zigeuner sind richtig schön.
> Das ist wahr, ich sage es, wie es ist. Beschreiben allerdings kann man Zigeuner nicht, [...] sie sind tot. Zusammengetrieben und erschlagen in jenen Jahren, an die wir uns erinnern, in jenen Gegenden, von denen hier erzählt wird. Wo soll man sie kennen lernen?
> Wer jetzt sagt: ich kenne welche, der denkt sich das bloß, der weiß nicht, was er redet, der meint die drei schwarzhaarigen Männer, [...] die im Kaffeehaus Musik machen und all das tun, was man (nur so als Mensch) vom Zigeuner erwartet. [...] Das meine ich alles nicht, ich meine Zigeuner, die man nicht beschreiben kann, also Habedank und diese Marie und noch einige andere. (3:60)

To accept this cliché with its false impression of domesticated civility diverts attention from the historical complexity of these gypsies and from the reality of their mass-murder. Bobrowski's own depiction of gypsies, and especially of this 'circus' draws instead from other sources, and in particular from a work by Günter Bruno Fuchs, the early

Zigeunertrommel, which was dedicated to the gypsies as a 'Volk der Klagefrauen und Geigenspieler, dessen Opfer die Grenzen aller Länder widerlegt'.[18]

The heterogeneity and anarchic temperament of this group render them totally inappropriate within any conventional 'socialist-realist' mode. Although his 'Dorfflötist' Geethe shares his middle name Vladimir with Lenin these are nothing but a romanticised rural 'Lumpenproletariat'.[19] They are social outsiders, motivated not by positive ideals of social equality but by the refusal as stated above 'sich zufrieden[zu]geben' (3:173) and by a sense of 'outsider' solidarity in face of the Grandfather's behaviour. There is no developed class consciousness. Their attempts to understand the social developments that face them remain unconvincing, and when they try to understand why the Grandfather's supporters act as they do they decide (with a great deal of assistance from the prodding narrator) simply that it is all to do with money: 'Na ganz einfach, [...] die einen, weil sie haben und es sich zusammenhalten soll, und die andern, weil sie haben wollen und was kriegen für Rumrennen'. Habedank's laconic 'Wirst schon recht haben' (3:170) concludes the discussion. This may be the last word in their attempt to sort the characters, but it hardly constitutes a serious attempt to understand.[20]

Apart from their private vandalism (i.e. the plank in the Grandfather's privy) the main weapon used by this group is that of art, a song that they sing holding the Grandfather up to ridicule as the suspect for the destruction of Levin's mill. This is another central aspect of the novel not present in the historical chronicle, but in emphasising it

---

[18] *Zigeunertrommel*, Halle 1956. Apart from the (truly cliché-ridden) Romantic image of the gypsy, German writers have been generally unprepared to be generous. Even Herder (*Ideen*, Book 16, chapter 5) could only condemn gypsies as 'eine verworfne Indische Kaste, die von allem, was sich göttlich, anständig und bürgerlich nennet, ihrer Geburt nach entfernt ist und dieser erniedrigenden Bestimmung noch nach Jahrhunderten treu bleibt'.

[19] After the brawl in the village pub, Geethe appropriately resurrects the words of his other partial namesake Goethe after the Battle of Valmy: 'Etwas ganz Neues. Und wir verfluchtige Hundezucht können verdammtnochmal sagen, wir sind zum Deiwel noch eins dabeigewesen Donnerschlag' (3:195).

[20] The narrator's own attempts to 'sortieren' (3:113f.) fail equally. Such sorting is 'schwierig oder einfach' (3:114) and leads to innumerable sub-groups of individuals acting for their own private reasons.

Bobrowski, as in his later *Litauische Claviere*, is commenting on a significant theme running through literary discussions of this period in East Germany, the question of the possible effect of art. It was a basic tenet of East German literary theory that works of literature could have a direct effect on the reader. For Stalin the writer had been the 'engineer of the human soul', and as late as December 1965, shortly after Bobrowski's death, Walter Ulbricht justified repressive measures against writers and artists with the rhetorical question: 'Sind wir der Meinung, daß ein paar Künstler oder Schriftsteller schreiben können, was sie wollen, und sie bestimmen die ganze Entwicklung der Gesellschaft?'[21] Ulbricht's comments refer negatively to undesirable works. Typical of the mood in the early 1960s (and it was a mood rather than a detailed theoretical argument) was the introduction to the SED program for the VI Parteitag. This had argued:

> Die im Kunstwerk gestalteten Erkenntnisse und Gefühle dienen der moralischen Veränderung der Menschen im Geiste des Sozialismus. Sie regen sie zu großen Taten für den Sozialismus an, erwecken in ihnen die Liebe zur Arbeit.[22]

Specific works were routinely praised as exemplifying the positive effects of art, and two such exemplary works were Harriet Beecher Stowe's *Uncle Tom's Cabin* and *Bitva v puti*, a recent Soviet novel by Galina Nikolaeva, translated into German as *Schlacht unterwegs*. In 1928 Friedrich Wolf's programmatic *Kunst ist Waffe* had praised Stowe, who

> mit einem Dichtwerk eine große politische Aktion heraufbeschwor [...]. Mit ihrem welterregenden Roman *Onkel Toms Hütte!* Sie war es, die 1852 die öffentliche Meinung der Nordstaaten gegen die Sklavenhalterdespotie der Südstaaten aufrief, die zum erstenmal Gleichberechtigung der farbigen Nigger forderte. Es kam zum Kampf und Sieg der Nordstaaten, daraus die 'Vereinigten Staten' hervorgingen.[23]

More immediately and with reference to the second work Kurt Hager's speech at the consultative meeting of March 1963 illustrated the

---

[21] Quoted in Werner Brettschneider, *Zwischen literarischer Autonomie und Staatsdienst: Die Literatur der DDR*, West Berlin 1972, p.27.

[22] *Programm der Sozialistischen Einheitspartei Deutschlands*, East Berlin 1963, p.135.

[23] Friedrich Wolf, *Aufsätze 1919-1944*, Berlin and Weimar 1967, p.78.

possible direct effect of art with reference to *Schlacht unterwegs* and argued:

> Unsere Auffassung darüber, wie Literatur bei der Lösung der ökonomischen Aufgaben helfen, wie sie zur Steigerung der Arbeitsproduktivität beitragen kann, ist in diesem Werk geradezu klassisch verkörpert.[24]

At the time of writing *Levins Mühle* Bobrowski was unwillingly caught up in this debate and in the same talk 'Benannte Schuld – gebannte Schuld?' in which he castigated the 'Philosemite' he put forward his hypotheses: 'Literatur ist machtlos' (4:443) but 'es muß getan werden, nur auf Hoffnung'. On these hypotheses he built an argument that outlined the effects that might *legitimately* be expected from literature. However limited these might be, Bobrowski tried to define them, and the terms he used were revealing: where Hager and others pointed to the positive and mass effects of literature, its ability to assist in solving mass social, industrial and economic problems, Bobrowski's vision of a possible effect, on which he based his hope, was cautious and individual: literature can 'benennen', it can 'befragen, dringlich befragen'. It is not, however, 'geeignet, Massenbewegungen hervorzurufen' (4:448), and Bobrowski illustrated this argument with exactly the same examples that Friedrich Wolf had used and that Kurt Hager was later to use. Of *Uncle Tom's Cabin* he commented: 'Die Sklaverei hat es nicht beendet. So etwas geschieht nicht als Folge von Literatur' (4:445), and he expresses only contempt for the exaggerated claims made for Nikolaeva's novel:

> Ich möchte also, daß Literatur etwas ausrichten soll. Aber man verlangt zuviel, wenn man gleich immer die Ergebnisse kassieren will. Also *Schlacht unterwegs* in 45 000 Exemplaren, und das Produktionsaufgebot ist gesichert.[25]

In place of such exaggerated expectations and claims, Bobrowski presents his own practice:

---

[24] *Dokumente zur Kunst-, Literatur- und Kulturpolitik der SED 1946-1970*, ed. Elimar Schubbe, Stuttgart 1972, p.862. In the 1970s this work still featured in official interpretations of the possible effect of art, and in the definitive *Zur Theorie des sozialistischen Realismus*, ed. Hans Koch, Berlin 1974, one finds the statement: 'Sowohl in der Sowjetunion als auch in der DDR wirkte [*Schlacht unterwegs*] nachhaltig und half bei der Überwindung einer veralteten Einstellung zur Arbeit' (p.142).

[25] The comment on this text was particularly topical since Galina Nikolaeva was, at that moment, visiting the GDR.

> Ich benenne also Verschuldungen – der Deutschen –, und ich versuche, Neigung zu erwecken zu den Litauern, Russen, Polen usw. Da ein solches Thema von historisch gewachsenen Vorurteilen und von aus Unkenntnis oder Voreiligkeit resultierenden Ressentiments weitgehend verdeckt ist, kann eine einfache Propagierung von Ansichten oder Empfehlungen nichts ausrichten. Ich beziehe mich also möglichst auf das, was ich selber kenne, ich will möglichste Authentizität, weil ich denke, daß 'wahre Geschichten' noch immer eher überzeugen. (4:447)

Levins Mühle forms part of this debate and provides an exposition of Bobrowski's arguments, illustrating the relationship between art and historical events through the relationship between the gypsies' song and the Grandfather's decision to retreat to Briesen. It is clear that the song is an irritant, disturbing the Grandfather every time he hears it. Its main achievement is, however, that it serves simply to remind the villagers of something they might otherwise have forgotten, and the Grandfather comments with considerable surprise that the story of his crime just will not go away, 'diese Geschichte, über die Gras wachsen sollte' (3:96). Although its influence extends beyond the village to include people such as Tante Huse, who are already predisposed to sympathy with Levin, the song converts no-one from the Grandfather's camp. It constitutes instead a focal point for opposition to the Grandfather, and it is typical of Bobrowski's cautious, realistic attitude that he criticises in his speech the ideology that concludes that art must have a significant direct effect, while presenting in his novel a story in which he stresses the importance of the song but also refuses to establish any *direct* link between it and the Grandfather's decision to move. This is not explained, and the Grandfather remains a 'Mann einsamer Entschlüsse' (3:208). All Bobrowski can do is hint at possible reasons: the pressure from other sources; the contempt in which he is held by sections of the community; the tampering with his privy; the public humiliation of the brawl in the pub;[26] finally, perhaps most significantly, the lack of support he experiences from the platoon of soldiers stationed in Neumühl, a lack of support brought about by his own arrogance and refusal to bribe the soldiers enough. In fact, Bobrowski hints at a number of social and economic circumstances as possible reasons for the Grandfather's retreat, while the song, literature, indeed art in general

---

[26] Indeed, the publican Rosinke allows this to happen for purely economic reasons: the Grandfather is not a frequent enough customer (3:194).

have little effect. As Bobrowski baldly stated in his speech: 'Ver-
änderungen in der Gesellschaft [...] geschehen auf andere Weise, nicht
durch Literatur' (4:445).[27] Despite the significance of art in the novel,
this modesty of claim is the over-riding factor.

Levins Mühle started with a half-quotation from Joseph Conrad that
looked back to the Napoleonic Wars and referred to a distant
Bobrowski. This initiated a number of references to Bobrowski's own
family, and it is clear that *Levins Mühle* presents an incident from this
family history, using considerable local colour and detail to add
'möglichste Authentizität', in order to create the impression of being
one of the 'wahre Geschichten' to which he referred (4:447). Bobrowski, however, repeatedly breaks through this fiction, as his narrator, after
initially questioning the moral legitimacy of telling the tale, more radically undermines the entire fiction by asking whether he, the narrator,
should not have set it somewhere else altogether. At first this is expressed only as a possibility:

> [wir sind] ganz hübsch vorangekommen in dieser Culmerländischen Ge-
> schichte, die übrigens auch um Osterode herum, dann aber später, oder um
> Pultusk herum, dann aber früher, spielen könnte, meinetwegen auch im
> Waldland um den Wysztyter See oder noch weiter nördlich, nach Litauen
> hinauf, dann müßte aber der Glinski Adomeit heißen und der Pilchowski, der
> jetzt Pilch heißt, Wilkenies und später Wilk, was ebenso litauisch ist, aber
> nicht so auffällt, der Wyderski müßte Naujoks heißen, der Gonserowski
> Aschmutat, der Urbanski Urbschies, oder die Geschichte könnte auch im
> Lettischen spielen, dann aber auch früher, solch eine Geschichte ist das. (3:55)

This idea is repeated and varied (3:115 and 3:196). By the end of the
work, however, the *historical* possibility (that the events presented as
happening in Neumühl could have taken place in many other places) has
become a *narrative* possibility, the source of new doubts for the
narrator:

> Und nun überlege ich nur, ob es nicht doch besser gewesen wäre, die ganze
> Geschichte weiter nördlich oder noch besser viel weiter nordöstlich spielen *zu
> lassen*, [my italics] schon im Litauischen, wo ich alles noch kenne. [...]
> Aber warum denn? Die Geschichte hätte an so vielen Orten und in so vielen
> Gegenden passieren können, und sie sollte hier nur erzählt werden. (3:222)

---

[27] Similarly, on a wider historical scale, the songs and stories concerning the Polish
Uprising of 1863 that are included in the novel do not lead to direct political action but
keep alive a memory that others would clearly prefer forgotten.

Bobrowski undermines his own fiction even more radically when he admits to deliberately transposing details of the two towns Briesen and Strasburg:

> Strasburg ist langweilig. Allerdings, und das haben wir bisher verschwiegen, ist es eigentlich die Kreisstadt. Also Briesen ist keineswegs der großmächtige Ort, zu dem wir ihn gemacht hatten. 3800 Seelen, ja das bleibt, zwei Kirchen und Wiezorreks Deutsches Haus auch [...] aber Kreisgericht, Katasteramt, Landratsamt, das alles ist eigentlich für Strasburg bezeugt. Aber wir können uns jetzt nicht daran kehren.
> Briesen liegt, was die Straßenverhältnisse anlangt, erheblich günstiger für unsere Geschichte, wenn sie schon in Neumühl spielen soll. (3:115)

The last comment raises, incidentally, the legitimate and unanswered question, why the story 'in Neumühl spielen soll'.

Even the fiction of the individual narrator is undermined, as he changes both geographical and temporal perspective. At the beginning of the novel he informed his reader: 'Ich sitze [...] einige hundert Kilometer Luftlinie westlich von jenem Weichseldorf' (3:10), and the time of narration is roughly Bobrowski's present. By the end, however, as Weiszmantel disappears into the winter of 1874, the narrator's position is quite different: he has moved close to the action and writes: 'Da lehnen wir am Zaun und sehn ihm nach, bis es dunkel wird. Dort geht er noch, ganz in der Ferne' (3:222). As the narrator had superfluously emphasised: 'Wir erzählen hier eine Geschichte' (3:168).

Despite its concentration on the historically insignificant events of a few weeks in 1874, the novel continues and develops the theme of the relations between the Germans and their Eastern neighbours, and refers in the passages just quoted to a historical and geographical entity far greater than that of late nineteenth-century Culmerland. It also presents a mass of topographical and historical detail, explains in passing the workings of a water-mill, writes of the flora and fauna of the area, lists at length the various culinary possibilities available for a quick snack[28] and shows how to cook a hedgehog ('für den, der es nicht weiß'). It presents a thumbnail sketch of Briesen ('3800 Seelen' etc.), and all this is evidently the product, if not of Bobrowski's own experiences then certainly of wide reading and, possibly, discussions with his father, who

---

[28] 'Sakuska. Gurken, und wenn keine Gurken, dann Sauerkohl, und wenn keinen Sauerkohl, dann saure Pilze, und wenn keine Pilze, dann Fisch, Quappen in Gelee [...] irgend

had known the area much better. The result is the interplay between factual detail and narrative distance that constitutes the novel's dual nature. *Levins Mühle* is a product of Bobrowski's deep love for his 'Ostvölker' and the lost regions of the East, and as such it involves a self-indulgent absorption in the past. It presents also, however, a 'Modellfall für das Verhalten der Nationalitäten untereinander' (4:465), or, as Bobrowski wrote in an apologetic letter to Gerhard Bobrowski of January 5 1965: 'Ich wollte allgemeine Verhaltensweisen zeigen, nicht individuelle – und außerdem mehr zur Gegenwart als zur Historie sagen' (*Marbach* 706).

Beyond the authentic retelling of a historical event, the 'Authentizität' of 'wahre Geschichten', beyond the 'Modellfall' and beyond the contribution to a contemporary literary discussion on the possible effects of art, *Levins Mühle* contains a further surprising dimension produced by a series of allusions to Hamann's 'Golgotha und Scheblimini', an edition of which Bobrowski had reviewed in the late 1950s (4:367-369) and with which he continued to be confronted in his work for the Union Verlag, as he prepared *Entkleidung und Verklärung* for publication. Bobrowski's own internal report on this anthology (see *Marbach* 408-10) was prepared in January 1962, well before the start of serious work on *Levins Mühle*, but on January 5 1963 he received the fifth volume of *Johann Georg Hamanns Hauptschriften erklärt: Mysterienschriften* (1962), at a time when, as he wrote in a letter of January 8 to Peter Hamm (*Chronik* 72), he had 'endlich wieder an den Roman gegangen'.[29] He was again working with Hamann.

In 'Golgotha und Scheblimini' Hamann had taken issue with Moses Mendelssohn's 1783 work *Jerusalem oder über religiöse Macht und Judenthum*. Hamann criticises this for its exaggerated rationalism and systematisation and in one context mocks what he sees as the dangerous individualisation of 'Recht':

> Ist aber das *Ich*, selbst im Stande der Natur, so ungerecht und unbescheiden, und hat jeder Mensch ein gleiches Recht zum *Mir!* und *Mir allein!* – so laßt uns fröhlich seyn über dem *Wir von Gottes Gnaden*.[30]

---

soetwas' (3:76).

[29] By January 21 he had completed the third chapter (*Chronik* 72).

[30] Johann Georg Hamann, *Sämtliche Werke*, vol.3, p.300.

Levins Mühle echoes this in dealing with the Grandfather's concept of 'Recht':

> Das hört sich an wie ein Zauberwort und lautet schlicht: Mein Recht. Beides groß geschrieben. Ganz klar, daß die Welt damit nicht bestehen kann. Mein Großvater hat also Sein Recht, es gehört ihm, aber natürlich soll es für alle gelten. (3;25)

Hamann also deplored in this work the tendency to work with abstract 'eternal verities'. He stressed instead the historical, factual nature of his christocentric religion:

> Weil ich von keinen *ewigen Wahrheiten*, als *unaufhörlich Zeitlichen* weiß [...] Der charakteristische Unterschied zwischen Judentum und Christentum betrifft also weder [...] *ewige Wahrheiten* und *Lehrmeinungen* – – noch *Cerimoniel=* und *Sittengesetze*: sondern lediglich zeitliche *Geschichtswahrheiten,* die sich zu einer Zeit zugetragen haben, und niemals wiederkommen – *Thatsachen,* die durch einen Zusammenhang von Ursachen und Wirkungen in einem Zeitpunct und Erdraum *wahr* geworden. (*Werke* vol.3, pp.303f.)

The corresponding passage in *Levins Mühle* occurs as the narrator reflects on Weiszmantel's new happiness:

> Wie kommt es, daß seine Lieder fröhlicher geworden sind?
> Es ist doch da etwas gewesen, das hat es bisher nicht gegeben. Nicht dieses alte Hier-Polen-hier-Deutsche oder Hier-Christen-hier-Unchristen, etwas ganz anderes, wir haben es doch gesehen, was reden wir da noch. Das ist dagewesen, also geht es nicht mehr fort. (3:221f.)

Hamann and Bobrowski emphasise the significance of the unique and factual rather than the general and theoretical. Both present a defence of the actual as opposed to the theoretical, an appeal to the primacy of reality over dogma, and in demonstration of this the expulsion of the Grandfather in *Levins Mühle* is not the result of the working out of 'eternal' Marxist Leninist laws of social development but is brought about by a single unique set of circumstances.

Such apparently abstruse points gain an added piquancy for the GDR if one bears in mind an early critical article by Robert Havemann, published in the GDR paper *Sonntag* on 28 October 1956, entitled 'Rückantworten an die Hauptverwaltung "Ewige Wahrheiten"'. Here Havemann argued: '[Der Dogmatismus] hat unsere Philosophie zu einem System allgemeinster Sätze über die allgemeinste Struktur der Welt zu machen versucht, zu einer Hauptverwaltung "Ewige Wahrheiten" (HEW)'.[31] With this *bon mot* Havemann was attacking the party organs responsible especially for sciences and the arts, the very ones that caused such difficulties for Bobrowski in his last years.

Even the 'Nein' of the last 'Satz' may be seen as echoing Hamann's repeated reference in his text to the 'sittliches Vermögen, *Ja!* oder *Nein!* zu sagen' (*Sämtliche Werke* vol.3, p.300). More indirect, but still recognisable, is a reference to 'Golgotha und Scheblimini' which Bobrowski applies in order to criticise the 'Großvater'. In the same context in which he criticised the individualisation of 'Recht' Hamann criticises those who demand things to which they are not entitled:

> [Der Mensch] hat also weder ein physisches noch moralisches Vermögen zu einer anderen Glückseeligkeit, als die ihm zugedacht, und wozu er beruffen ist. Alle Mittel, deren er sich zur Erlangung einer ihm nicht gegebenen und beschärten Glückseeligkeit bedient, sind gehäufte Beleidigungen der Natur und entschiedene Ungerechtigkeit. Jede *Lüsternheit* zum *Besserseyn* ist der Funke eines höllischen Aufruhrs. (*Sämtliche Werke* vol.3, p.299)

In *Levins Mühle* the narrator describes Weiszmantel's arrival at the grandfather's house. Weiszmantel and other characters have previously referred on many occasions to the Grandfather as a 'Teufel' or 'Deiwel':

> Wie der Deiwel heißt, der hier los ist, das weiß der Weiszmantel schon, jetzt bekommt er ihn zu sehen. Er wundert sich nicht, aber er denkt doch: Immer war der nicht so.
> Aber wie war er denn? [...] Du weißt das alles nicht richtig, Weiszmantel: nicht, wie man sich anstellt, wenn man etwas hat und es behalten will, noch weniger, wie es einem zusetzt, wenn man mehr haben will als man hat, schon gar nicht, wie einem zu Mute ist, der hier sitzt, in diesem Land, und weiß: er ist deutsch wie der Kaiser in Berlin, aber rundherum gibt es nur diese Polen und anderes Volk, Zigeuner und Juden, und nun, Weiszmantel, stell dir mal einen vor, bei dem das alles zusammenkommt: behalten wollen, mehr haben wollen, *besser sein wollen* als alle andern. (3:72, my italics)

The last phrase is the most significant. It characterises the Grandfather's attitude and that displayed during the entire history of the German presence in the East as Bobrowski interpreted it: 'besser sein wollen als alle andern.' The Grandfather, 'Deiwel' here as elsewhere in the novel, is guilty of producing just such a 'Funke des höllischen Aufruhrs' through his own version of this 'Lüsternheit zum Besserseyn'.

---

[31] Reprinted in Robert Havemann, *Die Stimme des Gewissens: Texte eines deutschen Antistalinisten*, ed. Rüdiger Rosenthal, Reinbek 1990, p.37.

These allusions in no way turn *Levins Mühle* into some form of religious drama, with the 'Deiwel' of the Grandfather defeated by the symbolically named Habedank and Weiszmantel. They do, however, indicate an alternative discourse and cast doubt on any attempt to read the work exclusively in terms of socio-economic circumstances, and commentators who have done so have reduced its significance.[32] In introducing this further dimension Bobrowski was attempting, yet again, to prevent (and indeed reject) such simplistic ideologically-based interpretations. As he demonstrates, the German who desires 'Ordnung' and feels 'deutsch wie der Kaiser in Berlin' is descended from Polish ancestors, while Poles have German surnames and Germans Polish. *Levins Mühle* emphasises the importance of confronting all aspects of one's past, as an individual and as member of a nation. Such a confrontation, in the spirit of enquiry which is assuredly *not* present in the Grandfather's selective use of his 'Geistererscheinungen', makes of history itself an anti-ideological corrective.

The narrator undermines the very tenets of the Grandfather's nationalism, and does the same for the purity of Christianity to which the 'Frommen' pay such lip-service, as, at the end of the novel the distinctly pagan Weiszmantel sets off into the distance and the narrator comments: 'Und Gott wird ihn schützen. Ihm wird es, denke ich, ganz recht sein, so, wie es der Weiszmantel macht' (3:222).[33]

Levins Mühle ends on a muted note of hope. The Grandfather is incorrigible, indeed the narrator has given him up, though Philippi still intends to irritate him. The various groups devoted to combating him have, however, worked together, if only once, and Weiszmantel's songs are happier because of what he has experienced. In addition, the narrative itself has established something quite new as it developed. At the beginning, as the discussion concerning the first sentence and the constant reference to an 'ich' make clear, the narrator presented himself

---

[32] M. and W.Dehn suggest that the novel '[gilt] vor allem [...] dem Verhältnis der "wirtschaftlich stärkeren" Leute zu den "wirtschaftlich Schwächeren"' in *Johannes Bobrowski: Prosa*, Munich 1972, p.31, and Gerhard Wolf makes a similar error when he claims: 'Die Untat beginnt völlig unscheinbar aus dem Alltag heraus, mit dem privaten Geschäft, und die Antriebe dazu liegen in der verfehlten Organisation menschlichen Zusammenlebens: im Kapitalismus', in *Johannes Bobrowski: Leben und Werk*, East Berlin 1967, p.73.

[33] It is the same sense of divine tolerance found in the short story 'Roter Stein'.

as misunderstood, facing, indeed almost opposed by a readership that
interpreted too quickly and superficially and that was happiest with its
'feste Urteile'. In its development the novel presents a number of shifts
from this singular 'ich' to a plural 'wir', implying new awarenesses on
the part of the reader. In describing gypsies, 'Richtige Zigeuner sind
richtig schön' the narrator initially appeared as an individual ('Ich sage
es, wie es ist') narrating a personal experience ('[...] hab ich an einer
Kirchenwand gelesen'). Returning to the subsequent fate of the gypsies
he turns to a collective 'wir': the gypsies have been 'zusammenge-
trieben und erschlagen in jenen Jahren, an die wir uns erinnern' (3:60), a
statement implying collective complicity. The same complicity is underlined in the discussion of the fifteenth 'Satz', where the narrator's use of
'wir' implies a community made guilty by its refusal to face the consequences of past sins, a refusal which constitutes its own *continuing*
sin: '[wir] nehmen uns unterdessen vielleicht stillschweigend aus'
(3:126). By the end, however, the narrator is presenting a shared
purpose between himself and his readers, a shift from an 'I' to a 'we'
which indicates that the sense of isolation and misunderstanding of the
first few pages has been overcome, and from the moment that 'unsere
Geschichte befindet sich [...] in Liquidation' (3:212) the narrator sees
himself as belonging to the community. The change is clear as the
narrator's position itself changes and his doubts from the beginning of
the novel are finally allayed in the last 'Satz', so that the entire novel is
embraced by the uncertainty of the beginning ('is it wrong for me to tell
the story?') and the certainty of the end: 'Nein'. The narrator and his
audience – this is the fiction – have come to share a common set of
moral values, directed against 'Grandfathers' of every persuasion who
just want to be left in peace with their prejudices, their 'Recht', their
'feste Urteile' and their guilt: 'Und dieses Philippische Nein, das soll
gelten. *Uns* gilt es hier für den letzten Satz' (my italics).

   Levins Mühle is designed to counteract expectations, to militate
against quick deductions and easy conclusions, to undermine accus-
tomed patterns of thought. Like Bobrowski's other works, it is directed
against the 'klarer Blick' based on ignorance or prejudice, emphasising
instead the significance of the often small detail, the inconvenient actual
fact so easily overlooked in following an ideological pattern. The work
constitutes an invitation to be exact, concentrating on detail rather than
the pattern which, perceived, imagined or imposed, would detract from
the actuality of how things were: 'und so ist es auch gewesen' (3:10).

This exposure of the inadequacy or failure of accepted patterns of thought constitutes the underlying motif of the work. It directly undermines the ideologies of nationalism, with particular reference to Bobrowski's theme of 'die Deutschen und der europäische Osten'; it pours scorn on the stupidity of anti-Semitism, but distances itself also from the simplistic and self-serving attitudes of the Philosemite; more indirectly it involves a common-sense critique of official cultural policies of the GDR, in particular its dogmatic insistence on the direct effect of literature. In this *Levins Mühle* makes a small but telling contribution to one of the literary debates of the early 1960s, a debate to which Bobrowski was contributing in his public utterances as well. While attempting all this, Bobrowski was also conducting a private dispute with members of his family from the Bundesrepublik who could not see the history of German involvement in the East as he himself did. To sustain debate on all these fronts simultaneously was a remarkable achievement.

8

LITAUISCHE CLAVIERE

Levins Mühle was completed in the summer of 1963. In 1964 and early 1965 Bobrowski wrote of his plans for a second novel, 'ein Roman mit 2 Personen' based on an incident from the Second World War.[1] By May 11 1965, however, this plan appears to have been abandoned, as he announces in a letter to Klaus Wagenbach that he has shortened this 'Kriegsgeschichte', his 'Bericht über Träume', to 80 pages and intends to start a new second novel, entitled *Litauische Claviere*, after he had finished it (*Marbach* 769). In the event Bobrowski abandoned the earlier project altogether and instead, in a burst of frenetic productivity between June 6 1965 and July 28 1965, wrote *Litauische Claviere*.

Such a complete change of plan within a few weeks is surprising but becomes less so if one recognises that some of the themes of *Litauische Claviere* reflect problems with which Bobrowski was directly and probably unexpectedly confronted in these weeks, and if one recognises that the work, arguably even more than *Levins Mühle*, represents a phase in the argument with the GDR concerning the role of art itself. Like *Levins Mühle*, *Litauische Claviere* offers a response to contemporary events and specific criticisms from this period.

In other important respects too the novel develops aspects of *Levins Mühle*. While the earlier novel looked at an area of West Prussia with its mixed German and Polish villages, the later depicts relations between the Germans and the Lithuanians sharing the mixed area of the Memelland, and both novels reach their climax in the juxtaposition of two sets of celebrations leading to violence. The problem of justice and its perversion in a mixed area is also raised. A further clear narrative parallel lies in the depiction of a love affair transcending boundaries. There is even a specific verbal link between two of the major protagonists: as Weiszmantel (3:222) walks out of *Levins Mühle*, he 'schwenkt ein bißchen den linken Arm'; when the 'Primgeiger' Gawehn is introduced at the beginning of *Litauische Claviere*, he has 'ein auffällig schlenkernder Arm, der linke' (3:227). A far more important link, however, one related to this figure of the artist, is formed by shared

---

[1] See his letter to Elisabeth Borchers of March 18 1964 (*Marbach* 768) and other references in 6:147f.

considerations of the possible significance of art, indeed of all cultural activity. In *Levins Mühle* this issue had been raised by the possible indirect contribution of the gypsy ballad to the Grandfather's decision to leave Neumühl. In *Litauische Claviere* this problem is more complex: the possibility, indeed the very legitimacy of writing an opera in German on the Lithuanian national poet Kristijonas Donelaitis (1714-1780) during a period of intense German-Lithuanian rivalry.

The novel also continues and develops the style of *Levins Mühle*. The narrator maintains his 'Hausrecht' over the characters: he interrupts the action, comments, criticises and warns, summarises because the characters would take too long to tell the story (3:283f.), imposes 'Sonnabendfarben' (3:243f.) to describe both natural phenomena and a coffee-service using the same colours. He deliberately makes unclear who is narrating a particular incident, so that a central chapter oscillates between a prose-poem by the narrator and a story told by one of the characters: 'davon reden wir jetzt, oder Storost redet selber: wie das war' (3:289).

The novel was completed at considerable speed, and this fact, in combination with its formal complexity, has led some critics to consider it incomplete,[2] while others have suggested that it is an even greater achievement than *Levins Mühle*.[3] It is certainly a difficult work, elliptical and allusive, with few concessions to the reader and with few of the narrative props of the realist novel, and the immediate response in East and West to its posthumous publication has been well summarised as 'eine durch Wohlwollen gedämpfte Ratlosigkeit'.[4] Instead of realistic techniques, the novel, especially in the last three chapters, develops a playfulness of narrative that allows the text to move freely between the allegorical, some elements of a superficially realistic plot, and a sequence of dreams or fantasies by one of the characters. The climax of this conflation of levels occurs when the novel is interrupted by the narrator himself, who proposes that a particular dream could form a

---

[2] Thus Johann Siering, 'Johannes Bobrowski: *Litauische Claviere*', in *Neue Deutsche Hefte,* 14 (1967), no.3, 157-9.

[3] See Hubert Ohl, 'Johannes Bobrowskis Roman "Litauische Claviere": Struktur und Thematik' in *Revolte und Experiment: Die Literatur der sechziger Jahre in Ost und West,* ed. Wolfgang Paulsen, Heidelberg 1972, pp.186-206.

[4] See H. Bosse, 'Johannes Bobrowski: *Litauische Claviere*' in *Neue Rundschau,* 78 (1967), 494.

sketch for a possible scene for this opera, while indicating also that his own fictional characters other than the dreamer are observing the same scene, trying to note down a musical rhythm. The narrator himself does not, however, move with ironic distance above his creation, but claims instead to be physically part of it. Just as the narrator at the end of *Levins Mühle* placed himself physically in the narrative: 'Da lehnen wir am Zaun und sehn ihm nach, bis es dunkel wird', so in *Litauische Claviere* the narrator extricates himself from participation in his own meta-fiction (his observation of the envisaged opera-scene within the novel) with the words: 'Da gehen wir besser ein Weilchen vor die Tür' (3:325).

By such means Bobrowski creates a number of links between the proposed opera and the written novel, and several of the comments describing this opera or other musical ideas clearly function as self-reflections of the novel: 'durchgehende Handlung kaum möglich' (3:229), 'ein paar ungewöhnliche Intervalle, bei ständigem Taktwechsel, fortwährendes Modulieren, die Fermate keine Fermate, das Ritardando kein Ritardando, – ein Erzählton vielleicht, aber doch wieder auch nicht ein Parlando' (3:237f.), while the theme of musical modulation is emphasised elsewhere by references to the concept of musical temperament. It is, as befits a novel on an opera, a work in which music plays a significant part.

The work consists of nine chapters, in which two humanistically minded Germans – a teacher, Voigt, and a musician, Gawehn – leave an unnamed town recognisable as Tilsit and travel across the River Memel to the Memelland. It is June 1936. They are planning to write an opera together about Donelaitis and intend to seek advice from a Lithuanian teacher Potschka, who has been assigned by the Lithuanian authorities to a school in the Memelland. Potschka is an ardent collector of Lithuanian folksongs and a passionate admirer of Donelaitis. Before leaving Tilsit, Voigt and Gawehn witness National Socialist brutality: they see an elderly pianist Elisat attacked by a Nazi Lenuweit for daring to sing songs in Lithuanian, an act of violence which *in nuce* anticipates the problems they face with their own work.

Their visit to the village Willkischken in the Memelland coincides with a visit by a certain Neumann, 'Rechtsanwalt Neumann, Memeler Führer einer neulich in Berlin gegründeten memelländischen Partei, treudeutsch und großdeutsch' (3:247). Voigt and Gawehn have a short but evidently very productive meeting with Potschka on the Saturday afternoon before Potschka leaves to spend the night with his girlfriend, a Memel German. It is an act of cross-national mixing disapproved of by the nationalist Germans, and as such a relationship that repeats the Levin-Marie liaison of *Levins Mühle*. That night a Memel German Josupeit is killed by Nazi supporters because he refuses to be transferred to the 'Reich'.

The next day being Sunday, Voigt and Gawehn attend church and are impressed by a sermon of reconciliation on 'Die großen Taten in verschiedenen Zungen' (3:275), although they also see that the sermon met with rejection from National Socialists present in the congregation. Gawehn returns to Tilsit inspired to continue work on the opera. That afternoon and evening the Memel Germans and Lithuanians hold separate celebrations: the German 'Vaterländischer Frauenverein' holds its annual celebration with a play about the humiliation of Queen Luise at the hands of Napoleon, while the Lithuanians perform a 'Festspiel' about their medieval King Vytautas. While attending the Lithuanian celebrations, Voigt has a long explanatory conversation with two Lithuanian intellectuals who harbour considerable doubts concerning his planned opera. Later that evening some Nazi supporters start a brawl, and one of them is accidentally killed by a Lithuanian. Voigt witnesses the accident, but his explanations are brushed aside as Neumann has the Lithuanian arrested. Voigt returns to Tilsit to work at the opera with a sense close to despair at what he has experienced.

At the centre of the novel (chapter 5 out of 9) and forming a story of its own almost completely detached from the rest of the work is a chapter devoted to the life of a poor peasant Indra Budrus and his own experience of reading Donelaitis. Bobrowski refers in a 'Nachbe-merkung' (3:332) to this chapter as being based on fact. Finally, in the last three chapters, the 1936 plot virtually disappears behind the construction of a fictional trigonometric tower which Potschka climbs, and here in particular the distinction between the voice of the narrator and that of his characters is lost in meditations on, among other things, the nature of time and the possibilities for the opera. Potschka is followed by a mysterious unnamed figure, 'der Schreihals', the embodi-ment of evil within the novel, who pushes him off the tower. Before he is pushed, Potschka experiences the series of dreams/fantasies to which I have referred above, and then wakes up, brought back down to earth by his girlfriend Tuta.[5] In the second of these three chapters the narrator presents the possible scene from the opera. At the end of the work Potschka appears to be starting to undergo some change of attitude in response to the dangerous political situation.

In view of this international situation, with the two nationalistically-minded countries Germany and Lithuania struggling for control of the Memelland, it is not surprising that the plan for such an opera is greeted with considerable reservations, and an important episode involves a discussion between Voigt and the two Lithuanians on Voigt's intentions. Voigt eventually convinces them that his intention is not to reduce the figure of Donelaitis to a 'Deutschenfeind' (3:287), but to point to German-Lithuanian 'Herrschaftsverhältnisse' (3:288), i.e. the earlier historical oppression of Lithuania by Prussia. Despite this clarification, the project is presented as – at least for the foreseeable future – doomed, and *Litauische Claviere* is infused with a sense of futility: all the good intentions presented appear to achieve nothing, while subsequent historical developments in this area, especially the German invasion of the Memelland in 1939, must negate any optimism.

Bobrowski returns here to the small villages of his childhood holidays, the area to which he refers when he writes that he grew up 'um die Memel [...], wo Polen, Litauer, Russen, Deutsche miteinander lebten, unter ihnen allen die Judenheit' (4:335). It is the area that forms the background for many of his poems, especially his earlier ones, but also for the short stories 'Begebenheit', 'Idylle für alte Männer', and 'Lipmanns Leib', which is set in Bittehnen. More than in almost any other mature work, Bobrowski makes use here of his memories of Tilsit and the villages of the Memelland to form the background to the text. He also, in part as a result of the freedom of narration that allows him to move so easily between times and places, presents a dense historical background to the area, from the Teutonic Knights and their 'festes Haus' built on the confluence of the Memel and the Jura but now lost (3:273), to the uprising of 1525 and the red-haired miller of Kaymen (3:276), to the passage of Napoleon's army and the various searches for his war-chest (3:283f.). It touches on the long history of the Lithuanian-Polish alliance and the Lithuanian Empire, and on the various Prussian

---

[5] Some critics have misread the text as ending with the death of Potschka after a fall from the tower. Since there is no tower to begin with, this is unlikely. It is a 'Turm, den es nicht gibt' (3:311).

academic societies established in order to preserve Lithuanian culture, but often having the unintentional effect of undermining its independence. It also extends into the twentieth century to include the 1930s with the two countries squaring up over the Memelland. On the Lithuanian side Bobrowski refers to the events of the 1920s and 1930s that left Lithuania with a right-wing, authoritarian government, but incidentally, and with typical disregard for the facts, confuses the various elements of this political scene.

The Memelland, largely German in culture if not language for centuries, had fallen victim to the imposed boundary changes of the end of the First World War and had been placed under French jurisdiction by Article 99 of the Treaty of Versailles. In January 1923, at the time of the French occupation of the Ruhr, Lithuania had invaded it without resistance from the French occupying forces, and in February 1923 the *fait accompli* of the partial annexation was officially recognised, and according to the 'Memelabkommen' and the 'Memelstatut' of March 1924 Lithuania was granted rights in the Memelland, although the area was accorded a relatively autonomous status. The period from 1924 saw piecemeal attempts by the Lithuanians to eradicate the specifically 'memelländisch' (i.e. German-Lithuanian) character of this area, with a series of bureaucratic moves, including replacing German teachers with Lithuanians. Potschka is evidently such an imposed teacher, and the tensions his imposition brings to the German community help to explain in part the animosity displayed by his headmaster Kankelat (3:250). On the German side, the novel indicates the attempts made to rescind this annexation and re-integrate the Memelland, though again, not as a mixed area but as a German homeland. It is Neumann's proud claim that Willkischken is a 'nahezu unberührt deutsches Dorf' (3:251). The Memelland was re-annexed and Germanised by Hitler's Drittes Reich a week after the march into Prague in March 1939.

Despite some critical comments on developments in Lithuania proper ('diese Voldemaras-Leute an der Regierung!' 3:287), Bobrowski's main criticism is not surprisingly directed at those Germans who intend to subvert the particular mixed character of the Memelland, namely Neumann and the 'Spießgesellen [...] Kumpanen oder Komplizen' (3:247) who support his Memelland Party. Here as in *Levins Mühle* Bobrowski takes considerable liberties with historical facts, and the organised suppression by Lithuanians of German organisations in the Memelland at the time was such that the two main representatives of

German 'culture' and aggression in the work, the 'Vaterländischer Frauenverein' and Neumann's party, would certainly have been illegal under Lithuanian law. A historical Neumann, leader of a 'Sozialistische Volksgemeinschaft', had in fact been sentenced in 1935 to a long period of imprisonment (6:180f.).

Compared to the 'höllischer Aufruhr' of the Grandfather, the violence of the Nazis here is significantly greater. The group around Neumann and their puppet-masters in Berlin share the Grandfather's contempt for the 'alien' culture that surrounds them, but are even more violent in their reaction. The assault by the Nazi Lenuweit in Tilsit and the murder of the Memel German Josupeit by Nazis have been mentioned above, as has the violent brawl which resulted in a second death, admittedly of one of the Nazis themselves.

In presenting this evil Bobrowski also develops the demonic imagery that he had used for his Grandfather. Apart from the cumulative effect, the comparison in *Levins Mühle* had remained largely conventional. In *Litauische Claviere* the association is direct, and the satanic attributes with which Gottschalk, the 'Schreihals' and Neumann are endowed are explicit. Initially Bobrowski has Neumann blasphemously parodying John the Baptist (Matthew 3: 11ff.) to proclaim his role and point to 'einen anderen, noch größeren Führer [...], der nicht Neumann heißt, wie er' (3:254). This is developed: the Nazi thugs are associated with heat 'wie in den Ofen geblickt' (3:268); they fear the light: 'es wird heller. Du wirst dich beeilen müssen' (3:271). A number of images of demonic evil occur as the narrator attempts to warn Josupeit of the danger of his association with his Nazi murderer:

> Und kein schwarzer Hund, tot auf deinem Weg? Dann wäre wieder ein Teufel tot. Der vielleicht, der dich erwartet.
> Umgedrehte Rasenstücke am Saumpfad links. Siehst du das nicht? Was sagt man darüber, erinnere dich.
> So versteckt sich der Teufel vor Perkun, das sagt man. Weißt du es nicht mehr?

Lithuanian folklore knows of many struggles between the Devil and Perkun, which Perkun generally won with human assistance.[6] Similarly, the narrator's final plea to Josupeit:

---

[6] See *Funk and Wagnalls Standard Dictionary of Folklore, Mythology and Legend*, ed. Maria Leach, London 1975, p.858.

> Nur noch ein Mittel: Den Rock ausziehn, durch den ausgekehrten Ärmel
> blicken. Dann siehst du ihn, den Satan, dann erkennst du ihn. (3:273)

This image of seeing the Devil by looking through a sleeve is also well documented.[7]

When Gottschalk kills Josupeit, the link to the Devil is made explicit: 'Zu unsicher, sagt der Teufel' (3:273).[8] Finally, during the brawl at the foot of the Rombinus, the same imagery is used: Gottschalk tries to stop Voigt from approaching and Voigt replies:

> Gehen Sie zum Teufel, sagt Voigt.
> Jetzt ist es genug. Da hat Voigt wohl das richtige Wort gebraucht. Gottschalk
> dreht sich um und ist verschwunden, wie aufgelöst, vor ihren Augen. (3:305)

It is only appropriate that Neumann, when he appears on the scene here, reveals almost superhuman qualities: he 'steht plötzlich da, wie aus der Erde gewachsen' (3:307).

Through such insistent association with pre-Christian and Christian 'devils', Bobrowski presents an image of National Socialists as uniquely evil. Here too, however, he does not present a work implying some Manichaean struggle of good and evil (though the all-pervading imagery of light *versus* darkness occasionally suggests it), and as in *Levins Mühle* the sources of the conflict are attached also to specific socio-economic situations: Voigt can refer to 'Herrschaftsverhältnisse' (3:288), while Gawehn, provoked by arrogant German comments on the state of the Lithuanian economy, explains the situation 'kenntnisreich und präzis' (3:239) entirely in economic terms.

The novel is set against the background of two nations manoeuvring to exclude the other from rightful historical interests in the Memelland. Between these two fronts German and Lithuanian intellectuals and artists meet to discuss co-operation and, faced with these international tensions, wonder how to respond. It is a situation with evident contemporary parallels in 1965, and four years after the building of the Berlin Wall Bobrowski even has Neumann adopt the tone of the post-war West German 'Revanchist' demanding a return to the borders of 1937, as he

---

[7] See the *Handwörterbuch des deutschen Aberglaubens*, ed. E. Hoffmann-Krayer and others, Berlin and Leipzig 1927-42, vol.7, col.1017.

[8] The combination of Christian and pagan elements in the warnings ignored by Josupeit itself forms an image of cross-cultural tolerance compared with the savage uniformity dictated by National Socialism.

has him refer with false pathos to the iniquity of the 'unnatürliche Grenze' (3:293) under which he claimed to have suffered.

The central theme of the novel is not, however, the danger of international conflict but, within such a situation, the value or otherwise of – at its broadest – cultural endeavour, more specifically the problems of the artist like Bobrowski whose activities appear to be esoteric and backward-orientated, and the novel is to be read as a discourse on the potential for wide-spread effects of any artistic endeavour. As is clear from the previous chapter, this issue had faced Bobrowski for many years but in *Litauische Claviere* he responds, both in the different behaviour of Voigt, Gawehn and Potschka, and in the comments by the narrator, to a specific set of criticisms raised against him in the immediate past, so that as well as forming the culmination of his treatment of the theme of 'die Deutschen und der europäische Osten' *Litauische Claviere* presents, as will become clear, an exercise in self-justification and explanation. Other immediate concerns also left their mark in the work, in particular Bobrowski's participation in a conference of writers in Berlin and Weimar, to which I will return.

The most significant factor that led Bobrowski to abandon his 'Bericht über Träume' and write *Litauische Claviere* was almost certainly the noticeably more critical attitude to his work adopted by journalists anticipating the cultural freeze of December 1965. In early 1965 Bobrowski was interviewed by Eduard Zak for the East German weekly *Sonntag,* published by the East German 'Deutscher Kulturbund', with the interview published April 4 1965 (4:489-93). They talk largely about *Levins Mühle* and Zak touches on delicate matters: reflecting East German concerns with contemporary themes he asks why Bobrowski has not used autobiographical material and points to the advantages of such material, in particular its suitability, 'Probleme aufzugreifen, die den Menschen bei uns zu schaffen machen' (4:491). In not doing this, he suggests, Bobrowski '[verzichtet] auf die Wirkungsmöglichkeiten dieser Literatur'. Echoing the continued insistence on the socialist-realist 'positive hero' Zak also complains that with Bobrowski's material one cannot identify with a hero. Such comments, to which Bobrowski replied with irony but also with apparent irritation, imply potentially serious criticism.

The interview was followed in the same paper, *Sonntag,* two weeks later by a potentially even more damaging article, by the author and critic Adolf Endler.[9] This issue was devoted to lyric poetry, and Bobrowski's appearance here twice in three weeks was an indication of his importance. Together with eleven other writers he had been asked to choose his 'best poem' and write something about it. When he refused, the journal itself selected the quite untypical 'Bericht' and Endler wrote an article accompanying it. Here, like Zak, he touched on a number of delicate areas. He admitted that Bobrowski's poetry was 'bedeutend', but qualifies much of what he says: it is discussed 'in kleineren Kreisen'; it is fascinating 'vor allem für Zunftgenossen'; it has 'direkte Nachfolge nur in den neueren Gedichten des christlichen Dichters Gottfried Unterdörfer' (and possibly Bernd Jentzsch).

In summarising the response of literary critics, Endler refers specifically to a review by Manfred Bieler as being unambiguously positive. Bieler was a close friend of Bobrowski (see 4:402f.), but he was also above all a controversial figure already at odds with the East German authorities, who fell victim to the December 1965 11th Plenum, and so the reference to him in the article was no positive signal. Even more potentially damaging, for all its qualifications, was the particular tradition in which Endler chose to place Bobrowski: he related him to Peter Huchel, evidently someone who had influenced Bobrowski, but also someone who had been severely criticised by the authorities. Endler then discussed both writers in the context of the 'Schwierigkeit, eine eindeutige Stellung zur Romantik und ihren realistischen Elementen zu gewinnen'. Referring to Bobrowski's '"sarmatische" Traumlandschaft' he insisted that Bobrowski was 'ein Romantiker'. He praised him for the 'humanistische, völkerverbindende Funktion seiner Lyrik' and for his 'Liebesbekenntnis zur armen Bevölkerung jener Landstriche', which he saw as a political act, but then continued:

> Gleichzeitig erscheint die Hinwendung zu jenen (inzwischen veränderten) Landschaften und ihrer untergegangenen (oder inzwischen gewandelten) Gesellschaft auch als eine romantische Abkehr von der Gegenwart. Ist Sarmatien Bobrowskis 'Mittelalter' wie Huchels 'Mittelalter' zuzeiten die wendische Mark ist, der es an die 'Wurzeln' geht? (*Marbach* 239)

Endler praises these works as 'künstlerisch glänzenden und menschlich tief bewegenden Poesien' and pleads against short-sighted polemical attacks on their 'schwere Verständlichkeit'. He insists that Bobrow-

---

[9] The following quotations are taken from passages of the text published in *Marbach*

ski's works do not represent 'Gleichgültigkeit des Menschen gegenüber den gegenwärtigen Entwicklungen', but he insists also on the need for an 'Auseinandersetzung' concerning Bobrowski's 'poetische Abkehr von der Welt der Gegenwart'.

Bobrowski had publicly acknowledged his indebtedness to Huchel in the interview with Irma Reblitz of late March 1965, where he emphasised the *human* element he found in Huchel's works: '[von Huchels Werken] habe ich es her, Menschen in der Landschaft zu sehen, so sehr, daß ich bis heute eine unbelebte Landschaft nicht mag' (4:488). The element that Endler chooses to emphasise is, however, much less acceptable: it is the apparent flight from the present into a mythical past. In what is surely a direct response to this criticism, Bobrowski has the narrator in *Litauische Claviere* repeat almost *verbatim* what he had insisted to Reblitz was his main point of contact with Huchel: '[Diese Landschaft] werden wir [...] bevölkern, mit Leuten, weil die schönste Landschaft ohne Leute eine entsetzliche Öde ist, schlimmer als die Hölle' (3:319). Such repetition indicates explicitly the extent to which the novel forms a response to external events, as indeed Voigt's proposed opera on a historical subject like Donelaitis at a time of such violence inevitably implies a response to Endler's expressed concern at the 'poetische Abkehr von der Welt der Gegenwart'. Bobrowski does not provide a specific answer to such questions, but in the three figures of Gawehn, Potschka and Voigt he presents, as I will demonstrate, an attempt at self-orientation through literary triangulation.[10] In Voigt and Gawehn, he creates complementary positive figures open to misunderstanding, while in Potschka he presents an initially negative image indicating what he himself does *not* intend with his works.

In Potschka he also raises some of the problems discussed in the 'Internationales Schriftstellertreffen' in Berlin and Weimar of May 1965. Unlike many of his other duties, this was one that he clearly relished, since it held out the prospect of contact with writers from the other part of Germany. Since the closing of the Berlin Wall the importance of such contact had formed one of the recurrent themes of his correspondence, and this conference presented a new opportunity for

---

238f.

[10] The notion of triangulation, the magic three, runs throughout this work: the three keyboards; the three main characters, the nine (3x3) chapters, of which the last three are set on the trigonometric tower.

'Gespräch'. He explained in a statement exactly what he hoped to achieve:

> Nicht so sehr einen auf Repräsentanz und imponierende Zahlen erpichten Kongreß, sondern vielmehr Gespräche, Gespräche der Autoren untereinander, über Sprach- und weltanschauliche Grenzen hinweg. Weil ich aus meinen Erfahrungen weiß, daß Mißverständnisse und Vorurteile weniger durch Erklärungen, die leicht zu neuen Mißverständnissen führen, als durch das lebendige Gespräch beseitigt werden, schon weil der Gesprächspartner als Person seine Auffassung repräsentiert. (4:493)[11]

The importance of such a 'Gespräch' was emphasised in an interview with *Neue Zeit* of May 13 1965, where he commented:

> Ich bin nicht für Kontakte um jeden Preis, sondern für nützliche, weil überlegte Gespräche. Wenn nicht alles täuscht, ist das Bedürfnis nach dem Gespräch – auch über weltanschauliche Begrenzungen hinweg – in letzter Zeit zunehmend intensiv geworden. Es geht konform mit einem steigenden Bedürfnis nach zuverlässiger Information. Für beides muß vielfältige Gelegenheit gegeben werden.

Asked in the same interview about the relation of 'Geist' and 'Macht' he emphasised again the centrality of 'Gespräch': 'Die Frage ist außerordentlich wichtig. Gerade an ihr dürfte sich das Gespräch, auch mit den ausländischen Freunden, entzünden' (4:495). These apparently innocuous comments flatly contradicted official concern that such meetings increased the danger of 'ideologische Koexistenz', and Bobrowski's public pleas must be seen in the context of the East German policy of 'Abgrenzung' against its neighbour.

This same issue is then explicitly raised in *Litauische Claviere*, as the narrator highlights a 'Gespräch' between Voigt and his Lithuanian

---

[11] A considerably earlier (June 11 1958) letter to Hans Ricke makes Bobrowski's sensitivity here very clear:

> Dich haben einige meiner Formulierungen erschreckt. Weißt Du, es hört sich leicht manches wie ein apodiktisches Urteil an, was im Grunde nicht so gemeint ist. [...] Und was ich so daherschreibe, mein ich zwar ernst, doch bedarf alles der Korrektur, die ein Gespräch ja fortwährend leisten sollte, wenn es richtig ist. Eben solch ein Gespräch führen wir wohl. (*Marbach* 295)

On April 20 1965 he applied this to his poetry in a letter to Gregor Laschen: 'Funktion des Gedichts ist das Gespräch, freilich oft am Rand des Schweigens. Auch gibt es Gegenstände (des Gedichts), die nur signalisiert werden können, durch Zeichen'. Quoted by Reichert, p.12.

colleagues: 'Die Herrschaften also werden jetzt ein Gespräch anfangen. [...] Ein Gespräch. Aber aus lauter Lücken' (3:285/288). The discussion between these comments concerns the central theme of the work, the legitimacy or otherwise of the opera, and leads, as will become clear, to just the development of understanding that Bobrowski espouses, as the mixture of bemusement and downright hostility on the Lithuanian side is gradually overcome through Voigt's evident personal integrity and through the realisation that the opera involved a significant element of self-criticism by the German.[12] It is an image for the ideal meeting that Bobrowski himself sought in his immediate surroundings.

Bobrowski's personal doubts about the possible effect of literature surfaced in the context of his two 'Thesen' from 'Benannte Schuld – Gebannte Schuld?', and they continued into the period immediately prior to *Litauische Claviere*: in discussing with *Neue Zeit* the May 1965 meeting in Weimar and Berlin, he restated his doubts with a critical reference to 'Zweckoptimisten, die der Literatur [...] Macht zuschreiben' (4:495). In *Litauische Claviere* the tension between the 'Thesen' is embodied in Voigt's progression from his initial unreflected and naive confidence to a final position of tenuous hope. At the beginning of the novel his enthusiasm 'carries him' ('trägt einen' 3:228), and even the incident with Elisat does not dishearten him. It is only when confronted in church with the painting of the 1525 uprising that he begins to question his artistic intention and asks instead whether only such a 'gemeinsame, unerträgliche Not' could have such a unifying effect:

> Andere Wege gab es nicht?
> [...] Aber wie soll das glücken? Klagen, Eingaben, Mahnreden, alles nichts? Die bitteren Worte des Dorfpfarrers nichts? Die alle gesagt werden sollen, in dieser Oper? (3:276).

The doubt is raised here but not developed.

The discussion with Storost and Saluga is surrounded by references to Voigt's hope: 'Was ihn da nicht im Stich läßt, in diesem Gespräch, ist, vorerst noch kräftig, die Hoffnung. Aber wird sie sich halten?'

---

[12] That the conversation is conducted in both German and Lithuanian, with the German speaking Lithuanian and the Lithuanians German (3:285), underlines the element of mutual 'give and take' here. A constant theme throughout the novel is the interchange of languages: in the priest's sermon, in this conversation, and in the numerous references to Lithuanian and German alternative names or words.

(3:285); 'Alles auf Hoffnung: Diese Oper. Dieses Voigt'sche Ja, ich denke' (3:288). After the brawl, and in view of the threatening injustice that Neumann intends, Voigt's confidence sinks, but here too Bobrowski suggests that hope remains. On the boat returning to Tilsit, Voigt and Storost look back, 'das Herz voll Ratlosigkeit', but this 'Ratlosigkeit' is set against the background of dark and light: they 'zurückschauen, obwohl es ganz dunkel ist und das wenige Licht nur dahinfliegt [...] manchmal schon so, als müßte es jetzt ertrinken'. This struggle of light and dark is itself an image of faintest hope, and the 'Ratlosigkeit' of Voigt and Storost is further qualified in an exchange between Voigt and the narrator: 'Was ist auszurichten? Und womit? Doch mit der Oper, Herr Voigt? Ja, vielleicht doch' (3:315).[13] Voigt's 'Ja, vielleicht doch' represents a realistic assessment of the possible influence of literature in such a situation.

The central discussion between Storost, Saluga and Voigt is, however, more than just a discussion on hope. It is paradigmatic, showing how a 'Gespräch' can break down 'Mißverständnisse' and 'Vorurteile', as the suspicions harboured by Storost and above all Saluga echo Endler's concerns, and Bobrowski uses Voigt to rebut them. Saluga, a clearly more nationalistic Lithuanian, had been responsible for turning Storost's 'Schicksalsdrama' into the 'Weihespiel' criticised by Potschka, and his view of German involvement in Lithuanian history is so critical that even the mild-mannered Voigt feels provoked to correct it. He appears to deny the validity of the tradition within which Voigt (and Bobrowski) stand: 'wir verdanken ausländischen Philologen sehr viel, gerade deutschen. Aber jetzt, was bleibt davon jetzt? Eine Art Volkskundemuseum, – ein imaginäres außerdem'. He even questions the integrity of those who had been involved: 'Oder liegt es ganz anders, ging es nicht um die Integration Litauens und also um seine Auslöschung?' (3:286). Voigt's intentions too are open to suspicion as Saluga comments: 'Ich finde den Vorwurf so schön wie reizvoll, wir müssen Ihnen alle dankbar sein, – aber was beabsichtigen Sie damit?'

---

[13] See the short story 'Dunkel und wenig Licht' (4:118-26), which ends on a note of praise for the stars, whose presence has an effect even though they shed no light on the earth:

Was wäre also schon groß, wenn es [die Sterne] nicht gäbe [...]
Da oben – da wäre es anders. Es ist jetzt nicht heller als es dann wäre, dunkler also würde es nicht. Anders, und ich weiß nicht: wie. (4:126)

Faced with this, Voigt has to define his own position. He makes it immediately clear that he does not intend to produce· an idyll. Nor does he denigrate Donelaitis by concentrating on his physical suffering, or trivialise his criticism of Germans as that of a 'Deutschenfeind' (3:287). Instead, he finally finds himself 'bei der äußersten Bedächtigkeit angelangt' and summarises: 'Er meinte die Herrschaftsverhältnisse' (3:288). These 'Herrschaftsverhältnisse' involved Prussian subjugation of the Lithuanians, and Voigt, and through him Bobrowski, clears his subject-matter of any suspicion that it is, in Endler's words, a 'poetische Abkehr von der Welt', a 'Mittelalter [...] [dem] es an die "Wurzeln" geht'. Voigt here, it transpires, is writing like Bobrowski about the 'lange Geschichte aus Unglück und Verschuldung, die meinem Volke zu Buche steht'.

Voigt here also provides Bobrowski with an opportunity to defend and explain another aspect of his position, as his insistence that the life of Donelaitis is not 'exemplarisch', 'vielleicht nicht, wahrscheinlich nicht' (3:287), is also directly relevant for an issue from Bobrowski's own time: the dogma of 'das Exemplarische' in socialist realism and its emphasis on exemplary lives. Voigt insists here on the validity of artistic interest in lives other than the great 'exemplary' figures, and by so doing implies a defence of such interest that leads (*mutatis mutandis*) directly to Christa Wolf's own defence of her choice of heroine in *Nachdenken über Christa T.*: 'sie ist, als Beispiel, nicht beispielhaft, als Gestalt kein Vor-Bild'.[14]

Bobrowski's vicarious self-defence embraces here his chosen subject-matter, but it extends also to his poetic style when Voigt describes Donelaitis as 'ein deutsch gebildeter Mann, – der sich einer Sprache bedient, damals, in seinen Werken, die seine Wirkung doch nur einschränken kann' (3:287). In context the comment refers to Donelaitis's choice of Lithuanian for his poem *Metai*, *The Seasons*, but it could refer equally to Bobrowski's own situation, as a writer who insists on his hope for some form of effect, but whose poetic language is all too open to the criticism of blocking the effect he claims to desire. In this too the suggestion of a literary response to Endler's and Zak's direct and indirect criticisms is strong, and the novel not only concedes here the difficulty of this language, but also provides a form of justification for it

---

[14] *Nachdenken über Christa T.*, p.46. Elsewhere, echoing Bobrowski's quotation from Hamann in *Litauische Claviere* (3:312) Wolf's narrator praises her heroine's writings with the words: 'Sie redet, daß man sie sieht' (p.89).

in the central fifth chapter on Indra Budrus. This chapter is loosely linked with the rest of the work as a short prose poem on the beauty of the Lithuanian landscape and as containing Storost's own thoughts on the life and death of Budrus. Storost explains that Budrus bequeathed his copy of Donelaitis's *Metai* to him, and jottings in the margins indicate that this work had accompanied the simple 'Kätner' throughout his life and provided comfort and inspiration: 'Das habe ich auch erlebt [...] Es ist wahr, wir leben so [...] Gott wird schon machen' (3:291). The chapter thus ostensibly presents a tale of interaction between art and life over the centuries and demonstrates what *degree* of effect and what *kind* of effect might justifiably be expected from literature. Bobrowski pointedly emphasises this, as he has Voigt and Storost link it with Saluga's 'Fragen und Zweifel':

> Und Storost sagt: Sie denken jetzt, das gehört auch in diese Salugaschen Fragen und Zweifel hinein.
> Und auf Voigts Ja: Sie haben wohl recht. (3:292).

At the end of the novel Bobrowski's 'Nachbemerkung' emphasises its authenticity:

> Die im Kapitel V verwendeten Züge aus dem Leben des Kätners Indra Budrus gehen auf einen 1912 niedergeschriebenen Bericht des litauischen Dichters Dr. Wilhelm Storost-Vydaunas [...] zurück. (3:332)

The implication of the episode is that even apparently esoteric literature such as Donelaitis's Lithuanian hexameters may have an unexpected resonance, may, in the musical idiom that is appropriate to such a work, 'strike a chord'. Literature may not have produced any mass effect, (the *Metai* certainly did not) but its positive value for the individual Budrus cannot be denied.[15]

The character of Voigt allows Bobrowski to express aspects of his own doubts but also to present a form of self-defence: the absent-minded intellectual with a bookish interest in an obscure eighteenth-century writer (the parallel with Bobrowski himself is overwhelming) is not thereby inevitably out of touch with reality. The character of

---

[15] In fact Bobrowski is here misleading any reader who confuses fiction and reality. While Budrus is indeed mentioned in Storost's work, and while he did indeed draw comfort from a book, (in which he indeed wrote in part the comments attributed to him by Bobrowski) that book had nothing to do with Donelaitis or even fictional literature. It was Thomas à Kempis's *De imitatione Christi*.

Gawehn, who is less important in this context, presents a different figure, that of the productive artist. He too is enmeshed in contemporary reality and clearly suffers under the loud nationalism of the times: 'wie war es heute schon laut im Stadttheater. Der Schmied von Marienburg, eine Oper, man streicht seinen Part'.[16] His few lines of biography imply that he has also suffered under the regime: 'Konzertmeister oder, wie er noch immer genannt wird, Primgeiger, als einstiges Haupt eines Streichquartetts von übrigens gutem Ruf'. His evident passion for music leads Bühnenmeister Schwillus to his 'altgewohnten Feststellungen...: Das sieht und hört nichts, Fiddel in die Hand, Noten vor die Nase, Künstler, dahinter ist die Welt zu Ende, Probe aus, da zieht er ab' (3:227), but as ever such convictions are misplaced, and Gawehn later explains 'kenntnisreich und präzis' the problems caused to the Lithuanian economy by German economic measures, 'die Kündigung der Handelsverträge durch die Reichsregierung'. Appearances deceive, and 'bisher hat vielleicht Bühnenmeister Schwillus recht behalten: Fiddel in die Hand, Noten vor die Nase. Aber jetzt nicht mehr' (3:239). To be an artist with an interest in creating such esoteric works does not mean that one is ignorant of current affairs. The 'altgewohnten Feststellungen' of Bühnenmeister Schwillus here join the 'feste Urteile' attacked in *Levins Mühle* (3:10).

Of the three figures of orientation, Gawehn is the least developed as a character, and his artistic creativity and clear political awareness coexist rather uneasily. Potschka's contribution is, on the other hand, much more complex, even though his role in the novel is very limited until the end. Although present to help Voigt and Gawehn in their search for inspiration for the opera, he is not present during any of the festivities, being, it seems, totally absorbed in either his cultural studies and collecting or his love-affair with Tuta. In the last three chapters, however, he is presented in relation to an imaginary trigonometric tower which, Bobrowski emphasises, does not exist (3:311), but from which Potschka observes his Donelaitis and from which he falls or is pushed by an unnamed Memelland Nazi. He observes events from the tower, but twice the tower itself is described as 'eine Art Bühne' (3:310/317) indicating that Potschka himself is also an object of observation.

---

[16] At such a time and place the nationalistic implications of such a title need no explanation.

The trigonometric point has a history in poetry of which Bobrowski must have been aware. Günter Eich saw his own poems as forms of 'Abmessung im Nichts'[17] and used the image poetically in 'Der Lübbesee'. In Bobrowski's immediate surroundings may be found the poem by Hans Magnus Enzensberger 'trigonometrischer punkt' (from the volume *blindenschrift*, Frankfurt/M. 1964) which Bobrowski included in his private anthology *Meine liebsten Gedichte*.[18] The image is, however, used centrally in the abandoned sketch for the 'Bericht über Träume', and this immediate pre-history is particularly significant, as it anticipates – in a very primitive fashion – the issues Bobrowski associates with Potschka's predicament. The sketch provides an essential insight into the Potschka episode.

In the sketch for this 'Bericht' a German soldier on sentry-duty at a camp for Russian prisoners of war is described:

> Soldat Wiedemann, oben auf dem aus Balken gezimmerten Turm – nach Art trigonometrischer Punkte, nur oben abgesägt sozusagen: statt der Spitze eine Art Laube als Abschluß. (4:240)

The tower provides Wiedemann with an escape from the greyness and misery of the camp. Here he can indulge his passion for music, with an improvised keyboard forming a particularly strong link to *Litauische Claviere*: 'Wiedemann greift sich das Brett mit den aufgezeichneten Klaviertasten und probiert eine neue Kadenz für ein altes Konzert. Töne' (4:240f.). He can also indulge his passion for plants:

> Da zieht er Kletterpflanzen, blaue Kronenwicke und rosa Ackerwinde, an Stöcken. [...] Es ist, als führe [die Laube] mit ihm davon, leicht schwankend, von den Tönen getragen, die Kadenz sinkt ab, geht auf ihr Ende zu, auf einen festen einigenden Akkord: hier, über der Erde. (4:241)

As a 'gebildeter Mensch' (4:240/241) he is 'über der Erde', above the brutal camp reality of 'Scheißhaus', 'Stacheldraht' and 'Leichen' and, for the prisoners, 'Meldung [...] vor drei Tagen. Bis heute keine Verpflegung'. Wiedemann's 'Bildung', his love of culture and beauty provide him on his version of a 'trigonometrischer Turm' with an escape from the horrors of the camp in which he plays his part.

---

[17] Günter Eich, 'Der Schriftsteller vor der Realität', quoted in S.Müller-Hanpft (ed.) *Über Günter Eich*, Frankfurt/M. 1970, pp.19f.

[18] Johannes Bobrowski, *Meine liebsten Gedichte: Eine Auswahl deutscher Lyrik von Martin Luther bis Christoph Meckel*, ed. Eberhard Haufe, Berlin 1985, pp.362f.

The similarity to Potschka's tower is clear. In the last three chapters of *Litauische Claviere* this relatively simple image is then developed into a narrative framework within which Bobrowski can present critically Potschka's dreams and fantasies. Potschka had throughout the book been an ambiguous figure whose fascination with Donelaitis had blinded him to the immediate danger. His response had always been to withdraw. He withdraws into his idyll of love with the German girl Tuta, even though this brings him personally into danger as a defiler of German 'purity'; he withdraws into his passionate collecting of Lithuanian folksongs, which, in a nice irony, endangers the house that he nearly burns down when he falls asleep while working at them; and he retreats into an absorption in Donelaitis so intense that he loses his own identity while making love to Tuta and adopts Donelaitis's, calling her by the name of Donelaitis's wife Anna Regina (3:264-6). It is not then surprising that Potschka is physically and mentally absent throughout the violent events of the story at a time when Voigt and Gawehn are at least aware of the threats to their cultural activities. As in the case of the 'gebildeter Mensch' Wiedemann on his watch-tower, so Potschka's 'Bildung', his culture, functions as a retreat from or a barrier against his contemporary situation. Initially at least it serves as an example of just the 'Abkehr von der Gegenwart' that Endler criticised and from which, in this figure, Bobrowski is distancing himself.

Here too Bobrowski's work preparing the Berlin/Weimar conference contributed significantly. Bobrowski had, as I have shown above, promised himself 'Gespräche' and provided an example of this in Voigt's 'Gespräch'. In the context of Wiedemann and Potschka and the uses and abuses of culture, the influence of this conference is even clearer: the conference had celebrated the defeat of National Socialism twenty years before but had also looked beyond that to the Paris 'Kongreß zur Verteidigung der Kultur und des Friedens' of 1935. One of the themes of the earlier conference had been summarised in some words by Bertolt Brecht in his 'Rede [...] zur Verteidigung der Kultur': 'Die Kultur ist gerettet, wenn die Menschen gerettet sind'.[19] The statement emphasised the importance of a direct link between culture and mankind, with no separate realm of culture which could be rescued over the downfall of humanity. In his interview with *Neue Zeit*,

---

[19] Bertolt Brecht, *Gesammelte Werke in zwanzig Bänden*, Frankfurt/M. 1967, vol.18, 241-246 (p.245).

(4:494f.) Bobrowski is confronted with this phrase and responds positively:

> Kultur meint ja nicht einfach einen Besitzstand, sondern ist nur als Bewegung denkbar, als ein Prozeß fortschreitender Humanisierung, als die Vermensch- lichung der Verhältnisse. (4:494)

Brecht's comment anticipates the situation in the unfinished 'Bericht' and in *Litauische Claviere*, in that in both works culture is misused, becoming a possession that cuts the possessor off from 'Humanisierung' and prevents him from making a contribution to the 'Vermenschlichung der Verhältnisse'. Brecht, from his Marxist point of view, saw that culture could only be saved if man was saved, and argued – in his 1935 speech – that this would only happen through a change of *'Eigentums-verhältnisse'* (*Werke* 18:245). Bobrowski, with this phrase almost certainly in mind, has his *non*-Marxist Voigt, speaking in *Litauische Claviere* in 1936, blame earlier *'Herrschaftsverhältnisse'*.

With Potschka as focal point, these last three chapters demonstrate the danger of aesthetic isolation in a critical historical situation. They present as scenes or sketches or visions three separate episodes from Donelaitis's life, episodes cut short in each case by the climbing figure of the murderous 'Schreihals'. At the end Potschka appears to have begun to understand that his own attitudes are endangering his 'living' Donelaitis, the embodiment for him of Lithuanian culture, language and patriotism. His attempt to preserve as his own possession this area of pure culture around Donelaitis will be thwarted by the political and social realities of his time, and under such circumstances he belatedly recognises the need for a new 'voice' that may communicate more actively between the ideals of the past, the present and the future, rather than seeing these different time levels, as he originally did, as disparate and effectively unconnected.

The three episodes are framed and interspersed with references to the tower, but are framed in particular by related images referring to time. The later images repeal in spirit and partly in vocabulary the earlier, as Potschka initially experiences the contradictoriness of his position but at the end attempts a resolution. Staring, in the imagery of the novel, into the past, he initially sees only distinctions:

> Hier ist Potschka. [...] Und von hier blickt man hinaus. Wo hinaus? [...]
> In eine Zeit. Wenn man das weiß: was das ist, Zeit.
> Das Gegenwärtige? Das schon immer, indem es bemerkt wurde, abge-

schlossen ist, vergangen, Vergangenheit geworden.

Das Zukünftige? Das immer herankommt, ganz nah heran, und nie eingetreten ist, immer draußen geblieben.

Die Vergangenheit? Abgeschlossen, abgetan, nicht mehr zu rufen, weil ohne Gehör. Erkennbar vielleicht in leblosen Gegenständen, Gestorbenes, in einem Augenblick unkenntlich geworden.

Aber man blickt darauf. Und worauf sonst? Als auf etwas, das man zu haben meint. (3:311f.)[20]

At the very end of the novel, the separateness epitomised in the idea that the past is 'nicht mehr zu rufen' is no longer seen as absolute, and Potschka responds to Tuta's appeal, 'Das von früher, das geht nicht mehr', by showing a determination at least to attempt to create the possibility of some fluidity, and the final words of the novel run: 'Herrufen, hierher. Wo wir sind' (3:331).

Between these two passages, which demonstrate the changes Potschka himself undergoes, Bobrowski's narrative voice invokes the episodes involving Donelaitis, each relating back to events or situations from the first six chapters. The first of these episodes, a visit to Donelaitis by his fellow priest Sperber, was mentioned earlier in the novel as a possible scene for the opera. In the dream sequence it is used to demonstrate the strength of character of Donelaitis in contrast to the fear and obsequiousness of Sperber who 'eine Patronatskirche [hat], da redet also sein Herr Baron: was zu beachten und was zu tun' (3:313). The scene culminates in an exchange that summarises the differences between the two, as Donelaitis argues: 'Antworten ist mein Amt' and Sperber insists: 'Es gibt Fragen, denen sich der Befragte versagen muß' (3:312). Donelaitis refuses to do this. The potential significance of such attitudes for the present hardly needs underlining, but it is illustrated within the novel through the incident after the brawl with Voigt and Kankelat. The two clearly witness the accidental killing of the Nazi thug

---

[20] The intellectual origins of this attitude to time have been related by Oliver Schütze in *Natur und Geschichte*, pp.220ff., to a passage from St. Augustine's *Confessions* (Book XI, ch. 14):

Diese beiden Zeiten, Vergangenheit und Zukunft, wie sollten sie seiend sein, da das Vergangene doch nicht mehr 'ist', das Zukünftige noch nicht 'ist'? Die Gegenwart hinwieder, wenn sie stetsfort Gegenwart wäre und nicht in Vergangenheit überginge, wäre nicht mehr Zeit, sondern Ewigkeit.

Bekenntnisse, Lateinisch und deutsch. Eingeleitet, übersetzt und erläutert von Joseph Bernhart, Frankfurt/M. 1987, p.629.

Warschoks by Antanas (3:306f.), but in his fear Kankelat responds to an appeal for help by denying that he has seen anything: 'Herr Rechts-anwalt, sagt er, ich denke, ich kuckte gerade nach der Seite. Hier nach dieser. // Und dazu eine Handbewegung' (3:309).

The second episode is the longest and depicts primarily a Lithuanian wedding feast which had also been considered as a possible scene for the opera. Central to this episode is the arrival of Donelaitis, 'der Bildung gelernt hat' (3:322), among his flock. In the scene he demon-strates that his 'Bildung' is not a possession that cuts him off from them, and despite his evident poor health he remains active in village life, contemplating the establishment of a spa for which his barometers could be useful. He can also, to an extent, control village life, as he placates his parishioners in a potentially violent situation: 'Tu deinen didelis peilis weg' (3:324).

If the first of these scenes illustrated Donelaitis's moral courage and the second his intimate involvement in the life of the village, the last scene illustrates his love of music but also provides a summarising image for the novel as a whole. Here, in one of the most complex scenes of the novel, Donelaitis, having manufactured the three 'Claviere' of the title, sets out to make music with two colleagues, Kempfer and Jordan, and their wives. Donelaitis and his colleagues play the instruments while their wives start to sing Bach's chorale 'In allen meinen Taten'. Unfortunately, the three wives start singing on too high a note, and it appears that they cannot 'come down' from there. The instruments will have to be tuned up, but Donelaitis is reluctant to do this, since he has already tuned 'einen guten Ton höher als früher üblich'.[21] He does not want to damage the frames by retuning so quickly:

> Aber wenn nun schon, dann mußte es heute sein. Morgen waren unsere Gäste wieder fort.
> Anna Regina, sagte ich, mach uns Kaffee.
> Das Stimmen unterblieb. Das Singen, für diesen Tag, auch.
> Anna Regina stand auf, einen herben Zug um den Mund. Aber sie ging.
> (3:330)

It is a frustrating end to a promising exercise, but although music has to be abandoned for the day, the scene ends with the parties continuing to act in harmony: the wives do not attempt to sing without their husbands' accompaniment, and the husbands, although the instruments they are

---

[21] For details of the historical shifts in tuning see 6:218.

playing are well tuned and in harmony (3:329), do not attempt to play
without their wives. Similarly, Donelaitis, despite his concern at having
to retune, evidently intends eventually to do so, while Anna Regina,
despite her obvious disappointment, does not try to insist on the retuning being undertaken immediately. The image is one of the frustration of total harmony, but hope remains in the willingness of all involved, despite visible disappointment and irritation, to 'give and take',
as a possible example of the compromises needed in order to maintain
the hope of an eventual harmony. Donelaitis has at least shown the way
in not insisting on an absolute level of tuning, but there is no easy, no
automatic solution.

In this scene Donelaitis raises in passing another important aspect of
musical harmony, the problem of absolute pitch:

> Daß am schönsten die verstimmten Claviere sind, die leicht verstimmten, vor
> allem in Oberlagen, das konnte ich doch nie jemand sagen, das hätte niemand
> verstanden. Und ich denke: mit Grund. (3:330).

The words appear to question the aesthetic value of absolute dogmatic
purity in musical tuning and gain substance as they follow earlier
allusions to the concept of musical 'Temperatur'. The first such reference is particularly significant, referring as it does to a speech by the
Nazi Neumann, which the narrator superfluously characterises as 'wenig
temperiert' (3:250). Later, in the context of raucous German celebrations, the narrator summarized: 'Und nun geht das Fest weiter und hat
eigentlich erst die richtige Temperatur' (3:299). Together the concern
with tuning and the word 'temperiert' suggest Bach's *Das wohl-
temperierte Clavier* (1722/1744) with its pragmatic and immensely
productive rejection of pure acoustic tuning in order to allow modulation – compromise – between the keys.[22] It involves an undogmatic
approach whose wider implications are well summarised by Scholes in
words that relate directly to the Lithuanian/German conflict in *Litauische Claviere*:

> Life is necessarily a compromise; perfect truth is unattainable, and so is per-
> fect tuning. [...] If in music we want to move easily among the keys, we shall
> have to accept approximations.[23]

---

[22] One of the self-referential musical descriptions of the text had referred to 'fort-
während Modulieren' (3:237f.).

[23] Percy A. Scholes, *The Oxford Companion to Music*, tenth edition, Oxford 1970,

At the end of this sequence of visions, this concluding 'Bericht über Träume', Potschka is awakened by Tuta. As elsewhere he has slipped into the first person in thinking and dreaming of Donelaitis. In one last vision he now experiences the death of Donelaitis, through the vision of Giltine, the Lithuanian snake-like divinity of death: 'Das Zeichen der Schlange geht in der Luft. Giltine kommt. Giltine sticht mit der Zunge' (3:328). Potschka's experience of this death is coloured by his almost hopelessly late realisation of the threat he himself faces. Donelaitis's death – placed unhistorically at the end of the day in which he, Kempfer and Jordan tried to play – indicates that Donelaitis has no time to retune. For Donelaitis at least 'das Stimmen unterblieb' (3:330) and there was no opportunity to make it good. Only in the present, with Potschka's 'death' at the hands of the Schreihals and 'recovery' at the hands of Tuta, is there an opportunity, though one threatened by the forces of intolerance and hatred. He is at least, unlike Wiedemann, no longer 'über der Erde', he has been brought 'down to earth'.

Bobrowski's Potschka, as the third figure of orientation within the novel, is clearly ambiguous. His own self-orientation from the trigonometric point had initially seen Donelaitis as a figure safely isolated from the present in a past which was 'abgeschlossen, abgetan, nicht mehr zu rufen, weil ohne Gehör'. Only at the end of the work can he see an alternative: 'Herrrufen, hierher. Wo wir sind'. His original view had emphasised the otherness of the past and could lead to the exaggerated attitude of the collector.[24] With this, an interest in the past could be made to exclude the present. His final self-imposed mission, that of 'herrufen', indicates the possibility of less rigid divisions, while maintaining the focal point of interest in the present. As Bobrowski commented more prosaically in the interview with the 'Deutschlandsender' (November 27 1964):

---

p.1013. Even equal temperament, itself a form of compromise, must not be applied dogmatically and needs another form of compromise within it. See *Bloomsbury Dictionary of Music*, P.D.Morehead, London 1992, p.146: 'In actual practice, piano tuners do not adhere to strict equal temperament, but adjust the octaves in the highest and lowest registers to make them sound right'. Donelaitis's words on 'die verstimmten Claviere' quoted above surely refer to this phenomenon.

[24] In a discussion at the Weimar/Berlin Conference Bobrowski commented: '[Potschka] versucht sich in die Historie des litauischen Volkes zu retten, also zu seiner National-kultur. [...] Er muß natürlich mit diesen Rettungsversuchen in Historie, in Nationalkultur Schiffbruch erleiden' (6:248).

> Ich glaube auch, daß es nicht Aufgabe des Schriftstellers ist, vergangene Zeit zu repräsentieren aus sich heraus, sondern immer von der Gegenwart her gesehen und auf die Gegenwart hin wirkend, daß sich also diese Bereiche, der historische Bereich und die zeitgenössische Zeugenschaft, ständig durchdringen. (4:475)

Litauische Claviere illustrates, precisely through Potschka's potential development, this 'Durchdringung'.

The events of the weekend could scarcely be more desperate: Potschka is under imminent threat because of his relations with Tuta; after his public insulting of the Nazi Lenuweit Voigt faces a very uncertain future in Tilsit, and there will be no legal redress for the attack on Elisat; Gawehn will remain in artistic exile. Meanwhile Josupeit is dead and Antanas faces a rigged trial accused of murder. The central question concerning the opera: 'wer wird sie aufführen wollen? Oder können?' (3:288) remains unanswered. The historical situation too could not be more desperate: within a few years the Memelland would be part of Hitler's Germany and there would be an end to any consideration of tolerance. The stories that occasionally trouble the Jewish Memelländer Herr Epstein with his 'rundes, fröhliches Gesicht' (3:242) will pale into insignificance compared with the coming 'Endlösung'. Before these historical facts, the proposed opera, the evident good will, the change of heart by Potschka all seem irrelevant.

As in *Levins Mühle*, however, this bleakly pessimistic view is counterbalanced by other factors which, like the Budrus incident, emphasise the other aspect, that of hope for the uncertain future: 'und ist mit Zuletzt dieser Tag gemeint?' (3:258); 'das Stimmen unterblieb [...] für diesen Tag' (3:330); 'mit einer Stimme, die ihre Laute noch finden wird, heute oder morgen' (3:331). Together with Voigt's own continuing hope these references to a time beyond the present imply something better for the future, in an attitude not of certainty but certainly of hope, and it is not surprising to find this hope implied in the words of the hymn that Donelaitis and his friends had wished to sing: 'In allen meinen Taten / laß ich den Höchsten raten [...] / der alles kann und hat' (3:329).

Litauische Claviere is a thematically over-burdened work in which Bobrowski attempts to synthesise many of the issues that confronted him in the 1960s: his specific 'Thema' and his continuing fascination with the past; his problems as an artist living under socially oppressive conditions; the irritating question immediately relevant in East Germany concerning the possible influence of literature; his own belief in the importance of 'Gespräch' to break down misunderstandings, itself under threat from his state; his love of music. All these different interests and complex and fluctuating issues are raised in an atmosphere over-shadowed by Zak's interview and Endler's article, as well as by his own work at the Berlin/Weimar conference. As Gerhard Wolf suggests the theme may well be 'das Zusammenleben der Völker, die Gleichberech-tigung verschiedener Stimmen nebeneinander', and in suggesting this Wolf implies that this relates to international relations.[25] More accurate, though also more general, are the words of the priest's sermon in praise of 'die großen Taten in verschiedenen Zungen'. This involves a plea for tolerance, for the acceptance of different 'voices': of Elisat's Lithuanian songs and of Donelaitis's hexameters, but also of Voigt's and Gawehn's opera and the new 'Stimme' that Potschka is in process of discovering. Above all, it involves a plea by Bobrowski that his own voice be accepted. Against a background of growing insistence on ideological purity and conformity, leading finally to the intolerance of the 11th Plenum in December 1965, the novel presents an appeal for tolerance, understanding and compromise.

---

[25] *Beschreibung eines Zimmers*, p.115

9

CONCLUSION

The political and cultural background against which Bobrowski wrote no longer exists. The state with which his last works attempted a form of artistic dialogue has gone, and fragments of the wall that protected it for decades now adorn mantelpieces and souvenir-cabinets the world over. Kaliningrad and Sovetsk, like the Sarmatia that Bobrowski, with Goethe's Iphigenie, could only 'mit der Seele suchen', now welcome the casual tourist.

Bobrowski's contemporary problems as a writer with a socialist state also belong to history. No German writer has to respond seriously to exaggerated claims on the possible effects of literature any more. Other more global problems have, however, imposed themselves, problems of which Bobrowski's works appear blissfully, indeed naively, oblivious: despite his acquaintance with Günter Kunert, there is no evidence of any fashionable 'ecological' element here. Bobrowski's concern initially with the past and then with the need to defend his own position obscured any vision of future dangers to his Sarmatian landscapes.

His final plea for tolerance towards different voices went, of course, unnoticed. Shortly after his death the notorious 11th Plenum of the Central Committee of the SED in December 1965 initiated a new round of repressive measures against, among others, his friend Manfred Bieler, his new acquaintance Wolf Biermann, but also Stefan Heym, Kunert and many others. A 'Lyrik-Debatte' (1966) in the journal *Forum* brought lyric poetry back into line, and with *Nachdenken über Christa T.* and its aftermath Christa Wolf herself was to experience for the first time the full weight of Party disapproval. The dialogue with the authorities was, for the time being, over.

There were, however, other forms of dialogue, especially between writers, and Christa Wolf acknowledged in December 1989 that while she had been working at her *Nachdenken* Bobrowski had been 'ein interessanter, indirekter Gesprächspartner. Das hat mir damals bestimmte Möglichkeiten eröffnet'.[1] Elsewhere she expanded on these possibilities:

---

[1] In an interview with Aafke Steenhuis. See Christa Wolf, *Reden im Herbst*, Berlin/Weimar 1990, p. 140.

Bobrowskis Art und Weise, sich frei in seinem Stoff zu bewegen, anachronistisch zu sein, den inneren Monolog zu behandeln, umgangssprachliche
Elemente in stilisierte Dialoge hineinzunehmen – das hat mir alles zuerst mal
einfach 'gefallen', wenn ich es las, und ich glaube schon, daß er mir auch
bestimmte technische Möglichkeiten des Schreibens eröffnet hat.[2]

The significance of Boehlendorff's 'Satz' is an issue referred to above,
as is the stylistic reflection of the 'indirekter Gesprächspartner' in
Nachdenken über Christa T. Such elements point to an unusual degree
of respect from the socialist writer for her Christian counterpart.[3] If such
a major and innovative writer drew marginally from Bobrowski, then
lesser writers were tempted to copy almost slavishly the 'new tone' of
Bobrowski's prose, so that Erwin Strittmatter could protest in a letter of
June 24 1969:

Bobrowskis Stil ist natürlich suggestiv. Christa Wolf hat für ihre *Christa T.*
auch in diese Bobrowski-Kiste gegriffen. Der 'Olle' Brezan [...] schrieb eine
ganze Geschichte in Bobrowski-Manier. In einer Nummer der NDL stand
diese Geschichte neben der eines jungen Bobrowskianers.[4]

Other GDR writers whose prose works were evidently immediately
affected by Bobrowski's prose included Wolfgang Buschmann and
Harald Gerlach, Helga Schütz and Friedemann Berger, but also the
major figure of Jurek Becker, whose *Jakob der Lügner* (1968) shows
the influence of the narrative perspective of *Levins Mühle*, and Fritz
Rudolf Fries, whose work *Das Luft-Schiff: Biografische Nachlässe zu
den Fantasien meines Großvaters* (1974) reveals the link even in the
subtitle.[5] For other writers Bobrowski was, if not an influence then a
defining experience, and Christoph Hein vividly remembers the novelty

---

[2] See Christa Wolf, *Im Dialog: Aktuelle Texte*, Frankfurt/M. 1990, p.59.

[3] That this respect extended beyond Bobrowski's prose and beyond the one work *Nachdenken* is indicated, incidentally, by the quotations from 'Die Memel' in *Kindheitsmuster*. See *Kindheitsmuster*, Darmstadt and Neuwied 1979, pp. 200f. Perhaps because of the Eastern setting, the novel contains a number of other echoes of themes also found in Bobrowski, as well as the question: 'Wie müssen die Verhältnisse beschaffen sein?' (p.295).

[4] Quoted in *Neue Deutsche Literatur* 23 (1975) vol.8, 119. Strittmatter is referring here to Jurij Brezan's 'Kraucecy' and Joachim Nowotny's 'Der kleine Riese', in *Neue Deutsche Literatur* 17 (1969) vol.2, 70-104.

[5] See Bernd Leistner, 'Der Erzähler' in *SZNB* 323-39 and his updating article 'Zur Nachwirkung Bobrowskis in der Literatur der DDR' in *Sankelmark*, pp.101-9.

of hearing Bobrowski read from *Levins Mühle* as an introduction to a completely new style of prose,[6] while Jürgen Fuchs recalls that while fleeing from NVA barracks on his first leave he 'führte Diskussionen über literarische Themen, sagte Gedichte von Bobrowski auf, fluchte'.[7] The fascination continues with a new generation of prose writers, and in 'Dies und das' Jens Sparschuh writes of Bobrowski's poems ironically but respectfully as one of his 'bevorzugten Lektüren', together with Kierkegaard's *Entweder – Oder* and his '"Wie helfe ich mir selbst"-Trabant-Ratgeberbuch'.[8]

The distinctiveness of Bobrowski's new prose as acknowledged by Wolf makes the impression of this prose on his contemporaries clear. Paradoxically, the very individuality of his poetry ensured that there was no direct succession, and the direct and identifiable influence of Bobrowski's poetic style has remained limited.[9] There were no clear major imitators. Bobrowski's insistence on the importance of the detail, the small-scale and regional encouraged, however, other writers to take their own regions seriously, and in October 1991 Kito Lorenc could talk of this effect:

> von dem unvergeßlichen, viel zu früh verstorbenen Johannes Bobrowski er-
> muntert, von seinen Gedichten der *Sarmatischen Zeit*, des *Schattenlands
> Ströme*, von ihm selbst ermutigt, den weitsprungbreiten sorbischen Bach
> Struga ernstzunehmen, zu den Quellen der eigenen Zeit zu gehen, den Sorben
> von sich und den mitwohnenden Deutschen von den Sorben zu erzählen.[10]

Bobrowski's influence beyond Germany and its Sorbian minority cannot seriously be measured, despite the occasional presentation of papers on 'Bobrowski und Litauen', 'Bobrowski und Polen' at specialist conferences in Germany and beyond.[11] His influence on East German publishing is more quantifiable, however, and it is difficult to believe

---

[6] In conversation with the author June 1995.

[7] See Jürgen Fuchs, *Das Ende einer Feigheit*, Reinbek bei Hamburg 1992, p.88.

[8] *Ich dachte, sie finden uns nicht: Zerstreute Prosa*, Cologne 1997, p.139.

[9] Bernd Leistner gives as an example of direct influence Harald Gerlach's 'Kiefern von Bory Dolnoslaskie' but draws a veil of discretion over other names. See *Sankelmark*, p.102.

[10] Unpublished typescript of talk delivered at Taylorian Institute, Oxford, October 1991. See Lorenc's work *Struga: Bilder einer Landschaft* (1967).

[11] See, as an example, *Sankelmark*, pp.57-78.

that the decision to produce a popular edition of the works of Donelaitis[12] had nothing to do with Bobrowski's own publicising of him in *Litauische Claviere*, while his behind-the-scenes participation in the publication of *Entkleidung und Verklärung* helped to introduce Hamann to a wider East German public. Hamann was never likely to be published in the popularising East German anthologies of Walter Victor, for whom Bobrowski had such contempt,[13] but the Union Verlag anthology is a very respectable second best.

Bobrowski's more lasting legacy lies elsewhere. As a writer who lived and suffered under two all-embracing ideological systems, he chose to use his works in order to question, to 'befragen und dringlich zu befragen'. Such questioning took many forms. Beyond the direct ('Wie muß eine Welt für ein moralisches Wesen beschaffen sein?') lay the implied questioning of official language inherent in the insistence on another 'voice', indeed on the importance of other voices in general. Within any closed system an emphasis on openness to others questions the automatic justification of its authority. It is central to Bobrowski's works that he should look almost always at the small and obscure, the 'loser' rather than the great and the famous: Hamann, not Kant, Buxtehude, not Bach, Boehlendorff and not Hölderlin, the River Drevenz, rather than the Vistula, but also the more specifically Eastern calamus and the 'Sproßer', the 'Polish' or thrush nightingale (*luscinia luscinia*) rather than the more common nightingale (*luscinia megarhynchos*). All such emphasis is a reflection of Bobrowski's concern at the 'Denken in Großräumen' (4:336) that corresponds intellectually to industrial globalisation. It was for him a dangerous process that reduced complexities to clichés, that encouraged the 'klarer Blick' that 'knows' without having to think, that selectively registers and thus remembers only what it will. For Bobrowski the most immediate manifestation of this was his contemporary German who attempted 'sich von seiner Nationalgeschichte [...] frei[zu]sprechen' (4:483). A wider contemporary application would, however, include all those whose ideologically limited view of themselves and their history blinds to the relativising power of the factual, the inconvenient historical detail, or even the

---

[12] Kristijonas Donelaitis, *Die Jahreszeiten: Ein litauisches Epos*, tr. and ed. Hermann Buddensieg, Leipzig 1970.

[13] See the epigrams 'Kostümfest' (2:236) and 'Walter Victors Gesammelte Werke' (2:237).

illogical or inexplicable desires or aspirations that contribute to the fullness of human existence. Again, the smugness of East German rationalist ideology provided a contemporary background, but such a mind-set is not limited just to the past.

In Bobrowski's concern with this he draws from the critical German writers of the Enlightenment, and above all from his 'Leib- und Magenheiligen' (*Marbach* 383) Hamann, of whom Isaiah Berlin once wrote, in words that could apply almost unchanged to Bobrowski himself:

> Any doctrine that stresses the general, the impersonal, the conceptual, the universal, seems to him likely to flatten out all differences, peculiarities, quirks – to obstruct the soul's free flight by clipping its wings in the interests of comprehensive inclusiveness. The ambition to 'Newtonise' all knowledge tends to work against sensitiveness to each fleeting particular, to lower susceptibility to empirical impressions – to stress form at the expense of content, uniformity at the expense of variety, fullness of life, the kaleidoscopic metamorphoses of actual experience that slip through the meshes of the most elaborate conceptual net. [...] Hamann is a champion of the individual, the complex and above all the unconscious and the unseizable.[14]

If this could be applied to Bobrowski's concerns, than a further passage from the same text applies not only to his concerns, but also to his fate in the united Germany:

> Hamann speaks for those who hear the cry of the toad beneath the harrow, even when it may be right to plough over him: since if men do not hear this cry, if they are deaf, if the toad is written off because he has been 'condemned by history' – if the defeated are never worth attending to because history is the history of the victorious – then such victories will prove their own undoing, for they will tend to destroy the very values in the name of which the battle was undertaken. (p.117)

Bobrowski himself wrote in and in partnership with a state that has now been 'condemned by history'. It is to be hoped that his works do not suffer the same fate. The introduction of a Johannes Bobrowski-Medaille as part of the 'Berliner Literaturpreis der Stiftung Preußische Seehandlung', awarded now to writers as diverse as Angela Krauß, Hans Joachim Schädlich, Max Sebald and (June 1998) Reinhard Jirgl and Ingo Schulze, makes such a danger less likely, while all serious

---

[14] *The Magus of the North: J.G.Hamann and the Origins of Modern Irrationalism*, Cambridge 1993, p.115.

readers will welcome the recent publication of the 'Erläuterungen' as volumes 5 and 6 of the *Gesammelte Werke*.

Beyond his death, neither the aesthetic quality nor the moral appeal of his works nor the concerns they addressed have lost their significance. At the end of his century they apply in equal measure to the 'ausländerfreie Zonen' of Magdeburg, to the dangerous simplifications of 'Ossi-Wessi' relations throughout Germany, and to the recurrent phenomenon graced with the name of 'ethnic cleansing'. Examples of such behaviour Bobrowski encountered in his own life and in his studies of German and Eastern European relations. As long as they continue his works will continue to speak quietly but persistently to readers from new generations.

SELECT BIBLIOGRAPHY

Works by Johannes Bobrowski
(significant publications/editions only)

'Gedichte', *Das Innere Reich* 4 (1943-44), pp. 351-4.

Sarmatische Zeit. Gedichte, Stuttgart: Deutsche Verlags-Anstalt, 1961.

Sarmatische Zeit. Gedichte, East Berlin: Union Verlag, 1961.

Schattenland Ströme. Gedichte, Stuttgart: Deutsche Verlags-Anstalt, 1962.

Schattenland Ströme. Gedichte, East Berlin: Union Verlag, 1963.

Levins Mühle. 34 Sätze über meinen Großvater, Frankfurt/M.: S. Fischer Verlag, 1964.

Levins Mühle. 34 Sätze über meinen Großvater, East Berlin: Union Verlag, 1964.

Mäusefest und andere Erzählungen, West Berlin: Verlag Klaus Wagenbach, 1965.

Boehlendorff und Mäusefest. Erzählungen, East Berlin: Union Verlag, 1965.

Boehlendorff und andere Erzählungen, Stuttgart: Deutsche Verlags-Anstalt, 1965.

Litauische Claviere, East Berlin: Union Verlag, 1966.

Litauische Claviere, West Berlin: Verlag Klaus Wagenbach, 1967.

Wetterzeichen. Gedichte, East Berlin: Union Verlag, 1966.

Wetterzeichen. Gedichte, West Berlin: Verlag Klaus Wagenbach, 1967.

Der Mahner. Prosa aus dem Nachlaß, East Berlin: Union Verlag, 1967.

Der Mahner. Erzählungen und andere Prosa aus dem Nachlaß, West Berlin: Verlag Klaus Wagenbach, 1968.

Literarisches Klima. Ganz neue Xenien, doppelte Ausführung, ed. Bernd Leistner, East Berlin: Union Verlag, 1977.

Literarisches Klima. Ganz neue Xenien, doppelte Ausführung, ed. Bernd Leistner, Stuttgart: Deutsche Verlags-Anstalt, 1978.

Gesammelte Werke in sechs Bänden, ed. Eberhard Haufe, East Berlin: Union Verlag, vols. 1-4 1987.

Gesammelte Werke in sechs Bänden, ed. Eberhard Haufe, Stuttgart: Deutsche Verlags-Anstalt, vols. 1-4 1987, vol. 5 1998, vol. 6 (ed. Holger Gehle) 1999.

Works edited/collected by Johannes Bobrowski

Gustav Schwab, *Die schönsten Sagen des klassischen Altertums*, East Berlin: Altberliner Verlag Lucie Groszer, 1954.

Gustav Schwab, *Die Sagen von Troja und von Irrfahrt und Heimkehr des Odysseus*, East Berlin: Altberliner Verlag Lucie Groszer, 1955.

Hans Clauert, der märkische Eulenspiegel, East Berlin: Altberliner Verlag Lucie Groszer, 1956.

Jean Paul, *Leben Fibels, des Verfassers der Bienrodischen Fibel*, East Berlin: Union Verlag, 1963.

Wer mich und Ilse sieht im Grase... Deutsche Poeten des achtzehnten Jahrhunderts über die Liebe und das Frauenzimmer, East Berlin: Eulenspiegel Verlag, 1964.

Meine liebsten Gedichte: Eine Auswahl deutscher Lyrik von Martin Luther bis Christoph Meckel, ed. Eberhard Haufe, East Berlin: Union Verlag, 1985.

Correspondence

Johannes Bobrowski/Peter Huchel Briefwechsel, ed. Eberhard Haufe, Marbach, 1993.

Selected translations into English of works by Johannes Bobrowski

'Poems by Johannes Bobrowski', trans. Christopher Middleton, *Times Literary Supplement*, April 28 1961.

Shadowlands: Selected Poems, trans. Ruth and Matthew Mead, London 1966.

I Taste Bitterness, trans. Marc Linder, East Berlin 1970.

Levin's Mill, trans. Janet Cropper, London 1970.

Selected Poems, trans. Ruth and Matthew Mead, Harmondsworth 1971.

From the Rivers, trans. Ruth and Matthew Mead, London 1975.

Michael Hamburger, *East German Poetry: An Anthology*, Oxford 1972, pp. 57-85.

Three German Stories, trans. Michael Bullock, London 1984.

Critical Works

Bibliography

Grützmacher, Curt. *Das Werk von Johannes Bobrowski. Eine Bibliographie*, Munich 1974.

Books/Dissertations

Adelsbach, Eva, *Bobrowskis Widmungstexte an Dichter und Künstler des 18. Jahrhunderts: Dialogizität und Intertextualität*, St. Ingbert 1990.

Albert, Peter, *Die Deutschen und der europäische Osten: 'Vergangenheitsbewältigung' als Historismuskritik im Erzählwerk Johannes Bobrowskis*, Erlangen 1990.

Behrmann, Alfred, *Facetten. Untersuchungen zum Werk Johannes Bobrowskis*, Stuttgart 1977.

Dehn, Mechthild and Wilhelm, *Johannes Bobrowski: Prosa. Interpretationen*, Munich 1972.

Deskau, Dagmar, *'Dunkelheit' und 'Engagement'. Zur Gestaltung des Geschichtsbezuges in der Lyrik Johannes Bobrowskis*, doctoral dissertation, Mainz 1973.

—— *Der aufgelöste Widerspruch. 'Engagement' und 'Dunkelheit' in der Lyrik Johannes Bobrowskis*, Stuttgart 1975.

Gajek, Bernhard, and Eberhard Haufe, *Johannes Bobrowski. Chronik. Einführung. Bibliographie*, Frankfurt/M. 1977.

Haufe, Eberhard, *Bobrowski-Chronik. Daten zu Leben und Werk*, Würzburg 1994.

Hoefert, Sigfrid, *West-Östliches in der Lyrik Johannes Bobrowskis*,

Munich 1966.

Keith-Smith, Brian, *Johannes Bobrowski,* London 1970.

Kelletat, Alfred (ed.), *Sarmatische Zeit, Erinnerung und Zukunft: Dokumentation des Johannes Bobrowski Colloquiums 1989 in der Akademie Sankelmark,* Sankelmark 1990.

Leistner, Bernd, *Der Epiker Johannes Bobrowski,* doctoral dissertation, Leipzig 1971.

—— *Johannes Bobrowski. Studien und Interpretationen,* East Berlin 1981.

Mauser, Wolfram, *Beschwörung und Reflexion. Bobrowskis sarmatische Gedichte,* Frankfurt/M. 1970.

Meckel, Christoph, *Erinnerung an Johannes Bobrowski,* Düsseldorf 1978.

Minde, Fritz, *Johannes Bobrowskis Lyrik und die Tradition,* Frankfurt/M. 1981.

Reichert, Stefan, *Das verschneite Wort. Untersuchungen zur Lyrik Johannes Bobrowskis,* Bonn 1989.

Rostin, Gerhard and Gerhard Wolf (eds.), *Johannes Bobrowski: Selbstzeugnisse und Beiträge über sein Werk,* East Berlin 1966.

—— with Eberhard Haufe and Bernd Leistner (eds.), *Johannes Bobrowski. Selbstzeugnisse und neue Beiträge über sein Werk,* East Berlin 1975.

—— (ed.), *Ahornallee 26 oder Epitaph für Johannes Bobrowski,* East Berlin 1977.

Scrase, David, *Understanding Johannes Bobrowski,* South Carolina 1995.

Schulz, Werner, *Die aufgehobene Zeit. Zeitstruktur und Zeitelemente in der Lyrik Johannes Bobrowskis,* Bern 1983.

Schütze, Oliver, *Natur und Geschichte im Blick des Wanderers. Zur lyrischen Situation bei Bobrowski und Hölderlin,* Würzburg 1990.

Stock, Alex, *Warten, ein wenig. Zu Gedichten und Geschichten von Johannes Bobrowski,* Würzburg 1991.

Tgahrt, Reinhard (ed.), with Ute Doster, *Johannes Bobrowski oder Landschaft mit Leuten. Eine Ausstellung und Katalog des Deutschen Literaturarchivs im Schiller-Nationalmuseum,* Marbach 1993.

Töteberg, Michael, *Johannes Bobrowski. Werkverzeichnis*, in *Kritisches Lexikon zur deutschsprachigen Gegenwartsliteratur*, ed. Heinz Ludwig Arnold, Munich 1978ff.

Wieczorek, John P., *Figures and Themes in the Works of Johannes Bobrowski*, doctoral dissertation, Oxford 1978.

—— (ed.), *Johannes Bobrowski (1917-1965)*, Occasional Publications of the Centre for East German Studies, The University of Reading, vol. 2 (1995).

Wolf, Gerhard, *Johannes Bobrowski. Leben und Werk*, East Berlin 1967.

—— *Beschreibung eines Zimmers: 15 Kapitel über Johannes Bobrowski*, East Berlin 1971.

Articles

Anderle, Martin, 'Sprachbildungen Hölderlins in modernen Gedichten. Celans "Tübingen, Jänner" und Bobrowskis "Hölderlin in Tübingen"', *Seminar* 8 (1972), 99-116.

Anon., 'The Pastoral Folkworld', *Times Literary Supplement*, September 21 1962.

Anon., 'The East End of Guilt', *Times Literary Supplement*, September 22 1966.

Barnouw, Dagmar, 'Poetry of Coexistence: Johannes Bobrowski on "The German East"', in *Mosaic* 6 (1972-73) no. 4, 21-38.

—— 'Bobrowski and Socialist Realism', in *Germanic Review* 48 (1973), 288-314.

Bayer, Oswald, '"In dem Lande, da man nichts gedenkt." Zu Bobrowskis "Epilog auf Hamann"', in *Zeitwende* 59 (1988), 239-46.

Behre, Maria, '"Rennen mit ausgebreiteten Armen." Johannes Bobrowskis Schreiben auf Hoffnung hin', in *Literaturwissenschaftliches Jahrbuch* 32 (1991), 307-28.

Behrmann, Alfred, 'Metapher im Kontext. Zu einigen Gedichten von Ingeborg Bachmann und Johannes Bobrowski', in *Der Deutschunterricht* 20 (1968) no. 4, 28-48.

—— 'Der hübscheste kleine Harlekin. Zu Johannes Bobrowskis "Im

Guckkasten: Galiani"', in *Revue d'Allemagne* 5 (1973), 387-97.

—— and Thomas Keilberth, 'Realien in der Fiktion. Dietrich Buxtehude im Werk Johannes Bobrowskis', in *Deutsche Vierteljahrsschrift für Literaturwissenschaft und Geistesgeschichte* 50 (1976), 238-58.

Beresina, Ada G., 'Johannes Bobrowskis Roman *Litauische Claviere*', in *Weimarer Beiträge* 20 (1974) no. 5, 91-106.

Bieler, Manfred, 'Sarmatische Zeit', in *Neue Deutsche Literatur* 10 (1962) no. 9, 141-4.

Bienek, Horst, 'Striche zu einem Porträt', in *Merkur* 20 (1966), 133-7.

Bischoff, Brigitte, 'Bobrowski und Hamann', in *Zeitschrift für deutsche Philologie* 94 (1975), 553-82.

—— 'Der polnische Zimmermann. Zu dem Gedicht "Joseph Conrad" von Johannes Bobrowski', in *Neophilologus* 59 (1975), 579-91.

Bohren, Rudolf, 'Johannes Bobrowski. Versuch einer Interpretation', in *Das Gespräch* 76 (1968), 3-23.

Böschenstein, Bernhard, 'Johannes Bobrowski: "Immer zu benennen"', in Hilde Domin (ed.), *Doppelinterpretationen*, Frankfurt/M. 1966, pp. 103-5.

Bosse, Heinrich, 'Johannes Bobrowski: *Litauische Claviere*', in *Neue Rundschau* 78 (1967), 494-8.

Brazaitis, Kristina, 'Kristijonas Donelaitis in Johannes Bobrowskis *Litauische Claviere* (Lithuanian Pianos): German Variations on a Lithuanian Theme', in *Germanisch-Romanische Monatsschrift* 38 (1988), 185-95.

Bridgewater, Patrick, 'The Poetry of Johannes Bobrowski', in *Forum for Modern Language Studies* 2 (1966), 320-34.

Buras, Jacek, 'Johannes Bobrowskis "Mickiewicz". Eine Interpretation', in *Weimarer Beiträge* 16 (1970) no. 1, 212-6.

Coghlan, Brian, '"So fremd vertraut..." Zum Prosaschaffen Johannes Bobrowskis', in Leonard Forster and Hans-Gert Roloff (eds.), *Akten des V. Internationalen Germanisten-Kongresses*, Bern 1976, vol. 3, 462-8.

Dinesen, Ruth, 'Johannes Bobrowski, "An Nelly Sachs". Eine Interpretation', in *Text und Kontext* 14 (1986), 310-21.

Elmore, Lee K., 'Bobrowski's Poems "J. S. Bach" and "Mozart"', in

Germanic Review 56 (1981), 70-6.

Endler, Adolf, 'Lyrik und Lyriker', *Der Sonntag*, April 18 1965.

Flores, John, 'Johannes Bobrowski: Shadow Land, of Guilt and Community', in *Poetry in East Germany: Adjustments, Visions, and Provocations, 1945-1970*, New Haven and London 1971, pp. 205-72.

Gajek, Bernhard, 'Autor—Gedicht—Leser. Zu Johannes Bobrowskis "Hamann"-Gedicht', in Reinhold Grimm and Conrad Wiedemann (eds.), *Literatur und Geistesgeschichte*, West Berlin 1968, pp. 308-24.

—— 'Johannes Bobrowskis Porträtgedichte. Zur Auseinandersetzung eines Autors mit seiner Gesellschaft', in Wolfgang Frühwald and Günter Niggl (eds.), *Sprache und Bekenntnis. Sonderband des literaturwissenschaftlichen Jahrbuchs. Hermann Kunisch zum 70. Geburtstag*, West Berlin 1971, pp. 403-22.

Glenn, Jerry, 'An Introduction to the Poetry of Johannes Bobrowski', in *Germanic Review* 41 (1966) no. 1, 45-56.

Grange, Jacques, 'Über Johannes Bobrowskis Erzählkunst in seinem Roman *Levins Mühle*', in *Archiv für das Studium der neueren Sprachen und Literaturen* 126 (1974), 271-86.

Grützmacher, Curt, 'Künstlergedichte von Johannes Bobrowski. Bildgestalt und sprachliche Form', *Sprachkunst* 5 (1974), 268-79.

Hamburger, Michael, 'In Memoriam Johannes Bobrowski', in *Merkur* 20 (1966), 131f.

—— *The Truth of Poetry*, Harmondsworth 1972, pp. 318-20.

—— 'Johannes Bobrowski: An Introduction', in *Art as Second Nature: Occasional Pieces 1959-74*, Cheadle 1975, pp. 131-3.

Hänsel, Edith, 'Eine Empfehlung für den Religionsunterricht. Johannes Bobrowskis "De homine publico tractatus"', in Klaus Wagenast (ed.), *Theologie und Unterricht*, Gütersloh 1969, pp. 362-70.

Harris, Edward P., 'J.M.R.Lenz in German Literature. From Büchner to Bobrowski', in *Colloquia Germanica* 3 (1973), 214-33.

Hartung, Günter, 'Johannes Bobrowski', in *Sinn und Form* 18 (1966), 1189-217.

—— 'Johannes Bobrowskis *Litauische Claviere*', in *Sinn und Form* 18 (1966), 1518-23.

—— 'Analysen und Kommentare zu Gedichten von Johannes Bobrowski', in *Wissenschaftliche Zeitschrift der Martin-Luther-Universität Halle-Wittenberg* 8 (1969), 197-212.

—— 'Bobrowski und Grass', in *Weimarer Beiträge* 16 (1970) no. 8, 203-24.

Haufe, Eberhard, 'Frieden ist uns versprochen. Eine Schlüsselfigur in Johannes Bobrowskis Werk: Dietrich Buxtehude', in *Neue Zeit*, December 24/25 1968.

—— 'Bobrowskis Weg zum Roman. Zur Vor- und Entstehungsgeschichte von *Levins Mühle*', in *Weimarer Beiträge* 16 (1970) no. 1, 163-77.

—— 'Johannes Bobrowski und Klopstock', in *Neue Zeit*, July 3 1974.

—— 'Zur Entwicklung der sarmatischen Lyrik Bobrowskis 1941-1961', in *Wissenschaftliche Zeitschrift der Martin-Luther-Universität Halle-Wittenberg* 24 (1975), 53-74.

—— 'Augenblick der Selbstbestimmung', in *Neue Deutsche Literatur* 29 (1981) no. 2, 143-7.

—— 'Zu Bobrowskis Erzählung "Im Gefangenenlager"', in *Sinn und Form* 34 (1982), 620-2.

—— 'Blick in die Werkstatt', in *Neue Deutsche Literatur* 30 (1982) no. 5, 133-9.

—— '"Schattenland Ströme." Zur Genesis eines Gedichtbandtitels von Johannes Bobrowski', in Norbert Honsza and Hans-Gert Roloff (eds.), *Daß eine Nation die andere verstehen möge*, Amsterdam 1988, pp. 333-47.

—— 'Barock im Werk von Johannes Bobrowski', in Klaus Garber (ed.), *Europäische Barock-Rezeption*, Wiesbaden 1991, vol. 1, pp. 817-27.

Hein, Manfred Peter, 'Schule der Freundschaft. Begegnungen mit Johannes Bobrowski', in *Gingkobaum* 11 (1992), 171-82.

Henkys, Jürgen, 'Der Liebe vertane Worte lernen: Bobrowski an die jüdischen Dichterinnen', in *Die Zeichen der Zeit* 7/8 (1972), 260-8.

Heukenkamp, Ursula, 'Johannes Bobrowskis Gedicht "Vogelstraßen 1957". Die zerbrochene Elegie', in *Weimarer Beiträge* 33 (1987), 803-14.

Heydebrand, Renate von, 'Engagierte Esoterik. Die Gedichte Johannes Bobrowskis', in Renate von Heydebrand and Klaus Günther Just (eds.), *Wissenschaft als Dialog*, Stuttgart 1969, pp. 386-450 and 525-32.

—— 'Überlegungen zur Schreibweise Johannes Bobrowskis. Am Beispiel des Prosastücks "Junger Herr am Fenster"', in *Der Deutschunterricht* 21 (1969) no. 5, 100-25.

Hoefert, Sigfrid, 'Bobrowskis Widmungsgedichte', in *Neue Deutsche Hefte* 12 (1965), 60-77.

—— 'Der Nachhall finnischer Dichtung in der Lyrik Johannes Bobrowskis', in *German Quarterly* 41(1968), 222-30.

—— 'Überliefertes und schöpferische Gestaltung in Bobrowskis "Die Seligkeit der Heiden"', in *Seminar* 4 (1968), 57-66.

—— 'Johannes Bobrowski und Adam Mickiewicz', in *Mickiewicz-Blätter* 43 (1970), 1-4.

—— 'Kunst und Literatur. Die Ikonen-Gedichte Johannes Bobrowskis', in *Monatshefte* 64 (1972), 218-28.

—— 'Der Nachhall Trakls in der Lyrik von Johannes Bobrowski', in *Modern Austrian Literature* 5 (1972) nos. 1/2, 7-13.

—— 'Zum Begriff der Sprache bei einigen DDR-Dichtern (Huchel, Bobrowski, Cibulka)', in *Muttersprache* 82 (1972) no. 3, 182-7.

Ingen, Ferdinand van, 'Des Dichters Bildnis. Zu Bobrowskis lyrischen Porträts', in *Dichter und Leser*, Groningen 1972, pp. 234-60.

Ireland, Leah, '"Your Hope is on My Shoulder": Bobrowski and the World of the "Ostjuden"', in *Monatshefte* 72 (1980), 416-30.

—— 'Two Clowns: New Dimensions of the Picaresque', in *Colloquia Germanica* 14 (1981), 342-51.

Ives, Margaret C., '"An Klopstock": A Reading of a Poem by Bobrowski', in *New German Studies* 7 (1979), 105-12.

Jäckel, Günter, 'Sarmatische Dorfgeschichte im "wissenschaftlichen Zeitalter"', in Günter Jäckel und Ursula Roisch (eds.), *Struktur und Symbol*, Halle 1973, pp. 40-54.

Jokostra, Peter, *bobrowski & andere*, Munich and Vienna 1967, passim.

—— 'Celan ist bestenfalls eine Parfümfabrik', *Die Welt*, October 30 1971.

Kähler, Hermann, 'Bobrowskis Roman', in *Sinn und Form* 17 (1965), 631-6.

Keith-Smith, Brian, 'The Chatterton Theme in Modern German Literature', in R.W.Last (ed.), *Affinities: Essays in German and English Literature*, London 1971, pp. 126-138.

—— '"Das lebendige Erzählen": Johannes Bobrowski. Dichter der Erinnerung und Erneuerung', in *Zeitschrift für Germanistik* 11 (1990), 678-85.

—— 'Johannes Bobrowski and the Romantics', in Howard Gaskell, Karin McPherson, and Andrew Barker (eds.), *Neue Ansichten: The Reception of Romanticism in the Literature of the GDR*, Amsterdam 1990, pp. 160-71.

Kelletat, Alfred, 'Griechisches Triptychon aus deutschen Gedichten: Peter Huchel — Johannes Bobrowski — Joachim Uhlmann', in *Festschrift für Konstantinos J. Merentitis*, Athens 1972, pp. 182-94.

—— 'Zur lyrischen Sangart Johannes Bobrowskis', in *Seminar* 8 (1972), 117-36.

—— 'Bemerkungen zu Johannes Bobrowskis Widmungsgedicht "An Klopstock"', in Lothar Jordan, Axel Marquardt and Winfried Woesler (eds.), *Lyrik von allen Seiten*, Frankfurt/M. 1981, pp. 412-28.

—— 'Notiz zu Johannes Bobrowskis Gedicht "Die Droste"', in *Beiträge zur Droste-Forschung* 5 (1978-82), 174-80.

—— 'Lyrischer Progreß im heimischen Planquadrat. Vom frühen Tilsit-Gedicht bis zur späten Sokaiter Fahre. Zum 75. Geburtstag Johannes Bobrowskis', in *Gingkobaum* 11 (1992), 148-70.

Kobligk, Helmut, 'Zeit und Geschichte im dichterischen Werk Johannes Bobrowskis', in *Wirkendes Wort* 19 (1969), 193-205.

Leistner, Bernd, '"Aus der fliegenden Finsternis, tief...". Johannes Bobrowski — Zur lyrischen Artikulation des Weltverhältnisses und zu einigen Schaffensproblemen in den Jahren um 1960', in *Weimarer Beiträge* 22 (1976) no. 9, 101-38.

—— 'Bobrowskis Gedicht "Hölderlin in Tübingen"', in Ingrid Hähnel (ed.), *Lyriker im Zwiegespräch*, East Berlin and Weimar 1981, pp. 97-134.

—— 'Wiederbegegnung', in *Sinn und Form* 40 (1988), 1308-15.

Lerchner, Gotthard, 'Intertextualität als ästhetisches Potential. Bobrow-skis "34 Sätze über meinen Großvater"', in *Zeitschrift für Germanistik* 9 (1988), 307-20.

Liersch, Werner, 'Aus der Hand der Vergangenheit', in *Neue Deutsche Literatur* 13 (1965) no. 2, 146-9.

—— 'Das Flüchtige fest machen', in *Neue Deutsche Literatur* 13 (1965) no. 12, 139-44.

—— 'Bewährung eines Themas', in *Neue Deutsche Literatur* 15 (1967) no. 5, 150-2.

Minde, Fritz, 'Das Zeichen-Gedicht. Bemerkungen zu Zeichen, Chiffre, Metapher und Symbol am Beispiel von Gedichten Johannes Bob-rowskis', in *Zeitschrift für Literaturwissenschaft und Linguistik* 8 (1978), 122-40.

—— 'Johannes Bobrowski', in Klaus Weissenberger (ed.), *Die deutsche Lyrik 1945-1975*, Düsseldorf 1981, pp. 45-75.

Mogridge, Basil, 'Pinnau und andere', in Leonard Forster and Hans-Gert Roloff (eds.), *Akten des V. internationalen Germanisten-Kongresses*, Bern 1976, vol. 3, 450-61.

Möller, Inge, 'Wölfe unter Schafen. Gesellschaftskritik in Johannes Bobrowskis Roman *Levins Mühle*', in *Der Deutschunterricht* 25 (1973) no. 2, 40-8.

Moulden, Kenneth, 'Johannes Bobrowski's "Kloster bei Nowgorod": An Essay in Interpretation', in *Seminar* 16 (1980), 37-46.

Müller, Joachim, 'Der Lyriker Johannes Bobrowski — Dichtung unserer Zeit', in *Universitas* 23 (1968), 1301-11.

Nalewski, Horst, 'Metaphernstruktur in Johannes Bobrowskis Erzäh-lung "Boehlendorff"', in *Weimarer Beiträge* 19 (1973) no. 4, 103-18.

Oellers, Norbert, 'Johannes Bobrowski', in Benno von Wiese (ed.), *Deutsche Dichter der Gegenwart: Ihr Leben und Werk*, West Berlin 1973, pp. 413-35.

Ohl, Hubert, 'Johannes Bobrowskis Roman *Litauische Claviere*. Struktur und Thematik', in Wolfgang Paulsen (ed.), *Revolte und Experimente*, Heidelberg 1972, pp. 186-206.

—— 'Casimir Ulrich Boehlendorff — historische und poetische Gestalt. Zu Johannes Bobrowskis Erzählung "Boehlendorff"', in

Jahrbuch des Freien Deutschen Hochstifts (1978), 552-84.

—— 'Licht aus Dunkelheit. Versuch über drei Gedichte Johannes Bobrowskis', in *Literatur in Wissenschaft und Unterricht* 24 (1991), 185-203.

Otten, Klaus, 'Das jüdische Element in Johannes Bobrowskis Lyrik', in Paul Sars and Harry Nijbeer (eds.), *Der Seelen wunderliches Bergwerk*, Nijmegen 1985, pp. 89-96.

Pielow, Winfried, 'Die Frauen der Nehrungsfischer', in Josef Speck (ed.), *Kristalle: Moderne deutsche Gedichte für die Schule*, Munich 1967, pp. 117-36.

Rittig, Roland, 'Zur Bedeutung der klassischen Odentradition für Johannes Bobrowski', in Günter Hartung, Thomas Hohle, and Hans-Georg Werner (eds.), *Erworbene Tradition*, East Berlin and Weimar 1977, pp. 148-93.

—— 'Bemerkungen zur Rezeption der klassischen Odentradition im frühen Schaffen Johannes Bobrowskis', in Hans-Georg Werner (ed.), *Friedrich Gottlieb Klopstock: Werk und Wirkung*, East Berlin 1978, pp. 287-302.

Roche, Reinhard, 'Ist Bobrowski zu schwierig? Leseempfehlungen zu seiner Kurzprosa', in *Der Deutschunterricht* 35 (1983) no. 5, 47-56.

Schäfer, Hans Dieter, '"... doch es fügt der Himmel nur das zertretene Bild zusammen"', *Welt der Literatur*, December 4 1969.

—— 'Johannes Bobrowskis Anfänge im *Inneren Reich*', in *Almanach für Literatur und Theologie* 4 (1970), 66-9.

Scherf-Deskau, Dagmar, 'Die Entwicklung des Geschichts- und Sprachbezugs in der Lyrik Johannes Bobrowskis', in *Sprachkunst* 8 (1977), 59-86.

Schmidt, Ernst Günther, 'Die Sappho-Gedichte Johannes Bobrowskis', in *Das Altertum* 18 (1972), 49-61.

Schmidt-Henkel, Gerhard, 'Momentaufnahme im Geschichtsprozeß', in Walter Hinck (ed.), *Geschichte im Gedicht*, Frankfurt/M. 1979, pp. 222-8.

Schwaderer, Richard, 'Heute, angesichts Hölderlins. Bemerkungen zu Johannes Bobrowskis "Hölderlin in Tübingen" und Paul Celans "Tübingen, Jänner"', in *Annali della Facolta di Lingue e Letterature Straniere de Ca' Foscari* 11 (1972), 463-472.

Schwarz, Peter-Paul, 'Freund mit der leisen Rede. Zur Lyrik Johannes Bobrowskis', in *Der Deutschunterricht* 18 (1966) no. 2, 48-65.

Scrase, David A., 'Point Counterpoint: Variations on the "Fest" Theme in Johannes Bobrowski's *Levins Mühle*', in *German Life and Letters*, 32 (1978), 177-85.

Seidler, Manfred, 'Bobrowski, Klopstock und der antike Vers', in Horst Meller and Hans-Joachim Zimmermann (eds.), *Lebende Antike*, West Berlin 1967, pp. 542-54.

Siering, Johann, 'Johannes Bobrowski: *Litauische Claviere*', in *Neue Deutsche Hefte* 14 (1967), 157-9.

Sölle, Dorothee, 'Für eine Zeit ohne Angst. Christliche Elemente in der Lyrik Johannes Bobrowskis', in *Almanach für Literatur und Theologie* 2 (1968), 143-66.

Streller, Siegfried, 'Zählen zählt alles. Zum Gesellschaftsbild Johannes Bobrowskis', in *Weimarer Beiträge* 15 (1969), 1076-90.

—— 'Johannes Bobrowski', in Hans Jürgen Geerdts (ed.), *Literatur der DDR in Einzeldarstellungen*, Stuttgart 1972, pp. 292-315.

Tismar, Jens, 'Zeit im Gedicht. Über Keller, Celan und Bobrowski', in Norbert Müller et al. (eds.), *Bausteine zu einer Poetik der Moderne*, Munich 1987, pp. 409-17.

Titel, Britta, 'Johannes Bobrowski', in Klaus Nonnenmann (ed.), *Schriftsteller der Gegenwart*, Olten and Freiburg 1963, pp. 51-7.

Waidson, H. M., 'Bobrowski's *Levins Mühle*', in Siegbert Prawer, R. Hinton Thomas, and Leonard Forster (eds.), *Essays in German Language, Culture and Society*, London 1969, pp. 149-59.

Wallmann, Jürgen P., 'Johannes Bobrowski: *Levins Mühle*', in *Neue Deutsche Hefte* 12 (1965), 151-3.

—— 'Johannes Bobrowski: zum 25. Todestag des Dichters am 2. September 1990', in *Literatur und Kritik* 25 (1990), 368-71.

Weber, Werner, 'Johannes Bobrowski: *Litauische Claviere*', in *Neue Zürcher Zeitung*, March 3 1968.

Weber, Werner, 'Johannes Bobrowski', in *Forderungen. Bemerkungen und Aufsätze zur Literatur,* Zurich and Stuttgart 1970, pp. 216-35.

Wernhauser, Richard, 'Johannes Bobrowski: *Literarisches Klima*', in *Neue Deutsche Hefte* 26 (1978), 576-8.

Wieczorek, John P., '"Die großen Taten in verschiedenen Zungen":

Johannes Bobrowski's *Litauische Claviere'*, in *German Life and Letters* n.s. 35 (1982), 355-67.

—— 'Christliche Elemente in der Lyrik Johannes Bobrowskis', in John L. Flood (ed.), *Ein Moment des erfahrenen Lebens,* Amsterdam 1987, pp. 120-39.

—— 'Questioning Philosemitism: The Depiction of Jews in the Prose Works of Johannes Bobrowski', in *German Life and Letters* n.s. 44 (1990-91), 122-32.

—— 'New Writing on Johannes Bobrowski (1917-1965): A Review Article', in *The Modern Language Review* 89 (1994), 406-16.

—— 'Johannes Bobrowski and Adam Mickiewicz', *German Life and Letters* 48 (1995), 413-21.

—— 'Saturn in Latvia: Johannes Bobrowski and the Events of August 1961', in Eoin Bourke, Roisin Ni Neill (eds.) *Schein und Widerschein: Festschrift für T.J.Casey,* Galway 1997, pp. 358-70.

Williams, A. F., 'Direct and Indirect Means of Historical Elucidation in Bobrowski's Short Stories', in *GDR Monitor* 18 (1987-88), 27-49.

—— 'Invisibility and Visibility in Johannes Bobrowski's "Rainfarn"', in *GDR Monitor* 23 (1990), 83-96.

—— '"Aber wo befinde ich mich?": The Narrator's Location and Historical Perspective in Works by Siegfried Lenz, Günter Grass and Johannes Bobrowski', in Arthur Williams, K. Stuart Parkes and Roland Smith (eds.), *German Literature at a Time of Change, 1989-1990: German Unity and German Identity in Literary Perspective,* Bern 1991, pp. 255-71.

Winter, Helmut, 'Some Aspects of Johannes Bobrowski's Poetry', in *Revue des langues vivantes* 37 (1971), 181-91.

Zimmermann, Werner, 'Rainfarn (1965)', in *Deutsche Prosadichtungen unseres Jahrhunderts. Interpretationen für Lehrende und Lernende,* Düsseldorf 1969, vol. 2, pp. 355-62.

Zukrowski, Wojciech, 'Nicht nur *Levins Mühle'*, in Manfred Diersch and Hubert Orlowski (eds.), *Annäherung und Distanz,* Leipzig and Halle 1983, pp. 283-9.

INDEX

—C—

—D—

—E—

—F—

—Z—